IN THE NAME
OF JUSTICE

THE THORNTON CENTER CHINESE THINKERS SERIES

The John L. Thornton China Center at Brookings develops timely, independent analysis and policy recommendations to help U.S. and Chinese leaders address key long-standing challenges, both in terms of Sino-U.S. relations and China's internal development. As part of this effort, the Thornton Center Chinese Thinkers Series aims to shed light on the ongoing scholarly and policy debates in China.

China's momentous socioeconomic transformation has not taken place in an intellectual vacuum. Chinese scholars have actively engaged in fervent discussions about the country's future trajectory and its ever-growing integration with the world. This series introduces some of the most influential recent works by prominent thinkers from the People's Republic of China to English language readers. Each volume, translated from the original Chinese, contains writings by a leading scholar in a particular academic field (for example, political science, economics, law, or sociology). This series offers a much-needed intellectual forum promoting international dialogue on various issues that confront China and the world.

Also in this series:

Yu Keping, *Democracy Is a Good Thing: Essays on Politics, Society, and Culture in Contemporary China*, 2009.
Hu Angang, *China in 2020: A New Type of Superpower*, 2011.

IN THE NAME OF JUSTICE

Striving for the Rule of Law in China

HE WEIFANG

BROOKINGS INSTITUTION PRESS

Washington, D.C.

Library of Congress Cataloging-in-Publication data

He, Weifang.
  In the name of justice : striving for the rule of law in China / He Weifang.
     p.   cm. — (The Thornton Center Chinese Thinkers series)
  Includes bibliographical references and index.
  Summary: "Assesses the evolution and state of legal reform in China covering
topics such as judicial independence, judicial review, legal education, capital
punishment, and the legal protection of free speech and human rights and how
reform contributes to the growing democratization of China"—Provided by the
publisher.
  ISBN 978-0-8157-2290-8 (hardcover : alk. paper)
  1. Rule of law—China. I. Title.
  KNQ2020.H4425 2012
  340'.11—dc23   2012036047

9 8 7 6 5 4 3 2 1

Printed on acid-free paper

Typeset in Adobe Garamond

Composition by Peter Lindeman
Arlington, Virginia

Printed by R. R. Donnelley
Harrisonburg, Virginia

Contents

Foreword by John L. Thornton   vii

Acknowledgments   xiii

Introduction by Cheng Li   xvii

PROLOGUE

    An Open Letter to Legal Professionals in Chongqing   1

PART I
JUDICIAL INDEPENDENCE: CHINA'S TREACHEROUS PATH

1   *The Ongoing Quest for Judicial Independence in Contemporary China*   9

2   *Mencius on the Rule of Law*   40

PART II
CONSTITUTIONALISM AND JUDICIAL REVIEW

3   *China's First Steps toward Constitutionalism*   63

4   *Constitutionalism as a Global Trend and Its Impact on China*   101

5   *Remarks Given at the New Western Hills Symposium*   125

PART III
THE EXPANSION OF LEGAL EDUCATION
AND THE LEGAL PROFESSION

6   *China's Legal Profession: The Emergence and
    Growing Pains of a Professionalized Legal Class*   133

7   *Foreign Models and Chinese Practice in Legal
    Education during the Reform Era*   144

PART IV
THE LEGAL PROTECTION OF FREE SPEECH

8   *Freedom of the Press: A Necessary Condition for
    Social Stability in China*   175

9   *An Open Letter to the CCP Politburo Standing Committee
    Regarding Media Censorship*   181

PART V
THE LEGAL PROTECTION OF HUMAN RIGHTS

10 *Challenging the Death Penalty: Why We Should
    Abolish this Barbaric Punishment*   191

11 *A Plea for Genuine Political Progress in China*   216

Notes   221

Further Reading: The Writings of He Weifang, 1984–2010   243

Index   249

Foreword

JOHN L. THORNTON

I have long believed that the rule of law is a critical civic virtue for the devel-opment of a just and thriving society. It is a view I have held in particular about China since the beginning of my involvement with the country more than twenty years ago. In those days, my enthusiasm for the topic was not usually matched by the Chinese officials with whom I interacted, but I felt confident that their views would change over time as China opened up to the world, especially the commercial world that would increasingly demand legal clarity as a condition for investing and trading.

I have also felt that the rule of law should top the list of perennial issues discussed when the leaders of the United States and other major nations meet with their Chinese counterparts. As both an internal and external strategic matter, the goal for the Chinese state should be, on the one hand, to provide clarity and certainty to its own citizens about their rights and responsibilities and, on the other, to reassure the rest of the world that China intends to inte-grate into the international system seamlessly and as a positive contributor to relations between states.

Therefore, I was heartened to hear Premier Wen Jiabao, in his meeting with a group of us from Brookings in late 2006, define the Chinese objective of "democracy" as comprising three primary components, one of which was the rule of law (the other two being elections and supervision based on checks and balances). Premier Wen stressed the need for continued reform to guarantee the Chinese legal system's "dignity, justice, and independence." That meeting catalyzed my research over the next two years into the topic of political evolution in China. In order to understand the state of the country's judicial system, I spoke to a broad range of Chinese and Western experts and practitioners, among them a vice president of China's Supreme People's Court and a professor at the Central Party School who had given lectures to the Politburo on the topic of the relationship between the constitution and the Communist Party.

These discussions and research led to an article in *Foreign Affairs* in January 2008 in which I concluded that, while they still had much further to go, on the whole the Chinese had made notable progress over the past three decades on this particular aspect of democratic evolution. In 1979, at the start of the era of reform and opening initiated by Deng Xiaoping, the entire country had only several hundred attorneys and was beginning to reopen the law schools that had been shuttered during the Cultural Revolution. From the time of the Anti-Rightist Campaign of 1957 to the end of the Cultural Revolution in 1976, the National People's Congress did not adopt a single new piece of legislation (other than passing pro forma the Constitution of the People's Republic of China in 1975). In fact, the legislature hardly met for nearly ten years during the Cultural Revolution.

By contrast, today there are more than 17,000 law firms operating in China and over 200,000 licensed attorneys. China has adopted 239 new laws in the past thirty years. Courts used to be staffed overwhelmingly with judges having little or no legal education, most of whom were demobilized military officers. In 1995 only 5 percent of judges nationwide held a bachelor's degree. Today the Judges Law and its amendments have established basic standards for new jurists that require a college degree, passing the National Bar Examination, and at least two years of prior legal experience. There is evidence that citizens are turning to the justice system in increasing numbers to try to resolve disputes and for protection of their legitimate rights from the interests of corporations and the state. According to government figures, from 2006 to 2010, approximately 10 million cases were litigated in China, another 5 million were resolved without litigation, and about 1 million cases involved legal aid.

Nonetheless, as the essays in this volume illustrate plainly, in too many instances China's justice system still falls well short of the letter and spirit of the codes on its books. Corruption is endemic. Collusion among police, prosecutors, and judges remains widespread. And the most fundamental obstacle to further progress remains the question of judicial independence—whether the ruling Chinese Communist Party serves the law or vice versa. The party controls the court system as a whole and keeps a tight rein on sensitive cases. It operates an extensive "inspection and discipline" system for party members separate from the legal system that applies to average citizens. At the heart of this complicated and imperfect reality sit the thinking and writing of He Weifang.

Given the consequential events that have occurred in China over the past year, a book addressing the state of rule of law in the country from the perspective of one of its boldest legal scholars could not be more timely. The fall of Bo Xilai and the related criminal cases against his wife Gu Kailai and the former Chongqing police chief Wang Lijun transfixed the country and drew intense scrutiny to its legal system. Yet nearly a year before the excesses in Chongqing were officially condemned—and while Bo and his mass campaigns were still at their height of popularity—He Weifang issued a widely circulated and debated "Open Letter to Legal Professionals in Chongqing," the first of his works collected in this volume. In the letter, He criticized local authorities, including police chief Wang by name, for their extralegal methods. He reproached Chongqing's lawyers and legal scholars, including those at his alma mater, the Southwest University of Political Science and Law, for staying silent or even cheering on official acts that they surely knew contravened Chinese law and due process. At the time Professor He published his letter, it was a decision not without personal risk. It was also unsurprising in that it was the sort of unblinking defense of principle that has marked his career. As a professor of law at Peking University, He Weifang has argued for two decades that the rule of law, however inconvenient at times to some of those who govern, must be embraced because it is ultimately the most reliable protector of the interests of the country, of the average citizen, and, in fact, even of those who govern.

In more ways than one, the events in Chongqing highlighted the central, if still tenuous, place the law is coming to occupy in today's China. Discussion of legal topics on social media platforms such as Sina Weibo, used by hundreds of millions of Chinese, draws intense interest. The Bo case underscored the view held by Professor He and others that accelerated progress toward rule of law is an essential condition if the country is to extend the progress it has made over the past three decades. My own view is that Bo's demise could in the end advance the rule of law in China if it pushes the Chinese Communist Party at the highest level to consider in earnest how to reconcile the power of the party with the legal system. The visibility and sheer difficulty of the case may force leaders to wrestle in a serious way with the relevant conceptual issues and systemic fissures. If this occurs, the prolonged national conversation about Bo and his associates could point the system in a healthier direction.

This is because, in part, some officials have already been thinking in forward-looking ways, others will come to realize that there is no alternative, and the public may demand that things be changed.

The rule of law should be of equal concern to the rest of the world that is invested in the development of a prosperous, stable, and open China. It is the necessary foundation for China's pursuit of political evolution and democracy. A nation in which respect for the rule of law has taken root is also more likely to abide by international legal norms. It would provide a more transparent and stable environment in which foreign enterprises could operate. These issues will only increase in consequence as China's economic, political, and military influence expands in coming decades.

Yet, surprisingly, even now there are few places to which an English speaker can turn to understand firsthand how leading *Chinese* think about this critical subject. While there are respected Western specialists in Chinese law, in general the outside world operates with an incomplete understanding of the country's legal system: its origins, development, and remaining challenges. This deficit can give rise to generalizations and oversimplification about a topic that plays an increasingly important part in the international community's engagement with China, whether it be in the realms of diplomacy, business, or human rights. The purpose of this volume is to help catalyze the process by which this situation may be remedied.

I first met He Weifang in 2007 when I was preparing the aforementioned article for *Foreign Affairs*. I sought him out because I wanted someone with a discerning mind who had lived at the center of the Chinese legal system during the country's reform era to critique the draft sections on rule of law. His forthright and trenchant comments, which improved the article measurably, reflected not only an understanding of the arduous path his country's legal system had traveled during the last century and a recognition of the advances of recent years, but also an unsentimental appraisal of its remaining deficiencies.

As a constructive critic, Professor He writes passionately and persuasively about the ways in which China's judicial system falls short. In his "Open Letter," He condemns the continuing use of so-called three chiefs conferences "in which the chief judge, the attorney general, and the police chief hold meetings and work in a coordinated fashion so that the cases are decided before they even go to trial. When the case is finally heard, it is a mere formality." Whether in commercial disputes, politically sensitive cases, or instances when the property of farmers has been expropriated by local governments and sold to developers, relevant laws can be ignored or distorted to fit the desired outcomes of those who hold the most influence. Ultimately, in

He's view, true rule of law in China can only be achieved when the party decides that it too must live, without exception, under the law's jurisdiction.

This debate goes to the heart of what course China will choose to take over the coming decades. In Professor He's view, greater rule of law must be established not only because it is the right thing to do but also to guarantee the country's continued stability. Public confidence in the neutrality and fairness of the courts is a condition for social order; citizens take to the streets when they no longer trust the efficacy of the system to address their grievances. A sound legal system is also essential for the next stage of China's economic development. The government's goals of creating an "innovation society" and a higher value-added economy depend on reliable protections for intellectual property. One former adviser to the Chinese central bank has argued that rule of law is a necessary "reform" for underperforming Chinese stock markets, which suffer from a lack of transparency and thus investor confidence. It has been suggested that the government create a central court to handle securities-related lawsuits to circumvent the undue influence of local governments.

As Brookings scholar Cheng Li recounts in detail in his introduction, Professor He's determined advocacy of a system in which no person or party is above the law has sometimes come at significant personal costs. Professor He had the temerity to criticize Bo Xilai's reign in Chongqing when far more powerful people in legal and political spheres dared not. Because of his propensity to speak and write the inconvenient truth, he has endured various penalties, including being "assigned" to teach for two years in the remote region of Xinjiang. That he has not been punished more severely is likely due to the widespread recognition and respect he has won for sticking to his principles. He's forthright advocacy of judicial independence has made him one of his university's most popular lecturers. His blog posts have received more than 16 million hits.

Not long after He Weifang and I met for the first time, he began his two-year "exile" in Xinjiang. He spent part of his time in the far west rereading the Chinese classics, some of which he acknowledged he had not read closely before. He's time in Xinjiang, if anything, appears to have reinforced his conviction that the rule of law must be China's foremost priority; upon returning to Beijing in 2011, he rejoined the debate with his open letter to Chongqing.

He Weifang is an intellectual and patriot in the best Chinese tradition. It is in China's interest to value and channel his insights for the good of the country. We in the West should read him carefully in order to better understand the hopes and fears of this rapidly changing nation, and envision a more promising scenario for its future development.

The Chinese struggle to create a nation ruled according to laws is not unique. While the specific obstacles and issues vary, every nation that has successfully established the rule of law has done so only after long and difficult effort. In his important book, *Making Our Democracy Work*, Supreme Court Justice Stephen Breyer traces America's own complex experience: "We simply assume today that when the Court rules, the public will obey its rulings. But at various moments in our history, the Supreme Court's decisions were contested, disobeyed, or ignored by the public and even by the president and Congress." He notes that in 1957, 170 years after the adoption of the U.S. Constitution, President Eisenhower had to send 1,000 soldiers of the 101st Airborne Division to Little Rock, Arkansas, to enforce *Brown* v. *Board of Education* and the constitutional right of black children to attend integrated schools. Such recent experience can usefully inform how we understand, empathize with, and give support to China's arduous and momentous task.

ACKNOWLEDGMENTS

As China undergoes rapid economic and sociopolitical transformations and continues to rise in stature on the global stage, the development of a stable and impartial legal system has emerged as a crucial issue. I am greatly honored to be the contributor of the latest volume of the Brookings Institution's Thornton Center Chinese Thinkers series, sharing my analysis of the complex nature of Chinese legal development with English readers.

I would like to acknowledge a number of individuals who greatly aided in the production of this volume. First and foremost, I sincerely thank Mr. John Thornton, chairman of the Brookings Institution and professor and director of global leadership at Tsinghua University, for his confidence in me and for his generous support without which this book project would simply not have been possible. Through our numerous conversations over the years, his remarkable insights and strong interest in rule of law in China have been truly inspirational. I am also profoundly grateful to him for finding time in his busy schedule to write the foreword of this volume. I would also like to thank Mr. Woo Lee for helping facilitate my one-on-one meetings with John in Beijing and for his own valuable input on the book project.

Deepest thanks go to Dr. Cheng Li, director of research and senior fellow at the John L. Thornton China Center at the Brookings Institution. He was instrumental in the launch of this project, in selecting original Chinese pieces for inclusion, in providing much needed explanatory footnotes for English readers, in checking the accuracy of the translation, and especially in editing and revising the manuscript. He was a constant source of support, and provided extensive consultation. I would also like to thank Dr. Li for his analytically keen and empirically rich introductory chapter. His research assistant, Eve Cary, was extremely helpful in the process, providing feedback and extensively editing the materials.

I must also thank the leadership at the Brookings Institution for their great support: Strobe Talbott, president; Martin Indyk, vice president and director of Foreign Policy; Ted Piccone and Michael E. O'Hanlon, deputy directors of Foreign Policy; and Jeffrey Bader, Kenneth Lieberthal, and Jonathan Pollack, senior fellows of the John L. Thornton China Center. A special note of appreciation goes to distinguished scholars in legal and other academic fields, especially Bill Alford and Niall Ferguson at Harvard University and Carl Minzner at Fordham Law School, not only for their interest and guidance in my work but also for kindly contributing their endorsements, which are included on the back cover of the volume.

During the past three decades, I have greatly benefited from professional exchanges with many overseas colleagues and friends, especially from reading their scholarly work. In addition to the aforementioned Bill Alford, I particularly wish to thank Masaki Abe, Tomoko Ako, Donald C. Clarke, Jerome A. Cohen, Alison W. Conner, R. Randle Edwards, James V. Feinerman, Paul Gewirtz, Jonathan Hecht, Nicolas C. Howson, Benjamin L. Liebman, Stanley B. Lubman, Frank Müntzer, Jonathan K. Ocko, Michael Palmer, Randall Peerenboom, Pitman B. Potter, Jeffrey Prescott, Harro von Senger, Ken Suzuki, Murray Scot Tanner, Karen Turner, among many others.

Several individuals have had a direct hand in helping to prepare the content and presentation of the project. I am grateful for the excellent translation work offered by Li Yunfeng, and equally excellent editorial assistance by Jordan Lee (Princeton University), Dr. Andrew Marble (freelance editor), and four very talented interns at Brookings: Kevin Wu (Yale University), Veronica Li (Stanford University), Lyric Chen (Harvard Law School), and John Langdon (Johns Hopkins University). At the John L. Thornton China Center, Kevin Foley, Teresa Hsu, and Iris An provided various help in keeping everything on track.

I would be remiss not to thank the Brookings Institution Press, including Janet Walker, managing editor, and Starr Belsky, copy editor, who efficiently and effectively edited the book. The successful publication of the book is also owed to the Brookings Institution Press's very capable team, especially Bob Faherty, director; Christopher Kelaher, marketing director; Larry Converse, production manager; Melissa McConnell, publicity manager; and Susan Woollen, art coordinator.

For any deficiencies and errors that might have survived all the assistance above, I, of course, bear responsibility. Any single volume that tries to explore the complicated, and often paradoxical, development of rule of law in contemporary China can be no more than an introduction. I hope that my English-speaking colleagues in the legal world and China watchers in general will be tempted to invest time and energy on this important subject, sharing their experiences, perspectives, and insights.

He Weifang
Peking University, Beijing
October 2012

Introduction

Fighting for a Constitutional China: Public Enlightenment and Legal Professionalism

CHENG LI

> *We are here not because we are law-breakers; we are here in our efforts to become law-makers.*
> —EMMELINE PANKHURST, leader of the British suffragette movement

> *The right rulings make a country great because the event is seen by all.*
> —STEPHEN BREYER, Associate Justice, U.S. Supreme Court

One evening in the fall of 2011, almost five months before the dramatic downfall of heavyweight political leader Bo Xilai, I sat in an auditorium at the Law School of Peking University listening to a panel discussion on China's judicial reforms.[1] The Beida Law Society, a student organization on campus, sponsored this public forum featuring He Weifang and Xu Xin, two distinguished law professors in Beijing.[2] The auditorium was crowded with several hundred people (mainly students and young faculty members but also some Chinese journalists). As I listened to this engaging and enlightening discussion, it occurred to me that I was witnessing a profound political movement unfolding for constitutionalism in the People's Republic of China (PRC).

I would like to thank Eve Cary, John Langdon, Jordan Lee, and Andrew Marble for their very helpful comments on an early version of this introductory chapter.

What struck me—and shocked me as a foreign visitor—was not only that the entire discussion was explicitly critical of the Chinese Communist Party (CCP) for its resistance to any meaningful judicial reform but also that the atmosphere was calm, reasonable, and marked by a sense of humor and sophistication in the expression of ideas. Both professors criticized the CCP's omnipresent role in the country's legal system, especially in regard to the infinite power of the Central Commission of Politics and Law (CCPL) of the CCP.[3] In the words of He Weifang, many recent well-known cases of injustice were largely due to the "invisible hand" of the CCPL. Both speakers called for a fundamental change in the role and presence of the CCPL, including the abolition of the politics and law commissions at all subnational levels.

As part of China's overall political reforms, He and Xu proposed prioritizing judicial reforms with a focus on judicial independence. They argued that judicial reforms are in line with the need for social stability and thus should be considered the least disruptive way to ease China's much-needed political transformation. They outlined several important systematic changes to China's legal system:

— transferring the leadership of judicial reforms from the CCPL to the National People's Congress (NPC) in the form of a yet-to-be-established judicial reform committee, one in which legal scholars, lawyers, and representatives of nongovernmental organizations would constitute more than half of the members;

— adjusting the role of the CCP from appointing presidents of courts and chief prosecutors to only nominating them (an independent selection committee, rather than the party organization department, would make these appointments);

— prohibiting interference by the CCP in any legal cases, especially by prohibiting judges from being CCP members and banning party organizations within law firms;

— reducing the power of both presidents of courts and chief prosecutors in order to enhance procedural justice; and

— establishing a constitutional review system, including a new constitutional committee and constitutional court.

In addition, Professor Xu presented a comprehensive plan for establishing a protection and guarantee system. He specifically addressed important issues such as how to ensure budget security for an independent judicial system, how to provide job security for legal professionals, how to prevent corruption and other power abuses in law enforcement, how the rule of law can ensure citizens' democratic rights including the development of the jury system, and how to protect the legal rights of vulnerable social groups.

The panel discussion was also politically and intellectually stimulating thanks to an interactive session with the audience that covered a broad range of questions from students. One questioner asked, "If judicial reform is the lowest-risk approach for China's political transformation, where does the strongest resistance come from?" Professor Xu responded bluntly, "The strongest resistance comes from the CCP leadership, and this is most evident in senior leader Wu Bangguo's recent statement widely proclaiming the 'five no's' for China."[4]

Another questioner opined, "Wasn't it a wise decision on the part of the former Libyan justice minister Mustafa Abdul Jalil to denounce the Libyan leader Muammar Gaddafi before the collapse of the regime?" Professor He did not directly answer this intriguing question but instead told the story of Qing dynasty minister (ambassador) to the United States Wu Tingfang, a U.K.- and U.S.-educated lawyer who decided to support Sun Yat-sen's 1911 Revolution because, as He said somewhat jokingly, "Wu wisely stated that 'the Qing dynasty cannot be saved (*meijiule*).'"

Still another questioner wanted to know, "What's the incentive for the CCP and powerful special interest groups to pursue judicial reform that may very well undermine their own power and interests?" Professor He replied, "It's a result of a domino effect—a natural and inevitable consequence of the fundamental change of state-society relations in China. From the perspective of CCP leaders, some may want to be remembered in history as having been on the right side."

This episode of openness and pluralism in intellectual and political discourse, though eye-opening and surprising for foreign observers like myself, is by no means unique in present-day China. In recent years an increasing number of well-known professors and opinion leaders have shown that they are not afraid of publicly expressing their controversial views, including sharp criticism of the CCP authorities. Such remarks would have been regarded as politically taboo or even "unlawful" just a few years ago. Never before in the six-decade history of the PRC has the Chinese general public, and especially the rapidly growing legal community, expressed such serious concerns about the need to restrain the power of the CCP and to create a much more independent judicial system.

Like He Weifang and Xu Xin, many other prominent legal scholars in the country frequently give public lectures and panel discussions on similar topics, with many of these events being webcast on the Chinese Internet.[5] In

November 2010, for example, the death of the distinguished constitutional scholar Cai Dingjian led to nationwide, year-long memorial activities honoring his advocacy for the rule of law in China.[6] Cai's last words, "Constitutional democracy is the mission of our generation," were widely cited in both the country's official media and social media.[7]

These instances do not necessarily mean that Chinese authorities have loosened control of the legal profession. On the contrary, liberal legal scholars and human rights lawyers are often among the main targets for harsh treatment, including imprisonment. Yet the movement for rule of law in the country seems to have already reached a moral and political high ground. It has gained further momentum in the wake of recent crises such as the defection of former Chongqing police chief Wang Lijun to the U.S. consulate in Chengdu, the downfall of Politburo member Bo Xilai and the subsequent murder charge against his wife, and graphic tales told by blind human rights activist Chen Guangcheng of torture and other abuses of power by Chinese law enforcement. Both the frequent manifestations of social unrest and the growing transparency of factional infighting in the CCP leadership in recent years further underscore the urgency of developing a credible legal system.

He Weifang and China's Legal Development: Objectives of the Volume

This volume is a collection of the English translations of He Weifang's representative work from 2001 to 2011. He Weifang has been at the forefront of the country's bumpy path toward justice and judicial independence for more than a decade. A proponent of reform rather than revolution, He's political and professional endeavors have largely paralleled the painstaking quest for rule of law in China during this crucial period of sociopolitical transformation. This volume examines some of the most important topics in China's legal development, including judicial independence, judicial review, legal education, the professionalization of lawyers and the selection of judges, capital punishment, and the legal protection of free speech, religious freedom, and human rights. In the volume, He also offers a historical review of Chinese traditional legal thought, enhanced by cross-country comparisons.

Though maintaining his characteristically optimistic personality, He is also keenly aware of the political, institutional, and cultural barriers to genuine constitutional development in China. To promote constitutional governance in a culture that lacks a strong legal tradition—and in a political system that is largely lawless—is an overwhelming task. This requires the country's legal scholars and other professionals, as a group, to be fully engaged in educating and enlightening the public (and elites as well) rather than merely pursuing academic and judicial research. Not surprisingly, Professor He is highly regarded for his dual roles as practitioner and thinker, as advocate and scholar, in the Chinese legal world. In addition to presenting a selection of He's important academic writings, this book also includes some of his public speeches, media interviews, and open letters, providing comprehensive and accurate accounts of his distinctive broader role as a public intellectual rather than as a more narrow, purely "ivory tower" scholar of legal studies.

With a few exceptions, most chapters in this volume are available to English readers for the first time. The US-based *Foreign Policy* magazine appropriately recognized He Weifang as one of the 100 top global thinkers in 2011.[8] The English-speaking world, including the China studies community in the West, however, has largely remained unfamiliar with He's scholarly writings and personal endeavors regarding China's legal development, reflecting a serious discrepancy in our understanding of the intellectual and policy discourse in this rapidly changing country.

To start the volume, this comprehensive introductory chapter aims to present the personal and professional background of He Weifang, the intellectual and political contexts essential to understanding his pursuits, and the legal and policy debates that his work has stimulated. This discussion can help readers grasp He Weifang's extraordinary contributions in the domains of public enlightenment and legal professionalism, which are the main focus of this introductory chapter.

Such an understanding of He Weifang and his remarkable endeavors is critical because, of all the issues sparked by China's ongoing economic and sociopolitical transformation, the development of the Chinese legal system is arguably the most consequential. The paradoxical trends of growing public demand for rule of law, on the one hand, and continued party interference in legal affairs, on the other, present an intriguing political phenomenon. How this battle will unfold has strong implications for the country's social stability, economic development, and political trajectory; and its ramifications go far beyond China's national borders. He's political and intellectual journey is a fascinating story of one man's courageous fight to promote justice within the world's largest authoritarian regime. His story enriches our more general understanding of the pluralistic and dynamic nature of present-day China. To a great extent, this timely volume provides invaluable insights and well-grounded assessments of the prospects of constitutionalism in China.

Public Enlightenment: Views, Values, and Courage

To better understand He Weifang's views, values, and courage, one needs to know something about the broader intellectual enlightenment movement in China. Public enlightenment (*qimeng*) has been an enduring aspiration of Chinese intellectuals in contemporary China. Over the past century, major sociopolitical crises at home, which were usually accompanied by strong ideological influences from abroad, often led forward-looking Chinese intellectuals to develop new ideas, views, and values in order to "wake up" the public and the nation. The May Fourth Movement in 1919, occurring in the wake of the collapse of the Qing dynasty, was a turning point in China's modern history and marked the first enlightenment movement in the Middle Kingdom. Hu Shih, one of the most prominent intellectual participants in the movement, characterized it as the "Chinese Renaissance" for its embrace of foreign ideas regarding science and experimentation.[9]

The Chinese intellectual ferment in the post-Mao era from the late 1970s to the late 1980s, especially its critical reflection on the decade-long political fanaticism and human suffering of the Cultural Revolution and the subsequent call for humanism, was often seen as the second enlightenment movement. In a sense, the post-Mao enlightenment was a strong wave of intellectual and public awakening that fulfilled the unaccomplished tasks of the May Fourth Movement.[10] Unfortunately, this second enlightenment ended tragically in the 1989 Tiananmen Square incident.

Toward a Third Enlightenment Movement in Contemporary China?

In the past few years, a third wave of public enlightenment has arguably been in the making—this despite the tight control, particularly over the media, that the Chinese authorities have maintained. A third enlightenment is the subject of a new volume, *The Enlightenment and Transformation of Chinese Society*, edited by Zi Zhongyun, a distinguished scholar and former director of the Institute of American Studies at the Chinese Academy of Social Science (CASS). In the book Zi pointedly asks, "Why do we need a 'new enlightenment' now?"[11] The answer lies, as she and other contributors describe, in the growing tension between rapid socioeconomic transformation and the stagnation of political reforms, between China's economic rise on the world stage and the party's ideological stance that resists universal values, and between revolutionary changes in telecommunication and the government's strict media censorship.[12]

In Zi's view, China needs a new enlightenment because of what she calls "obscurantism" (*mengmei zhuyi*), which refers to the efforts of those officials opposed to democratic change.[13] These officials and some conservative public intellectuals, as Zi describes, have spread the false notions that democracy does not fit with the Chinese people and that universal values are nothing but a Western conspiracy against China. She particularly warns against the danger of nationalism—leading to a tendency to perpetuate injustice in society in the name of the state's interest.[14]

According to PRC liberal intellectuals, enlightenment means that people are liberated from obscurantism and ignorance, from having blind faith in myths or in a dictator. One important aspect of the post–Cultural Revolution enlightenment movement was its strong critique of—and break from—the shadow of Mao worship.[15] What has been astonishingly disturbing in recent years, in the view of Chinese liberal critics, is the fact that Mao worship and myths about the "glorious" Cultural Revolution have resurged in the country—most noticeably in Chongqing under Bo Xilai, who himself, as many liberal critics believe, was very much a Mao-like figure in terms of the personality cult that surrounded him.[16]

Under these political and ideological circumstances, Chinese liberal intellectuals have begun mobilizing for a new wave of enlightenment. The overarching theme of this latest and ongoing intellectual ferment, as some prominent Chinese scholars observe, is rule of law and constitutionalism. According to Xu Youyu, a distinguished scholar at the Institute of Philosophy at the CASS, the enlightenment movement in the post-Mao era was heavily engaged in the philosophical discussion of humanism. In contrast, in this latest enlightenment movement Chinese public intellectuals are more interested in discussing law-related issues, including "rule of law, the protection of individual rights, and limiting the scope of authority and restraining the power of the government."[17] In Xu's words, Chinese liberal intellectuals seem to have highlighted "constitutional democracy" as the overall programmatic concept.[18] In the same line of thinking, Wei Sen, a professor of economics at Fudan University, believes that enhancing the awareness of the constitutionally granted rights of taxpayers is "a top priority for the 'new enlightenment.'"[19]

He Weifang shares similar views with Zi Zhongyun, Xu Youyu, and Wei Sen. As He argues forcefully in this volume, "constitutionalism and the rule of law are the best safeguards of liberty and the foundation of good governance in China." (See chapter 2.) He believes that "a rigorous system of auditing tax revenues, fiscal budgets, and government spending . . . is a very important manifestation of constitutional government" in democracies. (See chapter 3.) Early in his career, He recognized the daunting challenges confronting China's legal scholars. His LL.M. thesis in 1985 examined religious influences in the development of law in the West.[20] As He observed, the religious sentiment in the Western tradition that "everyone is equal before God" was what laid the cultural foundation for the legal consciousness, namely, that "everyone is equal before the law."[21] China has apparently lacked such a cultural foundation for this profoundly important notion of rule of law.

In his 1994 article on the comparative study of legal cultures, He Weifang described both the enormous difficulties and various effective approaches in transplanting the Western legal system to different cultural environments such as China:

> No legal system can be transplanted to another cultural circumstance without itself undergoing change, and that system cannot play the same role as it did in its original circumstance. Legal transplantation might be considered a two-way development. On one hand, foreign legal systems and ideas transform the native culture; on the other hand, they are themselves altered by the influence of that culture. During this process, some systems or ideas will be rejected because of sharp conflicts with native traditions; some will partly revise the native culture, establishing a new system different from both the system in its original place and the culture before transplantation; and lastly some systems and ideas may be absorbed by the native tradition completely. This can lead to the curious position where a transplant can even be believed to be an essential part of the native culture and defended as such by nationalists.[22]

He firmly believes that a "successful mixture of different legal cultures requires profound study of the foreign and native cultures."[23] In practice, He has long been committed to disseminating scholarly research to a much broader audience and to fully participating in the latest wave of the public enlightenment movement, especially spreading Western views of constitutionalism and what he believes to be universal values of the rule of law. Tellingly, He's life experience and intellectual journey personifies the nation's arduous struggle to make the rule of law more than just something that authorities pay lip service to or more than just documents sitting in libraries; He wants them to be legally binding and publicly recognized norms and practices. For He, the implementation of rule of law and coordination of judicial reforms through public discourse can be as important as the making of laws itself.

The He Weifang Phenomenon:
A Legal Scholar's Public Outreach

A native of Shandong Province's Muping County (located between Yantai City and Weihai City), He Weifang was born on July 17, 1960. He's father, a doctor in the People's Liberation Army (PLA), was demobilized to work in a civilian hospital when He was three years old. In the midst of the Cultural Revolution, his mother brought the ten-year-old He and two of his siblings back to their native village of Jianggezhuang (comprised of about 800 households) in Muping County.[24] He obtained most of his elementary and middle school education at schools in that village. When the PRC resumed its higher education entrance examinations in 1977, He took the exams but failed to be accepted as he scored only 4 of a possible 100 points on the mathematics test. He took the exams again the following year and was accepted. Although he chose the Department of Chinese Literature at Shandong Normal College as his preferred program, he was instead admitted to the newly reestablished law program at the Southwest College of Political Science and Law in Chongqing, a school he "had never heard of before."[25]

During his college years from 1978 to 1982, He was primarily interested in two broad subjects. The first was the "national madness of the decade-long Cultural Revolution," which was most notable for its political persecution, torture, and human suffering. The legal and judicial prevention of the recurrence of such a tragedy was a main concern for this young law school student.[26] This concern naturally led him to develop, especially in his junior year, a strong interest in a second broad subject: the "ideas of the European Age of Enlightenment." He thus became intensively absorbed in reading the classic works of Rousseau, Voltaire, Locke, Montesquieu, and Milton. At a time when books on law and the Western legal system were extremely rare in China, the writings of these great Western philosophers were enormously helpful to He's educational development.

As a law student, He conducted intensive research on church-state relations in medieval Europe. He wrote his undergraduate thesis on Catholic canon law and the role of religion in legal and judicial development in European states—a subject that he continued to focus on in his graduate studies under the supervision of Professor Pan Huafang at China University of Political Science and Law (CUPSL) from 1982 to 1985.[27] After receiving a master's degree, He remained at CUPSL as an instructor and research fellow at the Institute of Comparative Law. He was promoted to associate professor of law in 1992. He helped establish *Comparative Law* (Bijiaofa yanjiu), the PRC's first scholarly journal on comparative law, and served as deputy editor of this quarterly Chinese journal. For almost a decade, He also served as editor-in-chief of *Peking University Law Journal*, a prominent journal in China that covers both foreign and Chinese legal issues.

In the early 1990s, in collaboration with several other young legal scholars, He was engaged in a number of major translation projects of Western legal thought and systems textbooks.[28] He also served as editor of *Xianzheng yecong* (Constitutionalism studies), a translation series published by SDX Joint Publishing Company. He's instrumental role in translating important English language legal books into Chinese and his editorship of the journal *Comparative Law* greatly contributed to the dissemination of Western legal thought among Chinese law school students and the newly emerging legal professional community in the country. As He described, the Western legal system and intellectual evolution can serve as a mirror, reflecting some of the characteristics of Chinese legal development.[29]

In 1995, after having worked at CUPSL for a decade, He moved to Peking University where he served as an associate professor of law. His main faculty responsibility thus changed from research to teaching. Four years later, he was promoted to full professor. He has always been a popular professor on campus, including being named one of the "Top Ten Teachers" of Peking University Law School for three consecutive years (1998–2000) and receiving the title of the best teacher in the entire university in 2000.

Like many of his law school colleagues of the same generation, He had the opportunity to study in Western countries as a visiting scholar. In 1993 he participated in a two-month program on research techniques in social sciences at the University of Michigan in Ann Arbor. He was a visiting scholar at the East Asian Legal Studies program at Harvard University from July 1996 to January 1997. In addition, over the last two decades, He has frequently visited the United States, Japan, and European countries, giving lectures, participating in academic conferences, and attending court hearings. An admirer of American democracy, He has explicitly expressed his reservation about the notion of "moneycracy," the term that many critics in China and elsewhere used to characterize the U.S. political system. He observed, for example, "If a [Chinese] company can spend RMB 400 million to advertise a liquor product, it is really not so big a deal for Americans to spend $240 million to elect a president who will hold the position for four years or even eight years." (See chapter 3.)

Firsthand overseas experiences, especially extensive professional exchanges with foreign legal scholars, have not only enriched He's thinking on legal issues but also broadened his perspective in his efforts to promote the rule of law in China. He believes that China is in the midst of a crucial historical transition that needs many "Chinese Madisons" and "Chinese Hamiltons" to guide the country along the right track to constitutional development. He was profoundly inspired by his role model, Hu Shih, the aforementioned leading figure in the May Fourth Movement, a legendary figure in contemporary China. He's reference to these intellectual and political giants in both the West and China reflects his outlook on China's future political transformation rather than his own personal ambition. As He expressed in a number of interviews, "I will never be able to approximate the same level of Hu Shih's academic excellence, dedication to China's embrace of the modern world, and sense of how to maintain appropriate scholarly distance from political events."[30]

Fang Zhouzi, a well-known critic in the Chinese media, has criticized He Weifang for his lack of productivity in academic work and for his "trivial role" in legal scholarship. For Fang, He's contribution has not extended beyond a mere promoting of "legal literacy" (*falü puji*) in China. In Fang's judgment, He is not qualified to be a law professor at Peking University. Fang's criticisms of He, however, have elicited a strong backlash against Fang on Chinese online message boards.[31] Tong Zongjin, an associate professor at CUPSL, has used the fact that He's scholarly publications have frequently been cited by distinguished law professors in the United States to reject Fang's critique. Yuan Weishi, a well-respected Chinese historian, has also vigorously defended He's contributions from a broader perspective. According to Yuan, He has helped to shape legal development in China through his instrumental role in public enlightenment regarding the notion of civil society and judicial independence. In Yuan's words, "The impact of one powerful open letter or one profound public speech can be far more valuable than that of one hundred academic essays combined."[32]

He indeed has the ability to write so powerfully and speak so profoundly because he can draw from his scholarly work on comparative law and long-standing stance on the importance of legal professionalism. Having remained in close touch with the rapidly changing society in China, He has on a number of important occasions played a distinct role in either voicing vigorous dissent or winning a landmark battle in the name of justice. Thus the Chinese phrase "He Weifang phenomenon" first came into vogue several years ago to refer to the keen desire by public intellectuals to participate in political and policy discourse as well as the strong impact liberal legal scholars can have on public thinking and social norms.[33]

He Weifang himself has stated that he aims to serve as "a public speaker promoting basic judicial concepts." (See chapter 3.) In every year since 1998, he has delivered or participated in about thirty to fifty public lectures or panel discussions on college campuses (other than the institution where he has taught) and with local governments, nongovernmental organizations, and legal institutions (such as courts) throughout the country.[34] In some of his public speeches at colleges, students have waited for three to four hours outside the lecture hall in order to get a seat, with many having to sit on the floor.[35]

In addition to public lectures, He has been known for his public outreach through social media. Between 2006 and 2008, for example, He's blogs had a total of 3.7 million hits.[36] By the summer of 2012, his blog on sina.com had a total of 16 million hits.[37] Unlike most of his colleagues in China's law schools who usually devote their time to research and writings in academia, He has frequently written for popular magazines and has been interviewed by a variety of media outlets. Altogether, He has tendered several hundred nonacademic articles and media interviews during the last decade.

In 2001 He was selected by *China Youth*, a popular magazine in the PRC, as one of the top 100 young people who might shape China in the twenty-first century.[38] Within two years he had already begun to leave important marks on China's legal development. In 2003, for instance, in the wake of the tragic death of twenty-seven-year-old migrant worker Sun Zhigang who was beaten to death in Guangzhou, He and five other legal scholars in Beijing submitted a request to the Standing Committee of the NPC, asking that the "Regulation for Internment and Deportation of Urban Vagrants," adopted by the Chinese government in 1982, be considered unconstitutional. The news of the request circulated widely throughout the country. Within a month, Premier Wen Jiabao announced the abolition of the regulation, bringing to an end two decades of legal discrimination against migrants.[39]

He's provocative remarks at the famous New Western Hills Symposium in 2006, including his assertion that China's party-state structure is "a serious violation of the constitution and law" because it exempts itself from constitutional controls and proper registration as a legal entity, are considered the strongest critique of the CCP party-state in PRC history. (See chapter 5.) He argued that the CCP should be registered as a "corporate legal person" (*shetuan faren*), as otherwise the existence of the CCP itself is unconstitutional. He believes that the party should have its own bank account and the party and state should have separate coffers. The salaries of CCP leaders should also not come from the state coffer, which is based on income from the vast number of taxpayers in the country, but instead should come from party membership dues. In the symposium, He also proposed that the PRC should make a political transition on two fronts. The first would be to make a constitutional move to strip the

CCP of its control of the PLA, thus transforming the party army to the state army. The second would be to divide the CCP into two rival factions with a new mechanism of checks and balances within the party, eventually leading to a multi-party political system similar to that in democratic Taiwan.

Lately, He has taken a critical view of Hu Jintao's notion of the "harmonious society." In He's view, lawyers by profession are the products of a legal culture that respects dissent and conflict. He argues that "lawyers inherently conflict with prosecutors, with judges, and even with public opinion. Lawyers will lose their practical utility and professional purpose if a culture does not respect conflict. Genuine harmony in a given society should be based on the respect for conflict through legal process."[40]

In recent years, He's voice of reason was often in the limelight during major political events, such as the CCP's decision to close the liberal media outlet *Freezing Point* weekly in 2006 (see chapter 9); the Tibetan protest for religious freedom on the eve of the Beijing Olympics in 2008 (see chapter 11); the controversy over Bo Xilai's Cultural Revolution–style campaign, especially its disregard for the rule of law, in Chongqing in 2009–11 (see the prologue); the call for the launch of the judicial review process, which He characterized as the never-woken "sleeping beauty," following the bullet train crash in Wenzhou in 2011; and Chinese public outrage over the death penalty verdict in the financial fraud case of private entrepreneur Wu Ying in 2012.[41]

A Liberal Scholar on All Fronts: Consistency and Constraints

He Weifang has been known as a vocal opponent of the death penalty for over a decade. According to PRC criminal law, a total of fifty-five crimes are punishable with the death penalty, including tax evasion, embezzlement, bribery, and drug trafficking.[42] To abolish capital punishment—and to end the long history of cruelty in China's criminal system, especially public executions—has been one of the recurring topics of He's public lectures. (See chapter 10.) As a result of the indefatigable campaign by He Weifang and other liberal-minded public figures, in 2007 the Chinese authorities decided to instruct the Supreme People's Court to review all capital punishment cases. The number of executions dropped sharply from as many as 15,000 people annually in the 1990s to about 1,700 people in the year 2008, according to estimates by Amnesty International.[43]

In his public speeches, He constantly expressed the notion that the purpose of criminal law was not just retribution—and certainly not in any way to advocate for cruelty and violence—but to transform criminals.[44] The irony, as He pointed out, is that "while the state does not allow anyone to kill people, the state in fact executes people."[45] This manner of state behavior has an effect on the public psychology in any given country. In He's view, to the degree that the government is cruel, so is the public. He further argues that human beings cannot be without compassion and sympathy for each other. One's sympathy should extend even to criminals. (See chapter 10.)

He's liberal views are also evident in his comments on the sensitive issue of Taiwan and other controversial foreign policy matters. Regarding Taiwan, He believes that the mainland should respect the reality of the over sixty years of separation and existence of the Republic of China. In light of international law, the cross-strait relationship cannot be simply framed as a central government-province relationship. Taiwan has its own government, judicial system, passports, and territory. He believes that the mainland government should allow more international space for Taiwan. A truly close relationship between the mainland and Taiwan is, in his view, dependent upon the mainland's improvement in rule of law, human rights, democracy, and freedom.[46]

He is critical of the Chinese government's policy of supporting totalitarian regimes such as North Korea. He believes that a foreign policy that supports the dictators of North Korea is akin to suppressing the democratic demands of the Korean people. He challenges the notion that China's strategic interest in the Korean Peninsula should be driven by the need for a "buffer zone." He considers this professed "need" to be the external extension of the internal policy of "stability overrides everything" (*wending yadaoyiqie*), which means in this case that so-called stability comes at the expense of the freedom and human rights of the Korean people. He argues that today's narrow-minded "national interest" may be tomorrow's national liability or national scourge.

In response to the visit of blind human rights activist Chen Guangcheng to the U.S. embassy in Beijing in the spring of 2012, He Weifang commented on his microblog that such a visit was "consensual" and that CCP authorities should not make it a big deal by punishing Chen or condemning the U.S. government.[47] Not surprisingly, some conservative public intellectuals, such as Peking University professor Kong Qingdong, labeled He a traitor and a "running dog" of Western anti-China forces.[48] In fact, from time to time, He Weifang has expressed some reservation about certain aspects of Western countries' policies toward China. He argues that Western governments and politicians should deal with China in a more responsible manner, rather than solely expressing radical views so as to cater to domestic political audiences. Such domestically determined foreign policy pronouncements will only "fuel nationalism in China." (See chapter 11.)

Largely due to He Weifang's good reputation, especially among the country's youth, the Chinese authorities have been hesitant to persecute him. But this does not necessarily mean that He is exempt from punishment or threats by CCP hardliners for his liberal views and public outreach. In a number of instances over the past decade, He has been subjected to tremendous political pressure and faced with the possible loss of his teaching job.

At the end of 2007, the Guanghua Law School of Zhejiang University in Hangzhou invited He Weifang to join the faculty. In July 2008, He accepted the offer and resigned from Peking University. However, as He was about to move to Hangzhou for the 2009 spring semester, the Zhejiang University administration withdrew its offer. It was widely believed that He's signing of Charter 08, a manifesto that adopted the name and style of the anti-Soviet Charter 77 issued by dissidents in Czechoslovakia, offended the Chinese authorities.[49] Eventually, Peking University decided to reinstate him. For the following two years, however, He was assigned to teach in Shihezi, a small city in remote Xinjiang, as part of an exchange program.

He regards his two years in "exile" in Xinjiang from 2009 to 2011 with a resigned humor. He stated that for those two years he was following in the "footsteps of several renowned Chinese intellectuals, such as the writer Wang Meng and poet Ai Qing, who were exiled to Xinjiang during the Mao era."[50] In fact, these two years allowed him to reach out to a broader audience, both geographically and ethnically.[51] Yet when He finished his teaching assignment in Xinjiang and returned to Beijing in early 2011, he found himself in the midst of another political storm.

The Courage to Challenge Bo Xilai and Wang Lijun

Enlightenment movements—in China and elsewhere—often require political courage from those who attempt to challenge authority and power.[52] In his famous 1784 essay "What Is Enlightenment?" Immanuel Kant asserted that "hav[ing] the courage to use your own intelligence is the motto of the enlightenment."[53] Quoting the German jurist Rudolf von Jhering, He Weifang considers his professional pursuits in an authoritarian political system as a "struggle for the law." (See the prologue.) The tremendous personal danger He faced in his own struggle for the law was most evident in his courageous legal and political fight against Bo Xilai and Wang Lijun before their dramatic downfall.

Soon after Bo Xilai moved from Beijing to Chongqing, where he served as party chief from the end of 2007, this ambitious politician launched two idiosyncratic initiatives: "singing red songs" and "striking the black mafia" (*changhong dahei*). For the first initiative, Bo requested that both officials and ordinary Chongqing residents sing revolutionary songs to lift their spirits. This was a way for Bo to highlight his background as a communist princeling or member of the "red nobility," making him an ideal successor of the red regime that his father's generation established. This initiative also reflected Bo's Cultural Revolution–like mentality and behavior, with which he intended to mobilize the masses to achieve his ideological and political objectives.[54]

The second initiative was a police campaign that Bo launched in Chongqing in 2009 to arrest what he called the "gangsters of the underground mafia," who were often supported by corrupt law enforcement officials in the city. In June 2008, prior to launching this police campaign, Bo transferred his protégé Wang Lijun—then police chief of Jinzhou City, Liaoning Province—to Chongqing, where Wang served as executive deputy police chief. Then, in July 2009, Wang was promoted to police chief, and in the same month Bo and Wang mobilized a total of 30,000 police officers in the city to participate in the "striking the black mafia" campaign, which led to the arrest of 5,789 people.[55] According to *Chongqing Evening News*, Bo ordered the city's police to arrest approximately 9,000 criminals.[56] A handful of those arrested were quickly tried and executed, including Wen Qiang, the former executive deputy police chief and head of the municipal government's justice department. The execution was highly publicized across the country.

Before Bo's dramatic downfall, his ideological and political campaign had gained considerable momentum. Five of the nine members of the Politburo Standing Committee of the CCP, China's supreme leadership body, visited Chongqing, leading to speculation that these most powerful party leaders had endorsed Bo's campaign. Meanwhile, many distinguished PRC public intellectuals made pilgrimages to Chongqing. Some left-wing intellectuals called Bo's Chongqing development model the "Thousand Days' Reform," borrowing the term from the famous "Hundred Day's Reform" of the late Qing dynasty.[57] According to Kong Qingdong, Bo's "Chongqing model," which was known for its tough measures dealing with "underground mafia" on the political front, "singing red songs" on the cultural front, and the promotion of "common prosperity" on the economic front, paved the way for China's future development.[58] Wang Shaoguang, a professor of public administration at the University of Hong Kong, praised the Chongqing model of socioeconomic development as "Chinese-style socialism 3.0."[59] Quite popular not just among the Chongqing public, Bo's loud bravado earned him the title of "man of the year" in a 2009 online poll conducted by the national paper *People's Daily*.[60]

A large number of law professors and legal professionals in the country, however, expressed serious reservations about Bo's campaign at its outset.[61] He Bing, the associate dean of the law school at the China University of Political Science and Law, was one of the most outspoken liberal intellectuals who challenged the resurgence of Mao fever and the remnants of the Cultural Revolution exemplified in Bo's campaign.[62] He Bing sarcastically asked what the nostalgia for the Mao era espoused by Bo and other like-minded people tried to glorify: the political persecution of the Anti-Rightist campaign? The economic catastrophe that resulted from the Great Leap Forward? Or perhaps the sociopolitical chaos of the Cultural Revolution?

He Weifang, too, was deeply troubled by the Cultural Revolution nostalgia held by some in the country. A strong believer that the Chinese nation should seriously reflect on the terrible tragedy of the Cultural Revolution, He once poignantly reminded his countrymen that the famous writer Ba Jin's appeal for the establishment of a Cultural Revolution museum was sadly ignored. For the education of the future generations, He went on to argue, "The Chinese should do as the Germans have done: establish something like a monument for Jews who died in the Nazi era."[63]

Equally important, He pointed out that the way in which Bo Xilai and Wang Lijun dealt with crimes and the underground mafia in Chongqing was extremely troubling. He referred to the Nazis when making critical remarks on the ideological and police campaigns to the Chinese media in May 2011:

> I believe that the attempt to purify society through draconian methods was the idea of the Nazis. The mafia was a century-long problem for Italy. But under the rule of Benito Mussolini, it was effectively controlled, and the public was very happy. Many dictators in fact began their iron-fisted rule in the name of social justice, doing things that pleased the public. But consequently, liberty and independent intellectuals were soon in jeopardy. [64]

The Li Zhuang Case: Defending Lawyers' Rights

The direct confrontation between law enforcement in Chongqing, led by Bo Xilai and Wang Lijun, and liberal legal scholars, represented by people like He Weifang and He Bing, centered on the Li Zhuang case—arguably the most important trial in the PRC in the past three decades.[65] This was the case that He Weifang had warned could set "China's legal reform back thirty years."[66]

The case, however, turned into a big victory for the Chinese legal professional community. With its twists and turns and its far-reaching impact, the case constitutes a telling story about the effects of the enlightenment movement. For He, although the episode reveals the sad reality of political interference in legal affairs in the country, it also shows "the glimmer of the rule of law in China."[67]

Li Zhuang was a lawyer at the Beijing-based Kangda law firm. In November 2009, Li was commissioned by the relatives of a suspect named Gong Gangmo in Chongqing to be his defense lawyer. Gong, a rich private entrepreneur, was arrested during Bo's "striking the black mafia" campaign and was charged as "heading a mafia" of thirty-four people that was allegedly involved in homicide, bribery, illegal gambling, drug and gun trafficking, and other criminal activities. When Gong and other "mafia members" were arrested in June 2009, the Chongqing and national media called this prosecution "the first case of Chongqing's 'striking the black mafia' campaign."[68]

As a defense lawyer, Li Zhuang found that most of the charges lacked evidence. In addition, he found that the Chongqing police had horrifically tortured Gong and other suspects in this case. On December 10, however, a few weeks after Li took the case, his client Gong Gangmo reported to prosecutors that Li had encouraged him to fabricate his statement about police torture. The following day, Li was recalled by his law firm to Beijing and was suspended. One day later, the Chongqing police went to Beijing to arrest Li and took him back to Chongqing on charges of fabricating evidence.[69]

In January 2010, the court sentenced Li to a jail term of two years and six months. Li filed an appeal with the First Intermediate Court of the Chongqing Municipality. Surprisingly, during the appeal trial, Li pleaded guilty despite the fact that his defense lawyers stated that Li was not guilty. When the Chongqing Intermediate Court maintained the first trial conviction and handed down a sentence of one year and six months of imprisonment, Li screamed at the court, claiming that it had not kept its promise to exempt him from a jail term. Li revealed that his guilty plea had been the result of threats and pressure from the Chongqing authorities.

The Li Zhuang imbroglio took a further twist in April 2011 when Chongqing prosecutors attempted to level new charges against Li for falsifying evidence on a case three years earlier. The objective of the Chongqing police, as many observers believed, was to send Li back to jail again when his first prison term ended in June 2011. The Chongqing authorities' eagerness to give Li a longer jail term was widely interpreted as an effort to deny Li the opportunity to criticize Bo and Wang's campaign, which likely would have undermined the chances for Bo's promotion at the Eighteenth Party

Congress in the fall of 2012. Zhu Mingyong, a defense lawyer for the "mafia," bluntly stated at the court trial that the whole case against the "Gong Gangmo mafia was false," arguing that in order to justify the campaign, "the Chongqing police used illegal methods to convert a simple homicide case and a few common criminal cases into a complicated plot of organized crime by a mafia."[70] Zhu concluded by stating explicitly, "The director of this drama is the Chongqing Public Security Bureau."[71]

As the Chongqing police leveled new charges against Li Zhuang, the entire Chinese legal community became outraged. It demonstrated great unity and solidarity in condemning the Chongqing authorities for undermining the rights of defense lawyers and for disregarding the legal process. Hundreds of blog posts by lawyers and law firms in the country expressed their support for Li, proclaiming that the case against him was "an insult and threat to China's rapidly expanding community of lawyers."[72] Chinese liberal media outlets reported extensively on the latest developments of the Li case. *Caixin* magazine, for example, criticized the fact that Li's lawyers were not allowed to "exercise their legal right to read case documents, meet their client, or investigate the case."[73] In support of Li, a group of prominent Chinese legal scholars formed a consulting team for Li's defense, which included Jiang Ping, the former president of China University of Political Science and Law; Zhang Sizhi, the founder of *Chinese Lawyers* magazine and lead defense lawyer for the "Gang of Four" trial; Professor He Weifang; Professor He Bing; and a number of well-known lawyers such as Chen Youxi. Wei Rujiu, a member of the team, described their effort this way: "Defending Li Zhuang is defending the right to work as a lawyer in China and the ideal of justice."[74]

He Weifang's instrumental role in the Li Zhuang case cannot be overemphasized.[75] Immediately after Li's arrest, He was alerted to the political motivation of the Chongqing authorities. When the official media in Chongqing and elsewhere launched a campaign of character assassination against Li before the trial, including accusations of involvement in prostitution, He expressed his dissent. He argued that questions of Li's guilt or innocence aside, the original prosecution process lacked integrity. The flaws in the legal process were abundant; for example, defense requests for the case to be transferred to a court in a city other than Chongqing were rejected, witnesses in police custody were not allowed to appear at his first trial, and defense lawyers were denied access to witnesses whose statements contradicted Li's. He vigorously criticized the Chongqing court for severely depriving defense lawyers of some of the basic rights granted to them for criminal proceedings.

He Weifang's most important dissent was an "Open Letter to Legal Professionals in Chongqing" that he published on April 12, 2011. This letter, which has been chosen as the prologue of this volume, stands as a landmark in China's long journey for judicial independence and rule of law. By July 2012, the web link to the letter had received about a quarter of a million hits and over 14,000 comments on the author's blog. Additionally, hundreds of media outlets and websites also published or posted the open letter. In this letter, He highlighted the destructive and unlawful nature of Bo Xilai's "striking the black mafia" campaign, including its unambiguous rejection of "independent exercise of adjudicative and prosecutorial powers"—as was specifically evident in the Li Zhuang case. (See the prologue.)

Given subsequent events, his letter becomes even more important. In the letter He directly admonishes then police chief Wang Lijun that "respect for judicial independence is equally important for major power holders." He warned Wang that what happened to his predecessor Wen Qiang (that is, being purged and then executed) could also happen to him, because "without judicial independence no one is safe." Perhaps He's words affected Wang's decision, ten months later, to break his patron-client ties with Bo Xilai and defect to the U.S. consulate in Chengdu. This letter of remarkable foresight undoubtedly conveyed a much-needed warning to the nation about radicalism, violence, abuse of power, the rise of a demagogic dictator, and the complete retreat of justice and law.

On April 22, 2011, the Chongqing prosecutors suddenly decided to drop the new charges against Li Zhuang, and about two months later Li was released from prison. It seems that He Weifang and China's emerging legal community had won a public opinion battle on the importance of rule of law.

Legal Professionalism: Dimensions, Priorities, and Prospects

Public enlightenment about the rule of law, though important, cannot by itself lead to constitutional governance in a given country. Ultimately, the development of an independent judicial system requires legal professionalism—another domain in which He Weifang has made great contributions. The Chinese legal community's collective efforts to defend lawyers' rights in the Li Zhuang case is testimony to the remarkable advances in the development of legal professionalism that have occurred in post-Mao China, especially during the past two decades. Yet the priority that should be placed on the development of legal professionalism as well as the larger prospects for China's constitutional change remain topics of heated debate in the country. He Weifang's views on these issues represent the liberal perspective among

PRC legal scholars. A brief review of the development of the judicial system and the coming-of-age of Chinese lawyers and judges reveals how much China's legal professional community has accomplished during the past two decades, and how many daunting problems it has yet to overcome.

Overcoming Cultural and Political Barriers: Building a Legal System from Scratch

The Chinese legal tradition has been weak primarily due to what He Weifang calls the tight "integration of moral and political authority." As He observes, "Moral authority, intellectual authority, political authority, and religious authority were combined to form an insurmountable challenge to any attempt to limit the power of the sovereign in ancient China." (See chapter 2.) He has noted that Mencius, for example, the most prominent philosopher in the Confucian school of thought who also wrote substantially on law, "consistently emphasizes filial piety and assigns it a higher value than law." (See chapter 2.) He believes that this explains why in China's long history the norm of "rule by virtue" (*dezhi*) has consistently prevailed over other forms of governance such as rule of law (*fazhi*).

During the first three decades of the PRC, legal nihilism and legal instrumentalism dominated the public view of law in the country. A good example of legal nihilism was embodied in the remarks Mao made at the important CCP Politburo meeting in August 1958: "Every one of our party resolutions is law, and every meeting itself is law, and we can therefore maintain social order through resolutions and meetings."[76] The neglect of even a basic legal consciousness accounted for the fact that from 1949 to 1978, the PRC promulgated only two laws, one being the constitution itself and the other the marriage law.

In Mao's China law was largely seen as a tool of the ruling class to maintain its power and exercise its dictatorship. In the late 1950s and early 1960s, it was quite common for officials at various levels of the leadership to serve concurrently as public security chief, principal prosecutor, or court president.[77] Not surprisingly, prior to the late 1990s, when discussing the role of law in the country, Chinese authorities often used the phrase "to use law to rule the country" rather than "to govern the country according to the law."[78] These two phrases are fundamentally different in connotation. The former emphasizes the utility of law from the party perspective, and the latter emphasizes that no individual, group, or party should be above the law.[79] In 1996 the Institute of Law of the CASS convened a conference discussing these two Chinese phrases and concluded by adopting the second notion.[80]

Since economic reforms began in 1978, many top leaders who had suffered from the lawlessness of the Cultural Revolution, such as Deng Xiaoping and then chairman of the Legal Committee of the NPC Peng Zhen, have made systematic efforts to issue important laws. Over the years, many laws have been established in China, including the criminal law and the code of criminal procedure in 1979, the general principles of civil law in 1987, the administrative procedure law in 1989, the administrative punishment law in 1996, and the property law in 2007. The promulgation of these laws, in the words of He Weifang, has constituted "landmark events in China's legal development."[81]

The main motivation for the Chinese leadership to issue these laws has not been liberal legal thinking but rather self-interest, as the late Cai Dingjian—one of the prominent drafters of some of these laws—stated specifically in regard to the CCP leadership's desire to vindicate property rights.[82] China's transition to a market economy requires more laws and regulations, without which the economy would fall into anarchy. In July 1981, the State Council established the Research Center of Economic Laws, which was responsible for drafting large-scale economic legislation. From 1979 to 1993, among the 130 laws approved by the NPC, more than half were in the areas of economic and administrative law.[83]

According to the Chinese authorities, China's legal framework was largely established by the end of 2010. This legal system includes seven main functional areas: the constitution, civil and commercial law, administrative law, economic law, social law, criminal law, and litigation and nonlitigation procedural law. According to the official account, China has promulgated 239 laws in the reform era. The State Council has additionally issued 690 administrative rules and regulations, and local governments have issued about 8,600 local laws and regulations. Taken together, these developments are a substantial improvement over the legal vacuum of Mao's China.[84] Admittedly, many of these laws either have not been implemented or are insufficiently enforced, but they nonetheless represent an important foundation on which a more effective system can be built over time.

He Weifang on Lawyers and Judges:
Specialized Training and Professional Standards

Nearly keeping pace with this rapid emergence of a Chinese body of law has been a burgeoning legal profession.[85] In the early years of the PRC, the country had only four colleges that specialized in politics and law.[86] Only a few universities had law departments. These were all closed, moreover, during the

Cultural Revolution. In 1977 Peking University, Jilin University, and the Hubei Institute of Finance and Economics admitted law students for the first time since the Cultural Revolution, with the entire country registering only 200 law students that year.[87] Even then, the legal specialization remained as only part of the broad academic major called "politics and law" (*zhengfa*). By 1980 fourteen colleges and law departments in the country had admitted an underwhelming total of 2,800 undergraduate law students.[88] It is also interesting to note that in the early 1980s, there were only about 3,000 lawyers in the PRC, a country of approximately one billion people.[89]

By the end of 2010, however, this group had expanded sixty-eight-fold to 204,000 licensed lawyers.[90] In that year about 40,000 PRC nationals received licenses to become registered lawyers in the country. And in 2011 China's 640 law schools and law departments produced roughly 100,000 law graduates.[91] These numbers will continue to swell in the coming years. Meanwhile, the programs in legal studies—such as jurisprudence, constitutional law, administrative law, criminal law, civil law, procedural law, and environmental law—have over the past two decades become well-established professional subfields. As He Weifang recently described in a public talk, there were hardly any textbooks on law when he began his undergraduate study in 1978; now law-related books usually constitute one-fourth of the books in an academic bookstore.[92] In 2007 about 400 books and 70,000 scholarly articles on law, including translated works, were published in the country. In 2009 China had over 200 professional journals that focused on law.[93]

In addition, legal aid institutions and programs have begun to establish a presence in China. In 1992 China had its first nongovernmental legal aid institution: the Socially Vulnerable Group Protection Center at Wuhan University. Other legal aid institutions have since arisen, including Peking University's Women's Rights Legal Research and Service Center, Tsinghua University's Constitution and Citizens' Rights Protection Center, and the Oriental Public Interest Lawyers' Legal Aid Firm. These organizations have pursued many public interest litigation cases.[94] By the end of 2009, there were 3,274 registered legal aid institutions with 13,081 staff members in the country.[95] In 2010 a total of 8,189 Chinese volunteer lawyers worked on issues concerning protection of minors' rights, with the Beijing Children's Legal Aid and Research Center and the Beijing Legal Aid Office for Migrant Workers winning some important legal cases in this area.[96] A new phrase, "rights protection lawyers" (*weiquan lüshi*), was created during the past decade, reflecting the great strides made by a small but influential coterie of rights protection lawyers that have devoted their careers to human rights issues.

One of the most important contributions that He Weifang has made in promoting China's legal professionalism was his famous 1998 article on "Ex-Servicemen of the PLA Now Serving at Court."[97] The article boldly criticized the trend of ex-servicemen of the PLA, the majority of whom have not had any formal legal training, becoming a main source for judges in the country. He strongly criticized this practice as being akin to appointing demobilized servicemen to be medical doctors, saying that because a judge is as responsible as a medical doctor for the life and death of people, the position requires specialized knowledge and thus professional training.

For He Weifang, judiciary specialization (*sifa zhuanyehua*) should consist of many specific components, including professional training of lawyers and judges, separation between judicial and administrative functional areas in legal and law enforcement institutions, and ultimately an increase of judicial power and authority. By the nature of their profession, lawyers are responsible for containing state power. Yet lawyers are also professionally interested in developing legal norms to reshape state power. Lawyers can enable public resentment and grievances against the government to be expressed through legal channels rather than street protests. On many occasions over the past decade, He proposed that China should jettison undergraduate legal education in favor of the Western model of providing specialized legal training via postgraduate law schools. (See chapter 7.)

As for the professional specialization of judges, He argues that a judge must have received formal legal education and should possess both a capacity for superb legal thinking and an analytical mind. The relationship between the public security sector, prosecutors, and the courts should be well defined. Judicial power should be independent not only from external interference but also from internal restriction. According to He, both communist ideology and the traditional Chinese conception of law were the cause and consequence of "a judicial process dominated by laymen." (See chapter 1.) He argues that a sound legal system "is highly dependent on different legal practitioners having the same educational background." (See chapter 7.)

He's foresight and outspoken stance on the promotion of legal professionalism in China has yielded some very positive results. For example, the PRC established the judicial examination system in 2001. Not only are lawyers and legal scholars no longer considered state officials (as they were in China's recent past), they also now boast an unprecedented degree of political autonomy and a steadily increasing level of professionalism. At least partly because of He Weifang's initial advocacy, judges and judicial staff members now wear robes and use gavels in court.[98] Despite these advances, He is quick to say that Chinese judges are far from being able to maintain professional standards for judicial independence or even the spirit of judicial professionalism.

JUDICIAL INDEPENDENCE AS THE TOP PRIORITY

Legal development in China, like elsewhere in the world, is certainly not a linear process. The rapid expansion of and growing demand for professionalism in the Chinese legal community have paradoxically led the Chinese authorities, especially conservative leaders, to more aggressively strengthen the CCP monopoly over the legal system. As He Weifang observes in this volume, the party's supremacy over the judicial system has remained the defining feature of the Chinese legal system. The legal community and the general public "simply do not have a means to restrict the power of the top leader." (See chapter 2.)

In an article published in 2007, He criticized the phenomenon widespread at various levels of leadership in which the head of the public security bureau is simultaneously a member of the standing committee of the party committee or the secretary of the politics and law commission—an arrangement that effectively places police power higher than judicial power. He believes that this had led the police to become an important force in the maintenance of the CCP's monopoly on state power and in the suppression of any resistance to this system.[99]

What particularly troubles He Weifang and many other like-minded people is the recent return to a convergence of power between the police chief, the attorney general, and the chief judge at various levels of government in the form of the "three chiefs conferences." These "three chiefs" of vastly different functional areas often "work in a coordinated fashion so that the cases are decided before they even go to trial." (See the prologue.) Such a practice is most evident in the fact that the president of the Supreme Court is now supposed to report to the chairman of the Central Commission of Politics and Law or even to the police chief (minister of public security) on the work of the Supreme Court, rather than report to the NPC as China's constitution specifies. This has led He to pointedly ask: "How can a judiciary like this exercise effective supervision and constraint over police power?"[100]

Since a top priority of the CCP leadership is the maintenance of its own rule, it is no surprise that the police have become more powerful, not only in terms of their input into socioeconomic policies but also in terms of budget allocation. For example, the total amount of money used for "maintaining social stability" in 2009 was 514 billion yuan—almost identical to China's total national defense budget (532 billion yuan) that year. The Chinese government budget for national defense in 2012 was 670.3 billion yuan, while the budget for the police and other public security expenditures was 701.8 billion yuan (an 11.5 percent increase).[101]

Three factors have contributed to the growing power of the police force. First, the Arab Spring led CCP leaders to fear that they could face an outcome similar to that, for example, of the Mubarak regime. Second, business elites—especially those who work in state-monopolized industries such as banking, oil, electricity, coal, telecommunications, aviation, railway, tobacco, and shipping—have often bribed government officials and formed a "wicked coalition." This coalition constantly talks about the need for stability in the country but in fact is more concerned about maintaining its own interests.[102] Finally, the number and scale of group protests have increased in recent years, with some having become increasingly violent. In response, the authorities have often used administrative or political methods to fire local officials, crack down on protests, or apply what sociology professor Sun Liping and his colleagues at Tsinghua University have called "campaign-method governance" (*yundongshi zhili*).[103] These methods are largely arbitrary, being executed at the personal direction of individual leaders and often disregarding the role of law and the legal process.

The growing power of the Central Commission of Politics and Law—and the police force that implements its decisions—not only has generated much criticism from Chinese public intellectuals, especially legal scholars, but has also created a vicious circle in which the more fiercely the police suppress social protests, the more violent and widespread the protests become. As characterized by PRC scholars, "The more you are obsessed with social stability, the less you will have of it."[104] A popular sentiment in the country is particularly revealing: "Big protests lead to big settlements; small protests, small settlement; no protests, no settlements."[105] As He Weifang has insightfully pointed out, the rapidly growing power of the Internet and social media may not necessarily be conducive to the promotion of rule of law and legal procedures; sometimes Internet discourse is a distorting mirror, representing extreme views.[106]

In addition to the growing number of social protests, the rapid increase of petition letters also reflects the failure of the judicial system. Every year, all levels of the government combined receive over 10 million petition letters. Three recent remarkable events—Wang Lijun's defection to the U.S. consulate, the downfall of Bo Xilai, and Chen Guangcheng's visit to the U.S. embassy—have further revealed the major flaws in the Chinese political system in general, and its police and law enforcement apparatus in particular.

He Weifang believes that all of the recent phenomena resulting from the CCP authorities' heavy reliance on the use of police reflect an urgent need for an independent judicial system. He argues bluntly that China is in the midst of a race between a bottom-up revolution and judicial reform. This race will not require eighty—or even twenty—years to complete; it will likely occur much sooner. In He's words, the CCP has no other way to go (*wulu kezou*).[107] For He and many like-minded legal scholars, the judicial reform outlined in the beginning of this chapter is the approach with the lowest political cost and risk for what will be China's inevitable political transformation. He recently told the Hong Kong media that the tension between liberal leaders, such as Premier Wen Jiabao, and conservative leaders reflects the tension between the party's desire to surrender some of its power and privilege in order to promote rule of law, on the one hand, and the party's desire to retain its monopoly on power at all costs, on the other.[108] The recent discussion within the CCP leadership regarding the need to reduce the power and influence of the Central Commission of Politics and Law, if indeed adopted, is an encouraging development.[109] In a much broader context, China's judicial reforms and bold move toward constitutionalism should become top priority if the leadership wants to avoid a bottom-up revolution.

PROSPECTS FOR CONSTITUTIONALISM IN CHINA:
THREE CONTENDING VIEWS

China has a constitution, but its government does not adhere to constitutionalism. Since the founding of the PRC in 1949, China has had four separate constitutions, promulgated in 1954, 1975, 1978, and 1982, with the 1982 constitution having undergone four amendments, adopted in 1988, 1993, 1999, and 2004.[110] He Weifang believes that China's current constitution has two major defects. The first is "intrinsic, something that cannot be solved by minor amendments, because it was formulated at a time (1982) when constitutionalism was still seen in an ideologically tinged light. . . . The second major defect is that even this unsatisfactory constitution is not well implemented." (See chapter 3.)

According to Xia Yong, a well-known legal scholar who currently serves as director of the State Secrecy Bureau under the State Council, there have been three types of constitutions in the world: the revolutionary constitution, the reform constitution, and the constitution based on constitutionalism (*xianzheng xianfa*).[111] Xia believes that China is in the midst of transitioning from the reform constitution to constitutionalism. Only this third type can provide political legitimacy and enduring social stability because it contains the basic principle that "there is no other law above the constitution."[112]

Students of the Chinese legal system, however, have vastly different views on the future prospects of constitutionalism in the PRC. The three contending perspectives—pessimistic, optimistic, and pragmatic—have contrasting assessments of China's political and legal development at present.

Pessimists believe that the Chinese legal system is incompatible with constitutionalism. They believe that virtually all of the key elements of the current PRC constitution reflect the influence of both a Leninist approach to constitutionalism and the supreme authority of the party-state structure. The PRC constitution does not contain any provisions for constitutional adjudication or judicial review, which is often regarded as a foundation of constitutionalism. As some Western scholars argue, constitutionalism should entail creation of a state organ with the authority to legitimately interpret the meaning of the constitution and "determine whether any action by the state apparatus (or others) exceeds their authority to act under that framework."[113] There is no such independent state organ in China. Chinese courts are not given the ability to exercise such review power but merely apply the law with no power to interpret it when adjudicating cases.[114]

Pessimists often emphasize that in the absence of the supreme authority of the constitution, the rule of law loses any real significance. For the court, police, and prosecutor in the PRC, the primary concern is political accountability rather than legal accountability. Under these circumstances, any efforts on the part of legal professionals and the public to use the law against the party-state's autocratic rule and to demand constitutionally granted rights are akin to what some critics call "asking the tiger for his skin" (*yuhu moupi*).[115] As M. Ulric Killion argues, in the absence of a separation of powers, popular sovereignty, or independent judicial review, "neither liberty nor social rights will be protected."[116]

As both political structure and values are at the heart of constitutionalism, some pessimists point out that partly due to the Confucian cultural tradition and partly due to socioeconomic circumstances, the Chinese public does seem to enjoy economic liberties, rising living standards (for most), and newly obtained civil and political rights. Therefore the concerns of the Chinese public may profoundly differ from those of liberal legal professionals like He Weifang in the sense that they are not so interested in legal rights that involve political issues or institutional mechanisms that can impinge on the control of the regime. According to this view, the Chinese public places more value on the "competent leader" than they do on "competent law."[117]

In contrast, optimists believe that critics of the Chinese legal system, especially those in the West, seem too quick to reject the party-state political organization on the grounds that such a system is inherently despotic and thus incompatible with constitutionalism. As Larry Backer argues, the prevailing pessimistic view in the West about the prospect of Chinese constitutionalism is "both anachronistic and too simple-minded for the emerging possibilities in states like China."[118] For Backer, China presents "an interesting variant on constitutionalism."[119] He argues that in the case of China, one needs to "focus on party rather than state, grounded in separation of powers principles in which the administrative function is vested in the state while political authority overall is vested in the party under law."[120] An institutionalization of the role of the party leadership within the Chinese constitutional framework may therefore represent "the most appropriate way of further legitimating constitutionalism within the Chinese legal order."[121]

Other scholars challenge the conventional view that the Chinese constitution is static and unchanging. Instead, they believe that judges, lawyers, and Chinese citizens can use the courts as a mechanism for constitutional litigation—a process that Chinese legal scholars call the "judicialization of the constitution" (*xianfa sifahua*). Thomas Kellogg argues that attempts by actors inside and outside the government can make the Chinese constitution a legally operative principal document.[122] Along this same line of thinking, Xia Yong argues that although China has neither a Western-style separation of powers nor federalism, in reality the PRC's constitution recognizes three powers (legislative, executive, and judicial) and a functional division between central and local powers.[123]

Many optimists believe that the NPC can play a crucial role in constitutional adjudication and judicial review. Some argue that the foundation of constitutional review in the Chinese constitution already exists as the Division of Check and Filing under the Standing Committee of the NPC. This pronounced mechanism, created by an amendment to the Working Procedure in 2005, can be regarded according to the optimists as the first stage of the activation process.[124] Some foreign scholars also point out the fact that it took a long time for many Western constitutional democracies to practice constitutional review. As Michael Dowdle observes:

France's constitution, for example, did not articulate a practice of constitutional review until 1958, some eighty years after the initial establishment of her constitutional foundation, and that practice did not begin protecting the political and civil rights enumerated in that constitution until the 1970s. Britain developed a practice resembling judicial review only in the 1990s. The Dutch constitution, now entering its second century, forbids judicial review. Sweden's constitution articulates a judicial review practice, but as of 1987 Sweden had not yet resorted to this practice in its two-hundred-year history.[125]

Dowdle also argues that many of today's successful constitutional systems actually emerged out of environments in which neither democracy nor the rule of law initially enjoyed significant normative support from the public. Constitutional values are often the product rather than the cause of successful constitutional experience.[126]

It should be noted that optimists are divided into two broad and profoundly different camps: those who believe that the CCP can be a force for the promotion and implementation of Chinese constitutionalism, and those who believe a constitutional China can be achieved only after the end of one-party rule.

Yu Keping's call for fundamental political reforms represents the first camp. For Yu, constitutionalism means the constitution should be the ultimate basis of the operation of state power. Yu observes that the CCP constitution dictates that the "CCP should operate within the sphere allowed by the constitution and law," although in practice this principle has often been violated in the PRC.[127] Like other liberal scholars in the Chinese political establishment, Yu believes that "the CCP leadership cannot claim it governs the country by law unless the party is subject to the rule of law."[128] This does not mean that China should establish a law on political parties or move to a multiparty system but rather that the party should strictly comply with both the PRC constitution and the CCP constitution to regulate party affairs and member behavior. Specifically, Yu calls for political reforms in the three major relationships the CCP has with other institutions in accordance with the PRC constitution: the relationship with the NPC, with the government or the state council, and with judicial institutions.[129]

In the wake of the Bo Xilai crisis, an increasing number of liberal leaders and scholars in the CCP recognize the need to surrender some of the party's power and privilege. It is interesting to note that Wang Huning, a top aide to President Hu Jintao and former dean of the Law School at Fudan University, recently republished his 1986 article in which he argued that "public security, prosecutors, and the court merging into one" was one of the main reasons for the prevalent human rights violations, such as torture and vandalism, during the Cultural Revolution. He stated unambiguously that the

"Cultural Revolution could happen only in a country without an independent judicial system."[130]

The second brand of optimism that scholars have about China's constitutional future is not based on the scenario that the CCP may transform itself. Rather, this view holds that a bottom-up revolution can take place at any time, as the party has lost its legitimacy in the wake of many recent scandals, especially with regard to rampant official corruption. He Pin, a seasoned New York–based analyst of Chinese elite politics, believes that China's current political and socioeconomic problems—and its painful experiences during the decade-long democratic transition—are not caused by the public enlightenment movement for constitutionalism and democracy but are the consequences of a long-standing authoritarian and lawless political system.[131]

Zhang Lifan, a well-known scholar in Beijing, has argued that "China is not in danger, but the CCP is."[132] He states that many CCP elites do not care whether the CCP will collapse but instead are only concerned about the well-being of their own families. The large-scale outflow of capital in recent years, presumably by corrupt officials, further indicates the lack of confidence party elites have in the country's sociopolitical stability. According to a 2011 report released by the Washington-based organization Global Financial Integrity, from 2000 to 2009 China's illegal capital outflow totaled $2.74 trillion, five times more than the total amount from second-ranked Mexico.[133]

Optimists in both camps believe that an increasingly vibrant legal community in the country will likely contribute to the establishment of an independent judicial system. But neither camp of optimists can provide a convincing roadmap or model for a constitutional China. Understandably, many scholars take a pragmatic view. Randall Peerenboom, for example, argues that "legal reforms are path dependent and in that sense inherently local. Thus, no single model is likely to work everywhere given the diversity of initial starting conditions and the complexity of the reform process."[134] In a sense, the constitutionalism and democratization of a given country arise not by design but by necessity—the necessity to deal with contextual problems such as the abuse of police power and official corruption.[135]

Pragmatists reject the pessimists' cultural incompatibility thesis by referring to the World Bank's recent rule of law index: five East and Southeast Asian countries or jurisdictions—Singapore, Japan, Hong Kong, Taiwan, and South Korea—rank in the top quartile.[136] As pragmatists observe, these entities usually place priority on economic growth rather than civil liberty. Over time, however, "as the legal system becomes more efficient, professionalized, and autonomous, it comes to play a greater role in the economy and society more generally."[137]

Pragmatists recognize the long process facing constitutional development in countries such as China. They also believe, however, that one should not "dismiss the importance of transformative processes simply because at the present time they seem too subtle or glacial for our tastes."[138] Quite often the evolution of the legal profession and pressures from lawyers and civil society that "seem glacial today could suddenly revolutionize the system tomorrow."[139]

While pragmatists have serious reservations about both the possibility of the CCP subjecting its power to constitutional supremacy and the role of the NPC in exerting legal constraints on the party in the short term, they do believe it is worthwhile to make an effort on these fronts. As Ji Weidong, dean of Kaiyuan Law School of Shanghai Jiaotong University, recently stated, it may take decades or longer to make the rule of law a way of life. However, judges and lawyers as a group need to start moving right now. "Step by step, they will lead institutional change."[140]

As for He Weifang, it is difficult to characterize him as either an optimist or a pessimist, an idealist or a pragmatist. On the one hand, he is optimistic in that he has devoted his entire career to fighting for justice and constitutionalism in China. It is in part due to his tireless efforts that the country has witnessed remarkable growth in the legal profession. The victory of the landmark case of Li Zhuang and He's bold and effective challenge to some of the most formidable and ruthless politicians also may have enhanced his sense of optimism. On the other hand, however, he is soberly aware that party leaders wield unrestrained power, there is unprecedented official corruption, many high-profile lawsuits result in unfair verdicts, and civil rights activists are treated in an unlawful manner. What is truly remarkable about He Weifang is the fact that he seems to have combined, in a marvelously engaging and balanced way, both idealism and pragmatism in his search for a constitutional China.

Each reader, of course, will arrive at his or her own judgment of He Weifang's pursuits and analyses, the prospects for constitutionalism in China, and implications of its success or failure for the outside world. One can cogently argue, however, that the rule of law is of utmost importance to China, as it is elsewhere in the world. While this volume focuses on one truly extraordinary Chinese legal scholar's intellectual and political odyssey, it is also about the broader experience of China's journey into the twenty-first century—the country's painful search for a sound, safe, and sustainable political and legal system. Based on He Weifang's insights and foresight, the struggle for justice and rule of law will most likely become the prevailing issue in the next phase of China's political transformation.

The two epigraphs that open this introductory chapter remind us of equally arduous undertakings in Western democracies. Emmeline Pankhurst's courage and determination led to the victory of the British suffragette movement.[141] Justice Stephen Breyer's recent remarks made in China highlight the lessons learned and strengths derived from the growth of American constitutional democracy and its uncompromising adherence to justice.[142] These quotes remind us that He Weifang's words and endeavors, frustration and inspiration, courage and vision are by no means alien to Western readership. Perhaps more than anything else, this volume highlights the common aspiration, transnational values, and enduring human spirit in our rapidly changing world.

An Open Letter to Legal Professionals in Chongqing

Dear Colleagues in the Chongqing Legal World:[1]

For more than a year now I have wanted to write an open letter to discuss my views on the "campaign against the underworld" in Chongqing.[2] But because I had already written quite a number of commentaries on my own blog and for various media outlets, I feared I might make carping remarks or get all twisted up in an open letter, so I wrote the idea off. Several recent trends in Chongqing are nagging causes for anxiety. In my view, the various things that have happened in that city, however, may already pose a danger to the most basic notions of a society ruled by law. As a legal scholar, and as one especially engaged in the process of judicial reform, I believe I now have an urgent duty to openly express my unease and voice my concerns.

I am also motivated to write this letter because Chongqing is home to my alma mater, the Southwest University of Political Science and Law, and I have fond memories of the city. It was there in 1978, after a "long and arduous journey," that I began my sojourn in legal studies on that campus at the foot of Gele Hill.

Editor's note: This open letter first appeared in Chinese on the author's blog on April 12, 2011 (http://blog.sina.com.cn/s/blog_4886632001017xtf.html). The Journalism and Media Studies Center at the University of Hong Kong translated the letter into English and posted it to its website on April 17, 2011 (http://cmp.hku.hk/2011/04/12/11481/). This edited English version is based on an original translation.

I

In 1978 our teachers had also just returned to campus life after a "terrible decade" of suppression. In class they spoke of the lawless days of the Cultural Revolution, conveying countless episodes of misery and suffering. A number of teachers could not hold back their tears. We students had also experienced the Cultural Revolution firsthand, and all of us, in one way or another, treasured the study of law. We longed for a future in which we could establish rule of law in our homeland and hungered for the opportunity to get involved in this great project and do our part to defend civil rights and freedom. We decided we would never allow a tragedy like the Cultural Revolution to be replayed on this soil.

Now, thirty years later, so much has occurred in our beloved city that makes one feel like time has been dialed back, that the Cultural Revolution is being replayed, and that the ideal of rule of law is increasingly out of sight. I refer, of course, to the "campaign to crack down on criminal forces" that has been taking place in Chongqing for two years now (and also the business of "singing red songs," of course, but let us set this issue aside for now).

Throughout the "campaign against the underworld," we have witnessed the steady increase of campaign-style law enforcement and administration of justice. Within just eight months, Chongqing's local authorities rounded up close to 5,000 supposedly "criminally involved" persons by mobilizing informers (or so-called "letters and denunciations by the masses"). In addition, over one hundred "special case teams" carried out countless wholesale arrests, prosecutions, and trials with so-called "Chongqing speed."

The Chongqing police, prosecutors, and courts worked in concert, preparing cases without any separation of responsibilities or checks on each another's discretion, as evident in the diary of Judge Wang Lixin, posted to the official website of the Supreme People's Court prior to the hearing of the Wen Qiang appeal case.[3] Moreover, so-called three chiefs conferences have occurred for a number of cases, in which the chief judge, the attorney general, and the police chief hold meetings and work in a coordinated fashion so that the cases are decided before they even go to trial. When the case is finally heard, it is a mere formality. Thus the institutional goal of ensuring that the three branches check each other is forsaken. My colleagues, do you not believe that these methods run absolutely counter to the independent exercise of adjudicative and prosecutorial powers as clearly stipulated in our nation's constitution and criminal procedure law?

In the course of trial proceedings for the Li Zhuang case, we saw quite clearly that even the court's minimal neutrality had vanished.[4] For instance, Li Zhuang and his defense attorney had requested that witnesses appear in court to be cross-examined during the trial. I have no doubt that Judge Fu Mingjian, who officiated the trial, understands all too well the importance of face-to-face cross-examination, as this was the topic of a research paper he wrote at the Southwest University of Political Science and Law. It argued for the need for witnesses to appear in court for cross-examination. In this case, however, the collegiate bench [of judges in Chongqing] rejected the defendant's request, claiming that the witnesses were unwilling to appear in court. Please, won't you all consult your criminal procedure law to see whether or not court appearances by witnesses are determined by their willingness? Seeing as the seven key witnesses in this case were in Chongqing police custody, the written statements they provided might well have been coerced out of them or written for gain, and their testimony must be checked in person. Only then can we really be sure whether Li Zhuang instigated others to provide false testimony. Nevertheless, the court in Jiangbei District—where I studied during my university years—arrived at a guilty verdict in the case, based solely on this so-called testimony that had not been challenged through cross-examination.

In the midst of this hearing, something extremely strange happened: Li Zhuang, who had firmly denied his guilt during the first trial, suddenly pleaded guilty. When the court announced that because of his confession, Li Zhuang's sentence would be reduced from thirty months to eighteen months, Li Zhuang, feeling humiliated and angry at having been hoodwinked, shouted out: "My confession is fake. I hope the court would not convict me according to this plea bargain, as my confession was induced by the Chongqing Public Security Bureau and prosecutors."[5] Li Zhuang's words show that he did not truly admit guilt.

The issue before us is, supposing the legal profession did not cooperate, could these judicial dramas continue to be perpetuated? Those involved might make excuses and say that they personally harbor doubts or even resist in their hearts the process or outcome of the adjudication of the cases, but can one really resist the overwhelming power wielded by the government? Admittedly, this is a very thorny problem, but there is at least a clear line between passive obedience and active bootlicking. It is chilling how some prosecutors with solid legal training have disregarded basic legal concepts and endorsed various illegal actions. This signifies a failure of legal education in our country.

Here I must express my disappointment with a number of law professors in Chongqing. Even if these professors, because of their roles, have no choice but to listen to their superiors, it is still entirely within their power to maintain at least a minimal degree of independence. Faced with a wholesale disregard of the basic standards of rule of law, it is understandable that one might not wish to directly voice his or her reservations, but remaining silent is a better option than voicing open support. The history of law in many countries reveals that, in terms of protecting the basic standards of rule of law, an important mission of legal scholars is to provide and reinforce support for fundamental principles and theories for professionals working in the field. At the same time, they have a sacred duty, as [the German jurist] Rudolf von Jhering put it, to "struggle for the law." Scholars must issue clear, firm criticism and opposition to intrusions on judicial independence, violations of legal procedure, and conduct that infringes upon civil rights and freedom. Regrettably, a number of my colleagues in the legal world have failed to do this. To the contrary, even before the initial verdict came out in Li's case, these scholars were singing in unison in support of the trial proceedings and possible outcome in official newspapers, making statements completely at odds with the five procedural rules. You can see online how various people commented on the case, doing damage to the dignity of academia and especially the dignity of the Southwest University of Political Science and Law. I can't for the life of me understand what motivated these colleagues to act this way.

Finally, I have a few words for Chongqing's chief of police, Wang Lijun.[6] In November 2010, you were given a concurrent post as an advisor to doctoral students at the Southwest University of Political Science and Law. As it happens, I too advise doctoral students at the university, so at this point I might as well engage a fellow scholar in a bit of conversation. While you are only a chief of police, you are a person of real consequence since authorities in Chongqing have assigned the "campaign against the underworld" such high priority. I harbor several concerns about the "thunderbolt" nature of the campaign you are spearheading. First, if the guiding principle contains hints of social purification, as it appears to some, the campaign and its result could be quite dangerous. There are always aspects of human nature that cannot be changed, and a healthy society, then, should probably adopt an attitude of tolerance toward certain human weaknesses. There is an inherent tension between order and freedom, and if order is emphasized too strongly, then freedom will suffer in the balance.

Second, while we all oppose and resent criminal activity and wish to deal with such activity in accordance with the law, we must also recognize that for "black society" [criminal gangs] to have developed in Chongqing to the terrifying degree you note, this must surely mean that serious problems have also emerged in "white society" [or "clean society"]. For example, as justice has faltered, enterprises have had to rely on means outside the law to ensure the security of their business activities and property. While campaigning against criminal elements is a necessary component, dealing with the problem at its root means building the relevant systems to ensure that government administration is in accordance with the law and that the courts are just.

Third, assuming that in the process of meting out justice, the government employs means that are illegal, such as extracting confessions by torture, violating suspects' rights in litigation, or even intimidating defense lawyers in criminal cases, the long-term consequences of employing these means will be quite serious. The government's use of illegal means to combat illegal activity leaves people with the unfortunate impression that might is right, that "black" means can be used to deal with "black" phenomena. Moreover, excessively severe penalties upset the expectation of fair treatment, and this letdown of expectations angers the family members of those who had been found guilty and the convicted who might one day be released from prison, fostering frightening forces of social resentment. For many years we've seen that the perpetrators of many of the most grievous crimes in our society were those viciously treated in previous "strike hard" campaigns and then released at the end of their terms. Mr. Wang, since you have been in law enforcement for so many years you must be even more cognizant of this than I am.

Fourth, even though under the current system police departments have more power than the courts, I am confident you must understand, given your role as an advisor to doctoral students, that one important measure of the rule of law in a country is the ability of the courts to limit police power. Police must respect the courts, accept the independent examination and supervision of prosecutors, and protect the independence of courts and judges. In actuality, respect for judicial independence is equally important for major power holders. While Wen Qiang [former police chief in Chongqing] was still in favor with the Chongqing leadership, he likely had little idea of the value of judicial independence. But once Wen fell out of favor with the authorities, he must have had a rude awakening, realizing that without judicial independence no one is safe.

My colleagues, writing this letter also prompts me to think of death. While not all the numbers have been released, there have been many people in Chongqing, including Wen Qiang, who have been sentenced to death since the "campaign against the underworld" began. Death comes to us all, but for the state to deprive a person of his or her life is a grave matter. I saw pictures on the Internet of the city organizing citizens in the singing of "red anthems." Red banners fluttered in the wind—red as far as the eye could see.

The color of these flags was also the color of blood. The "singing of red anthems" and the "campaign against the underworld" invoke a common color, and one cannot suppress all sorts of complicated memories.

Whether one is on top for a time, or lives his or her life in ignominy, in the end death will visit us all. Those criminals sentenced to capital punishment will only go sooner than the rest of us. Decapitation and firing squads leave behind dreadful scars, a trauma without a cure. The ancient Greek playwright Sophocles recognized this plight. Let me use his words, then, to close this letter:

> No ceremony, no wedding songs, no dances and no songs . . .
> Just death! The end of us all is death.
> The best would be not to be born at all.
> But then, if he is born, the next best thing for him would be to try and return to where he came from in the quickest possible time!
> While youth and its careless mind lasts, no thought is given to what pain, what misery will, most certainly, follow.
> Murder, mayhem, quarrels, wars will come before the inescapable end.
> The hateful old age, frailty, loneliness, desolation and your own misery's neighbor, is even more misery.

I wish you all happiness, and offer a salute to the rule of law.

PART I

JUDICIAL INDEPENDENCE:
CHINA'S TREACHEROUS PATH

CHAPTER ONE

THE ONGOING QUEST FOR JUDICIAL INDEPENDENCE IN CONTEMPORARY CHINA

On September 23, 1821, an accident occurred while an American ship from Baltimore, named *Emily*, was loading cargo in Guangzhou. A woman on a nearby boat fell into the water and drowned. Her family accused a crewmember from the *Emily*, Francis Terranova, of hitting the woman with an earthen jar, which caused her death. The Americans insisted that the woman fell into the water inadvertently and Terranova had nothing to do with her death. The local magistrate of Panyu County heard the case on October 6 on the ship *Emily*, where the trial was held. According to British scholar Hosea Ballou Morse's account, the hearing was a complete sham:

> He [the local magistrate of Panyu County] asked the Americans what defense they intended to put forward, and they delivered their defense as follows: "Our evidence can prove, that the Jar which is said to be the instrument that caused the death of the woman, was safely delivered by the accused into her hands, and that she fell overboard at the distance of thirty feet and upwards from the ship *Emily*, that she was seen from on board the *Hero of Malown* (an English ship laying near the *Emily*) to fall overboard whilst in the act of sculling her boat, that no jar or any such instrument was thrown at her, or caused her falling into the water, that

The original Chinese version of this chapter first appeared in the author's chapter (of the same title) in Su Li and He Weifang, eds., *Ershi shiji de Zhongguo—xueshu yu shehui* [Twentieth-century China: academia and society (the volume on law)] (Jinan: Shandong renmin chubanshe, 2001), pp. 172–213.

from the relative situation of the boat to the ship, it was impossible to strike the woman on the side of the head on which the wound was inflicted, and that the jar could not have cut the hat in the manner in which it was cut—We declared as our belief, that the boat, having been swept by the strength of the tide some distance from the ship, the woman in her anxiety to regain her station had by a misstep fallen over-board and in the act had struck her head against the pivot on which the scull moves, or the sharp edge of the boat which caused her death.[1]

Then prosecution witnesses delivered testimonies, which, in the eyes of the defense, were either self-contradictory or not indicative of what had really happened at the incident site at all. However, "the magistrate denied any argument for the defense . . . claiming that having seen the corpse of the woman and the earthen jar with his own eyes, he was convinced that the accused was guilty and that even if his judgment erred, it was the mandate of Heaven. He stood up from his seat in great rage. The trial seemed to have already been brought to an end."[2]

To the astonishment and dismay of the foreigners, the local officials of Guangdong had the accused executed by strangulation within forty-eight hours without waiting for the final decree of the emperor. Moreover, "the report submitted to the emperor contained distorted information on the evidence and adjudication."[3]

The *Emily* incident was concluded quickly, but the clash of legal systems and legal concepts between China and the West in their early interactions became a very difficult, ongoing problem.[4] Although Western powers' colonialist policies were responsible for the modern military conflicts between the West and China, one must admit that if China's legal and justice system had not been so unreasonable either in concept or actual practice, many disputes would have been resolved fairly without resulting in war.[5] However, it was China's failure in said war and the subsequent Western oppression that naturally led many Chinese to question the traditional legal system—in particular, to reflect on the judicial system as well as on the reform of law and the judiciary.

With its long history and advanced civilization, China is proud of its tradition of written law. According to the famous Japanese legal scholar Shiga Shuzo, the Chinese legal system achieved great accomplishments over the course of its development.[6] Why then did Westerners become increasingly intolerant toward China's legal system and its enforcement in the early modern era? What exactly was the classical judicial system in China?

It is necessary to review the basic structure of the old judicial system as it provides context for its evolution in this century. In light of the theme and limited length of this chapter, I will only focus on the most basic characteristics in general terms.

Old Tradition

China's classical judicial system developed gradually through a long process of historical evolution, along with its political, economic, and other social systems. It also shared the same axiological implications with the other systems. With the recognition that judicial function is an essential part of government, the importance of the judicial system in China's traditional government structure was unique in the world. Therefore the main characteristics of this judicial system can be summarized by examining the relationship between the structure of government and society.

The government structure of ancient China can be divided into two levels: the central government and subnational governments. At the higher level, the central government included the "three departments" (the Department of State Affairs, the Chancellery, and the Secretariat) and the "six ministries," among which the Ministry of Punishment (*xingbu*), the Censorate (*duchayuan*), and the Court of Judicial Review (*dalisi*) were more concerned with law. Of course, the emperor was always the paramount authority when legal disputes or other issues were involved. But as far as the everyday life of ordinary people was concerned, the central government, or even government at the provincial level, was not that important. When disputes arose among people concerning reasons or amounts that were not significant enough and that failed to be solved privately, or when misdemeanors were involved, they would turn to the county government for help.

County officials were at the end of the power network by which the whole country was ruled. These officials were appointed by the central government and were responsible for collecting taxes, maintaining social order, and resolving disputes. Included in those functions was what we would today call the judiciary, which was very important at that time.

Much research has been done on the traditional judicial function of local officials.[7] But here I want to explore the characteristics of this judicial tradition and its potential influence on today's society from another perspective— one that emphasizes the impact of the social systems and sociological factors on the actual work of the judicial system, as well as on the relationship between knowledge and power.

CONCENTRATION RATHER THAN SEPARATION OF POWERS

The most distinctive structural characteristic of the traditional Chinese local government was that there was no arrangement whatsoever for the separation of powers. The county magistrate had comprehensive responsibilities. The three basic governmental functions, namely, the enacting of rules (legislature), the execution of rules (administration), and the resolving of disputes (judiciary), which are taken for granted today, rested entirely with the magistrate alone. Although he was subject to the supervision of higher government, within the local government, he held absolute power and was beyond the supervision and check of any entity. All others working inside the government served as the magistrate's consultants or assistants and had no authority at all to check the magistrate's power. It was because of this fact that Wang Huizu, a famous consultant in the Qing dynasty, remarked, "Among the existing powers, except for that of province governors, the most important one is that of county magistrates. . . . Why? They have concentrated powers."[8]

The concentration of power was obvious in the judicial process. According to Ch'u Tongtsu's description, "[the] magistrate heard all cases under his jurisdiction, civil as well as criminal. And he was more than a judge. He not only conducted hearings and made decisions; he also conducted investigations and inquests, and detected criminals. In modern terms, his duties combined those of judge, prosecutor, police chief, and coroner, comprising everything relating to the administration of justice in its broadest sense, and the failure to carry out any of these duties incurred disciplinary actions and punishments, as defined in the many laws and regulations."[9]

To people today who have read Montesquieu's works and firmly believe in the value of separation of powers, and who hold the view that "power tends to corrupt, and absolute power corrupts absolutely," the government model from the past with its highly concentrated powers is most frightening. Indeed, there exist countless examples in the traditional politics of China that testify to the various defects of this despotism. But there is no system that is without at least some advantage. The highly concentrated powers in the county governments helped improve efficiency. Without other parallel powers to those of the magistrate, without an independent judiciary, a corrupt official could pervert the law and exploit the people at his will, but an upright and incorruptible official could also give full play to his administrative talents without any impediment. From the perspective of "rule by man," unity in government often made it difficult for people to gain rights to which they were entitled because there was nowhere to turn other than to this sole government. But on the other hand, the costs to people of dealing with the government (including bribery costs) remained low because of the uncomplicated nature of government, and they were spared the trouble of coming to terms with the blinding array of government agencies that people today have to face. In addition, in a society with agriculture as its leading pillar, the simplicity of this government also helped reduce the number of officials and thus avoided imposing on people's livelihoods through high taxes.[10]

Of course, from the perspective of establishing a modern judicial system, the most significant impact of this traditional model of a highly centralized government is that it prevented the knowledge and development of judicial independence. It did not even provide a context for this principle. Although there have always been so-called upright and incorruptible officials and strong expectations of fair and honest judges, those were moral requirements of officials and quite apart from the notion of judicial independence.

RULE OF KNOWLEDGE

Still, the lack of institutionalized checks on this kind of government causes significant concern for modern observers. How could powerful county officials not become dictators? In fact, the traditional selection process for county officials contributed to important restrictions on the use of powers by these officials.

The Imperial Civil Service Examination system (*keju kaoshi*) had a significant influence on the traditional political and legal system.[11] It meant, first of all, equality. Gaining political powers was no longer solely decided by blood or status. There were, at least in a formal way, more equal opportunities open to people of obscure birth to compete for political positions. Furthermore, the standard for this competition was not physical ability, but *literae humaniores* based on Confucianism. Although it became rigid over time, the widespread use of Imperial Civil Service Examinations resulted in the administration of social affairs by the intelligentsia. In order to prepare for the exams, people needed to become extremely familiar with the ancient classical works and explanations of those works by Confucian masters of the past. Examinees were required to give persuasive explanations of some views themselves. Thus the process of preparing for the exams was also a process of Confucianization. The political philosophy of Confucianism and related theories became deeply etched in the minds of prospective county officials and constituted a potentially effective check on the use of power in the future.

It should also be noted that the combination of the above two features guaranteed the authority and legitimacy of the traditional government. Because the possibility of becoming an official was open to anyone, unfairness deriving from selection standards based on status or blood disappeared.[12] Even people who failed could only criticize themselves for not being capable enough and admire or envy those who succeeded. As a result, this equality made reasonable the differences between the rulers and those being ruled and reinforced people's obedience to their rulers.

RULE OF UNSPECIALIZED KNOWLEDGE

Although the imperial examinations represented the traditional model of rule, with the knowledgeable ruling the ignorant, they did not promote the division and specialization of knowledge but rather impeded it by narrowly emphasizing the Confucian standards and poetic techniques. As Max Weber pointed out, "The educational qualification, however, in view of the educational means employed, has been a 'cultural' qualification, in the sense of a general education. It was of similar, yet of a more specific nature than, for instance, the *humanist* educational qualification of the Occident. . . . The Chinese examinations did not test any special skills, as do our modern rational and bureaucratic examination regulations for jurists, medical doctors, or technicians. . . . The examinations of China tested whether or not the candidate's mind was thoroughly steeped in literature and whether or not he possessed the ways of thought suitable to a cultured man and resulting from cultivation in literature."[13] Though people who succeeded in those exams were involved in the judgment and resolution of disputes, because of the singleness of their knowledge and background, the officials' judicial activities were not able to contribute to the growth and development of independent and specialized legal knowledge.[14]

In fact, the traditional Chinese legal concept was a direct result of a judicial process dominated by laymen. In Western history, the independence of legal professionals as a group originated with and was connected to the restrictions inherent to the accessibility of the profession, based on the pursuit of profits. In fact, a profession could not obtain broad social resources without the establishment of a so-called abstract expertise system. Judges apply strict legal procedures to their assigned cases and make decisions without interference. Those decisions become unshakable once they obtain procedural validity. All of those principles are taken for granted in the West.

But in China, the judges were not lawyers, and they usually did not specialize in law. When they dealt with disputes and cases—mostly what we would label as civil cases today—there was no certainty of law. What they were applying was a combination of law, ethical standards, and the community's customs. As the origin of modern law, this provided no clear boundaries

between the different sources of this mixed body of rules. When local officials handled cases, they were not able to apply different legal rules and
sources as the judges do today. At the same time, because of their training for
the imperial examinations, in order to support certain decisions in a case,
they always relied on resources from the teachings of Confucianism or historical works, which had no legal implications. When the records of some of the
"famous trials" are seen from today's point of view, they are more valuable as
literary or rhetorical references than legal documents.[15]

Judicial Proceedings without Adversity

The lack of involvement of lawyers in legal proceedings further reinforced
the uncertainty of rules, which had been established by county magistrates
rather than by lawyers. Even though dialecticians, such as Deng Xi and
Gongsun Long, had appeared in court representing petitioners from very
early times, Confucianism and Taoism adopted a negative attitude toward
them. They were considered to know only logic but not right or wrong, and
thus posed a threat to the social order. The joint influence of Confucianism
and Taoism inhibited the development of logic as a discipline throughout
China's two thousand years of history.[16] According to Chinese American historian Tang Degang, it was this different legal concept that created the sharp
contrast in the development of logic between China and the West.[17]

Of course, there always existed the profession of the pettifogger. Although
pettifoggers have always been despised by the government, according to the
research of the Japanese scholar Fuma Susumu, pettifoggers became more
active during the thousand-year period between the Song dynasty and the
Qing dynasty. Based on abundant research, Professor Fuma concluded that
they existed against all odds, within the loopholes of the judicial system.[18]
They met both their clients' needs and shared interests with government officials. However, the work of advocates then was quite different from that of
lawyers today. For example, they could not represent clients and argue in
court. Almost all of their work was done outside the court. As a result, the
claims of parties could not be developed into an exploration of legal theory.
Rules of evidence could not be created without the participation of lawyers.
Neutrality and passive jurisdiction amid professional confrontation were not
possible either. As a result, officials in local government played a dominant
role in the proceedings. At the same time, even though the pettifoggers did
survive as a profession, their exclusion from the social mainstream, in addition to the fact that most pettifoggers were people who had failed the imperial exams, made them a powerless group that lacked support from legitimate

sources. This humble class's influence on social affairs was further impaired by the lack of a guild, which usually establishes a set of professional guidelines to gain wide support for the conduct of business activities. During the process of constructing a modern legal system and structure, people repeatedly confronted the problem of lack of legal professionals.

In sum, this review of China's old government structure and the operations of its judicial system indicates that some of its characteristics still exist today and might be a potential impediment to the process of creating a new legal system in China. To some degree, the evolution of a modern judicial system in China was the outcome of both a collision between and a fusion of traditions and foreign knowledge, which occurred in connection with changes in China's social structure and social life.

After the mid-eighteenth century, despite China's increasing contact with the West and the constant legal clashes during the process, the Chinese were not particularly interested in the legal system of Western nations. Even missionaries to China seldom made efforts to introduce their law. This was partly because the Chinese people were traditionally more interested in knowing about things they already had, and partly because the deeply held beliefs of the Middle Kingdom made it difficult to acknowledge any superiority of the "barbarians." As a result, when the Western powers arrived with guns in the nineteenth century, the Chinese were equipped to confront them only with disdain, an underdeveloped social structure, and an army that was incapable of confronting foreign powers due to its poor management system.

Under such pressure from the outside, China's legal system began to change. Because of this, the Chinese first had to make superficial alterations. For example, without the pressure from the West, especially the tremendous impact of the Western invasion of Beijing after the Boxer Rebellion and the Eight-Nation Alliance, the Qing dynasty would not have made fundamental changes to its traditional legal and judicial systems, which had been in place for more than two thousand years. But Western influence made it increasingly evident that the traditional legal system was not effective enough to retain control of such a large country with a growing population. Some progressive thinking asserted that changing the legal system was the only way for China to survive.

Experimentation in the Separation of Powers in Modern China

The defects of China's traditional governance model had been fully exposed by the time of the Qing dynasty. Under the absolute monarchy of the emperor, there was naturally no separation of powers. In addition, the system was beset by many other flaws, such as an outdated bureaucratic establishment and temporary organizations (such as the unofficial Grand Council [*junjichu*]) coexisting with and encroaching upon the authority of official organizations. To prevent any potential threat from any single powerful official, each administrative organization had at least two heads, and one official could hold multiple posts in different organizations, resulting in confusion, low efficiency, and a lack of responsibility. This mechanism also existed for official posts outside the imperial court, such as between the governor-general and the provincial governor. High-ranking officials often did not have the specialized knowledge required for performing their duties, and many responsibilities were given to petty officials who, with a meager salary, often resorted to all sorts of malpractice, which damaged the government's image among the people.

This government structure had been criticized by scholars as early as the late nineteenth century. In 1865, for example, the Englishman Robert Hart observed that although the Chinese system was formulated with considerable prudence, the system had become too worn-out to be effective. The local officials were mostly corruptible and self-indulgent, and officials in the capital were overburdened with often overlapping responsibilities. He also held that good scholars did not always make good officials as they often lacked knowledge of practical matters. He predicted that if these defects could not be remedied, it would be difficult for the government to rise to new challenges.[19]

Conversely, some Chinese acquainted with the political and legal system in the West expressed their appreciation of the system. In 1877 Ma Jianzhong sent a letter to Li Hongzhang from Europe:

> I have been in Europe for more than one year. When I first came here, I thought the rich and powerful European nations were only concerned with developing their manufacturing capacity and military strength. Later, as I review their legal codes and literature, I have come to realize that their richness lies in their protection of businesses and their power stems from their national solidarity. . . . Their schools bring up a great number of talents, and their parliaments have a good knowledge of the concerns of the ordinary people. Their manufacturing and military strengths are merely the natural results of these factors.[20]

In his letter, Ma Jianzhong explicitly expressed his commendation and admiration of the separation of powers and the independence of the judiciary in the West. "With the separation of the executive, legislative and judiciary powers rather than concentration and mutual interference, their national affairs are handled in great order . . . everyone may take initiative and so has more self-esteem."[21]

During the Hundred Days' Reform (*wuxu bianfa*), the reformists gave more straightforward criticism of the country's traditional government structure.[22] Kang Youwei, for example, presented a lengthy memorial to the emperor calling attention to the shortcomings of the existing government organization.[23] According to Kang, it had become imperative to initiate government reform at both the central and local levels. He pointed out the main structural problem of the central government: "The six ministers are inundated with myriad affairs while petty officials, great in number, have no clearly defined responsibilities. At the imperial court session every day, the officials simply stand by waiting for orders. . . . Petty officials are neither assigned to a specific duty nor hold their positions on a part-time basis. . . . Facing such a messy state of things, even a sage will be at his wit's end." Concerning the prefecture and county-level governments, the problem is that "one official is put in charge of military, judicial and cultural affairs so that it is simply impossible for him to attend to them all." As a result, officials were primarily concerned with preserving themselves rather than serving the people. Even worse, bribery and the sale of official positions were commonplace.[24] In the memorial presented to the emperor, Kang Youwei proposed that the bureaucratic system should be reformed so that every official has clearly defined responsibilities and authority, that the practice of one official holding multiple posts be changed, and that efficiency of local governments be improved by, for example, canceling superfluous government positions. By 1898 he advocated an even more radical proposal to overhaul the existing government system and put in place a new government structure with separation of powers like that in the West.[25]

The Hundred Days' Reform eventually failed, which greatly frustrated the reformists. However, seen from the perspective of China's legal evolution, this frustration was like a rest in a musical composition: the short period of quiescence after the failure was soon followed by an even greater wave of calls for reforms. At the turn of the century, when the legitimacy of the traditional government model was universally doubted and challenged, and with increasing internal and external crises, foreign concepts and knowledge had a growing impact on this time-honored land and culture. And an increasing number of people aspired to follow the developmental path of the West.[26] In 1901 the Qing court, pressured from within and without, had no choice but to declare the implementation of "political reform," and the measures subsequently launched embraced almost all the propositions of Kang Youwei and, in some respects, even surpassed them.[27]

During this period, Yan Fu translated in full Montesquieu's masterpiece *The Spirit of Laws*.[28] As a matter of fact, long before the translation of this work advocating for the separation of powers, Yan Fu had already expressed his strong dissatisfaction with China's classical legal system and attached great importance to the role a sound legal system can play in bringing about social change. He once recalled a conversation with Guo Songtao, the Qing's ambassador to England: "During my visit to Europe, I once attended court hearings and when I came back, I felt at a loss. On one occasion, I said to Mr. Guo Songtao that of the many reasons that make England and other European nations rich and strong, the most important one is the guarantee of justice. And my view was shared by Mr. Guo."[29] In addition, Yan Fu also held that the assertion that China was too populous to implement democracy was wrong.[30] In comparison with the specious viewpoint later aired by Sun Yat-sen that "the freedom enjoyed by the Chinese is not too little, but too much," Yan Fu clearly pointed out that although "forgiveness" was advocated in China, there was no freedom here in the Western sense of the word.[31] He was of the firm conviction that a prosperous and strong China should rely on civic-minded citizens, the safeguard of civil rights, local autonomy, and national intelligence.[32]

It merits noting that, while advocating such values as democracy and freedom, Yan Fu often mentioned the absence of specific governance techniques in China. "From the three dynasties of the Xia, Shang and Zhou onward, an untold number of people, from emperors and high-ranking officials to masters and scholars, who have set their minds on ordaining conscience for Heaven and Earth, securing life and fortune of the people, continuing lost teachings for past sages and establishing peace for all future generations, but as far as specific techniques for achieving these goals are concerned, in the span of more than 4,000 years of an endless cycle of conflict and peace, there has almost been no progress at all."[33] He advocated for the division of labor and believed that good governance lies in the technical competence of bureaucrats: "The matters of legislation and diplomacy are not things every man is capable of. With the advancement of civilization, the division of labor becomes more specialized. To govern a country well, like in a business, one must have the proper aptitude and receive proper education."[34] He held that the neglect of specific techniques in ancient China had much to do with the convergence and concentration of talents in the officialdom due to the Imperial Civil Service Examination system.

> If the spirit of equality prevails in a country, then all professions only represent a division of labor and are equally indispensable, and there is

no differentiating between the respectable and the humble. And people may have varying attainments in what they do but are equal as individuals. Everyone does their best in their own trades and then all matters will be well attended. In China, however, due to its excessive emphasis on civil accomplishment, all talents across the country are concentrated in the officialdom, so that those who are intelligent and able disdain to engage in practical trades, and even if they find themselves in such trades due to circumstances, they find no delight in engaging in the business for a whole life.[35]

In addition to translating *The Spirit of Laws*, Yan Fu also wrote articles especially discussing the separation of powers and expounding on the principles of judicial independence.

Due to the introduction of the principle of separation of powers to China and the criticisms of China's existing governmental structure, by the early twentieth century the idea of the separation of powers had moved from private discussion into official discourse. On the sixteenth day of the ninth month of the thirty-second year of the reign of Guangxu (November 2, 1906), the commissioner of reorganizing the governmental system presented a memorial to the emperor on reorganizing the ministries of the central government:

> The government system of constitutional countries features primarily the separation of powers of the executive, legislative and judicial branches, where they are complementary to and are checked by each other, with an excellent design and exceptional effectiveness. This provides an ideal example of how old problems are rectified and accountability is established, as instructed by his majesty. In the case of China, methinks that there are three reasons for the difficulty of rectifying longstanding problems and establishing accountability, as follows:
>
> The first is the indiscrimination of responsibilities and authorities. The officials in charge of both administration and legislation tend to make unfair laws out of the needs of administration without consulting public opinion. Those in charge of both administration and the judiciary tend to change laws out of their own prejudices. And those in charge of both legislation and judiciary tend to take advantage of it and make draconian laws, departing from laws' basic purpose of safeguarding the rights of the people. . . . .
>
> The second is the lack of clarity of officials' duties. For government to be effective, responsibilities should be clearly divided, and for decisions

to be effective, accountability should be established. But as it is today, one government department often has six heads, which means that six persons hold one position, and it can be sure that half of them are redundant. Likewise, one official often holds positions in different government departments, which means that one person holds multiple positions, and it can be sure that such a person must be wanting in real expertise. Multiple persons holding one position has the disadvantage of dawdling in work while one person holding multiple positions has the disadvantage of neglecting duties. As a result, the worthy are restrained from doing the right things, and the unworthy are contented with passing the buck. . . .

The third is official titles not matching their duties. The Ministry of Personnel is given the duty of appointing personnel, yet does not have the power of evaluate personnel, and the Ministry of Revenue is responsible for finance, yet does not have the power of statistics.[36]

Although the separation of powers was discussed only from the perspective of reorganizing the governmental system, and the Qing court did not seem to really intend to push the mechanism, it was exactly at that time that China formally bid goodbye to the traditional government model and embarked on the path of Westernization. Indeed, both the five-power constitution model adopted by the Republic of China and the "one-government, two-branch" model (under the People's Congress) adopted by the People's Republic of China were nothing but variations of the separation of powers of the West and retained its basic framework.

The Tortuous Path of Judicial Independence in Modern China

Judicial independence is an inherent requirement of the principle of separation of powers. It is true, as clearly shown in the analysis of China's old tradition of government, that the absence of a tradition of separation of powers is an important reason for the lack of judicial independence in ancient China. But seen from a sociological perspective, there is another reason for it: that is, an independent legal profession and the resulting legal scholarship and knowledge tradition had never emerged here. More broadly speaking, in the absence of a social environment and social resources safeguarding judicial independence, the concept of judicial independence is bound to be nothing but a hollow-sounding theory advocated by the minority. Even if it is enshrined in the official discourse, it is still no more than lip service without substance.

FORCED SEPARATION OF POWERS

In modern China, the principle of judicial independence was, from the very beginning, something forced upon it by the outside world. As discussed earlier, with the increase in contact and legal conflicts between China and the West, foreigners were increasingly dissatisfied with China's laws and legal system. Therefore, in the Treaty of Nanjing and the Treaty of the Bogue signed after the Opium Wars, provisions were made not only for the cession of Hong Kong, the opening of ports, and tariff agreements, but also for the exclusive application of British laws and courts to British citizens in China, that is, consular jurisdiction. This last provision was not perceived by the Chinese at the time to be of any significance at all. "In the eyes of people during the reign of the Daoguang emperor, it was only natural that foreigners should be governed by their own laws. They saw it as the most convenient and straightforward way of handling things."[37] However, concurrent with the conflicts between Western powers and China was the dissemination of Western concepts of the national state and sovereignty, and under the influence of these concepts, consular jurisdiction began to be seen as a disgrace to the state and nation. After the Boxer Rebellion, there was a rising demand within China for changes in the existing laws and legal system in imitation of the Western model, and consular jurisdiction, while safeguarding the interests of Westerners in China, intensified the conflict between China and the West.[38] With this backdrop, in the Renewed Treaty of Commerce and Navigation between Britain and China signed in the twenty-seventh year of the reign of the Guangxu emperor (1901), there was a special provision that read: "China shall commit itself to aligning its legal system to other countries, an endeavor for which Britain agrees to give all necessary assistance, and Britain agrees to abandon its consular jurisdiction in China when China's laws and adjudication practices are soundly established."[39] It was only then that China began to reform its legal system officially.

This reform, largely initiated under external pressure, had its intrinsic flaws. For example, whether the government, the primary actor behind the reform, was sincere about the cause was open to debate.[40] There were other factors seriously affecting the reform process, such as disagreement among officials with different views, difficulty in coordinating among different government departments, and increasingly intense conflicts between the ethnic minority Manchu and the ethnic majority Han Chinese. Above all, because this reform had a strong utilitarian orientation, decisionmakers seldom considered the reform's far-reaching effects and the basic elements required for the formation and administration of the new legal system, contenting themselves with a perfunctory reproduction of the Western system.

In the ninth month of the thirty-second year of the reign of Guangxu, the Qing court ordered that "the Ministry of Punishment be changed to the Ministry of Justice in charge of the judiciary and the Court of Judicial Review to the Supreme Court in charge of trials."[41] This order immediately triggered much talk about a series of issues, such as how the power was to be divided between the Ministry of Justice and the Supreme Court, how to determine the qualifications of judicial officials, how to coordinate between the old system and the new system, and what model all levels of local governments were to follow to ensure judicial independence. Among the memorials submitted to the emperor on the those issues, one memorial entitled "Proposal on Strict Separation of Government Administration and the Judiciary," submitted by Imperial Censor Wu Fang, showed remarkable insight and deserves some space for discussion here.[42]

Unlike most officials, who primarily concerned themselves with the establishment of the cabinet system of government and the legislative body, Wu Fang held that given the circumstances at the time, the separation of the legislature and the executive could not be achieved any time soon, but overall, judicial independence was practical and feasible.[43] Besides, according to Wu Fang, judicial independence was completely feasible not only at the level of the central government but also at the level of local government, refuting the view that China should not hurry to introduce judicial independence:

> It is generally agreed among men of broad vision at home and abroad that an independent judiciary is the kernel of our present endeavor toward a constitutional government, and they are all looking forward with great anticipation to the establishment of the judicial system. Efforts in this direction, however, have been obstructed by some buttoned-down officials accustomed to the old ways and resisting new things with misleading half truths. Their arguments, in summary, consist of no more than three points: 1), the nationals are not well educated enough for the system; 2), the talents in legal affairs are inadequate; and 3), the power of executive officials will be eroded. The view that the Chinese people are not suitable to be judged by an independent court is simply nonsensical because even within the foreign concessions, consular jurisdiction applies to all people including Chinese, and no objection has ever been raised against the application to Chinese on the grounds of their legal illiteracy.

It pains my heart to think that while the Chinese are entitled to fair trials and due process in foreign concessions, they are denied the right by their own government. As for the argument pointing at our inadequacy of talents in adjudication, it is seemingly right but actually wrong, because, although government officials were only responsible for administration of civil examinations, labor and taxation and were not necessarily acquainted with adjudication, when they took the office of an executive position, they were at ease in handling adjudication matters. Now if the executive and the judiciary are separated, so that officials are enabled to devote themselves completely to one duty and do it well rather than being distracted by two different duties at the same time and resulting in poor performance as was the case in the past, and the poor performance was not due to lack of intelligence but to the fact that the officials were overburdened. This should not be taken as an argument for China's lack of talents. At last, the view that the separation of powers will lead to the erosion of authorities enjoyed by officials in the past is particularly one-sided, because officials' authorities are given by the state and they are respected and revered even if they do not adjudicate on cases in person. If behind the view is the fear that with the establishment of the new system they would not be able to resort to intimidation and brutal force for private gains as they could in the past, such officials would not be tolerated in this sagacious dynasty. Your humble servant observes that there was no separation between the executive and the judiciary in the West in the ancient times and it came about only when their legal system developed to a certain stage.

With the separation between the two governmental bodies, the executive officials can devote themselves completely to the administration of the government without any occurrence of abuse of power, and the judges can devote themselves completely to safeguarding the lawful rights of the citizens through fair trials. If an independent judiciary interfered with the performance of duties of executive officials, Western countries would not have abandoned their old practices and embraced the separation of powers. If the combination of executive and judicial powers does not threaten the long-term stability and prosperity of our country, it is well to keep it for a while for gradual change, but the fact is that, given the development of world affairs and the grievances and hardships suffered by the ordinary people, we have come to a point where our country's stability and prosperity will be put in jeopardy if the judicial independence is not institutionalized immediately without delay. Your humble servant prays Her Majesty the Empress Dowager and His Majesty the Emperor to consider this.[44]

Wu Fang not only forcefully demonstrated the importance of judicial independence for the elimination of consular jurisdiction but also explicitly analyzed its great significance in internal affairs:

It is my observation that civil disorders in history have mostly had two causes, the first being heavy exploitation and taxation and the second being unfairness in adjudication. . . . The independent judiciary in Western countries was established as a countermeasure against the arbitrariness of executive officials, and over some one hundred years since then, has contributed to the civil harmony, prosperity and national strength of these countries. In the case of China, however, adjudication has always been in the charge of prefectural and county heads and executed by their secretaries, leading to all kinds of malpractice and dishonest dealings and bringing great suffering to ordinary people as well as giving rise to various factors threatening national stability, so that a mechanism meant to have justice done ends up estranging the people from the government. The primary reason for this is that prefectural and county heads are full of various duties where they need to attend to both government administration and civil and criminal trials and as a result, the worthy of them are exhausted and the unworthy of them become unscrupulous. What's more, competent adjudication requires great familiarity with laws and with the details and particulars of each case, something it is impossible for executive official to accomplish given their already crowded agendas. However, if an independent judiciary is established so that the executive officials concern themselves exclusively with government administration and judges with adjudication, then all ills will be removed.[45]

This argument for judicial independence is so cogent and powerful that it still speaks to today's readers. Regrettably, arguments like this were uttered too late, and no more than five years later, the Qing dynasty collapsed. The time allowed to the decisionmakers was too little to implement a reform of such magnitude in such a vast country. Besides, there was little accumulation of knowledge concerning institutional development at that time. Just as Wu Fang said, "adjudication requires great familiarity with laws," but when it came to specific questions, such as in what aspects the responsibilities of the judiciary differ from those of the executive and what institutional arrangements should be made, very little thought had been devoted to them. The impact of court ministers' memorials and the emperor's decrees on society was also open to question.

Regarding private discourse, I mentioned earlier the famous translator Yan Fu's exposition on the separation of powers. In fact, he also expressed a number of insightful opinions on judicial independence. For example, in the preface to his translation of Adam Smith's *The Wealth of Nations* (published during 1901–02), he made special mention of the unique features of the Western judicial system:

> The biggest difference between China and the West in the institutional framework of government, without doubt, lies in law. The legal system of the West has its origin in Greek and Roman antiquity and has evolved and undergone great changes over a long period of time before reaching its present state. In summary, it has eight unique features. The first is the study of law as a specialized discipline. The second is the legal profession. The third is the jury system. The fourth is the legislature controlling the enactment and revocation of laws. The fifth is that the salary of public servants is being provided by citizens. The sixth is public justice being classified into the two kinds: civil and criminal. The seventh is that judges determine the conviction of the accused. And the eighth is that judges are all very well paid. These are only the major differences. With these features, Western countries safeguard the integrity of their legal system and ensure justice.[46]

In a note appended to his translation of *The Spirit of Laws* by Montesquieu, Yan Fu further explained the principle of judicial independence to his countrymen:

> In China, adjudicators are servants of the emperor. The justice and judiciary bodies are established only as agents of the emperor. That's why verdicts issued by the Ministry of Justice are subject to the approval of the emperor who is also responsible for rehearing provincial cases of capital punishment. All of these policies are diametrically different from the practices in Europe. Laws are regarded as supreme in Anglo countries and do not yield to any other power. Each law is formulated in accordance with the Constitution, and upon enactment, does not allow any change to it, not even a single word of it.[47]

The above observation was indeed brilliant, but the reform undertaken by the Qing court in this direction was too late to save itself from ultimate collapse.

After the Qing dynasty was replaced by the Republic of China, the mission of judicial reform was left to the builders of the new republic.

Judicial Independence during the Beiyang Government Period

This was an age of radical change. With the overthrow of the feudal monarchy and the establishment of a republic, people were stirred by elation and hope, eager to build a brand-new modern nation after the previous chaos and revolutions. The Provisional Constitution of the Republic of China, promulgated in the first year of the Republic of China, offered a portrait of the new country. It would be a country where citizens are entitled to a series of political and legal rights, with a parliament representing public opinion and exercising the power of legislation, and a president elected, empowered by, and responsible to the parliament. Concerning the judiciary, the constitution had the following provisions: "The judiciary shall be composed of those judges appointed by the Provisional President and the Chief of the Department of Justice"; "Judges shall be independent and shall not be subject to the interference of higher officials"; and "Judges during their continuance in office shall not have their emoluments decreased and shall not be transferred to other offices, nor shall they be removed from office except when they are convicted of crimes, or of offenses punishable according to law by removal from office."[48] These provisions, with their high degree of explicitness and rigor, were the most thorough among all provisions concerning judicial independence adopted in China in the twentieth century.

Unfortunately, the Beiyang era in which the well-ordered constitution was formulated was an age beset by political chaos. On the one hand, the political stage was a complete mess with warlords manipulating the government, elections and appointments dominated by blatant fractional struggles, and money and private relationships playing an important role; on the other hand, the constitution was approached with an idealistic attitude intolerant of any concession and compromise. "Chinese expectations for the probity of politicians in a constitutional order were probably unrealistically high. Normal political compromises were seen as betrayals, tactical shifts as evidence of lack of principle."[49] Ultimately, "the Constitution failed to check conflicts and lead to solidarity as the broad mass of the Chinese people expected . . . the constitutional system exhausted its own vitality through its members' absorption in factional struggles."[50]

When it comes to the judicial system in this period, however, there was a somewhat different state of things. Shen Jiaben and Wu Tingfang, both important officials in charge of judicial reform in the late Qing dynasty, retained important roles in the establishment of a new legal system after the Revolution of 1911 (Xinhai Revolution).[51] Shen Jiaben was reputed to be a "matchmaker between Chinese and Western laws," while Wu Tingfang was the first Chinese to receive a complete legal education in the West and the first ethnically Chinese barrister in history.[52] Since 1902 they had been given the important task of reforming the country's legal system. From their positions in the new government, they introduced many changes to the traditional legal system by abolishing various cruel punishments, prohibiting the use of torture in interrogations, drafting a civil procedure law, translating foreign legal works, and establishing legal schools for developing specialized talents, which laid a good foundation for legal development in the Republic of China period.[53] After the Revolution of 1911, Wu Tingfang served briefly as the chief of the Department of Justice for the Nanjing Provisional Government, but due to the short duration of the provisional government, he did not make a far-reaching contribution to the development of the legal system in this position. Even so, he published a work entitled "Preliminary Suggestions on the Governance of the Republic of China" (*Zhonghua minguo tuzhi chuyi*) in 1915, and in two chapters arguing for the importance of the judicial system, he cogently and poignantly aired his views on the subject:

> As the Western saying goes, to determine whether a country is civilized, one should check whether its judiciary is independent and whether its law enforcement is strict and impartial. The idea underlying this saying is that the judiciary is the central pillar on which the whole country's governance rests rather than something superficial. China's legal system, in contrast, has always been foreign to the concept of judicial independence, and for more than two thousand years, the three powers of legislation, administration and judiciary had been controlled by a single person from the central government down to local governments. . . . This diametrical difference between Chinese and Western laws used to give rise to a lot of conflicts between China and the West, especially in international affairs. And China's legal system was slighted due to its administrative officials' interference with the judiciary.[54]

Wu emphasized, in particular, that the key to judicial independence is "the judge being given exclusive and unchallengeable rights to adjudication . . . the judge is the representative of the law and the judicial power shall not be interfered by the monarch or president. A verdict, once issued, cannot be set aside unless referred to a competent judicial organ at a higher level and reheard by duly authorized judges."[55]

As a matter of fact, the judiciary enjoyed a higher degree of independence during the Beiyang government period than in the Nanjing Nationalist government period. Take the relationship between the judiciary and political parties, for example. There was an act governing the organization of courts that banned any judge from joining any political party or organization or from being elected to any national or local congress. In December 1912, the Department of Justice issued an order requiring all judges who had joined any political party to declare their withdrawal from their party.[56] In March of the following year, the Department of Justice in a reply to a report from Guangxi Province ordered the Higher Court of Guangxi Province to ensure the removal of all judges from their political affiliation.[57] In the meantime, it announced a list of judges serving on the Supreme Court, the Higher Court in the capital, and local courts, showing that they either had no political affiliation or had withdrawn from their parties.[58] By 1915 the ban on political affiliation was extended to county magistrates in charge of judicial affairs.[59]

Judicial independence during the Beiyang government period was also reflected in the application of the challenge system. In 1915 the Department of Justice issued an order banning all judges, prosecutors, and lawyers who served as clerks at courts and procuratorates from engaging in the legal profession within three years after their departure from their offices. This ban was not revoked until 1927.[60]

It should be admitted that the banning of judges from political affiliation during the Yuan Shikai administration had the obvious political motive of constraining the political and legal influence of the Kuomintang and the Republican Party.[61] In spite of its expedient nature, this regulation, if adhered to perennially, would still likely become a fixed, effective system. Indeed, such cases abound historically both in China and foreign countries. Besides, political calculation is only one among many possible reasons for the creation of the regulation, including people's enthusiasm for the newly introduced judicial system and the reasonable guidance of institutional development from the chiefs of the Department of Justice, who almost all had received excellent legal education.[62] Extra efforts were made to accelerate the abolition of consular jurisdiction in China and ensure the high professional caliber of senior judges.[63] When commenting on national affairs in 1923, Liang Qichao, who once served as the chief of the Department of Justice, observed that the measures and policies put forth by the government since the founding of the republic had generally been unsatisfactory.[64] Relatively speaking, however, the development of the judicial system was among the few successful endeavors.[65]

PARTISAN CONTROL OF THE JUDICIARY

In spite of institutional progress in judicial development, the political scene in the Beiyang government period went from bad to worse, beset by political division and wars fought among powerful warlords, so that the country was a republic only in name and a despotic state in essence. This ultimately led to the Northern Expedition in 1926 and the establishment of the Nationalist government in Nanjing in the following year, ushering in nearly a decade of relative national unity.[66] During this period, the development of the judicial system underwent a drastic shift from judicial independence and political neutrality to the subordination of the judiciary to the ruling party, that is, partial political control of the judiciary.

Xu Qian, who served as chief of the Department of Justice and chairman of the Judicial Committee of the Nationalist government in Guangzhou from August to December 1926, was the earliest advocate of partisan control of the judiciary. He graduated from the Law School of the Imperial University of Peking and, according to Zhang Guofu, had the experience of

> assisting Shen Jiaben in judicial reform in the late Qing, promoting cooperation between Kuomintang and the communist party in 1924, and participating in the May Thirtieth Movement led by Li Dazhao in 1925. He also accompanied Feng Yuxiang on a visit to the Soviet Union in 1926. With this background, particularly with the influence of Li Dazhao and his Soviet visit, he came to the conclusion that the judicial system of the warlord-dominated Beiyang Government was reactionary and he therefore made the determination to reform that system.[67]

With this introduction, the following remark from Xu Qian will come as no surprise: "The law under the traitorous [Beiyang] government is by its nature non-revolutionary and indeed counterrevolutionary and meant to serve the interest of the privileged bourgeoisie by suppressing ordinary people and the proletariat. . . . Since we are determined to carry out revolution, it behooves us to overthrow the counterrevolutionary law. Our revolution should be a thorough one and against not only the traitorous government but also its judiciary."[68] Xu expressly called for demolition of the principle of judicial independence:

> The old judicial concepts such as "judicial independence" and "judges without political party affiliation" are often taken for granted, but they are today among the principal obstructions to the advancement of our

party's doctrines and revolutionary spirit. The judiciary, if given independence, may go counter to our political guidelines and give rise to
conflicts if revolution is advocated politically and yet prohibited judi-
cially. Therefore, the judiciary must be subjected to politics. This new
system, indeed, has materialized in the Soviet Union where not only
the executive and the legislature are integrated but the judiciary is also
not independent.[69]

If what Xu Qian advocated represented the views of the leftist wing of the
Kuomintang government, then the elaboration on partisan control of the
judiciary by Ju Zheng, a founding member of the Kuomintang and the head
of the Supreme Court, represented the mainstream views of the party. In an
article published in 1934, he made a clarification on partisan control of the
judiciary, where the concept was divided into the two aspects of "political
identification of judges with the party" and "application of party doctrines to
adjudication." "Political identification of judges with the party" does not
mean that all judges shall be Kuomintang members; it means that "judges
shall be selected from candidates with a good understanding and strict adherence to the party's doctrine. They don't have to be Kuomintang members but
must identify themselves with Three Principles of the People. In a nutshell,
partisan control of the judiciary is not the judiciary being staffed by party
members but its being guided by the party's doctrines."[70]

Departing from political expediency-based arguments, Ju Zheng attempted
to rationalize partisan control of the judiciary from the perspectives of the philosophy of law and jurisprudence. He held that there is no legal principle that
holds true anytime and anywhere, and those who hold such ideas are "poisoned by the eighteenth-century theories of the natural law."[71] The following
argument illustrates his application of Marxist concepts:

> The law is a superstructure, rather than a castle in the air, which has
> the social structure as its base; in other words, it must fit in with the
> economic system. The specific modes of production and their corre-
> sponding economic systems in all eras of all societies reflect the diverse
> needs of people living in those eras and result in various social ideolo-
> gies and world outlooks. Therefore, every society, every ethnicity and
> every era have their distinctive world outlooks: the world outlook is
> something with particular temporal and spatial coordinates. . . . The
> law is the embodiment of the part of the whole world outlook that
> concerns with the understanding of "justice."[72]

Ju Zheng also used Hans Kelsen's pure theory of law and legal realism, which he called "two great epoch-making achievements in modern legal theory," to demonstrate the absurdity of the "old theory of separation of powers," the inseparability of legislature and judiciary, and the need to apply party doctrines to adjudication, that is, "party doctrine-based adjudication," which requires that the judge shall:

> 1) refer to party doctrines where the law does not provide for; 2) turn to party doctrines for solutions to specific problems for which the relevant provisions of the law are too abstract to be operable, and ensure that the law's provisions do not go beyond the bounds explicitly set by party doctrines; 3) invigorate the law where it is too rigid and impractical; and 4) declare the invalidity of legal provisions if they obviously contradict the actual social life and there is no other applicable legal provisions by citing specific party doctrines.[73]

Partisan control of the judiciary was greatly advanced in the decade after 1926 when the Committee for Judicial Reform established by the Nationalist government in Guangzhou passed a resolution that not only explicitly revoked the ban on judges joining political parties but also required that all judicial officials must be Kuomintang members and have a good reputation and at least three years of experience in legal affairs.[74] The requirement of at least three years of professional experience shows that the decisionmakers did not replace professional competence completely with political loyalty. However, as seen from how this was put into practice later, political loyalty always had priority over professional competence.[75] Indeed, the government introduced a series of measures to strengthen the party's control of the judiciary. In the newly established judge training school, for example, a total of 200 candidacies were especially reserved for Kuomintang members with appropriate educational backgrounds (graduation from a legal education program of three years or more).[76] In addition, candidates recommended by the party headquarters of the Kuomintang for judicial posts enjoyed priority over other candidates.[77] And cases involving members of the Communist Party (counterrevolutionary cases) were heard by juries composed of Kuomintang members selected by local party committees of the Kuomintang.[78] These measures, among others, made the judicial system so politicized that the judiciary was almost turned into the internal affairs department of the Kuomintang.

In retrospect, partisan control of the judiciary was a deviation, or, indeed, a regression, for the past century of judicial development in China. However, it should be pointed out that partisan control of the judiciary was not only part of the Kuomintang's endeavors toward comprehensive control of the country's social affairs but also an extension of the guideline of "using the political party to run the state" (*yi dang zhi guo*) advocated by Sun Yat-sen.[79] Given the historical conditions then, this practice was inevitable.[80]

Some Comments

A review and study of history does not easily reveal specific laws to be followed by later generations in order to avoid the past's detours, because history is not a drama in which every actor from kings and heroes to ordinary people has well-defined roles and lines. In the case of the history of China in the last century, with the country torn by revolutions, wars, and changes in political regimes in the first fifty years and divided between two governments in the second fifty years, there were too many drastic changes to find in them any meaningful set patterns. It was one hundred years full of major events, during which there were a great many missed opportunities, man-made disasters, unexpected changes, tragically pursued and impossible endeavors, and conflicts of and alternations between reason and sentiment. It was a grand history jointly created by people half consciously and half unconsciously.

However, I am still of the conviction that the survey and study of history is capable of enlightening later generations. According to Benedetto Croce, "The deed of which the history is told must vibrate in the soul of the historian . . . the past fact does not answer to a past interest but to a present interest, in so far as it is unified with an interest of the present life. . . . Every true history is contemporary history."[81] Besides, different narrations of the same history are also a competition of different views and a contest of wisdom. They present diversified perspectives on the same things that happened in the past and enable us to better understand where we are now and where we are going.

A survey of the legal history of modern China shows that over the last century, China has always endeavored to build itself into a modern country, but due to internal trouble and outside aggression, the establishment of a reliable legal and judicial system has proven difficult. There is a Western saying, "In times of war, the law falls silent" (*inter arma silent leges*), that provides profound insight into the nature of law.[82] Law, per se, is a mechanism of using peaceful coercion to restrain violence among parties, but in a society constantly ravaged by wars or other intense conflicts, it is impossible for the law to effectively restrain such violence. In the meantime, the establishment and development of the legal order can also be a source of problems. Admittedly, there is no place for legal order where there is no conflict, but for legal order to be maintained, the conflict must be kept within a reasonable limit, where parties or classes in conflict may, through mutual compromise, come up with a system of rules with which they all shall comply. In the course of time, this system may, in some aspects, become out of step with the needs of life, but even so, the attempts to update this system should not evolve into wars but be brought into fruition in the form of a new system through a new round of compromise among conflicting parties. It goes without saying that between the new and old systems there is often a relationship of aggregation and inheritance rather than abrupt rupture. This continuity of history cannot persist without the factor of time, without a reasonably long period of social stability.[83] To use an old Chinese maxim, "Social order and general prosperity do not come by without one hundred years of sustained efforts."

In this respect, however, how much time—that is, peaceful time without the presence of wars or intense social conflicts like the Great Cultural Revolution—have the Chinese really had to wholeheartedly develop the country's institutional system? A calculation finds that it is no more than some thirty years. Furthermore, the two periods constituting these thirty-some years were separated by a war and were characterized by different ideologies and prevailing legal theories, so that the former period could hardly serve as the foundation for the latter period's development. This is an important social reason why China's legal system has not embarked on the right path to this day.

The incompatibility, like that of putting a square peg in a round hole, is reflected not only in the different institutional systems and concepts over the past one hundred years but also, and more important, in the fact that the Chinese cannot identify a possible conjunction between today's efforts toward judicial reform and the country's older traditions. Regarding the judicial system, as shown by the earlier brief analysis of China's old judicial tradition, it is true that the old tradition contradicts some of the basic value orientations today, but this does not mean that it has no strong points worth being integrated into today's system. Take the imperial examination system, for example. In spite of its overemphasis on general erudition at the expense of specialized knowledge, the form it takes and the value assigned to knowledge-based adjustment of social relationships still show considerable rationality. The rationality of this system, however, has never been done justice, and the whole imperial examination system was abandoned in favor of the so-called masses orientation, which has led to the arbitrary selection of judges and ultimately undermined both people's trust of the judicial organs and the judicial organs' credibility in society. To this day we are still mired in the vicious cycle of judges being denied independence in judgment on the grounds of their general incompetence in legal affairs, which in turn is attributed to their being denied independence in judgment. Consequentially, judicial independence remains unachieved, and the competence of judges remains unimproved. In China's efforts to establish a strict examination system and a more sophisticated, legal expertise–based judicial appointment system, it is advisable to draw on Japan's experience in applying the spirit of the imperial examination system to the establishment and shaping of the legal profession in modern times.[84]

The departure of China's old government system from the separation of powers, as discussed earlier, still has influence in various aspects of government and society today. For instance, although China has put in place a government system divided into the people's government, the court, and the procuratorate, people inside and outside this system have difficulty getting accustomed to it. The relevant officials only pay lip service to this system while in reality they attend to matters in their own way. A county head does not truly believe that he must comply with the decisions made by an ordinary judge in legal matters, and even the judges themselves do not have the courage to go through the procedures in strict accordance with the law when handling cases concerning local government departments or individuals without giving consideration to the opinions of high officials.[85] Ordinary people are simply at a loss about how to deal with this government system. On the one hand, the government's power has penetrated deeply into grassroots life, but on the other hand, the government, with its dizzying number of departments, has become so bureaucratic that the people do not know where to turn for solutions to their problems. Additionally, this superficial separation of powers not only fails to ensure the real independence of various branches of government but also significantly sacrifices the administrative efficiency of the old system, making ordinary people victims of bureaucratic buck-passing.

This is exactly the source of the challenges facing judicial independence. The court, as a later offshoot of the government, needs the support of social resources. However, as the logic of the internal operation of government organs does not support judicial independence, the court faces "survival" pressure, despite the independence and supreme prestige granted to it in the formal codes. The obvious result is that the court has to accept the authority of powers not recognized in law and its role therefore as a tool, and yet it must try to expand the scope of its powers at every opportunity. The expansion of power obtained this way, however, only ends up pushing it further from independence.

The malfunction of the separation of powers system and the difficulty of achieving judicial independence in China are associated with both a lack of in-depth discussion among China's intelligentsia about the kind of judicial system to be established in the country, and with the limited dissemination of major judicial concepts among the public. From the survey of judicial independence in China over the past century, it can be readily seen that judicial knowledge was not well developed during that period; even today, some prevalent judicial concepts are ambiguous or misleading. Most prominently, there is little serious discussion in legal circles of the reasons why it is necessary for judicial powers to be separated and independent from executive powers. The boundary between these two powers should also be reflected in the criteria for appointment of personnel, the ways in which powers are exercised, institutions' internal administration models, the relationship between organs and the public, and other aspects. It is exactly due to the ignorance of the differences between the two powers in such respects that an administrative, or rather nonjudicial, model has been adopted by the courts for a long period of time.

The hierarchical system of judges is a good case in point. In this system, adopted in imitation of administrative or even military systems, judges' positions follow a hierarchy like that of administrative officials, and inside the court, judges of higher ranks enjoy institutionalized powers, such as the ability to interfere in cases heard by judges of lower rank. Although this system of domination by top-down rankings has always been taken for granted and greatly facilitates the control of court activities, the nature of this control is completely administrative and against the intrinsic requirements of the judicial profession and decisionmaking. Unlike administrative organs or the military, the activities of judges are highly case specific. The judge exercises his powers of office in the court where he makes decisions, not just in the final judgment but also in decisions concerning specific matters in the course of adjudication and in interaction with all parties concerned in the case. With the constant need to make decisions, if the judge cannot decide on relevant matters independently, the efficiency of adjudication will be directly affected. Besides, judicial decisions rely heavily on the evaluation of statements of the parties concerned and witnesses and require the judge's close observation.[86] Indeed, this intrinsic requirement of adjudication is what determines the principles of direct trial and oral evidence in modern legal proceedings. But the hierarchical system prevents the judge from making independent judgments because of the influence from judges at higher levels of office, that is, their "superiors." It is taken for granted that judges should rely on and comply with their superiors for decisions. This model undoubtedly increases the uncertainty of adjudication and provides a channel by which illegitimate powers interfere with judicial activities.

This hierarchical system of judges blinds those living under it to the possibility that there could exist a diametrically different system where every judge is independent and there is no subordination among judges, and where the judge's sole responsibility is to understand the law and administer justice. Regardless of titles and positions, every judge is one among equals.[87] This equality is not just among judges in the same court or courts of the same level but also among judges of courts at different levels. It is true that a higher-level trial court can change the judgment issued by a lower court (strictly pursuant to applicable laws), but this should be understood in terms of the division of labor rather than of rank; nor does this fact indicate any significant change in the criteria of appointment and emolument for judges in different courts.[88]

Another characteristic that is associated with, or indeed is an adaptation to, the hierarchical system of judges is the administrative structure of courts. The appeals process in the modern court system, by which a preliminary trial may be followed by a second appeal trial, is designed to provide a channel for the correction of possible mistakes in judgment. In the two-tier court system, for example, a concerned party not satisfied with the preliminary judgment may take his or her case to the appeals court, which will then review the preliminary judgment, usually with an emphasis on whether the preliminary court followed due process and whether there were any mistakes in the interpretation and application of the laws. The appeals court then decides either to return the case to the original court for retrial or to uphold the preliminary judgment; in the latter case, the original decision becomes final and legally binding on the parties concerned. The fact that appellate courts have the power to change preliminary court judgments does not imply that they are administratively superior to lower courts; the former does not have leadership or supervisory power over the latter. If the two become administratively affiliated, then there should be consistency in their will and behaviors, and the higher courts should be responsible for the decisions the lower courts make. In this case, the lower courts must turn to the higher courts for directions before making any decisions and strictly follow the higher courts' instructions. Under such a scenario, the appeals system would no longer make sense. Therefore, in some countries that adhere to the rule of law, the higher courts and the supreme court attach due importance to safeguarding the independence of lower courts.

China's judicial framework, it is true, adopts the concept that the relationship between higher and lower courts is different in nature from that existing between different levels of administrative or procuratorial organs. For instance, the relationships between higher and lower courts and between higher and lower procuratorates are differently provided for by law. According to article 132 of the Constitution of the People's Republic of China, "The Supreme People's Procuratorate directs the work of the people's procuratorates at various local levels and of the special people's procuratorates. People's procuratorates at higher levels direct the work of those at lower levels." Article 127 of the same constitution stipulates that "the Supreme People's Court supervises the administration of justice by the people's courts at various local levels and by the special people's courts. People's courts at higher levels supervise the administration of justice by those at lower levels."[89] However, the framework is one thing while the actual operation of the legal system is quite another. In spite of the different phrasing concerning the relationship of courts and of procuratorates in the constitution, the meaning of the word "supervise" as it is used concerning the relationship between higher and lower courts is not that straightforward. In some instances, the boundary between "supervise" and "direct" is very thin. A good example is the rising number of cases in which lower courts turn to the higher courts for direction concerning specific legal matters. This case referral system, under which the lower courts, rather than make judgments independently, refer cases to higher courts for directions on what judgments to make, is deemed by the mainstream an important element of "nonprocedural supervision on trial work." In addition to case referrals initiated by the lower courts, the higher courts may, on their own initiative, give instructions to lower courts about cases deemed as "having major impact." In such respects, there is simply no difference between courts and procuratorates in organizational structure.

This situation has various causes, including long-term instability in society and academic research, the traditional overemphasis on general principles and neglect of specific systems, a mainstream perspective that exaggerates social character and underestimates the role of sound systems, and class ideology that prevailed for a long period of time in China's institutional development. In addition to these noticeable factors, I think there is another important cause, namely, the failure to realize that institutional development, in essence, is a process of knowledge accumulation, and that the difference in the degree of soundness of different institutional systems reflects the difference in the command of knowledge of the people operating the systems. With regard to the judicial system, although China has introduced a modern framework, people inside and outside the framework still approach and operate it with traditional concepts, thus engendering incompatibility in many matters. The new system was introduced with the intention of avoiding the defects of the traditional system, but if the new system cannot run smoothly while the order of the old system has been undermined, it is inevitable that defects of both the old and new systems will emerge, with the paradoxical result that with more new rules there is less order.

In today's China, the knowledge dimension of the institutional system is especially significant and merits emphasis. In the past, the advocates of a new system often only concerned themselves with "grand discourse" on values and oversimplified the complicated process of institutionalization into a number of provocative slogans, which to a certain extent intensified ideological conflict and hampered success. For example, as a slogan, "judicial independence" is something so good and desirable that some would risk their life to achieve it while others would regard it as horrible and consider anyone advocating for it a rightist who should be suppressed by imprisonment. However, a rational survey of the theories and practices of judicial independence shows that the judiciary should be independent because independent courts are better able to accomplish their mission of settling disputes. In the meantime, an independent judiciary has the double effect of restraining the government from abusing power and safeguarding the rights and interests of citizens—as well as channeling public dissatisfaction into the courts and allaying it through the legal process, thus preventing citizens from resorting to violence for solutions to their suppressed grievances.[90] Like anything in the world, judicial independence is not perfect, and its realization has a price. Independent jurists have their private interests, specialization has its blind spots, and the pursuit of judicial independence is likely to distance the court system from the external world. As the saying goes, "One cannot have one's cake and eat it too." Humankind can only strike the best balance possible, otherwise those pursuing judicial independence with an idealistic vision will get disillusioned after achieving it, while those attempting to suppress judicial independence will end up seeing the disappearance of social order with the departure of judicial independence.

CHAPTER TWO

MENCIUS ON THE RULE OF LAW

In what follows I would like to discuss the legal dimension of Mencius's thought and, more broadly, the relevance of Confucianism to the development of China's rule of law today. The relationship between Confucian teaching and the rule of law has captured the imagination of Chinese intellectuals in recent years—actually, I should say ever since 1840. For more than a century, we Chinese have been grappling with the issue of how to strike a balance between the tradition we inherited and the modernity we seek. A good example is the May Fourth Movement and its stirring slogan "Down with Confucianism," which unleashed an intellectual revolution in China.[1] Here I think of Mr. Wu Yu from Chengdu, a strong critic of Confucian ways, who was recruited by Peking University. Although it caused him a lot of trouble, he still went on a crusade against Confucian ethics, almost to the point of opposition for opposition's sake. In fact, there is even a view that since the May Fourth Movement, countertradition has become a new tradition. Western ideas, such as socialism, were borrowed and applied. And it is true even today: you have people like me who believe that constitutionalism and the rule of law are the best safeguards of liberty and the foundation of good governance in China. This is a cause to which I have always been committed.

Editor's note: The original Chinese version of this chapter is based on a talk by the author at the Beijing bookstore Sanweishuwu (三味书屋) on January 2, 2010. Chinese transcripts of the talk have been widely circulated, with the authorization of the bookstore, on various Chinese websites. The author provided the Chinese transcript of his talk for this volume.

The British say that "history is another country." It is true, especially in the case of China. I sometimes joked with my colleagues who study China's legal history: "Your research has little more than archaeological value." What I meant is, their research only tells how the Chinese legal system has developed—or failed to develop, to be precise—and why we have essentially adopted the Western system. My specialty, as you know, is Western legal history. As far as I am concerned, our current legal system—the penal code or civil laws alike—is largely based on Western laws. The Property Rights Law—and questions like "Can the government pull down this house or not?"—is a case in point. It has its roots in the Western legal tradition going back to ancient Rome. So from my perspective, although in our law schools Chinese professors teach Chinese students using Mandarin, it is Western stuff that is being taught. Remember that witticism from Qian Zhongshu's novel *Fortress Besieged*: "Studying overseas in China"?[2] That's also what this is: we in fact study foreign or Western materials in Chinese classrooms.

This assertion, of course, is highly controversial, but it causes no problem for Neo-Confucians who hold that China's classical theories can still be used to solve China's contemporary cultural problems. But when it comes to institutional problems as related to constitutionalism, democracy, and rule of law, we must turn to the West for solutions. It merits mentioning that what the so-called third wave of Confucianism is committed to is precisely the integration of the classic Mind Confucianism and Western constitutionalism, and this is a basic orientation of Neo-Confucians. As many people are aware, Mr. Jiang Qing has spared no efforts in recent years to advocate for a return to the true Confucian tradition.[3] His work, *Political Confucianism*, has been published unabridged in Taiwan, but the mainland version, published by Sanlian Publishing House (SDX Joint Publishing), has been heavily censored because some of his views are too unorthodox. His basic premise is that Marxism has proven to be a wrong path for China, as is Westernization toward a constitutional government safeguarding democracy and freedom. The author does not buy the idea of integrating classic Confucianism and Western constitutionalism, either; instead, he holds that Western constitutionalism should be thrown away altogether. According to him, China has its own profound political tradition, and there is no need to borrow ideas from the West. The book is an attempt to rediscover China's own political tradition. He once said to me that China should not learn judicial reform from the West because we have Confucius as our guide, who was not only a great educator, philosopher, and thinker but also a great jurist and judge. He said that he would count China's judicial reform as successful when Confucius's statue is erected at the entrance of the

Supreme People's Court. These ideas leave us to ponder the question: what on earth is the proper path of development for China?

As friends here know, I was transferred last March to teach at Shihezi University in Xinjiang for two years. I noticed on the Internet that many friends showed great concern about my transfer. In a post entitled "Settled down in Shihezi," I received more than one thousand replies from friends across the country, many leaving their real names in support. As a matter of fact, my transfer to Xinjiang was a sound move for Peking University because it both made the university accountable to some authorities and could protect me from persecution. My transfer to remote Xinjiang, far away from the political center, was a good thing for Peking University, and it was not a bad thing for me as well in 2009—a politically sensitive and troubled year. At this time last year, I did not expect to see any substantial changes in China within the following one or two years. In this period, it seemed desirable to leave this politically troubled area and pursue some good reading in beautiful Xinjiang. As indicated in a doggerel poem I wrote there, "Zhuangzi, Mengzi, and Shihezi" [*laughter*], this was a period for me to read some Chinese classics.[4]

The education I received during my childhood was in large part counter-traditional and, at least formally, rejected any learning of traditional literature. The works of Mao Zedong were the only objects for reading, and there was simply no chance to seriously read Chinese classics. It was only due to the "Criticize Lin, Criticize Confucius" (*pi lin pi kong*) campaign launched by Mao Zedong after the Lin Biao incident that I began to familiarize myself with some Confucian doctrines.[5] I still remember telling everyone around me the stories of how Confucius attempted to restore the old ways. As for *The Works of Mencius*, to be frank, I had never read it with any seriousness before, even if I had bought the book long ago. It is indeed very well put that classics are books that everyone recommends but nobody reads. So it was only after I was transferred to Xinjiang that I began to read Mencius in earnest and with diligence.

As we all know, Mencius was a highly peculiar figure among thinkers in the pre-Qin period.[6] He was well known for his uncommon eloquence. In his annotation to *An Oral Autobiography of Hu Shih*, Mr. T. K. Tang (Tang Degang) made interesting mention of Mencius's eloquence. For instance, Mencius once argued with the utopian socialist Chen Xiang until the other was left defenseless and speechless. But rather than being triumphant, Mencius said indignantly, "Indeed, I am not fond of disputing at all, but I am compelled to do it!"[7]

Given my academic background in Western legal systems, I read Mencius with a special eye to the legal dimension of Mencius's thought, especially its relevance to the development of China's rule of law today. I wanted to find out what Mr. Jiang Qing was referring to when he said that classical Confucianism has its own great political tradition, and what Confucianism has to say about the rule of law and its applicability in contemporary China.

The first thing we encounter today when we discuss the relationship between Mencius and the rule of law is Mencius's predicament about how to restrict monarchical power. It is an important issue in any monarchical state, and even for republics, because the question of how to restrict the powers of the state's top leaders remains. China is arguably the first country in the East to establish a republic. There used to be a view that if the Qing dynasty were ruled by the Han rather than the Manchu, China might have established a constitutional monarchy long ago. However, the deep-seated conflict between the minority Manchu and the majority Han, and the resulting nationalism and radicalism on the part of the Han Chinese, made it very difficult to establish a constitutional monarchy. A similar hypothesis is that if China had come under pressure from Western powers during the Han-ruled Ming dynasty and not during the late Qing dynasty, a constitutional monarchy would also likely have been established.

I do not agree with these views because from the Qin dynasty onward, there had never been any possibility of establishing a strict legal or institutional system to restrict monarchical power. The Chinese either submitted themselves to the emperor's unscrupulous use of his paramount power or rose in revolt and overthrew the existing dynasty. No effective attempts were made to establish a system that allows the existence of the sovereign but restricts his power. I think this problem not only persisted in the ancient times but has remained almost unchanged in modern times, with the only difference being that the name of the supreme leader changed from emperor to generalissimo and then to today's president and general secretary. In a word, we simply do not have a means to restrict the power of the top leader. After he was elected as the general secretary, Comrade Hu Jintao reiterated that the whole party should supervise the work of the Central Committee, and particularly the general secretary himself. Well, we do want to supervise, but we have no means to do that. [*Laughter*] How are we to supervise them, the country's powerful top leaders? They are nowhere to be seen. And when you write any critical articles, they are censored or deleted. So there is simply no way to supervise them.

When reading Mencius, I find that he ran into the same tricky situation as well. There were many dialogues between Mencius and the King Xuan of Qi on monarchical power. When it comes to the relationship between the sovereign and his ministers, we see a significant development in Mencius's thinking about Confucius's treatment of the same subject. According to the summarization by Mr. Hsiao Kung-chuan, this is reflected in three aspects.[8] The first is the nurturing of the people. Mencius emphasizes that a well-governed state must include a harmonious relationship between the sovereign and his subjects, where the people are well fed and live a good life rather than existing in hunger and suffering. The second is Mencius's proposition that the people are more important than the ruler. In his own words, "The people are the most important element in a nation; the spirits of the land and grain are the next; the sovereign is the slightest." This marked a great development of Mencius's thought beyond that of Confucius. He holds firmly that "those who win the hearts of the people win the world." Third, unlike Confucius, who often looks at the positive sides of things and expounds on them without any mention of the conflicting sides, such as what to do when conflicts arise between the king and his ministers, Mencius explicitly defines the king-minister relationship as one of mutual reciprocity. Just as Mr. Yi Zhongtian once observed, there is a major difference between reciprocity and equality: the king and his ministers cannot be said to be equals, but there does exist a reciprocal relationship of power and responsibility.[9] Mencius said, "When the prince regards his ministers as his hands and feet, his ministers regard their prince as their belly and heart; when he regards them as his dogs and horses, they regard him as another man; when he regards them as the ground or as grass, they regard him as a robber and an enemy." This remark was very radical and revolutionary in Mencius's time.

Among the kings with whom Mencius talked, I think King Xuan of Qi was the most striking. Always candid and outspoken, he told Mencius of his weaknesses for wealth and women. The two had many interesting conversations. One day Mencius said to the king, "Suppose that a person entrusts his wife and children to the care of his friend while he travels to a faraway place, and that, on his return, he should find that his friend had caused his wife and children to suffer cold and hunger. How ought he to deal with this friend?" The king said, "He should cast him off." Mencius said, "Suppose that the chief criminal judge could not regulate the officers under him, how would you deal with him?" The king said, "Dismiss him." Mencius proceeded, "If within the four borders of your kingdom there is not a good government, and people are suffering and dying of hunger by the thousands, what is to be done?" The king, nonplussed, looked to the right and left.[10] He then asked Mencius about the latest songs of Song Zuying.[11] [*Laughter and applause*] As I read *Mencius*, I find that King Xuan of Qi was indeed a very interesting person.

Another time, King Xuan of Qi asked Mencius, "Was it so, that Tang banished Jie of Xia, and that King Wu smote Zhou of Yin?" Mencius replied, "It is so in the records." The king said, "May a minister then put his sovereign to death?" Mencius said definitely, "He who outrages the benevolence proper to his nature is called a robber; he who outrages righteousness is called a ruffian. The robber and ruffian we call a mere fellow. I have heard of the cutting off of the fellow Zhou of Yin, but I have not heard of putting a sovereign to death in his case."[12] Mencius was unequivocal in his stance.

As we know, there is a great difference between the conversations of pre-Qin scholars and Plato's dialogues. Mr. Zhu Guangqian once observed that in the early stage of human civilization, when knowledge was disseminated through dialogues, there were two most eminent dialogists: one was Mencius, and the other, Plato.[13] But I think there is a major difference between Mencius and Plato. Plato's dialogues are often long and systematic, often involving several persons. Take *The Republic*, for example. It starts with a dialogue between Glaucon and Socrates, which was then joined by Thrasymachus. They talked and argued and debated, and their dialogues culminated in a book 400,000 words long. I do not think *The Republic* is a record of real-life dialogues, as it is presented, but rather was written by Plato, the master dialogist. The worst form of dialogue is what happens in the press conference, where the reporters ask questions and receive answers. Suppose I am a reporter, and I have questions to ask Mr. Li, who is a bookstore owner. I ask him, "What qualities do you think a bookstore owner should have to be successful?" And he gives me a three-point answer. And I ask again, "What difficulties have you faced in operating your bookstore?" And he gives me an answer. Here I am nothing but an asking machine, and there is little fun to speak of.

The best form of dialogue is when three or four persons of comparable intelligence argue and debate on a serious topic of common interest, each trying to convince the others and win them to his side. Plato's dialogues belong to the second category. They attempt to answer such questions as, what is good, what is bad, what is justice, and how does one build an ideal state? Such dialogues require rigorous logical reasoning. Therefore, one has to keep a concentrated and clear mind in order to understand *The Republic*. The philosophical dialogues in the pre-Qin period in China, as recorded in the *Analects of Confucius*, the *Works of Mencius*, or other works of the period, all basically follow the pattern of a short series of Q&A's in different settings. This aphoristic and unsystematic presentation of wisdom marks a huge difference from the Greek and especially Platonic systematic method of dialogue.

Mencius made quite a few remarks on the relationship between the ruler and his ministers, but they are sporadic and without elaboration, leaving the question to posterity. For example, there is the following story from the time of Emperor Jing of Han who, like King Xuan of Qi, also enjoyed discoursing with scholars. One day two scholars were invited into the presence of the emperor. The first was Yuan Gusheng, who was an expert on the *Book of Poetry* and was allegedly also from the state of Qi, and the other was named Huang Sheng. When the three of them picked up the topic of "whether Tang and Wu had received Heaven's Mandate," Huang Sheng expressed his explicit opposition to Mencius's stance, saying: "Tang and Wu did not receive the Mandate, and moreover they were murderers." Yuan Gusheng, who was a staunch follower of Mencius's theory, refuted:

> It is not as you say. Now, King Jie and King Zhou were uncultivated and disorderly, and the heart of the kingdom completely turned toward Tang and Wu. Because the kingdom's heart had turned to them, Tang and Wu punished kings Jie and Zhou. The people of kings Jie and Zhou would not obey them and turned to Tang and Wu. Because Tang and Wu had no other alternative, they were established as kings themselves. Is this not receiving the Mandate?

Ancient people liked to use metaphors in debates. Now Huang Sheng made a retort by way of a metaphor of the shoes and hat, saying,

> Even if a hat is worn-out, it must be put on the head, and even if shoes are new, they must be put on the feet. Is this not so? 'High' and 'low' have their distinctions. Now, even though Jie and Zhou had lost the Way, they were nonetheless high rulers, and even though Tang and Wu were sages, they were low ministers. Now, if a ruler fails in his behavior and the minister does not rectify his speech and correct his mistakes in order to honor the Son of Heaven, but instead punishes his ruler on the basis of his mistakes and replaces him on the throne, is this not murder and usurpation?

Yuan Gusheng, not convinced, turned to proof by contradiction and said, "If it is certainly as you say, then was it not murder when Emperor Gao, the founder of the Han, replaced the Qin and made himself the Son of Heaven?"

This question, of course, put Huang Sheng in a difficult position. Sensing an intellectual dilemma that could potentially challenge his claim to Heaven's Mandate, Emperor Jing put an abrupt stop to the debate, saying, "In discussing one's learning, he cannot be considered stupid if he avoids talking about Tang and Wu receiving the Mandate."[14] So this question was left unsolved, and it remained an unanswerable question in China's 2,000 years of intellectual history. This demonstrates the first aspect of Mencius's predicament.

Indeed, the predicament of how to deal with a ruler treating his own people ruthlessly was not just for Mencius, but for China as well. In fact, Huang Sheng's argument has obvious flaws. First of all, the metaphor comparing the relationship between the ruler and his ministers to that between hat and shoes is not appropriate because unlike a hat that does not hurt one's head, a ruler is capable of abusing his subjects. Second, he did not give a solution to the scenario when ministers following the normal procedure fail to make the ruler change his ways and the ruler's ruthlessness continues.

However, once Mencius did touch on the topic of what to do when the "normal procedure" fails. The occasion was when King Xuan of Qi talked with Mencius about the relationship between the ruler and his high ministers. Mencius distinguished between high ministers, who are noble and relatives of the prince, and those who are of a different surname. Concerning high ministers who are noble and relatives of the prince, Mencius said that "if the prince has great faults, they ought to remonstrate with him, and if he does not listen to them after they have done so again and again, they ought to dethrone him." Hearing this, the king looked moved and changed countenance, for he was a very straightforward and spontaneous person who did not bother to hide his real feelings. When the king's countenance became composed, Mencius went on to speak of high ministers who were of a different surname from the prince: "When the prince has faults, they ought to remonstrate with him, and if he does not listen to them after they have done this again and again, they ought to leave the State." This means, in Mencius's words, "getting upon a raft and floating about on the sea." Nevertheless, Mencius only discussed how high ministers should get along with the prince and did not mention what an approach commoners like Chen Sheng and Wu Guang should take when they are dissatisfied with their ruler.[15]

Another major challenge facing Mencius was what criteria to use to decide whether a monarch has regressed into what he called a "robber and ruffian." Take Comrade Kim Jong-il, for example. In pictures taken with pretty female soldiers, he looks congenial and approachable. Is he a despot? How are we to determine whether the paramount leader of a country is or is not a despot? Some monarchs may be less than intelligent. As we know, the position of monarch is inherited by birth, not earned by virtue. You cannot sit the imperial examination to contest for the position of monarch. Yet intelligence is not something that can always be inherited, and a father of vision and great ambition may beget a tardy or cowardly son. And there is the intelligence of the mother to consider. So there is no direct link between intelligence and blood lineage. A monarch with low intelligence cannot make sound decisions and may fall under the sway of those around him, becoming a puppet. Is a mentally retarded monarch a despot? Perhaps not. Nor is one who caused great damage due to unsound decisionmaking. Some point to the high percentage of corrupt despots among rulers in Chinese history simply because one-third of them are generally regarded so. However, there is no unanimous agreement on this generalization.

In a letter to Guo Moruo, Mao Zedong admonished him "not to criticize the First Emperor of Qin, for the last word remains to be said about burning the books and burying the scholars."[16] In fact, as far as "burning the books and burying the scholars" is concerned, Mao Zedong went much farther than the First Emperor of Qin, as the number of intellectuals killed during the various political campaigns that he launched far outnumbered those scholars buried by the First Emperor of Qin. History always repeats itself. In the case of Chiang Ch'ing, Roxane Witke, the author of her biography *Comrade Chiang Ch'ing*, once published an article in *Time* magazine to introduce the book.[17] The book was translated into Chinese with the title *Empress of the Red Capital*. In the Great Cultural Revolution, the whole of China was thrown into chaos and countless lives were lost. Wasn't that despotic rule?

History is full of recurring themes. Every generation is adding to the historical record. To answer the question of who were despots and who were not, perhaps we have to rely on history for judgment; but historical judgments by their nature are made by those in the future rather than contemporaries of the historical period. Liu Shaoqi once said, "Fortunately, history is written by the people," but when it was the people's turn to write history, Liu had long since passed away.[18] When the future set about writing the history of the preceding period, the disasters made in that period were beyond repair.

In a well-governed state—or rather, a sound political system—there is an important mechanism by which mistakes can be rectified quickly after their occurrence rather than when it is too late to reverse the negative effects of those mistakes. Then how does one establish such a rectifying mechanism? Not long ago, when commenting on a case in which a woman petitioner to

Beijing was illegally arrested by the Liaison Office of her native Tongbo County in Henan Province and then raped, I said that the rapist certainly deserves punishment, but who was responsible? Wasn't it the Liaison Office of Tongbo County in Beijing? Shouldn't it be held responsible? What is the legal basis for preventing people from making petitions in Beijing? If the local governments spare no efforts to intercept petitioners to Beijing, what is the point of establishing bureaus and offices for complaints, and isn't this equal to making the directors of those bureaus and offices mere figureheads? Why are those authorities of the local governments so determined to thwart local people's attempts to make petitions in Beijing? Why are protests allowed and seen as legal and legitimate in other countries? In the United States, for example, hundreds of thousands of people came to the streets of Washington in protest against the Iraq War. I think it is rigid ideology that underlies all the suppressions of people's protests, and the result is a superficial harmony where nothing except for eulogies and praises of the government is allowed. Such a harmony is indeed terrible, resulting in an environment where those in leadership positions make gross mistakes and never bother to rectify them.

The second aspect of Mencius's predicament was what procedure to follow to determine that a monarch has regressed into a "robber and ruffian." In the parliamentary debates in the early period of Britain, a recurring issue was how to judge whether the king acted beyond his proper power. A procedure was then put into place for this purpose. A state usually has a mechanism, either in the form of a constitution or other regulations, that provides a framework for the exercise of powers. In 2003, after the Sun Zhigang incident, four peer scholars and I submitted a proposal to the Standing Committee of the National People's Congress demanding that measures be taken about the incident in accordance with the provision of article 71 of the constitution.[19] According to the article, the National People's Congress (NPC) and its Standing Committee may, when they deem it necessary, appoint committees of inquiry into specific questions and adopt legally binding resolutions in the light of their reports. The NPC does have such a committee, and we may well call it the "Article 71 Committee." After the incident, we made it clear that we do not trust the provincial government of Guangdong because it had happened there, and the provincial government then said that it would establish a special committee for the incident, with membership comprising personnel from the province's people's congress, department of public security, and department of civil affairs. This meant that those whose policies and enforcement led to the incident were going to investigate it. Of course we would not trust them, not because they were not CCP [Chinese

Communist Party] members or that they were morally unworthy, but because it went against procedural justice for them to make the investigation, and it was absolutely impossible for us to believe in their impartiality. We demanded that a neutral and independent agency be put in charge of the investigation. Accordingly, we called for the establishment of a special committee under the NPC to investigate the Sun Zhigang incident in particular, and the implementation and legitimacy of the Measures on Aid and Management of Urban Vagrants and Beggars in general. For instance, a public hearing should be held to give the public definite information on what really happened in the Sun Zhigang incident, who would be held responsible for the incident, and what measures would be taken to retain the balance between maintaining urban order and safeguarding human rights, in addition to an update in relevant legislation. If these measures were taken, it would really be fine.

You must remember what happened in Britain after the mysterious death of David Kelly, an arms expert at the Ministry of Defense. As you know, a special committee chaired by famous senior judge Lord Hutton was set up, and a public hearing was subsequently held. During the hearing, even Prime Minister Tony Blair was summoned to provide information under oath. How desirable it would be if a similar committee would be established by the NPC here in China for similar cases, especially so if He Weifang were to chair it, and then I would surely perform my duties the best I can. [*Laughter*] I would produce a solid report and propose various suggestions for legislation on behalf of the NPC. But the reality is always cold and disheartening. You know, it has been some thirty years since our current constitution was formulated, promulgated, and took effect in 1982. During this long period, the procedure provided for in article 71 of the constitution has never been initiated. The article may well be called a "Sleeping Beauty" article, for it has been sleeping undisturbed all these years. I have always hoped that the NPC would exercise all powers and perform all duties conferred upon it by the constitution, but it seems ever inactive and passive. It did not dawn on me why it is so until a friend said to me, "Why, if you don't enter this system, you never realize that it was established precisely to be inactive and meant to be nothing." This is really a thought-provoking revelation. Why have some constitutional rights become mere lip service? What drives their enforcement?

The third predicament concerns the enforcement of the political system in place. There is a story about the adoption of the English charter the Magna Carta. It happened that in 1215 King John of England asked his barons for money to continue wars with France because the previous unsuccessful wars had drained the country's treasury. But the barons refused and said that the king should not levy taxes at his own will, and they would instead establish a parliament to take charge of the country's finances. The king was outraged and threatened them, saying that his army may lose to foreign armies, but it was more than capable of teaching them a lesson. A war broke out between the king's army and the barons' own armed forces. As a result, the king's army was defeated, and the king was forced to sign the Magna Carta.

Dear friends, as you may have found, there are many interesting things in English history. Take the rebellion of the barons we just talked about, for example. The barons defeated the king, but they did not dethrone the king and have their leader replace him, as would surely have been the case if it happened in China. No, they did not do that; they demanded that the king sign the Magna Carta, which set down a series of rules for the king. The charter covered various provisions meant to limit the powers of the king and even provided for a legal procedure under which the king had to obtain the approval of the barons to levy taxes, and his exercise of power would be subject to the supervision of the barons. For example, it stipulated that no person could be deprived of his life, liberties, and properties unless by a legal procedure, and every accused would be entitled to a fair trial. These provisions, though enacted hundreds of years ago in England, remain goals we have been struggling for in China, where many people are put in prison or even killed without receiving a fair trial, and some people are deprived of freedom for expressing their own independent thoughts. The due process of law embodied by the Magna Carta, of course, was not achieved at one go but over a period of time. Anyway, the year 1215 was a very important one in the English history of constitutionalism.

Here we come to the third aspect of Mencius's predicament: how to create a force powerful enough to align the exercise of power by the monarch and all officials at large with the needs of the people? This force may not necessarily come in the form of a legal provision but may assume some other form, such as a unique social system and a compromise-reaching mechanism among different classes of conflicting interests. The king is a person, but he represents a class, and within the noble class, there are nobles with different religious backgrounds as well as secular nobles, and they may have conflicting interests. Today, we have such entities as the middle class, civil society, the self-governing body of university administration, farmers' federations, and workers' unions—even a cab drivers' union. These entities can take unified action to protest and safeguard their interests because they are organized and capable of exerting pressure on other groups. A well-organized society with considerable strength to confront the establishment is very important for maintaining effective restrictions on the monarch's power. To the contrary, the worst society is one that has a monarch with unchecked power, where the people are not well organized or united. It is impossible for such a society to achieve benign development.

Recently I have been reading a book entitled *Confucian China and Its Modern Fate* by American sinologist Joseph Levenson.[20] A very striking feature of this book is that the author begins his analysis of China's bureaucratic politics with a discussion of Chinese traditional painting. According to the author, literati-officials liked this literary and artistic activity, and the evolution of Chinese painting, in particular, is a mirror of the Chinese literary tradition, which places emphasis on spiritual fidelity rather than formal fidelity. Therefore a person who has not mastered sketching may be a master of Chinese painting. What concerns him is not to give a reproduction of nature; indeed, realism in painting is sometimes disparaged. For example, in Chinese landscape painting, the water surface has the reflection of the mountain, but the reflection is by no means an exact mirror of the mountain. The author sees in this a general aesthetic inherent to officialdom and a link between this perspective and the absence of professionalism in the bureaucracy in China. The literati-official class, especially the bureaucratic class based on the imperial civil examination system, had a deep-seated bias and opposition against technical things and a blind worship of moral and spiritual things. As a result, an expertise-based bureaucracy with a clear division of labor never emerged in the more than 2,000-year history of feudal China. According to Western constitutional theory, and as shown by history, such a bureaucracy is a necessary condition for effective restriction of the monarch's power.

This connection is demonstrated by an interesting anecdote about Sir Edward Coke, the chief justice of England, and King James I. The king demanded to hear a case by himself, but Sir Edward Coke declared that such a proceeding was not warranted by law. The king replied that the law was founded on reason, and he had "reason as well as the judges." Coke then said,

> True it was that God had endowed his majesty with excellent science and great endowments of nature; but His Majesty was not learned in the laws of his realm of England, and causes which concern the life or inheritance or goods or fortunes of his subjects; they are not decided by natural reason, but by artificial reason and judgment of law—which law is an act that requires long study and experience before that a man can attain to the cognizance of it.[21]

In a word, however richly endowed by God the king might be, the law had to be administered by professionally trained judges pursuant to a fixed set of standards.

Do we still face this problem today? Well, suppose you caused a serious traffic accident resulting in death due to a violation of traffic rules. You come to your lawyer and ask whether you will be given a death sentence. And you are told that this is a traffic offense, and according to article 133 of the Criminal Law, anyone who commits a traffic offense resulting in injury or death is punishable with a maximum of seven years of imprisonment, regardless whether you are guilty of drunk driving or driving without license and no matter how many persons are killed in the accident, for this is how the law currently stands. However, your offense is more serious because you abandoned the scene without coming to the rescue of the victim, and the victim died due to untimely treatment, and in this case, according to the law, you are punishable with a maximum of fifteen years of imprisonment. Hearing this, you are overjoyed and relieved, feeling assured that you will not receive the death sentence. However, your lawyer warns you that it is still too early to feel relieved because whether you are to receive a death sentence is not just up to the law but also up to how the public feels about what happened. If the public is outraged, and all demand that you be given the severest punishment, then you will be in great trouble, and therefore your lawyer is really not so sure whether you are doomed or not.

I think this is very bad for a country's legal system because the laws are not the only criteria for judgment. In fact, things have become so bad that folks are losing trust in the courts and prefer to handle disputes in other ways, privately. The Sun Weiming case in Chengdu is a good case in point to demonstrate the arbitrariness of China's legal system.[22] Some may say that he deserves the death sentence because his drunk driving claimed four lives. But do not forget that he was driving to drop off his parents. The 9/11 hijackers who were determined to die in their terrorist acts did not bring their parents with them. Did Sun Weiming mean to take his parents along and die with them? Of course not. He dropped off his parents, and when he said goodbye to them, his father cautioned him to be careful when driving because he had consumed some liquor. He reassured them and said that he would be careful. But the accident still happened. The Chengdu Intermediate People's Court gave him a death sentence, to take effect immediately. Although it was changed to a life sentence in the second-instance [appeals court] hearing, it still constituted a gross breach of the law. Now it has become common for drunk drivers causing death to be given life sentences. There was a similar case in Nanjing recently. But it is simply wrong to give arbitrary interpretation of laws. When the law becomes a plaything, it is really horrible.

I do think there was advocacy for professionalism in the government in the early period of Chinese history, and the advocate was none other than Mencius, who placed a particular emphasis on technocracy in the governance of the state. During an interview with King Xuan of Qi, Mencius said to him,

> If you are going to build a large mansion, you will surely cause the master of the workmen to look out for large trees, and when he has found such large trees, you will be glad, thinking that they will answer for the intended object. Should the workmen hew them so as to make them too small, then your Majesty will be angry, thinking that they will not answer for the purpose. Now, a man spends his youth in learning the principles of right government, and being grown up to vigor, he wishes to put them in practice; if your Majesty says to him, 'For the present put aside what you have learned, and follow me,' what shall we say? Here now you have a gem unwrought, in the stone. Although it may be worth 10,000 taels, you will surely employ a lapidary to cut and polish it. But when you come to the government of the State, then you say, 'For the present put aside what you have learned, and follow me.' How is it that you herein act so differently from your conduct in calling in the lapidary to cut the gem?

By this comparison Mencius put across the importance of special knowledge for state governance.

A little earlier I mentioned a debate between Mencius and Chen Xiang, a disciple of Xu Xing. Xu was the master of another philosophical school advocating that princes and ministers should cultivate the ground equally and along with their people, and eat the fruit of their labor, and that they should prepare their own meals, morning and evening, while at the same time they carry on their government. To express the theory in today's terms, it would be equal to requiring the nine members of the Politburo Standing Committee of the CCP Central Committee to plow the fields in the morning and hold meetings in the afternoon, and the members of the National People's Congresses and the judges of the Supreme People's Court to toil in their own fields while discharging their official duties. This would be the ideal state in the eyes of Xu Xing.

Mencius, of course, was very opposed to this ridiculous theory, and asked Chen Xiang, "I suppose that Xu Xing your Master sows grain and eats the produce. It is not so?" "It is so," was the answer.

"I suppose also he weaves cloth, and wears his own manufacture. Is it not so?" "No. Xu wears clothes of haircloth."

"Does he wear a cap?" "He wears a cap."

"What kind of cap" "A plain cap."

"Is it woven by himself?" "No. He gets it in exchange for grain."

"Why does Xu not weave it himself?" "That would injure his husbandry."

"Does Xu cook his food in boilers and earthenware pans, and does he plough with an iron share?" "Yes."

"Does he make those articles himself?" "No. He gets them in exchange for grain."

Mencius then said,

Then getting those various articles in exchange for grain is not oppressive to the potter and the founder, and the potter and the founder in their turn, in exchanging their various articles for grain, are not oppressive to the husbandman. How should such a thing be supposed? And moreover, why does not Xu act the potter and founder, supplying himself with the articles, which he uses solely from his own establishment? Why does he go confusedly dealing and exchanging with the handicraftsmen? Why does he not spare himself so much trouble?

Chen Xiang replied, "The business of the handicraftsman can by no means be carried on along with the business of husbandry."

Mencius resumed,

Then, is it the government of the kingdom which alone can be carried on along with the practice of husbandry? Great men have their proper business, and little men have their proper business. Moreover, in the case of any single individual, whatever articles he can require are ready to his hand, being produced by the various handicraftsmen—if he must first make them for his own use, this way of doing would keep all the people running about upon the roads. Hence, there is the saying, "Some labor with their minds, and some labor with their strength. Those who labor with their minds govern others; those who labor with their strength are governed by others. Those who are governed by others support them; those who govern others are supported by them." This is a principle universally recognized.

Here Mencius was arguing for the importance of the division of labor. This thought, however, failed to take root and blossom in ancient China.

Next I want to talk about Mencius's thought as it relates to international law. Was there legal thought on international relations in the pre-Qin period? In my opinion, though greatly different from the modern concept of the sovereign state, Mencius's thought on the relations of states still deserves our study. W. A. P. Martin, also known as Ding Weiliang, was the inaugural president of the Imperial University of Peking (today's Peking University). He translated the *Elements of International Law* in 1860 and was among the earliest figures to disseminate concepts of international public law in China.[23] This was exactly the subject and, indeed, a challenge faced by Lin Zexu when he went to Guangzhou to ban imports of opium from foreign countries.[24] He was considering seizing the opium goods in foreign vessels, but on second thought he decided to acquaint himself with the common practice of foreign countries in such cases first. He began to search for books in this field and was introduced to *The Laws of Nations*, written by the famous Swiss jurist Emmerich de Vattel. It was 1839. He had his assistant Yuan Dehui, who was born in Malacca and versed in both Latin and English, translate the part of the book on seizure of goods, but the translation was unintelligible to Lin Zexu because some of the most essential abstract terms did not have ready Chinese equivalents then, such as "right" and "liberty," and the translator was unable to express their meanings. Then Lin Zexu turned to a missionary and doctor called Peter Parker who was running a hospital in Guangzhou. The missionary translated some parts of the book into Chinese as required, but his translation was still quite beyond Lin Zexu. Anyway, based on the rough ideas he got from the translation, Lin wrote a letter to Queen Victoria about the opium trade. I have read the English version of the letter. It was sternly written, as if addressed to the chief of a tribe. In the letter, Lin Zexu asked the queen to have her people well managed. This was the first dissemination of concepts of international law in China. By the 1860s, W. A. P. Martin arranged for a full translation of *The Laws of Nations*. He even wrote an article entitled "A Review of Classical Chinese Thoughts on International Law," in which he introduced some of the basic rules governing the relations of states in ancient China.[25] For example, a battle shall not commence unless both sides have prepared. This was a rule governing warfare in ancient China.

In fact, Mencius had many interesting thoughts on wars, international relations, sovereignty, and human rights. To put it briefly, first, he put human rights above sovereign rights, rejecting today's popular principle of "noninterference in international affairs," in the belief that a sovereign suppressing his own people is illegitimate. According to him, it can be an option for a state to overthrow the ruler of another state if the ruler is tyrannical and his subjects are asking for help. Therefore, if Mencius lived today, he would surely nod to the Iraq War led by the United States. This is the first aspect of Mencius's thought on interstate relations.

Second, when it comes to interfering in the internal affairs of another state, it should be considered whether this interference is welcome to the state's ordinary people or not. This, however, is difficult to decide, especially in the absence of public opinion polls. For instance, it is really not clear whether the Iraqi people welcomed the war or not. In the terrible period of the Great Cultural Revolution in the 1960s, when everyone lived in terror and a great number of people were put in prison, would it have been welcome if U.S. forces had invaded China then? There is a story that several years ago, when a camera crew was shooting a scene in Jiaodong, Shandong Province, my hometown, several actors dressed as Kuomintang soldiers tried for fun to scare an old man working in his field, and with guns in their hands, they said to the old man, "Old Man, what are you doing?" The man turned around and, taken aback at the sight of them, cried with sentiment, "Oh, I have waited for your return for so long!" This, however, was only an individual case. The overall popular sentiment is not quite clear.

Third, the tyrant is punishable, even by death, as a consolation to the people badly treated by him. However, Mencius did not mention what procedure is to be followed to decide how to punish the tyrant—for instance, by a special tribunal. But Mencius, in an interview with King Xuan of Qi, said that "when the people all say, 'this man deserves death,' then inquire into the case, and when you see that the man deserves death, put him to death. In accordance with this we have the saying, 'the people killed him.' You must act in this way in order to be the parent of the people." Does this procedure apply to the punishment of a tyrant?

Fourth, the conquest of another state should cause as little damage and disruption to that state as possible. Mencius hoped that warfare would be conducted so that ordinary people on both sides are undisturbed by it and carry out their life as usual. He thinks this is the best way to show respect to the people of the state being conquered. It is not permissible to slay or imprison ordinary people, or pull down the ancestral temple of that state, or remove its precious vessels to the conquering state.

The fifth point is particularly interesting, for it answers the question of whether U.S. forces should continue to stay in Iraq after the overthrow of the former regime. According to Mencius, after the conquest is completed with the dethronement of the despot, the conquering state should work with the conquered state to put in place a new sovereign. A question remains: Isn't it good for a benevolent and virtuous king to conquer other states and put the whole world in his charge so that the kingly way can be applied universally and all people can benefit from it? Behind the withdrawal of the army and the enthronement of a new king from among the local people seems to be the idea of respect for what we call territorial integrity, but it is not promotion of the kingly way. Did Mencius advise King Xuan of Qi so because in his eyes the king did not have what it takes to be a king to unify the whole land?

What follows is the last aspect of Mencius's legal thought. His stance against the rule of law was reflected when he answered the question asked by Tao Ying about law: "Shun being sovereign, and Gao Yao chief minister of justice, if Gu Sou, the father of Shun, had murdered a man, what would have been done in the case?" Mencius said, "Gao Yao would simply have apprehended him." "But would not Shun have forbidden such a thing?" "Indeed, how could Shun have forbidden it? Gao Yao had received the law from a proper source." "In that case what would Shun have done?" "Shun would have regarded abandoning the kingdom as throwing away a worn-out sandal. He would privately have taken his father on his back, and retired into concealment, living somewhere along the sea-coast. There he would have been all his life, cheerful and happy, forgetting the kingdom."[26] This is how Mencius answered the question. This issue, of Confucianism's opposition to rule of law, particularly putting filial piety above compliance with the law, is treated in a book entitled *An Ideal State of Law: A Virtual Dialogue between Socrates and Mencius.*[27] When reading his works, we see that Mencius consistently emphasizes filial piety and assigns it a higher value than law. This is a very intricate and tangled aspect of the legal thought of Confucianism as a whole.

Finally, I would like to summarize what I have discussed in some brief points. First, Confucianism faces a legal predicament, which stems both from its intrinsic theoretical framework and from the unique traditional social structure of China. As we know, every thought has its social background, and a thinker is always a product of the society in which he lives. To cite an Arab saying, "People resemble their times more than they resemble their parents." Therefore, Mencius's thought should be understood in the context of the closed social structure of his time more than two thousand years ago. I think the predicament of Confucianism at large is more or less related to the traditional social structure.

Second, the integration of moral authority and political authority is a deep-seated problem in China's political and legal history. Great thinkers were always those whose thoughts were endorsed by the imperial court, and these thoughts were then imposed on all people of the state. In this way, moral authority, intellectual authority, political authority, and religious authority were combined to form an insurmountable challenge to any attempt to limit the power of the sovereign in ancient China. Even today, it is inconceivable for us to think how the great German philosopher Kant, a commoner who never held any government post and throughout his life never went out of the small city where he lived, managed to become well established as the greatest thinker in his country, even during his lifetime. His status as a great thinker hinged exclusively on his own thought, without the precondition of government endorsement. Indeed, his views often went against the orthodox thoughts of his time.

Third, there were attempts at technocracy in the early period of ancient China, but they were thwarted ultimately by Confucianism's strong moral orientation and the enduring imperial civil examination system. There was little success in establishing a division of labor in government and professionalization of some government posts. There is even regression in some respects today. For example, the president of our Supreme People's Court is a layperson who never received a single day's training in law or served a single day as a judge, but nevertheless he can be and is the president of our Supreme People's Court. This shows the magnitude of the challenge we still face today.

The introduction of Western legal thought into China since the beginning of modern times has afforded the best opportunity for China to extricate itself from the old trap and move toward a brand-new future, but due to the country's long history of autocracy, this path is necessarily extremely difficult. But whenever we face challenges, we can draw encouragement and inspiration from the following words of Mencius: "Humanity subdues inhumanity as water subdues fire. Nowadays those who practice humanity do so as if with one cup of water they could save a whole wagon load of fuel on fire. When the flames were not extinguished, they would say that water cannot subdue fire. This is as bad as those who are inhumane. At the end they will surely lose what little humanity they have."[28] I hold the firm conviction that in spite of the huge challenge before us, if we draw extensively on the best of cultural, spiritual, and institutional creations that humankind has hitherto contributed, and at the same time embrace and give new expression to our classical discourses, then our extrication from our predicament will not be as distant as we may imagine.

PART II

CONSTITUTIONALISM AND JUDICIAL REVIEW

CHAPTER THREE

CHINA'S FIRST STEPS
TOWARD CONSTITUTIONALISM

Zhang Shaoyan, moderator: Dear students, distinguished guests, ladies and gentlemen, good evening! It gives me great pleasure to introduce this evening's guest speaker, Professor He Weifang! [*Applause*] A graduate of the class of '78 from our university, Professor He is no stranger to this audience. Like many of you, I am also an ardent admirer of his. Professor He really needs no introduction, but let me just highlight one thing about him: he was named by *China Youth* magazine in 2001 as one of the most influential youths who would shape the future of China in the twenty-first century! [*Applause*] And he was the only entrant from our legal profession! [*Applause*]

Author's note: I would like to thank my students Xiang Lei and Wan Lihong for their diligent work in preparing this manuscript based on my oral presentation, my Ph.D. student Zhang Weiwei for her careful proofreading, and my old friend Zhang Shaoyan for not only moderating the panel discussion but also offering very helpful comments on the manuscript.

Editor's note: The original Chinese version of this chapter was based on a lecture by the author delivered as part of a moderated panel at the Southwest University of Political Science and Law in Chongqing on March 17, 2003. The moderator of the lecture was Zhang Shaoyan (张绍彦), professor of criminal law of the Southwest University of Political Science and Law. All presenters of the panel were faculty members of the Southwest University of Political Science and Law, and included Li Changqing (李长青), associate professor of jurisprudence; Liu Junxiang (刘俊祥), lecturer; Song Yubo (宋玉波), associate professor of constitutional law; Fu Zitang (付子堂), professor of jurisprudence; Lu Yunbao (卢云豹), lecturer; Luo Jun (罗军), associate professor; Wang Xuehui (王学辉), associate professor of administrative law; and Mo Jiangping (莫江平), associate professor of constitutional law. The English version omits some of the panel discussion.

He Weifang: I am sorry to jump in, but actually there were two. The other one was Xia Yong, who was my classmate here.[1]

Zhang Shaoyan: Oh yes, thank you for correcting me. I just came back this afternoon from Beijing where I am doing Ph.D. studies at the Law School of Peking University. Here I want to mention that Professor He was chosen as one of the "top ten young professors" of the Law School of Peking University and voted "the most charismatic teacher"! [*Laughter and applause*] Now let's welcome Professor He to give his lecture, "China's First Steps toward Constitutionalism."

He Weifang: Dear teachers and students, good evening! Let me tell you how excited I am to see so many of you—little did I expect a lecture on the constitution to be so popular among the students here. [*Laughter*] One explanation, I guess, is that I was quite successful in advertising my lecture. In my comments as a panelist last night, I kept telling you I was to give a lecture that would be a good follow-up to the one you had just heard. Besides, I think many of you are here not because of me but because of my capable colleagues here who are from this university—though I must confess I privately blamed them for attracting such a crowd and making it almost impossible for me to get in! [*Laughter*]

Reminiscences of My Alma Mater

It has been nearly twenty-one years since I graduated from Southwest University of Political Science and Law (SWUPL) and twenty-five years since I went to study at the university from my hometown in faraway Shandong. To be exact, the university at that time was still called Southwest College of Political Science and Law, which we jokingly referred to as Rotten College of Political Science and Law because the first sight of it was indeed a very far cry from what we had expected of it.[2] The truck that transported us to the college was stuck on the muddy road after rain while Dongshan Building of the college was already in sight, and we had to get off and carry our baggage to the building, which was our dormitory then. Time really flies, and almost in the twinkling of an eye, I have already been in, if not past, my middle age. [*Laughter*]

As time passes, I find my feelings for my alma mater growing increasingly strong and deep. Mr. Qian Zhongshu once said in an article that one's memory of one's hometown and motherland cannot be compared to the memory of a mathematical formula.[3] While the memory of a mathematical formula fades away in the course of time, the memory of one's hometown and motherland is like characters inscribed on a tree that become increasingly clear and discernable and unforgettable as the tree grows. I cherish the same feelings for SWUPL. Every time I hear a piece of good news from SWUPL, I will ask several alumni to have a drink in celebration [*applause and laughter*], but when I hear that some teachers have been transferred to other universities such as Xiangtan University and China University of Political Science and Law . . . [*laughter*], I have mixed feelings. Some of them are transferred to Peking University and become my colleagues, like Professor Yi Tian, and they help to further strengthen the Law School of Peking University, but I cannot help feeling worried about the brain drain from SWUPL. That is why I have mixed feelings.

This year marks the fiftieth anniversary of SWUPL. Its alumni around the country are all contemplating doing something for the university. The SWUPL Alumni Association in Beijing has decided to publish a series of monographs entitled "SWUPL Academic Library," consisting of fifty representative works of fifty SWUPL alumni of remarkable accomplishment and fame in academic and legal education circles. I believe this sort of thing has been done for the anniversary celebrations of many other universities. [*Applause*] In addition, I also had the pleasure of attending the inaugural ceremony of the SWUPL Alumni Association in Guangdong, where I made a speech entitled "The Spirit of SWUPL." I learned during the ceremony that our moneyed alumni in Guangdong are planning to make more donations to the university, which I suspect may be of more practical value than our enterprise in Beijing. [*Laughter*]

My Country and Myself

Professor Zhang Shaoyan just gave me a highly complimentary introduction, which I hardly deserve. As for the title of being one of the top 100 young people to influence twenty-first-century China, I have no idea whether my influence is a good or bad one [*laughter*], though of course I hope it is good. But frankly speaking, it is not easy to influence Chinese society, for our country is so huge and has a very time-honored historical tradition. As for other aspects, I don't think I have much to recommend myself, especially in academic research. In this regard, to be honest, I feel quite unworthy before you, particularly so in the presence of other young colleagues, because I have not made much of an academic contribution, and my efforts have mostly been socially oriented. There has even arisen a term for my approach, called the "He Weifang phenomenon": a public speaker promoting basic judicial concepts. If you are into online reading and news, you will know that quite a few objections and criticisms have been directed toward me on the grounds that I am sacrificing my academic responsibilities. However, I have my own stance and believe what I do has its meaning.

I think even among scholars there is certain division of labor. Some scholars prefer to bury themselves deep in their books, studying metaphysical and unfathomable knowledge. In fact, there is a special need of these scholars. Professor Jiang Shan, a graduate of the class of '79 from our university and now teaching at Tsinghua University, is just such an example. Even today I find his works highly incomprehensible [*laughter*], though he comforts me that his books are written for the Chinese 1,000 years from now. [*Laughter and applause*] It is true that we do need some scholars to write for our posterity 1,000 years from now, though they may be at a disadvantage because wherever they go, they pass unnoticed and whatever they write goes unread. In the past, when he was teaching at SWUPL, he was once assigned the task of giving lectures to an adult education class on jurisprudence, which as you can imagine proved a disaster for the students. [*Laughter*] He gave the students textbooks, which were actually a work of his, and the students strongly protested against it because they said the book was not so much a textbook as a sleeping pill. [*Laughter*] On a serious note, however, I still believe that there is a need for people to disseminate the knowledge developed in the ivory tower among the public in a manner welcome and easily accessible to them, and I think this is a worthwhile endeavor for a scholar to pursue! In fact, most of my efforts in recent years have gone into this work, particularly in connection to the country's judicial system and reform.

Professor Lu Yunbao and I used to be colleagues teaching foreign legal history. This afternoon I also paid a special visit to Professor Lin Xiangrong, who taught me in my college days and ushered me into the field of foreign legal history—though I later found that the study is a rather solitary affair and that its value was not really appreciated until I turned to the study of China's contemporary judicial system and used my knowledge of foreign legal history to examine the status and prospects for the rule of law in China. The Western legal landscape does make an interesting and illuminating contrast with China's legal situation, revealing many discrepancies and inconsistencies between the two. I noticed that although China's modern system was borrowed from the West and assumed a more or less similar structure, things often proceed differently between China and the West. This spurred me to think more about China's judicial system. What are the problems of China's existing system? As it turns out, this work, as it advances, always encounters a wall that prevents further progress, and that wall is China's constitution, or the constitutional situation in China.

China's judicial system is an important component of its constitutional system, and the judicial system cannot be studied without touching on constitutional issues. China's accession to the World Trade Organization (WTO), for example, was based, among other things, on the Chinese government's solemn committment that the country has an independent judicial system that performs judicial review of executive and legislative activities. The judicial review system originated in America and, ultimately, in England. During the WTO negotiation, Chinese representatives, none of whom was a legal professional, asserted that China has an independent judicial system to review government behaviors, but this was and is far from the fact. Following the philosophy that "the end justifies the means," all kinds of committments, regardless of whether they would be honored, were made to gain accession to the international organization. With the commitment to judicial independence being explicitly made, whether the court has such power immediately becomes a major question facing China's constitutional system. When we study the judicial system, this question is inevitable and must be answered.

The Conscience of Constitutional Jurisprudence

Dear students, you may not know, but it is a fact that when we were studying on this campus, teachers of constitutional law were the group of people who were most troubled by conscience because they had to say untruthful things to their students, such as that bourgeois democracy is hypocritical and bourgeois parliament is all about deceptive and empty talks while our democracy is the most real. We were told that the people are the master of this socialist country of ours and that the year 1949 was a monumental year in Chinese history because the People's Republic was established, and in the words of Chairman Mao, the Chinese people had finally stood up, bidding goodbye to the miserable old society dominated by imperialism, feudalism, and bureaucrat-capitalism, which weighed like mountains on the backs of the Chinese people.

But have the Chinese people really stood up? Do the Chinese people really have the opportunity to manage their own country? Has the constitutional provision that "all power in the People's Republic of China belongs to the people" really been made a reality rather than empty lip service? The students were full of questions and doubts as their teacher made such high-sounding statements, their eyes oozing with distrust. I believe that the teacher also sensed this distrust from the students, but he had no choice and dared not tell the students that it is our democracy that is hypocritical [*laughter*] and that the separation of powers is in fact a very good thing. During that ideologically fervent period, everything we were taught about the constitution was completely politicized and full of falsehoods. Every time they returned home from classes, teachers of constitutional law would speak to themselves with a sigh: "Gosh, I again pulled the legs of my students." [*Laughter and applause*]

Another problem is that as this state of things continues, constitutional jurisprudence is becoming the least attractive subject in China's legal education. I do not think talented students will choose to study China's constitution because there is simply no use in studying it in the first place. In fact, the appeal of constitutional study to students has not only not increased, but decreased! I myself have never attended any meeting of the Chinese Association of Constitutional Law. Professor Song Yubo in this audience is a constitutional scholar, and he has occasion to attend these meetings. I have the impression that people studying constitutional jurisprudence always have sorrow written in their faces [*Laughter*] because they do not know what to do with the predicament they face.

Constitutional Rights: Text and Reality

I took part in an intellectually stimulating academic seminar last evening. I heard a jurisprudential scholar say that China is now at the dawn of a new age of constitutional government. Indeed, there is strong advocacy for it in the media. In an interview with *Southern Weekend*, I said something to the effect that "the first priority is to give substance to the existing constitution." It is a shared view among legal scholars that China's current constitution has two major defects. The first is intrinsic, something that cannot be solved by minor amendments, because it was formulated at a time (1982) when constitutionalism was still seen in an ideologically tinged light and the influence of the Great Cultural Revolution had yet to dissipate. The second major defect is that even this unsatisfactory constitution is not well implemented!

Take, for example, the constitutional provision that "citizens of the People's Republic of China enjoy freedom of speech, of the press, of assembly, of association, of procession, and of demonstration." Dear students, when one day you get rich and wish to start a newspaper, I am sure your application will be turned down because running newspapers is the exclusive business of government agencies and CCP [Chinese Communist Party] organs in this country, where there is no privately owned newspaper at all. In sharp contrast, there is almost no government-run newspaper or television in America. Even those giant international media organizations like CBS and CNN are privately owned. It was not that long ago that I learned through the autobiography of its female chief editor that the world-class influential newspaper *Washington Post* was also a family-run newspaper. In China, however, there is no privately owned press. If you are so unaware as to take written laws seriously and apply for the establishment of a newspaper or television station, it will be rejected outright; that is to say, it is prohibited by internal policies.

The Constitution of the People's Republic of China also grants Chinese citizens the freedom of procession and demonstration; that is, we may express our dissatisfaction with the local government or other people, or protest against actions of foreign governments, such as the U.S. invasion of Iraq. But in reality, while people around the world come to the streets to express their protest, all we can do is protest in cyberspace. There were students of Peking University who applied for a procession but were told that "it is not allowed." Of course, the government's worries were understandable because although the students applied for the procession in the name of protesting against the United States, one can never be sure that students will not deviate from their stated cause and cry slogans of a quite different nature [*laughter*], so it can be troublesome. In a rare case, as I already mentioned last evening, a group of Peking University students did get the nod to make a procession, but the condition was that they must proceed northward of Peking University, in the direction of the countryside—and a sparsely populated area, for that matter. [*Laughter*]

The Constitution of the People's Republic of China also grants the freedom of religious belief, but what does it mean? I once said when talking about the judicial system that the freedom of religious belief has many dimensions, and one of the dimensions, to put it simply, is that it is their own business what citizens choose to believe, and it is none of the business of anyone else or of the government, not to mention any political party. This constitutional freedom, to be frank, has not been fulfilled yet.

The Logic of Constitutional Argument

During last evening's seminar, a big theoretical puzzle arose among participating scholars. Professor Zhang Zhiming kept criticizing the weakness of the argument made by legal academia about constitutional government, and he often expressed the hope that those of us aspiring to construct or reconstruct authority will come up with a more vigorous and compelling argument so that the government cannot but accept it. What baffles me very much is how we can display our strength. How are we to argue for the constitution's intrinsic spirit? The truth is that it is impossible to employ constitutional means to make clear to all the value of the constitution and to subject everyone, including top CCP and government officials, to the provisions of the constitution. Even today I still want to ask Professor Zhang Zhiming about the kind of rigorous and compelling argument he means. He once gave me an explanation, but perhaps due to my dim-wittedness, I failed to make full sense of it.

As I see it, the rise of constitutional authority and the prevalence of constitutional government are not completely driven by scholars. The argument made by scholars, of course, has its own role to play. Previous arguments for such values as democracy, freedom, rule of law, and human rights in China, I think, had something amiss in that they tended to give the impression that those values are good only for the people but not for the government—or for top officials. As a result, it is exactly those who pursued democracy who ruined democracy! Therefore, a comprehensive perspective is needed. Be it democracy or rule of law or freedom, all things have two sides.

EXPERIENCING DEMOCRACY

Democracy, by its very nature, means rule of the people, where the people take part in the management of the state. If this system is truly followed, the state dignitaries in Zhongnanhai will truly be our servants, doing whatever we tell them to do rather the other way around. [*Laughter*] This sounds disrespectful to the CCP, but in fact this philosophy is exactly in line with the party's proclaimed doctrines, according to which the party does not have its own interest and is committed to making the people the master of the country. However, such remarks are still sensitive and tend to cause trouble. So I will try not to be too radical in this speech, and later when you ask questions, I also hope you will take care not to go to extremes. [*Laughter*]

I think democracy has immense, immeasurable value. I once wrote a small article for *Southern Weekend* but was told that the article could not be published because it was politically sensitive. I said that the article only puts across the idea that democracy is good and not dangerous, with detailed arguments. The editor replied that the message behind the article was prohibited, and the article was not published. It was later included in my book *The Detailed Rule of Law,* under the heading of "The Magic of the Ballot Box."[4]

The Magic of the Ballot Box

I think the ballot box is a magical thing that works wonders. For example, it can shift decisionmaking risks. As you know, any decisionmaking involves risk, and as a result, it becomes very important who participates in the process and who makes the decisions. In a democratic country, ultimately it is the people who are the decisionmakers for state affairs, such as selecting their president or making laws, and they do so by way of casting a ballot. The people are responsible for the kind of president they elect, like Clinton with his sex scandal. So there is a risk-shifting mechanism, something that is more or less like a marriage. Marriage under the democratic system is based on free love, while that in a despotic or antidemocratic system is a forced arrangement effected by the parents. If the governor of a province is appointed rather than elected, the people of the province of course will complain if the governor does a bad job, just as one will complain about a forced arranged marriage if it turns out to be joyless. However, one has only oneself to blame if one's marriage based on free love turns out to be a nightmare. The same thing is also true of decisionmaking in a democratic system. Should the Three Gorges Dam be built? If it is decided through a democratic process, whatever consequence it may incur, nobody except for the people themselves will be held responsible. This is a very effective conflict- and risk-shifting mechanism. The maintenance of social order is the most basic issue faced by every society, and it has to be based on a shared expectation of relations among people. The social order comes from general compliance with the law. Why will the people comply with the law? The same shifting mechanism can also be seen here. The law is made by representatives elected by the people; that is to say, ultimately the law is made by the people themselves and therefore is generally complied with.

The Beauty of Debate

Western parliaments give every citizen the impression that his own will is reflected in the legislative process. Take parliamentary debate within the United States as an example. The representatives do almost nothing but debate. They can debate as briefly as one minute and as long as more than ten hours straight. They are professional speakers, mastering all styles of speech with excellent effect. In fact, in most parliaments, members are trained as lawyers and have received formal instruction in the art of speaking. Due to the great importance of debate in parliamentary sessions, many turn themselves into professional debaters.

The professionalization of deputies to the National People's Congress has also been put on the agenda. According to reports, a total of twenty deputies, all with legal or economic backgrounds, are to become professional deputies and members of the Standing Committee of the National People's Congress. However, if the annual sessions of the National People's Congress last only three and a half days (up to now I still have not figured out what this year's sessions are all about), then the professionalization of congressional deputies is nothing but empty talk. In Western countries, the parliament has sessions for 180–250 days every year, that is, more than half of every year, where they debate and debate. Why do we want debate? Because it is through debating that parliament members perform their duties of speaking for the interests of the groups of people they represent. Besides parliamentary debates, there are also all kinds of hearings that often accompany the enactment of specific legislation. If the U.S. Congress is to enact a law about China or adopt or amend a treaty with China, for example, it will hold a legislative hearing where experts on China issues and those on other pertinent issues are invited to debate on the subject matter.

All these things, in essence, are part of the art of state governance and a Foucauldian exercise of power. They give people the conviction that although they are not parliament members themselves, they are represented by the parliament and that their will is reflected in the legislative process and embodied in laws. This also gives laws justification and legitimacy and makes people willing to comply with them. In nondemocratic countries, legislation takes no consideration of the people's will, and the people have no means to have their will reflected in legislation, resulting in lawmaking that becomes the exclusive business of a few persons wielding unchecked power. Laws enacted under such a system will only be regarded with resistance, and this explains why ordinary people, including many legal scholars, jump at every opportunity to take advantage of the loopholes within laws. Why don't they identify with such laws? Because they deem these laws rules that do not reflect their own will and are forced upon them! If most people in a society hold the belief that the legal system only embodies the will of a small group of people, it is natural that they will not be willing to comply with the system or bother to maintain the social order.

Governance Cost

Up to now I have demonstrated the value of democracy from the perspective of decisionmaking control. Aside from this value, democracy through the ballot box has another benefit, that is, it reduces governance cost. As we know, every government faces a governance cost. The amount of this cost varies greatly from country to country. It is very low in some countries, though. Take the United States as an example: it is an extremely difficult thing and costs a tremendous amount of money to win the White House. There is an article entitled "The Money-Paved Path to the White House" that gives a vivid account of this.[5] Those of us who disparage American democracy and label it as "moneycracy" will be glad to read the article and contrast it with a superior air to China's system, saying that no such expenditure is needed in China. But as a matter of fact, $240 million is not really so great an amount for the election of the U.S. president, and it is part of the federal expenditure of taxpayer dollars. It is especially so when we hear of the report that the Shandong-based, little-known liquor brand Qinchi Liquor paid up to RMB 400 million to win the CCTV Prime Advertising Resource Bid. If a company can spend RMB 400 million to advertise a liquor product, it is really not so big a deal for Americans to spend $240 million to elect a president who will hold the position for four years or even eight years. And furthermore, how the money is spent is clearly recorded and can be checked at any time.

The key to the cost of governance issue is that the election of the president under the democratic system greatly reduces or even eliminates the possibility of power usurpation. As long as the president is elected following due procedure, you have to submit to his leadership. You cannot bring down Bill Clinton because of the Lewinsky scandal, accusing him of moral culpability and then taking his place, because under the democratic system a person aspiring to the presidency has to run through a democratic procedure provided for by law and cannot do it in any other way; otherwise he runs the risk of going against the voters, and that is a doomed approach.

It happened that I was in the United States during the general election after Clinton's first term of office. During that period, I watched TV every day because it was broadcasting the presidential race between Republican Robert Dole and Clinton. By the way, I would like to introduce you to an excellent TV channel named C-Span in the United States. In fact, I have always suggested to CCTV that the channel be introduced to China. Sometimes it can also be watched online. It is a political channel that does not have a single advertisement and broadcasts congressional debates, bipartisan competitions, and lively press briefings. For a political animal, it is the most joyous thing to watch the channel every day. [*Laughter*] The fact is that I was indeed reduced to a political animal in that period, and every day I watched TV about the fierce competition between the two presidential candidates.

After some time, the election result came out, and the first person to congratulate Clinton was none other than Robert Dole himself, who was still attacking him yesterday. What followed was the inauguration ceremony as the presidential motorcade proceeded slowly along Pennsylvania Avenue. The swearing-in ceremony was performed by Chief Justice Rehnquist, where Clinton placed his hand on the Bible and was sworn in as the president of the United States of America. At that moment, I found my eyes were wet. [*Laughter*] I am not a sentimental person, but at that very moment, I was really deeply touched. In human history, the regime change of a country as vast as the United States and with a population of more than 200 million should have been accompanied by bloodshed and cruel wars. Indeed, even today, the handover of political power in many countries around the world is by no means peaceful. But in the United States of America, except for a disruption during the American Civil War, the solemn presidential inauguration ceremony, where the country's highest power is handed over by the outgoing president to his popularly elected successor, has been held on Capitol Hill every four years for over 200 years, since the founding of the country. Therefore, the country has been blessed with a lasting peace.

This country's mechanism for ensuring the peaceful handover of political power leaves no room for conspiracy and gives every presidential aspirant the opportunity to attain the highest power through a duly democratic procedure. In the United States, a coup is out of the question. The U.S. military is always politically neutral and independent and is absolutely prohibited from interfering with government affairs. For the president's part, he also has no fear of being criticized in newspapers. During the Lewinsky scandal, President Clinton was greatly humiliated. The newspapers were full of corny jokes poking fun at him; one cartoon featured the Clinton presidential library with its door marked with three X's, meaning that the library is full of pornographic material.

A hilarious joke has it that after Clinton dies, his wife Hillary also dies, and she goes to heaven and St. Peter offers to show her around. At one point, they come to a huge room full of clocks. Hillary asks, "What's up with these clocks?" St. Peter explains, "Everyone on earth has a clock that shows how much time he has left on earth. When a clock runs out of time, the person dies and comes to the Gates to be judged." Hillary thinks this makes sense but notices that some of the clocks are going faster than others. She asks why. St. Peter explains, "Every time a living person tells a lie, it speeds his clock." Now Hillary asks with concern which clock is Clinton's. St. Peter replies that both hands on Clinton's clock spin so fast that the clock is used as a ceiling fan. [*Laughter and applause*] So you see how sarcastic American newspapers are toward their president, who has command of the three armies and often delivers lofty speeches before the people. However, his power over the three armies is not affected in the least. During the Kosovo conflict, no military general dared to doubt Clinton's power on grounds of his misconduct in the White House, and his orders were strictly followed. In addition to the sex scandal, Clinton had engaged in other dishonorable acts such as evading military service during the Vietnam War and using marijuana when he was young. All these things were exposed. But the military submitted to him as always. What kind of strength is this? Why did no general dare to defy him or submit to him in appearance but then complain to former president George Bush, saying that his successor was incompetent and had deviated from the lines he set down, and suggest that he do a southern tour.[6] [*Laughter and applause*] No, there is no such thing in America.

So we find that under the democratic system, national leaders do not have to take pains to maintain their power. This significantly reduced cost of governance is one of the most valuable things brought by democratic politics. National leaders are spared the trouble of constantly guarding against threats to their power because there is no room for the formation of unconstitutional political cliques. Another benefit of democratic politics is that former leaders are well protected. When the president completes his term and leaves office, he becomes an ordinary citizen and comes back to his friends and can do many beneficial things. After leaving the White House, Bill Clinton, for example, is now having a very good time. Last time he gave a speech in Shenzhen he fetched $200,000. There is no one to supervise or monitor him. Unlike leaders of some nondemocratic countries, he does not have to make a choice between holding onto power until being buried in Babaoshan or being put into prison or placed under house arrest.[7] No political figure likes the prospect of being put into prison or placed under house arrest after stepping down from power.

It is said that Chairman Mao spent his last days in bed unable to speak, only able to use his fingers to gesture. When he moved his fingers in some way, those beside him said that Chairman Mao's latest direction was to "fight selfishness, repudiate revisionism," and a nationwide political campaign was started. Before his death, Mao jotted down a note, with the first part being, "With you in charge, I am at ease," and gave the note to Hua Guofeng, designating him as his successor.[8] Later, when Jiang Qing was tried, she said, "You only know that the first part of Chairman Mao's note is 'With you in charge, I am at ease,' and that is referring to Hua Guofeng. But why do you ignore the second part, which is, 'When in question, turn to Jiang Qing.'" [*Laughter and applause*] If a country's leader keeps his grip on power to the last moment of his life, it is perhaps a disaster for both the people and himself.

I think such an argument and comprehensive interpretation of democracy and its values is convincing. When expounding on judicial power and judicial independence, the famous French political thinker Alexis de Tocqueville always proceeds from two perspectives. On the one hand, an independent judiciary indeed imposes restrictions on the exercise of state power, but on the other hand, it also provides a mechanism by which the people can have their dissatisfaction addressed within the legal framework rather than turn to the desperate resort of revolt. Tocqueville's approach is highly illuminating.

DIMENSIONS OF CONSTITUTIONAL GOVERNMENT

Although some adjustment needs to be made in argumentation, I must return to the main subject: what are the factors that make constitutional government a reality? Here it is proper to give a brief survey of the social foundation and historical development of Western countries. This may help to explain why the constitution is revered as the foundation of all laws and policies in Western countries, while in other countries the constitution is only an empty promise. This is also a question that I want to ask many experts in this audience. In my opinion, there are two secular factors and two spiritual factors that have shaped constitutional development in the West. These four factors are very important. Of the two spiritual factors, the first is Christianity.

Religion as a Transcendent Force

Christianity originated in Asia and was not an indigenous religion of the West. It gradually spread around the Western world during the period of the Roman Empire. And it was a history written with tears of blood, because at first it was deemed by the government to be heretical and Christians were persecuted. However, in spite of persecution, it grew so fast that eventually it was formally recognized as the official religion of the Roman Empire. It conquered the Western world and turned it into a Christian world where almost every Westerner was Christian, especially during the Middle Ages.

We know Christianity is a spiritual force that shapes people's monotheistic belief in the one true God as a trinity of persons: the Father, the Son (Jesus Christ), and the Holy Spirit. All Christians go to church every Sunday to say their prayers and Catholics make their confessions, a process through which their spirituality undergoes profound changes. This spiritual force also has great influence on secular rulers. A Christian ruler will subscribe to the doctrine of original sin, believing that everyone is guilty of sin due to the fall of man after Adam and Eve were tempted by the serpent, the embodiment of Satan, into eating the fruit from the tree of knowledge of good and evil, in disobedience of God. According to the doctrine, everyone is born with sin, and life is a process of redemption. We live to make atonement for our sin, and we need to confess constantly, always keeping in mind that we are not extraordinary, we are not divine, we are all ordinary persons, that everyone, be it a king or emperor, has original sin. This concept is extremely important because there is but one step from equality before God to equality before the law. It imposes strong restriction on secular powers, sustaining the sober consciousness that no one person in the world should be arrogant or imagine himself to be always great, glorious, and correct. It is humanly impossible to never make a mistake. As it is generally acknowledged that there cannot possibly be such a person, it constitutes a rigorous restriction on the ruler's thought and behavior. I think this restriction is immensely effective.

On the other hand, Christianity is not merely a theological system, but it also has a strong presence in the secular world as an institutional social entity. Aside from the Bible that is read by everyone, Christianity has a tangible infrastructure that takes the form of churches, which play an important role in the life of Christians. Furthermore, there is the Holy See, the central government of the Catholic Church. By the Middle Ages, the Holy See became the biggest landowner in the Western world because Christians willed one-tenth of their property to the Catholic Church. Will-making is a time-honored tradition in the West, but the practice is unpopular in China because it is thought to be inauspicious. At any rate, with the constant accumulation of property given to the Catholic Church through wills, it came to possess an increasing amount of land and, in consideration of the great significance of land in the Middle Ages, gained further prominence in politics. Furthermore, the [Catholic] Church divided the actual world into two parts, one spiritual and the other secular. In the secular life, one must comply with the laws of the king, but in the spiritual life, one must comply with the orders and decrees of the church or the pope.

There is a biblical saying, "Render unto Caesar the things which are Caesar's, and unto God the things that are God's." This statement calls for an explanation of what belongs to Caesar and what belongs to God. Take marriage, for example. By common sense, marriage certainly belongs to the secular life, but it is not so according to Christian logic because, as it reasons, the union between husband and wife cannot be understood merely in the secular sense as a means to serve the purpose of procreating and rearing offspring; it

also symbolizes the union between Jesus Christ and the church. This interpretation makes marriage something divine. In fact, in the Middle Ages,
divorce was prohibited since marriage was considered to stand for the eternal
relationship between Christ and the church; in the same vein, polygamy and
polyandry also were not permitted to exist. Strict monogamy represents one
of Christianity's most profound transformations of Western society.

Even China's current marriage system is the result of learning from the
West. You know, our traditional practice was not monogamy but polygamy,
which was allowed for a long period of time in Chinese history. But according to Christian doctrine, polygamy is not to be tolerated. In the West, the
wedding ceremony is traditionally held in church, attended by marriage witnesses and the relatives and friends of the bride and bridegroom, and officiated by the clergy. During the ceremony, the bride and bridegroom will be
asked a number of questions, such as "Will you honor and be true to each
other as man and wife in good times and in bad, in sickness and in health for
the rest of your lives?" And they both will answer, "Yes, I will." [*Laughter*]
And then melodious wedding music will echo in the church. At that moment
we feel deeply the solemnity and greatness of love. This scene committed to
the memory will also serve as a deterrent when one day the husband is
angered and about to bully the wife. [*Applause*] This explains why there is
more domestic violence in China than in Western countries.

Many other spiritual fields, including those that are closely related to constitutional government such as freedom of speech, academic freedom, freedom of the press, and freedom of expression, were traditionally also governed
by the church. This has to do with the usual lack of interference by secular
power in these fields. The history of university independence, for example, is
not one of struggle with the crown but with the church. This history is best
illustrated by the statement that "the wind may blow through it—the storm
may enter—the rain may enter—but the King of England cannot enter."[9] An
independent university is a sacred place where it is completely our own business what we think and what we choose to believe in, and the government
shall not interfere with it. Up to today, these values still exert huge influence
on Western politics. There is no president in the Western world delivering a
"May 31 speech" and asking the whole nation to study it.[10] This very notion
would have been inconceivable to President Clinton. The "May 31 speech"
was so extensively studied that on the external wall of a slaughterhouse in a
remote mountainous area in Sichuan was painted a slogan that read: "Let the
spirit of the 'Three Represents' be the guide of our slaughtering work!"[11]
[*Laughter and applause*]

Dear students, you know, the price of the democratic system is that government leaders no longer play the role of thinkers! Since the beginning of modern times, there have been almost no Western leaders who were also great thinkers. Great thinkers are all found among scholars in universities, and government leaders are only implementers of their thought. For example, Ronald Reagan was an advocate of new classical macroeconomics while Theodore Roosevelt was an advocate of Keynesian economics. In Western countries, government leaders listen to professors, while in China, the opposite is true. The result is that it is not easy for great personalities to emerge among Western leaders and that those who govern us in China are not necessarily noble and great. The absence of great personalities in the political scene may lead to some problems, but the democratic system gives all elected leaders sufficient credibility and legitimacy. In nondemocratic countries, every paramount political leader is also the paramount spiritual leader. In the Mao Zedong era, Vice Chairman Lin Biao had a famous flattering saying that "every sentence of Chairman Mao's works is a truth; one single sentence of his surpasses ten thousand of ours." If this is the case, what have we to say? Therefore, it can be said that in such a country, the only thinker is the paramount leader. However, this gives rise to a serious issue: that is, when secular power and spiritual power become highly centralized, we will be deprived of the last vestiges of freedom of expression and thought.

The combination of state power and spiritual power has a history. The two were completely separated in Western Europe and were combined to a certain degree in Eastern Europe, where the Orthodox Church was followed. In China, where the saying that "the sage's [Confucius's] words are above carping comments" used to be commonly cited, state power and spiritual power were completely integrated. Chinese intellectuals did not have freedom of speech, even though Confucius had died 2,000 years ago. In this case, the secular paramount leader became the only person to interpret the sage and decide what is in accord with the sage's thought and what is not. I think this is a great trap.

Many of you may have read the *Works of Gu Zhun*. Gu Zhun, in my opinion, was one of the most extraordinary thinkers in twentieth-century China.[12] Even when he was sent to work in the countryside during the Cultural Revolution (1966–76), he was still studying Greek history and Western history. When studying medieval history, he observed with a sigh that in the age of separation between church and state, although the lowest class of people might have nothing to benefit from the system, it gave those of higher classes the opportunity to avoid persecution by switching their allegiance between the church and the state. It was a strict rule that the king's soldiers should not enter the church. If one offended the secular ruler, he could seek shelter with the church, and vice versa. But things in China, he went on to say, were different. If one offended the highest ruler and spiritual leader, he could do nothing but stretch out his head—for decapitation. [*Laughter*] In spite of the lapse of forty years, that sigh of his, pregnant with meaning, still echoes in contemporary China, and the force behind the sigh is deeply felt. This force, divine and powerful, is what has made constitutional government in the West possible and a reality.

Tradition of Natural Law

The second spiritual factor, in my opinion, is the natural law tradition. As all of you are well trained in law, I will not expand on this, and the time available to me also does not allow for a lengthy discussion. The natural law tradition imposes a strict limit on secular power, including legislation in the Western world. The enactment of laws is by no means arbitrary and unscrupulous. In the famous ancient Greek tragedy *Antigone*, the female protagonist Antigone buried the body of her rebel brother, who was killed outside the city, in violation of the king's edict. She believed that she should not obey the order and must bury her dead brother. When questioned by the angry king why she dared to go against the edict, she said that she was acting in accordance with the law of the gods, which is superior to man's law. This Greek belief in natural law profoundly influenced the legal and political system of the whole Western world! During the dark medieval times, there appeared a great theologian called Thomas Aquinas. He proposed that rigorous restrictions be placed on secular power and put divine law above positive law. He held that the people have the right to rebel against government and that the government or ruler's power must be obtained through legitimate means. If forgers of money are punished, those who obtain power through illegitimate ways shall also be punished. The people are justified in overthrowing such persons through violence. This thought is indeed powerful and heart stirring.

In Chinese history, although we have Mencius, who made such observations as "Heaven sees according to what my people see; Heaven hears according to what my people hear" and "people are more important than the ruler," the whole approach gives the impression that advisors were admonishing rulers with maxims like "Water can carry a boat; it can also sink a boat," and such arguments are very weak. In contrast, Thomas Aquinas's concept is powerful and empowering because it draws its strength from the natural law system. Natural law was revived in Germany after World War II and is most conspicuously reflected in the German constitution's respect for natural law. That constitution subjects laws to be enacted after due democratic procedure to necessary restrictions, which is to say, even if the overwhelming majority of the citizens support the enactment of a law that persecutes Jews, the law must not be adopted by the parliament. In a word, natural law is a powerful tool for restricting legislative power in a democratic system.

Pluralistic Interests and Class Society

There are two secular factors that have also shaped the development of constitutionalism in the West. The first factor is the formation of different social classes and interest groups. For instance, a landlord has five sons, each of whom inherits forty hectares of land, and after the five sons themselves beget five sons each, then each grandson will only inherit eight hectares of land. In this way, the landlord's property is increasingly segmented among his descendants until the individual land ownership loses any political significance. The peasant economy, however, was favored by Chinese emperors because such an economy made it impossible for the formation of a powerful landlord class. In antiquity land and class had important political significance, as I mentioned earlier when talking about the confrontation between the landlord class and the king in medieval times. Such a large-scale land ownership system, which served as the foundation for confrontation among comparable political groups, was absent in China, however. This also explains the long-term lack of rigorous protection for private property in China.

Another contributing factor to China's failure to form a class society, as I pointed out in a former article, was the Imperial Civil Service Examination, which undermined a stable class structure. I will only discuss this point briefly here since I covered it in some depth in our lecture hall about the year before last. This system was an open and fair one that opened the privileged officialdom to all persons, regardless of their backgrounds, as long as they were smart and industrious enough. In history there was a village scholar in Chenjiazhuang, by the Yellow River, named Chen Shimei, who married a virtuous wife and had a son. He was sparklingly intelligent and exceptionally industrious and eventually won first place in the Imperial Civil Service Examination. During the final imperial examination, presided over by the emperor himself, the emperor was so impressed with Chen's handsome appearance and scholarly erudition that he found in them a worthy candidate to marry his daughter. The emperor asked Chen Shimei about his marital status and was given the untruthful answer that he was still single, which gave rise to a popular folk tale and opera.

In the Western world, however, it was inconceivable and impossible that a king would marry his daughter to a commoner. No matter in feudal times or modern times, royal and noble families attached paramount importance to the purity of their own bloodlines, and family members were not allowed to marry at their own will. Whom the king of the England can marry is subject to constitutional precedents, and any violation will send the nation into a constitutional crisis. King Edward VIII found himself at the center of such a crisis when he announced his marriage to Mrs. Wallis Simpson, who was not eligible to become queen as a divorcee with living ex-spouses. Therefore, the high degree of upward social mobility in China engendered by the Imperial Civil Service Examination was foreign to the Western world.

There are many poems singing of the dreamlike vicissitude brought by this social mobility over time, including, "I saw them build the courtesan's quarters, saw them feast and make merry. But I saw, too, how the building collapsed," "Swallows that once nested in late Premiers Wang's and Xie's grand halls are now turning to common people's houses to pay their calls," and "A peasant at morning may appear in royal court at evening," to name but a few. What was the consequence of this state of things? The answer is that China failed to develop a politically structured class society comprising stable groups such as peasants, landlords, capitalists, politicians, warriors, and nobles, and the resulting loose social structure made it impossible for continued and stable class interests and the necessary class struggle and conflict to take shape, creating a social environment unfriendly to the growth of constitutional government. Even if a constitution is put in place, it is nothing but an empty promise, superficial banner, and hollow sounding slogan. It is true that these were only historical factors, but these factors, be it the overall structure, or the protection of private properties, or the bureaucratic system, have not undergone any fundamental change since the beginning of modern times. Therefore, it can be said that it is inherently impossible for a constitution and constitutional government to emerge in Chinese society and that our constitution is arguably bound to be an imported thing.

Taxation and Representation

The fourth factor is quintessentially secular: taxation, which is a very important infrastructural condition for the development of constitutional government. Not long ago, I wrote an article about this for *Southern Weekend*, but its title was changed by the editor from the rigorous "Taxation as the Foundation of Constitutional Government" to the enfeebled "The Significance of NPC Review of Government Budget." However, there have also been times when I gave my article a moderate title, but it was changed to a radical one. For instance, I once wrote an article commenting on a new policy of the Kunming Municipal Procuratorate that stipulated that colorful Chinese idioms—such as "fleeing helter-skelter," "a cornered dog will leap over a wall," and "joining in villainy"—shall not be used in legal papers, but the original neutral title was changed by the editor to the colorful "Sweep Colorful Expressions out of Legal Papers," with the changed title itself giving the impression of irrationality. I got so frustrated with their tampering with my articles that I told them to "either publish my articles untampered with, or return them to me." I may be a little domineering to say that, but I was really irritated by their meddling.

Regardless, taxation is a very big issue. Only recently Ms. Liu Xiaoqing got herself into trouble because of this.[13] I am very sympathetic to her. She is a well-respected film artist especially popular among people of my generation. She is also Sichuanese, very versatile in performance. Ms. Liu was our iconic film star in our youthful days, but now she has been put into Qincheng Prison, and I miss her all the time. [*Laughter*] I myself have certain grudges about taxation, and I do not like to pay taxes, though some taxes are unavoidable, such as the bicycle tax that one has to pay to get a bicycle license plate and ride a bicycle lawfully in Beijing. But the biggest question I want to ask is how our tax payments are used. The taxation may be justified; the slogan that "it is a sacred obligation of every citizen to pay taxes in accordance with the law" is everywhere to be seen. But if we have the obligation to pay taxes, we also have the right to know how our tax payments are used. In rule-of-law Western countries, there is a rigorous system of auditing tax revenues, fiscal budgets, and government spending, and this is a very important manifestation of constitutional government.

We all know of the Great Charter of Liberties or Magna Carta, a quasi-constitutional document of England issued in 1215, and the history of this document was closely related to the issue of taxation. At that time, the tyrannical King John drained the treasury due to several failed wars with France and had entered into a conflict with Pope Innocent III. He gathered his barons together to raise funds from them because without money, no further war was possible. But the barons, who sided with the Pope, rejected the king's request, enumerating his mistakes in spending and launching wars and demanding that from then on, the power to declare wars rest with the "parliament." Of course, there was no parliament as such back then, but it was demanded that the fiscal budget, fiscal spending, and taxation be subject to the review and approval of a council composed of the representatives of the barons before implementation. In the subsequent 100 or nearly 200 years since then, every king, when ascending the throne, was required to sign the Magna Carta, which became an important mechanism to restrict the king's power. The concept of "no taxation without representation"—the famous slogan during the lead-up to the American Revolution—had its roots in the events surrounding the signing of the Magna Carta more than five centuries earlier.

Dear friends, do you have deputies in the National People's Congress? In spite of its name—"people's congress"—are the deputies really elected by the people? What do they have to do with the people? In this so-called People's Republic, the word "people" is everywhere to be seen, to the point of abuse. We used to have "people's communes," our government is called the "Central People's Government," our country is called "the People's Republic of China," and we have many other entities bearing the name "people," such as "the People's Court," "the People's Police," "the People's Procuratorate," "the People's University," and "the *People's Daily*," and we use "People's Currency" [RMB] issued by the "People's Bank." [*Laughter and applause*]

But the deputies to the People's Congress are not elected. We do not know how our tax payments are used. I believe there are several issues that will attract increasing attention. The first, of course, is the direct election rather than appointment of deputies to the People's Congress. Direct election of deputies to represent us in the People's Congress would be the principal foundation of legitimacy for the People's Congress. A second source of legitimacy would reside in the people's deputies fulfilling their duty to review the government's fiscal expenditures and revenue. In this regard, some issues deserve attention. Those of you who are in the field of constitutional research may have long concerned yourself with the need to significantly reduce the scale of the National People's Congress. Personally I think it is appropriate for China's parliament to have 700 members rather than the current nearly 3,000 members. A 3,000-member meeting is impossible for effective deliberation of issues and can only be an occasion where the audience listens to speeches and reports. Of course, there is also the discussion session, but that is not plenary but group based. There is the Sichuan group, Chongqing group, Guizhou group, and so forth. Each group is presided over by the provincial party chief and governor, who make speeches while the deputies listen, which is basically no different from the provincial party meeting, only the venue of the meeting has changed from the provincial capital to Beijing. [*Applause*] Therefore, the scale of the National People's Congress should be decreased to make it possible for parliamentary style debates, and more of them! Our attention should be called to all these issues.

Not long ago I wrote an article on dialectics. You may have read Aristotle's *Rhetoric*, a significant part of which is devoted to oration. There are three kinds of oration, including political oration, litigation oration, and ceremonial oration. Oration has a long history in the Western world. The *History of the Peloponnesian War* features a good number of orations of varying genres, the most famous of which is Pericles' solemn, heartfelt, and stirring Funeral Oration. In my foreign history class, I once read this speech with feeling to my students, and then read President Reagan's Challenger disaster speech. All of the students felt that the two speeches had striking similarities and were excellent in their own ways. In order to strengthen their understanding, I again read the speech of Hua Guofeng at the funeral of Chairman Mao. [*Laughter*]

It was generally agreed that the Chinese speech is so colorless and, above all, lacks originality. I think the study of oratory is of great importance. Is there oration in the real sense of the word in China's National People's Congress? You know, the most important element for the development of the art of oration is confrontation between opposing forces. No confrontation, no debate, no oration so to speak. In the 2,000-year literary history of China, one of the least developed literary genres is oration. Of course, it is not to say that there was no debate in China's 2,000 years of history. We know two great philosophers who discussed with their disciples about learning, but only a small part of these discussions are preserved. The works of Confucius and Mencius are both records of short dialogues and lack lengthy comprehensive debates, and the limited debates follow an expository style and are very different from their Western counterparts. With regard to oration, it can be said definitely that there was no lengthy public oration at all. I think public oration is an art that should receive more academic attention.

I think it is also reasonable that some parliament members who fail to defeat their opponents in debate throw shoes at them [*laughter*], because a divided, fractious parliament is more like true representative government than a puppet parliament. [*Applause*] We should constantly improve our system so that we know clearly where our tax payments have gone. This is a question I have always been much concerned with. Who is spending our money and how? Take military spending, for example: the National People's Congress does not review it at all. Regarding this matter, I am just calling a spade a spade for I myself am a CCP member. Where do the salaries of the CCP's professional officials come from? Does the CCP have a treasury independent from the national treasury? The CCP cannot treat the national treasury as its own, yet it draws money from the national treasury and uses it to hold its own national congress. Shouldn't this be reviewed by the National People's Congress? I read an interesting news report recently that Taiwan's Kuomintang has downsized its party newspaper (the *Central Daily News*) from more than 100 employees to several dozen due to financial problems. It is really impressive that several dozen people run a daily newspaper much more comprehensive and interesting than the *People's Daily*! This news report also indicated that the Kuomintang has its own party treasury. Do you know how many people are employed to run the *People's Daily*? It is a ministerial level entity, and though there are no exact data, its staff numbers in the thousands, with journalists across China and around the world. Who pays their salary? Of course, the eight democratic parties are also run using the taxpayers' money because they do not have their own party treasuries, either, because they are not even registered in the first place. [*Laughter*]

In rule-of-law countries, political parties, as a form of juridical association, must be registered in accordance with the law. After registration, they are subject to strict regulation. They have the capacity to be sued as well as to sue. As the CCP is not formally registered, it can neither be sued nor sue. The eight democratic parties are not formally registered, either. All of their funds are drawn from the national treasury. It is the taxpayers who foot the bill for them. Scholars of the time criticized the Southern Song dynasty because though its territory had been reduced by half, the number of its officials had doubled. The fact is, even if the number were doubled again, it would still be far fewer than the number of China's officials today because there was no party system then. [*Laughter*] Those in this system not only are excellently paid but also enjoy superior welfare benefits. I think all these things have constitutional significance. Of course, these remarks represent my loyalty to the party, otherwise I would not have made these unwelcome observations! [*Applause*] In a word, taxation is another secular factor that will play an important role in advancing constitutional government in China.

Rule of Law and Legal Professionals

Of course, there are some other reasons that I have discussed in my speech on the judicial system and that I therefore do not expand on here. I think judicial independence also provides a very important opportunity to advance constitutional government in China. More efforts should be devoted to this in the future. Professor Zhang Zhiming had an observation this afternoon that the realization of rule of law in China will be a historic deal. That is, it would be a historic process through which different forces arrive at a balance of interests. Based on this view, I think constitutional government has just made a start in China, and the road ahead remains a long one.

The aforementioned four factors are all very important. An additional factor, in particular, is our legal professionals who, with their professional knowledge, specialized skills, special lingo, and well-informed decisionmaking logic, play a crucial role in maintaining the judicial review–based mechanism regulating the exercise of power. As a legal professional myself, I am particularly concerned with the development of China's judicial system, though, of course, it does not affect our efforts to push for advancements in other areas. Every time I come back to my alma mater and see young students studying industriously in classrooms, I feel that they are having their minds "formatted" by legal knowledge and principles. Yes, I think the acquisition of legal knowledge is a process of mind formatting that gives the students a legal perspective and trains them to always think like a lawyer. With the graduation of one class of legal students after another, the concepts of rule of law and democracy will be spread to every corner of society, transforming this society and how it functions in the process, and gradually putting the whole country with its political, administrative, legislative, and judicial systems on the track of rule of law and constitutional government. This great turning point, the one that the Chinese people have long struggled for over 2,000 years and sacrificed for over generations, is at hand today! At last, I would like to share with you my optimism that with the presence of our legal professionals, there is a tremendous prospect for constitutional government in China, though the process has just started. Thank you all. [*Long applause*]

Zhang Shaoyan: From now on, students who have questions may write them down on notes and pass them on to the rostrum. Given Professor He's special background, you may also ask questions outside the subject matter of his speech. As we have all enjoyed to our hearts' content his exciting speech, I propose we give a warm applause to show our thanks. [*Warm applause*] You know, this speech is the longest one ever delivered at the Legal Forum of the Southwest University of Political Science and Law. I had meant to remind him on several occasions, seeing that he was really tired and sweating, but I still refrained for fear that it might offend the audience. [*Laughter*] Now let us invite other scholars to make brief comments on issues touched on by Professor He in his speech, and reserve more time for our students and Professor He. [*Applause*]

Li Changqing: My question is very brief. I think the constitution is the product of struggle and compromise between different interest groups. Do you think China meets this condition today, and if not, how is the condition created? Thanks! [*Applause*]

Zhang Shaoyan: Now it is Professor Liu Junxiang's turn. [*Applause*]

Liu Junxiang: Just now Professor Li Changqing said that China currently does not have the conditions for constitutional government, but I do not agree with this view. My question is what purpose it serves to set sail for constitutional government in China. According to Professor He, the Western-style constitutional government can stimulate China's own constitutional government. How does this stimulation work? Thanks. [*Applause*]

Zhang Shaoyan: Now let us invite Professor Song Yubo to make a comment.

Song Yubo: My first question concerns the legitimacy of how the constitution is made. Our constitution, as Professor He already mentioned, was made by the National People's Congress, but the problem is that the deputies to the congress are not representatives of the people, and no one knows how they become the deputies. My second question is that the legislature, even if it is legitimate, should be subject to restrictions in the exercise of power. For instance, we contemporaries do not have the right to confer the rights of our descendants to any organization or political party, and it is not allowed in the constitution to confer the executive power of the state to an organization, and to do so without any conditions or restriction on term. And the foundation of the constitution should also be legitimate. What is the function and purpose of the constitution? It is not meant to serve any political party or organization but to safeguard the fundamental rights of citizens and maintain the balance between state power and civil rights. In spite of the constitutional provision that "all power in the People's Republic of China belongs to the people," there is no institutional channel by which this provision is made a reality. This is about the legitimacy of the foundation of the constitution. And the last is the legitimacy of the implementation of the constitution. There is no supervision over the implementation of the constitution or mechanism addressing any constitutional violation. All these aspects are concerned with the legitimacy of the constitution. I would like to know Professor He's opinions of these issues. Thanks. [*Applause*]

Zhang Shaoyan: Now let us invite Professor Fu Zitang to make a comment. Professor Fu is an expert on jurisprudence and a Ph.D. from Peking University. [*Applause*]

Fu Zitang: I would like to ask Professor He two questions. My first question concerns the object of reference for our study of constitutional government. I do not know whether you feel the same way or not, but I do have the impression that when speaking, Professor He always made laudatory references to the

West, saying how good the American system is, how good the British way is, and so on and so forth. But the thing to remember is that, after all, we are living in China. Where are we going to find constitutional government? From where does constitutional government bud forth? Is it possible that constitutional government grows within the indigenous culture of China? Can we not achieve constitutional government without imitating the West? We do not have a religious tradition, and we lack a natural law spirit, so we cannot achieve constitutional government? This is the first question I would like to ask Professor He.

The second question concerns the relationship between constitutional government and rule of law. The two conditions that I cited from Professor He, in essence, are not the conditions for constitutional government but for rule of law; they are the two Aristotelian elements of rule of law. We have to clarify the two concepts of constitutional government and rule of law. What on earth is the relationship between constitutional government and rule of law? What is the starting point of the constitutional government that we study? In fact, I think constitutional government is the starting point but not the whole of rule of law. Besides constitutional government, what other things do we need? Thanks. [*Applause*]

Zhang Shaoyan: Thanks to Professor Fu Zitang for his comment, which reminds me of an important rule that I failed to announce before Professor He's speech, that is, we should not flatter each other. The good thing is that up to now I have not seen any sign of this. [*Laughter*] Now it is Professor Lu Yunbao's turn to make a comment.

Lu Yunbao: Many years ago I once joked with Wang Renbo, saying that if He Weifang were in a Western country, he would very likely run for the presidency. [*Laughter and applause*] The lucky thing is that while we lost a politician, we gained a brilliant scholar. Professor He's speech was thought-provoking. The speech's title, "China's First Steps toward Constitutionalism," in particular, reminds me of the "preparation of constitutional government" more than one hundred years ago [*laughter and applause*], then of the "three stages of constitutional government" put forward by Sun Yat-sen after the 1911 Revolution—military unification, political tutelage, and constitutional government. According to Sun Yat-sen, the stage of political tutelage would last about six years, followed by the stage of constitutional government. However, several decades after Sun Yat-sen put forward his three-stage constitutional government theory, constitutional government was still nowhere to be seen. In that period of the Republic of China, a Peking University student pasted half a couplet on the door of his dormitory that read: "There is military unification, there is political tutelage, but why has there never been constitutional government?" When asked about the other half of the couplet, he said, "There is no other half until we have constitutional government."

More than one hundred years since the "preparation of constitutional government," constitutional government has remained a tricky issue facing Chinese intellectuals, and facing Chinese intellectuals alone. The first priority of Chinese politicians has always been the elimination of their political opponents, and it has been so since the beginning of modern times. They are a little like the gladiators of ancient Rome in the sense that once they throw themselves into the arena, they have no way to leave it unless they do away with their opponents. [*Laughter*] To stay on the scene, they resort to every conceivable means, and when the goal is attained, it becomes a political one-man show. Up till now, we have seen no top-down efforts to prepare China for a constitutional democracy through political reform and reconciliation. Can such a political environment become the cradle of constitutional government? I do not think so; instead, it can only be a workshop of so-called great leaders and helmsmen. [*Applause*]

We may say that apart from bureaucrats and farmers, there are intellectuals who can play a positive role in promoting constitutional government. But in this country, what on earth are intellectuals capable of? In the past more than 100 years, Chinese intellectuals were either reduced to being the tools of power politics or cheap mouthpieces for farmers. Of course, in the recent period, we have people like Professor He, who actively tries to bring the benefits of constitutionalism home to the bureaucracy. Professor He wrote quite a few articles in *Southern Weekend* preaching to the bureaucracy as well as the public that constitutional government and freedom of the press are good for both the public and bureaucrats. When reading this argument, I almost burst into laughter, imagining to myself the possible reaction of those officials who read the articles. They would likely think to themselves, "Professor He, we won't take your bait!" [*Laughter and applause*]

Suppose they accept rigorous supervision over themselves, what will happen? First, they will have to cough up their ill-gotten gains, and if the supervision continues, some of them will likely be put into prison. Then what can Chinese intellectuals do for the cause of constitutional government? I have great doubt about that! I don't know whether Professor He shares this doubt, but I am highly pessimistic about it. As I see it, in this country, constitutional government is not feasible either through the top-down bureaucratic approach or through bottom-up preparation. If Professor He attempts to introduce the concepts of freedom and constitutionalism to farmers, when he finishes speaking and asks them what is freedom, they will say, "We are free after you finish talking." [*Laughter and applause*] So I think when Chinese farmers are struggling to stay employed and have their stomachs filled, and are asked what is freedom, they will only understand it as unemployment and being hungry. In a way, the ideas of freedom and constitutional government are too abstract and distant for most Chinese, especially rural people. That is why I am always pessimistic in this regard. The last question I want to ask Professor He is, since he often mentioned democracy in his speech, can a democratic state be called a constitutional state? Thanks. [*Applause*]

Zhang Shaoyan: Now let's invite Professor Luo Jun to comment. [*Applause*]

Luo Jun: Be assured I will keep it brief. [*Applause*] Professor He's speech was so romantic and vivid that it was really unforgettable. [*Laughter*] It is a real treat to hear his speech. What I want to say is that the world in which we are living cannot be said to be a judicial world but rather an evil-law world. The Western rule of law is based on and grows from the basic assumption that human nature is evil. In fact, we say that human nature has its good as well as evil aspects. Based on Kant's argument for free will, what constitutionalism can do is start from free will and channel it toward goodness. Constitutionalism is by no means an all-good system, as it seems to be, but a necessary evil for human society. Professor He said that China's constitutional system has begun to take shape. I do not know how it is proceeding. Is it like what the song says, "If you ask which way to go, the way is under your feet?" [*Laughter*] Let's paraphrase that: what is the way to go for China? And Professor He's answer is that it is constitutional government. But I have to remind you that the road toward constitutional government is full of traps. The question I want to ask Professor He is: does constitutional government in China need a transcendent justice? To put it another way, does it need a theological dimension? [*Applause and laughter*] If there is not such a dimension in the case of China, how will our constitutional government grow? And in the absence of a theological dimension, from what source does constitutional government draw its nobility? [*Applause*]

Zhang Shaoyan: Now it is Professor Wang Xuehui's turn. [*Applause*]

Wang Xuehui: I have two questions. My first question is: what is the core concept of constitutional government? My second question is about Professor He's view that taxation is the foundation of constitutional government. In my opinion, both constitutional government and rule of law are the game of the rich. It must be based on certain economic infrastructure. Does China have the economic foundation to promote constitutional government? Given

China's present economic foundation, what do you think of the possibility and feasibility of rule of law and what you call constitutional government? [*Applause*]

Zhang Shaoyan: Now let us invite Associate Professor Mo Jiangping to share his views. He is a teacher and scholar of constitutional law.

Mo Jiangping: I also have two questions. Both Professor He in his speech and Professor Li Changqing in his comment assume that the presence of different interest groups is the foundation of constitutional government. And then Professor He mentioned China's Imperial Civil Service Examination as a factor detrimental to the formation of different interest groups and consequentially the formation of constitutional government. However, I do not see any relationship between the two. To the contrary, I think that in comparison with Western culture, which maintained a rigid class system, Chinese meritocracy based on the Imperial Civil Service Examination was not only not detrimental but in fact beneficial to the growth of constitutional government. I do not know whether it is that I failed to understand Professor He or that he did not make his point clear. So I have some puzzles and put them forward as a reminder. My second question concerns another puzzle of mine, about taxation as the foundation of constitutional government. As the saying goes, "There is no dynasty or emperor that does not impose taxation." Why was there not constitutional government in feudal times? Thanks! [*Applause*]

Zhang Shaoyan: The time is limited, so I do not make my own comment. Now let us invite Professor He to give a response to the above comments and answer the questions of students. [*Warm applause*]

He Weifang: Although you do not stand on the platform, I think you can well understand my present predicament of being asked certain questions to which I do not think I am fully capable of giving well-informed answers. Anyway, I would like to use the remaining time to offer my responses to the questions and comments raised. Some responses have to be brief, of course, not because of the lack of time but because of the lack of my knowledge. I think it is a great privilege of a scholar to be able to give a speech at this forum because very few universities will arrange for nine peer scholars to attend and hear the speech and make unflattering but truthful comments. I was told that President Jiang Bixin had a hard time the last time he came here. [*Laughter*] Of course, I am also aware that even some seemingly complimentary words should not be taken at face value. One example is Professor Wang Xuehui's comparing me to a preacher and missionary. In fact, this comparison carries with it certain criticism and the hope that I will go beyond this role and produce more scholarly output. Well, in what follows, I briefly answer the raised questions one by one.

Professor Li Changqing's question is that though the conditions for constitutional government did not exist in ancient China, have those conditions become ripe today? You know we are undergoing a profound social transformation, which comes as an indirect result of what China suffered more than one hundred years ago, the disaster that was described at that time as unheard of in the country's 5,000 years of history. So what situation do we face today? Historian Tang Degang observed in a book that throughout Chinese history, there have been two profound transformations.[14] The first was the transition from the "nine squares" system to the system of prefectures and counties, which was completed during the Qin and Han periods. He pondered this issue when he was studying at the Central University in Shapingba in Chongqing during the period of the Republic of China. According to Tang, this transition of China's administrative system was of paramount significance and influenced Chinese history over the subsequent 2,000 years. Two thousand years after that, especially after the Opium Wars in 1840, Chinese society underwent another major transformation, which came as the result of the disastrous encounter with the West and the lesson that the country's traditional governance model had run its course and that the only viable option was to learn from the West. In his opinion, just as it took 200 years to complete the transition from the "nine squares" system to the system of prefectures and counties, it will also take some 200 years from the firm establishment of democratic politics and rule of law in China; that is, this vision will not materialize until 2040, by which time I will already be 80 years old. Tang compared this historical transition to a tough journey through the precarious Three Gorges. This will be a crucial period for our nation, and all parties involved, especially the country's leadership, must be cooperative and make concerted efforts to make the process progress smoothly and prevent any military, political, or diplomatic disruption, otherwise the vision will not come true in 2040 as expected but will perhaps by the time I am 180 years old.

A direct result of the disastrous encounter with the West is a deep-rooted cultural inferiority complex among the Chinese. Before 1840 all Western things were held in contempt, but after that, they have always been held in great esteem. Many prominent figures in modern Chinese history, from Sun Yat-sen to Mao Zedong, have advocated learning from the West, though there were occasional deviations from the direction toward the Soviet Union. Chinese society, especially as respects its class structure, had never been a market economy society in its more than 2,000 of history until 1992, when

Deng Xiaoping initiated a market economy–oriented reform, beginning another major social transformation.

I think a market economy is based on and leads to the diversification in social interests and the emergence of the middle class. There are many popular advocacies that I do not agree with. For example, the idea that we need an organization to represent the interests of the broadest number of people, in effect, more or less strangles the opportunity for the development of constitutional government. As a matter of fact, as our society becomes increasingly diversified, what we really need is diversified political parties representing the interests of different social groups. [*Applause*] A capitalist class is nothing to fear. Our society has tolerated the presence of capitalists. Indeed, they have been allowed to join the Communist Party. In fact, they may well establish a party of their own. [*Applause*] The primary reason why I joined the Communist Party was that I thought it represented the poor, but now it has come to represent the rich, making me feel as if overnight I returned to the era before the liberation of China. [*Laughter and applause*] My answer, in a word, is that the reality of a multiplicity of interests should be recognized, and a corresponding diversified political system should be established.

The question asked by Professor Liu Junxiang is a very hard one for me to answer and gives the impression that by saying that the ship of constitutional government has set sail in China, we have broken a bottle of champagne. [*Laughter and applause*] On the other hand, it is unmistakably palpable through my speech that China's conditions for constitutional government are not yet completely ripe. If so, isn't it contradictory to say that the ship of constitutional government has set sail in China? Is it that the ship setting sail is an unfinished one? [*Laughter*] Of course, any metaphor for the starting of constitutional government, be it a ship or a vehicle, is awkward and problematic because the emergence of a constitutional government has its own highly distinctive dimensions. The understanding of constitutional government and the development of the constitutional system itself both are a groping process toward increased depth and clarity. In fact, the acquaintance with the concept of constitutional government has been relatively recent, even among constitutional scholars like Song Jiangping. That is, it is only in recent years that legal scholars at the prestigious Southwest University of Political Science and Law have come to an increasingly sophisticated understanding of the principles of constitutional government. With the increasing awareness of constitutional government, the official response to it is also becoming increasingly positive. In the past, people advocating such ideas would be put into prison, but things are different today. The present forum, where we have open discussions about the relevance of constitutional government to China, is a good example. I myself am quite outspoken when espousing constitutional government, and the government also shows considerate tolerance of such expressions, which I think is a very important sign that China is changing for the better in its political environment. Therefore, I think the issue mentioned by Professor Liu Junxiang is something that will unfold naturally, and perhaps one day, regarding some of the factors discussed, a decisive step will be taken in China toward the right direction of constitutional government. This, however, does not mean that I am preaching legalism. What I advocate, as a matter of fact, has been put forward by Professor Liu Junxiang. There is still some conceptual and theoretical research that is needed to form a more comprehensive argument for constitutional government. In this respect I think I also need to devote more effort.

Professor Song Yubo is a constitutional scholar. His comment can be said to be a succinct summary of the major questions covered in my speech, such as how to go about institutional development, what legitimacy is required, and how to ensure constitutional legitimacy. I totally agree with his views expressed in his comment.

Professor Fu Zitang put forward two sharp questions. His first question concerns the object of reference for constitutional research, underscoring his view that in our constitutional studies, we cannot always make reference to Anglo-American practices since we are here in China, pushing for China's own constitutional government, and Western practices cannot generate solutions to all the problems we face. This question is very thought provoking. It reminds me of American sinologist Paul A. Cohen's book *Discovering History in China*, in which he criticized John K. Fairbank's "impact-response" approach.[15] According to Cohen, the social changes in China since the late Qing dynasty have all come about to meet the intrinsic needs of Chinese society. This is his conception of history. It can be said that China's discovery of constitutional government by itself is already part of the effort to develop and promote constitutional government. But in this effort, it is also necessary to reinterpret our history and draw on resources for constitutional government from China's own history and social fabric; in this regard, I totally agree with Professor Fu. In fact, I also made some effort in this direction by rediscovering China's traditional political system, which was, in fact, very different from the stereotypical image of being despotic, ruthless, and suppressive. One of the very fine aspects of the system was the strict accountability of officials. Each magistrate was fully responsible for the governance of his prefecture, following a highly centralized administrative system as opposed to division of labor and separation of powers.

Today, we have put in place a complicated government system based on separation of powers, only to find that what is meant to be restricted cannot be restricted and accountability of officials cannot be clearly established. If a country is not well governed, who should be held responsible for it? In ancient times, it was certainly the magistrate, who would be severely punished and replaced by another official. But today, for example, if the county of Panyu is badly governed, who should be held responsible: the party chief or government head of the county? If the county has deteriorating law-and-order situations, the county's party head will shift the blame to its government head. The government head will say it is the public security bureau to blame. The public security bureau will say it is because the court is negligent in law enforcement. The court again will shift the blame to the procuratorate. At last, even the county's Communist Youth League committee will be dragged into the scene. In a word, both accountability and honor are so divided among different departments and officials that neither is taken seriously.

Therefore, I think China's traditional governance system has its own merits. Although we do not need to reinstate the system, we should not lose sight of its merits, especially as respects accountability. In a sense, a modern democratic system lacking in administrative efficiency and division of labor is even inferior to our former highly accountable despotic system! [*Applause*] One hundred years ago, when the Manchu-ruled Qing dynasty was overturned, many Manchu people residing in the Forbidden City, young and old, all cried like babies because they felt that the empire was lost to others, as if the empire had been their own exclusive property that therefore was greatly treasured; but today, who treasures this country? [*Applause*] I have a strong sympathy for the concept of "creative transformation." We also need certain mechanisms and efforts to reinterpret and rediscover our tradition.

The second question asked by Professor Fu regards the relationship between constitutional government and rule of law. I think the answer has already been given in his own comment, that is, constitutional government is the precondition and foundation of rule of law. I completely agree with this view.

Professor Lu Yunbao painted a very pessimistic picture of the prospect of constitutional government in China, which I think is very incongruous with my role as a passionate preacher and missionary of the cause since the defining characteristic of any preachers or missionaries is their faith and confidence in what they preach and in the attainability of their goals. However, as they say, profound pessimism is better than shallow optimism. I think what Professor Lu Yunbao conveys is just such a profound pessimism. However, this pessimism actually does not affect our endeavor to pursue constitutional government at all; instead, it points out two aspects where more improvements should be made. In the past twenty or thirty years, there have been many people devoted to what could be called a rural enlightenment movement. For example, some women went to the countryside to popularize such concepts as democracy and feminism only to be met with indifference and apathy, and they came back disappointed and disillusioned, believing that people in the countryside do not really bother themselves with such things. When I got closer to this problem, however, I found that things are quite different in the countryside. Not long ago, it was reported that four villagers in Anhui Province were beaten to death as they went to the head of their village and demanded to check the village committee's accounts. Many people were appalled by the news but were puzzled as to why they asked to check the village's accounts. Obviously the villagers believed that they had the right to ascertain how the money they paid was used. This, in fact, shows an awakening of constitutional consciousness in the countryside, especially the realization that villager autonomy is something closely linked to their own interests. In the past, we tended to explain democracy, freedom, and human rights in a way that gave farmers the impression that these things have no relevance to rural life and are very abstract and distant from their everyday lives; so it was only natural that they would feel indifferent and apathetic to such efforts. However, if we explain to them how the system works and how many benefits it will bring to them, their response will be very different and positive. Farmers are also reasonable beings driven by self-interest, and they do not like the idea of their money being taken away without knowing how it is used. So based on my own life experience and my subsequent research, I do not agree with the view that farmers are apathetic or lack constitutional consciousness.

In his comment, Professor Lu Yunbao also expressed his doubt as to what degree government officials will accept admonitions and become convinced that, among other things, the freedom of the press is also in their own interests. I once even wrote an article titled "Treat Officials Well" in which I expressed the view that the absence of freedom of the press puts officials on the crater of the volcano so that they are far more likely to become another Wang Baosen rather than Kong Fansen.[16] Why? Because without the freedom of the press and the ensuing media supervision, Chinese officials, especially those at the level of bureau or above, exercise almost unchecked power, which inevitably leads to corruption.

As for Professor Luo Jun's comment, I agree with his view that constitutional government is not all perfect and has its flaws. However, I do not think constitutional government has anything to do with traps. Although the Chinese characters for "constitutional government" and "trap" sound similar, they have nothing in common, let alone equating the one with the other. As for the religious dimension of constitutional government, since we believe in Marxism, there is no place for any religion, and therefore it is impossible for us to worship constitutional government or establish a theology-based jurisprudence. This is determined by China's national conditions.

Professor Wang Xuehui asked two questions. The first is what the core concept of constitutional government is. I don't quite like the term core concept, nor have I given any thought to it. I think all aspects of constitutional government are important, and we cannot say which is the most important. But I do agree with Professor Wang's observation that constitutional government is the game of the rich. As for whether China has the capacity to implement constitutional government or not, I think it takes time, and although it cannot be achieved at one go, the goal can be attained gradually. The Imperial Civil Service Examination brought about such social mobility that today's peasant could be tomorrow's top official, as was the case with Chen Shimei. It generated an illusion and made people discontent with their own class. The Imperial Civil Service Examination also hindered the division of social labor and the formation of stable classes and interest groups, making it all but impossible for the emergence of constitutional government. China had a strong intellectual tradition that went against the division of labor. Among the many thinkers in Chinese history, which of them ever paid any attention to the division of social labor? Aristotle studied not only politics, philosophy, and rhetoric but also zoology. Never had Confucius or Mencius ever mentioned anything about zoology. What they liked to discuss was how to be a gentleman and the like. As these issues were already covered in my speech, I do not say any more about them here.

Zhang Shaoyan: Thanks to Professor He for his brilliant comments. In what follows, Professor He will answer questions from students. [*Applause*]

Student: There is a widely shared view that rule of virtue is a regression from rule of law and a return to China's old tradition of "moral enlightenment and prudent punishment," which in essence was rule of man. What do you think of this issue? In the words of a Western jurist, the nineteenth century was for criminal code, the twentieth century for civil and commercial law, and the twenty-first century for constitutional government. When do you think China will enter into the twenty-first century?

He Weifang: Good question. Rule of virtue is an issue that is not so easy to expand upon. How does one define virtue? Can it be codified? State governance means the imposition of a set of rules to be followed by everyone, but virtue cannot break down into specific rules. Just as a friend recently commented here, isn't virtue a Kantian moral imperative inside a person's mind? Who can extract this moral imperative and turn it into a moral code? How can we determine who is morally noble or ignoble? In Chinese history, there were indeed times when highly esteemed, morally impeccable rulers did well in practicing rule of virtue. But in an increasingly pluralistic society, any attempt to impose the moral standards of a few persons to all people is morally condemnable! [*Applause*]

In fact, a survey of China's more than 2,000 years of history shows that periods when rule of virtue was emphasized were often those when hypocrisy ran rampant. In spite of the truth that no one is so noble as to completely rid himself of self-interest, that impossible standard of selflessness was once imposed upon us, and we were asked to follow the example of Lei Feng, to be unselfish and utterly devoted to others. Lei Feng, so we were told, studied the *Quotations from Chairman Mao* every day and gave his hard-earned money to help others, deeming it a great pleasure. He was therefore turned into an exemplary figure for everyone else to learn from. In our childhood days, we were admonished to do away with any thought of self-interest. However, it was exactly in that age that those calling for selflessness had their self-interest best served, marrying one wife after another, building themselves luxurious mansions, and watching the most erotic Western films while the ordinary people could only watch stereotyped propaganda films. [*Laughter*] So those who are most fervent in preaching moral lectures are often the most wanting in morality. Qian Zhongshu had a witticism that God punishes man with three things: the first is war, the second is epidemic, and the third is moralists. [*Laughter*] In fact, it is nothing for a moral moralist to preach moral standards; the most spectacular form of moralizing is that done by a morally bankrupt moralist who has an axe to grind. [*Laughter and applause*]

Furthermore, rule of virtue may lead to cruel persecution and sanction of those failing to comply with the prevailing moral standards. Indeed, the criminal penalty in ancient China might well be thought of as an extension of rule of virtue. One was killed when thought to be morally incurable. Furthermore, there was a complicated hierarchy of how the death penalty was to be administered, such as decapitation and hanging. The execution of death sentences was seldom a straightforward thing. In many cases, executions were publicly performed and deemed a public festival, especially in the case of slow slicing or death by a thousand cuts, where the condemned was killed by using a knife to methodically remove portions of the body over an extended period of time. There are photos featuring such horrible scenes, shot by Westerners. Why were executions made a ritual? Because they acted as a form of legal education. The executions were performed primarily not to punish but to maintain rule of virtue. Therefore, our past practice in setting up a minority group to oppose and attack was in fact an inevitable result of rule of virtue. In this sense, rule of virtue is indeed a regression and should be shunned.

Student: You said that constitutional government could not take root in traditional China due to its loose class structure. How do you arrive at this conclusion? Is it that only when all classes from farmers to the rich to the elite are contented with and confined to their own classes will constitutional government have the foundation for growth?

He Weifang: This question, though a little radical, is yet very interesting. In fact, as early as ancient Greece, there were political philosophers arguing for the justification of various social classes and taking the contentedness of people with their own classes as a prerequisite for social order. They argued that people of different classes were made of different metals such as gold, silver, bronze, and iron and were meant to perform different social functions accordingly. The result, of course, is long-term control of the ruling class over the ruled, but this in fact is also a prerequisite for the growth of constitutional government. Under this system, the ruled usually will not revolt against the ruler unless they feel forced to. This is a very interesting process. The worst scenario, however, is where the ruler appoints one person from his subjects to lead the government today and replace him with another tomorrow. Nothing that will incite resistance against the establishment should be done, for it is not good for social progress.

OK, I have to stop here. I hope there will be more opportunities to exchange ideas with you. [*Warm applause*]

Zhang Shaoyan: Thanks to Professor He, thanks to our guest commentators, thanks to you all. Goodbye. [*Warm applause*]

CHAPTER FOUR

CONSTITUTIONALISM AS A GLOBAL TREND AND ITS IMPACT ON CHINA

Many Western-educated, enlightened Chinese intellectuals in modern China, most notably Yan Fu, advocated that China should learn from the West not only in building warships and armaments but also in developing sound legal and political systems. That is, we should look beyond the outer strengths of Western powers to see their institutional and cultural contexts, which foster such strengths. We came to notice the existence and great significance of a constitution in these countries very early, and made various efforts toward constitutionalism, including the formulation of a quasi-constitution after the manner of the West in the late Qing dynasty. Since then, China has had its own constitution, but to our dismay, it always fails to play the role assigned to it. Various rights granted in the constitution are not strictly guaranteed, and the mutual checks and balances of power provided for in the constitution have never been implemented.

This lip service given to constitutionalism in China is very disappointing. Suffice it to compare the stern reality with the heart-stirring provisions in the

The Chinese version of this chapter was based on the author's lecture at the Guangdong Academic Forum, co-organized by the Sun Yat-sen (Zhongshan) Library, *China's Reform Forum* magazine, the Guangzhou Social Science Association, and the *Southern Metropolis Daily*, and held at the Zhongshan Library in Guangzhou, on July 28, 2004. This version has omitted the author's discussion on Guangdong's sociopolitical development at the beginning of the lecture and the question-and-answer section.

Author's note: I would like to thank the four host institutions for their thoughtful arrangements for this lecture and for providing full transcripts, in which I have made some changes and added subheadings.

country's constitution, that the people are the masters of the country, that the fundamental mission of all state organs is to serve the interests of the people, and many more, so much so that people reading the text of the constitution in 200 years and taking it literally would almost glorify this period as "the good old days" and imagine with envy how happy a life the Chinese were enjoying then. It would give the false impression that the government's powers were subject to strict limitation in law, private properties were legally protected, the protection of human rights was taken as an important mission, and citizens' freedom of person was inviolable. People in 200 years, if they are not armed with solid historical and sociological knowledge of this period and take the text of the constitution literally, will have no way of knowing that, as a matter of fact, those rights enshrined in the constitution were in reality not duly guaranteed at all.

This situation in China, where there is a constitution but no constitutional government, has been studied by quite a few scholars. Andrew Nathan, a U.S. expert on Chinese affairs, in his analysis of the disillusionment accompanying the pursuit of constitutionalism in modern China, pointed out how the country's officialdom was full of anticonstitutional practices. It has been customary for officials to appoint or promote those associated with them, such as their relatives, townsmen, or classmates, who usually formed a clique to advance their own interests and to oppose other cliques, with the result that constitutional politics could not be implemented. It is true that contemporary party politics has similar characteristics, but they are considered "vestigial traits" and are completely different both in nature and function.

Another factor detrimental to constitutional government is the difficulty in reaching a compromise among conflicting interests, and the relationship among different cliques is often hostile and absolutely irreconcilable. Political leaders not only wield great power but also believe that truth is right in their hands, so that they both promulgate government decrees and dictate what is right or wrong, thus precluding any possibility of competitive and cooperative opposition. This combination of paramount power in both the administrative and intellectual sense is, so to speak, destructive to constitutionalism, so that dissidents must choose either total submission or armed revolt. The Kuomintang, for example, used to preach that all powers and truths rest with Generalissimo Chiang Kai-shek, the party's political and military leader; the CCP, however, didn't buy it and rose in revolt, with the pronounced mission of building China into a democratic country with press freedom and a neutral military. The encounter between the CCP and the uncompromising Kuomintang finally led to the civil war.

In 1949 the People's Republic of China was established, and this new socialist state, at least initially, was embraced by the Chinese as a brand-new social system completely different from the traditional bureaucratic empire, one that filled them with exhilaration as if they were in heaven. In the 1950s, almost every Chinese was bathed in joy and jubilation in the firm belief that the Chinese people had finally stood up and risen to become the masters of the country while bidding goodbye forever to the exploitation and suppression of the past. This social atmosphere was vividly reflected in the example of the painter Huang Yongyu who, upon returning to China from overseas in the 1950s and seeing a traffic officer in Tiananmen Square, was so excited that he ran straight to him and shook hands with him, saying: "Comrade, you are doing a good job! I've finally come to the bosom of the motherland!" Most people at the time were like him, believing that China had finally embarked on the broad and bright road toward communism.

However, as subsequent history proves, it is simply impossible for us to transcend our history. It is not difficult to change a country's name, but it is extremely difficult to change its customary pattern of governance and tradition. Having undergone many vicious political campaigns and power abuses on the part of the government that trampled human rights and freedom, we have come to the bitter realization that even in a socialist state, the constitution is still necessary, that the law remains indispensable, and that the government's power must be restricted to safeguard the people's freedom and rights and to prevent them from being infringed upon by the government.

In this age of globalization, China's institutional development is increasingly subject to influences from the external world and intertwined with other countries, especially developed countries. If we take an overall view of the whole world in terms of constitutional development, we can identify a number of steadily rising trends. What are they then? As time does not allow me to undertake a detailed review of them, I only mention the major ones.

Trend 1: Increasing Justification for Constitutionalism

The first trend is that constitutional government, or a system by which the government's power is legally constrained to safeguard civil rights, is constantly gaining in justification and legitimacy. This trend is very obvious and easily sensed. Constitutional government or rule of law emerged in the West more or less by chance. England was the first country to establish a constitutional government. In that country, with a small population, it was possible to put in place a set of definite legal procedures and rules by which the people could participate in the country's political affairs. In 1215 English barons united in revolt against the king, who was finally forced to consent to their demand to limit his power. The barons had no interest in starting a civil war but instead forced the king to sign a document stipulating that no tax could be levied without their agreement. The concept behind it, that is, that a tax cannot be imposed without taxpayers' consent, has obvious constitutional significance. After that, a concept arose among the English, and it eventually evolved into the stirring slogan "No taxation without representation," which united the people of the thirteen colonies in North America in their pursuit of independence.

The point is that the government must exercise its power as authorized by the people and shall not exceed the scope of authorization. The norms formed under the influence of this concept, along with other factors, gradually led to the establishment of England's constitutional regime. Even though Britain to this day does not have a written constitution, that fact does not affect its claim to be a constitutional state. In contrast, although the Soviet Union and many former Eastern European countries did have brilliantly worded constitutions, they could not be considered constitutional states. Indeed, since the beginning of modern times, it has become something of a norm for a new country to formulate an impressive constitution, but it has not always been easy to give substance to those constitutional provisions. In many places in the world, the advancement of constitutional government still faces considerable resistance, and this resistance often has complicated historical and cultural origins.

Taking China as an example, to limit the power of the government or emperor was always a very difficult thing because the emperor had natural legitimacy as the Son of Heaven, and to go against his will was to go against that of heaven. Throughout the history of China, the emperor's power never faced any serious limitations. Although he was subject to certain restrictions, such as "the ancestors' mandates" mentioned in the *Rites of Zhou*, these restrictions were generally based on written passages, which allowed multiple interpretations and therefore lacked the force of constraint. It was not until the late Qing dynasty that a serious effort was made to reform the country's governmental structure as a result of influence from the West. Given the 2,000 years that the imperial system had been continuously in place, it was inconceivable at the time to end the system altogether, and therefore only a mild approach to reform was possible. The reform, a forced one in nature, encountered quite a problem in choosing the object of imitation.

France, then a republic seething with public unrest and protests, was considered an inappropriate model for China to follow. The United States, though not yet a major power, still attracted considerable attention, but it was not a monarchy. The country's leader, called the president, was elected by citizens and had a fixed term. This arrangement, of course, could not be borrowed by China. The search finally settled on Britain, then the wealthiest country in the world. It was also the country from which China suffered the most at the time. We are all familiar with the Sanyuanli Anti-British Incident, let alone the Opium Wars.[1] By learning from Britain, the reformers hoped that China would also become equally powerful. Besides, the British model had another attraction: it was a monarchy. For the Chinese at the beginning of the twentieth century, a government system without an emperor was still beyond imagination. Anyway, it was eventually realized that Britain was the most difficult—and should have been the last—candidate to learn from. The first reason is that British law was too complicated. One hundred years back, the most urgent task faced by China was to reconstruct its political and legal systems to bring them into line with those of the West. To reach this goal, the most convenient way was to copy the West's legal system, and even directly translate its laws and adopt them as China's own. The same approach was also taken by such countries as Japan and Turkey in their initial endeavor to adopt Western legal systems. In the case of Turkey, it translated Switzerland's civil code, and to keep its law scholars and practitioners abreast of the latest developments in the field, it also kept continuously updated on the Swiss courts' interpretations of the civil code. In Japan, Eto Shinpei, who was in charge of the formulation of the country's legal code, gave the scholar Mitsukuri Rinsho the task of translating the French penal code. The task proved very difficult because Mitsukuri specialized in Dutch, not French. He reported to Eto that he could only get a very rough idea of the code's meaning with the aid of the dictionary, and it was beyond him to translate it into Japanese; but he was asked to go ahead with the task, and if there were some translation mistakes, it was no big thing. The work was eventually completed, and after the title was changed from the French penal code to the Japanese penal code, Japan had its own set of laws. These examples indicate the urgency and eagerness of some countries to learn from the West, and they also reflect the relative ease of copying the law of continental European countries.

As far as convenience was concerned, the most difficult laws to copy were those of Britain and the United States. Unlike the laws in continental European countries, which are generally compiled into a single-volume statute book, British law is not contained in such a book but rather consists of a voluminous collection of precedents that serve as points of reference for future cases that are of a similar nature. Such a framework makes for a very arduous learning process, and it also makes it impossible to distill such material into a statute book in a short time.

The second challenge of copying British law came from the firmly established tradition of local autonomy in British constitutional government, something that was highly foreign to and incompatible with China's tradition of centralized government. In China the mention of "local autonomy" brings to mind horrible scenarios of warlords dominating their own regions and local despots bullying ordinary people, and therefore the most desired state of the country is a unified country under a centralized government. Even today, it is difficult to implement local autonomy in China. That explains Sun Yat-sen's famous remark that "the freedom in China is not too little, but too much." He said that in allusion to the disunity of the nation at the time. Given these circumstances, Sun placed great emphasis on centralization and unity. In a way, Sun's political theory (especially the views he held in his later years) is even closely associated with quite a few drawbacks in China's current system, especially as it relates to the relationship between the ruling party and the state and the power of the leaders. Local autonomy is a very important tradition of Britain's political system, and its trait of harmony between this local autonomy and national unity is the most difficult to copy.

Then reformers focused on the British constitutional monarchy, which bore the closest resemblance to China's traditional governance system and therefore appeared most acceptable. However, a largely neglected fact about the British monarchy was that the monarch had only a ceremonial position without substantial power. So later it was realized that China's monarch should also have a symbolic position, but this was something extremely difficult to achieve, given the absence of such a tradition in the country. Therefore, it was decided that the British system could not be copied.

Then the German system was considered, and this time the Qing imperial officials finally felt assured, believing that the German system was what China should follow to become an important force on the world scene, like the Western capitalist powers. It had become a very urgent goal at this point, and so China began to learn increasingly from Germany and Japan, which had risen in power by learning from Germany. In the development of political or legal systems, Germany exerted a major influence on the modernization of quite a few East Asian countries. In a word, China finally embarked on the path toward an economically prosperous and militarily strong country by following the example of Germany. In the 1920s and 1930s, China's legal system was essentially based on that of Germany, either directly or through the Japanese model. However, the lack of freedom in the German system was also transmitted to China's system. The fact that Germany eventually embraced Nazism also indicates some inherent flaws in its system.

Returning to the present, the West's constitutional system is gaining increasing legitimacy and is recognized almost universally worldwide, at least in words if not in deeds. Even countries not really practicing constitutional government have their own parliaments, elections, and constitutions providing for a certain degree of separation of powers and extensive civil and political rights. This has been particularly true after the 1990s. The legitimacy of constitutional government has been so widely recognized that it can be described with Francis Fukuyama's classic expression: the end of history.[2]

At this point, attention should also be given to another aspect of the trend toward increasing justification for constitutionalism, one that may be closely related to nationalism. The global spread of the Western system and the establishment of its supremacy have also elicited complicated reactions; they are not always gladly accepted, without resistance, around the world. In other words, this system, after being introduced, failed to bring about the same anticipated effects, and as a result people lost confidence or patience in the process; even some early enthusiasts gradually changed their former stance. In China we have such examples as Kang Youwei, Liang Qichao, and Yan Fu, who turned conservative and embraced traditional Confucianism in their later years. In fact, there was a two-way change after the introduction of the Western system to China, that is, it both changed China's traditional system and was changed by the Chinese culture and various informal mechanisms. As often happens, foreign things that are introduced to China gradually become part of Chinese culture. If they do not undergo the process of localization, they will not be able to survive in China; however, if localization is so radical that they are changed beyond recognition, the introduction itself becomes pointless. In Shakespeare's *A Midsummer Night's Dream*, a person was changed into a donkey, and the other person cried, "Bless thee! Thou art translated!" The introduction of a Western system into China is just like this. After being introduced and localized, it has become something very different from its original form.

Taking China's National People's Congress as an example, it is a product of learning from the West's parliamentary system, but it lacks some of the essential functions of the original system. The most conspicuous absence is parliamentary debate, an inherent characteristic of parliamentary politics. In Britain, the birthplace of the modern parliamentary system, the parliament is designed to facilitate debate between the ruling party and opposition parties on an equal footing, following rules of order in the presence of the presiding speaker of the parliament. However, debate is rarely seen in China's People's Congress. One of the reasons, of course, is that the deputies, numbering more than 3,000, are too numerous to debate together.

This also reflects the flaw of the classification of parliament members in China. In Western countries, members of the parliament are, first of all, classified in accordance with their party affiliation. When we watch a TV interview with a member of the U.S. Congress and note that his name is displayed followed by "D.," we know that he is a Democrat. The seats in Western parliaments are also arranged according to party affiliation. However, this set of rules does not apply in China, where 80 percent of the deputies are CCP members. Even those who are not CCP members support and owe allegiance to the CCP. Given this state of things, there is indeed no substantial ground for them to debate with each other.

This evolution and degeneration of the Western system in China fills its advocates with disappointment, disillusionment, and even despair, and they come to the bitter realization that China should carve out a path of development of its own. Similar sentiments are also shared by other people in other countries, such as Lee Kuan Yew of Singapore, who advocates for the assertion of Asia's own values or uniqueness. In a word, people in East and Southeast Asia have gradually redirected their efforts toward developing this region's own set of discourse on political and legal systems and culture to confront the West. This kind of thinking has also emerged in China. Despite 100 years of development, constitutional government in China remains premature.

There is hope for a feasible theory of constitutional government based on the local culture. Professor Jiang Qing is an advocate of Confucianism in contemporary China. In his recent work *Political Confucianism,* he explores the issue of how Confucian political theory can answer the need to advance rule of law, democracy, and constitutional government in contemporary China.[3] As we know, proponents of contemporary Neo-Confucianism generally share a conviction that traditional Confucianism has an excessive emphasis on the mind but fails to address the development of political and social systems. Although Mind Confucianism helps to foster the formation of a noble character, it does not indicate how to enable political and legal systems to maintain a good order. It is good to have "inner sageliness" (*nei sheng*), but it is difficult for that to blossom into "outer kingliness" (*wai wang*). The result is that in spite of lofty pursuits among traditional literati-scholars, as embodied by such heart-stirring mottos as "Be the first to bear hardships and the last to enjoy comforts" and "To bring a heart to heaven and earth, to bring livelihood to the general population, to continue the lost teachings of past sages, and to bring about peace to ten thousand generations," China's political chaos and social unrest always formed a sharp and cruel contrast to what literati-scholars pursued. As they came up with more and more fancy dictums and maxims, China's actual reality only went in the opposite direction and became increasingly corrupt. That is why some representative Neo-Confucian scholars are advocating that while it is important for us to embrace traditional Mind Confucianism to foster the nation's soul and character, it is also necessary to draw upon Western political and legal theories and integrate Western values, such as democracy, liberty, separation of powers, judicial independence, and safeguarding of individuals' rights. Only when this integration succeeds will Confucianism be able to enter into the so-called third stage of its development.

Professor Jiang Qing, however, takes exception to this integrative effort. According to him, Confucianism has its own profound teachings on politics and law, but due to traditional obsession with Mind Confucianism—which was sometimes even equated with Confucianism as a whole rather than being part of it—these teachings have been neglected for a long period of time, just as the saying goes, "The eyelash, immediate to the eye, yet is not seen, and the Tao, which is within everyone, yet is often sought elsewhere." What Jiang commits himself to is rediscovering the political and legal aspects of Confucianism and their relevance to China's contemporary development concerns, and his book *Political Confucianism* is part of this ambitious effort of his. He holds that the Western political system and its underlying theories have serious flaws, such as their blind emphasis on democracy and equality before the law, which grants equal rights to the worthy and the unworthy alike, and he thinks this is not fair. In his logic, a country is in a bad way if every citizen, be it a mean person or a great man like Confucius, has a vote of equal weight. Instead, he advocates for inequality before the law and the formal establishment of core Confucian concepts such as "moral enlightenment having priority over punishment" (*de zhu xing fu*) and "the purpose of punishment being the elimination of punishment." He also advocates that the state be led by Confucian scholars and those who are capable of carrying on the country's historical and cultural traditions. Professor Jiang Qing once told me that my efforts would be better served if I tried to have a statue of Confucius erected at the entrance of China's supreme court, and he thinks that Confucius has a fair claim to have his statue also erected at the site of the Hague-based International Court of Justice. Confucius, who once served as the chief justice of the state of Lu, says in the *Analects*, "In hearing litigation, I am like any other body. What is necessary, however, is to cause the people to have no litigation."

In my opinion, Jiang Qing's endeavor to reinterpret the classic Confucian tradition on politics is commendable and deserves respect, but his theory, if used to reconstruct China's political and legal systems today, will prove inadequate and even lead to ridiculous situations. And the inevitable result cannot be completely attributed to China's absorption of Western thought since the May Fourth Movement, because if this were the case, one would not be able to explain why China failed to create a good social order through Confucianism in the long, 2,000-year period before the late Qing, and why Chinese society was always full of social inequality and injustice so that social tension had to be periodically alleviated by way of violence.

In a word, the efforts of non-Western countries to carve out a new path different from the Western model in developing their own political and legal systems are respectable, but their chances of success are slim. These constantly renewed but always unsuccessful efforts, while showing the perseverant spirit behind them, also serve to prove the justification and irresistibility of the Western model. In addition, I think one point that the advocates of this kind of theory should keep in mind is that unlike other fields, the application of a novel theory to the building of a political or legal system is a matter that requires the greatest degree of prudence possible, because once such a theory is put into practice, it will put at stake the livelihoods and even lives of many people, with consequences no scientific experiment can measure.

Trend 2: The End of the Socialism-Capitalism Dichotomy and Its Impact

The second trend is that the traditional confrontation between the socialist camp and the capitalist camp no longer has influence on the development of constitutional government. Before 1990 a significant part of the world belonged to the socialist camp, but subsequently the Soviet Union and all Eastern European socialist countries changed color, and even Mongolia turned to capitalism, so that there are only a few socialist countries left, including China, North Korea, Vietnam, and Cuba. And among these there is much conflict—for instance, North Korea refuses to recognize China as a socialist country. Indeed, using the criteria of socialism during the Cultural Revolution, today's China indeed cannot be counted as a socialist country.

China is now building a socialist market economy, and the term "market economy" is seen in a highly positive light. In his southern tour in 1992, Deng Xiaoping drew a circle around Guangzhou and made it the place where socialism and a market economy—which were considered mutually exclusive in the past—were to be reconciled, and he called the combination a socialist market economy. The CCP is never dogmatic but always pragmatic, if not opportunistic. In China there are many things that you can do, but you cannot talk about them, and this, in fact, is also a great wisdom. However, there is also a price to pay. In the attempt to cross the river by feeling for stones, one may cross it eventually, but one may also drown midway through.

Anyhow, during the preceding century, the socialist system was humankind's grand experiment to explore a new type of social system, and it set for itself the lofty goal of eliminating all the ills of previous social systems, the capitalist system in particular, and creating a new world of grand harmony without suppression or exploitation. At first, the experiment attracted many supporters full of high expectations of what was to come. The Chinese writer Hu Feng wrote a poem after 1949 announcing that "a new epoch has begun!"[4] Everyone was of the firm belief that with the establishment of the socialist system, the future would be immensely beautiful, and China had embarked on the thoroughfare from socialism to communism. No one at the time expected that this social system would bring about serious man-made disasters with its various campaigns such as Stalinism and the so-called Great Cultural Revolution. It is through these disasters that we begin to reflect on socialism and capitalism as well.

Drawing lessons from the past half century—nearly one century if the Soviet Union is taken into account—we have to admit that humankind cannot transcend the historical stage in which it finds itself. In retrospect we find that it is often those endeavors to turn the human world into heaven on earth that have brought humankind the greatest suffering. Today, few people are calling for marching toward communism or cherishing any fancy for a society without a state system, law, or police. Instead, we are promoting the coexistence of different systems of ownership, and we have had the first constitution in the history of socialist China that explicitly provides for the protection of private property. It is extraordinary if we think of the meaning of the Communist Party, which, as its name indicates, is committed to "all properties for all." [*Applause*]

Behind the constitutional protection of private property is a profound change in the political philosophy embraced by the country's leadership. Traditional socialism has its own political philosophy based on a set of assumptions, among them the assumption that in a socialist state, a constitution is not necessary because the state is led by the most advanced of all classes, the proletariat, whose political party, the Communist Party, is composed of members belonging to an extraordinary category of persons—a theory similar to Plato's in *The Republic*. The Central Committee of the Communist Party, in turn, is composed of the most exceptional members of the party, and the Politburo, again, is composed of the greatest members of the Central Committee. These Politburo members are the finest of all humans, the cream of the crop, who are endowed, above all, with the extraordinary capacity of discovering and grasping truths of social development and leading the country toward the brightest future. With them as our leaders, everything is assured. And with such a political party to lead the country, there is simply no need for separation of powers or constitutional government.

In the period when such a doctrine held sway, it was neither imaginable nor practical to establish a legal system limiting the power of top leaders and the government. Therefore, back in the 1950s, China could not be a rule-of-law rather than a rule-of-man country. Lin Biao described Mao Zedong as the Great Teacher, Great Commander, Great Leader, and Great Helmsman, and it is said that even Mao himself found the expression too exaggerated and said that he did not need so many titles, that he only wanted to be a great teacher of the country. As a matter of fact, for the paramount leader to be the whole country's teacher has a major implication: it entails a combination of both political and spiritual control, where the paramount leader enjoys not only the greatest secular power but also the highest spiritual power. This is perhaps an inevitable result of traditional socialism. The reason for the coexistence of suppression of religious belief and a thriving cult of personality in socialist countries in the past is that the paramount leader was considered the savior of the people, like a sun that gives them warmth. In a social environment like that, it is impossible to practice constitutional government.

Today, however, we no longer believe in the possibility of a person or group having exclusive possession of the truth. We are all independent individuals and know that both the government and political parties should be subject to the regulation of law, and that without such legal restriction, the people will suffer terribly. This is a precious lesson we draw from the bitter experience of the past. That is why we call for constitutional government today. The Sun Zhigang incident that happened here last year had a great social impact and was brought to a close with the abolition of the custody and repatriation system. However, we did not think that this was enough, and we demanded the establishment of a constitutional review system to rectify any unconstitutional acts of the government, including the highest level of the government, and bring a timely halt to any laws and administrative regulations that are considered unconstitutional. Although this goal was not achieved then, we have noticed that the Standing Committee of the National People's Congress is now considering the establishment of a relatively independent organ for constitutional review. It was reported the other day that this organ has been established, in the form of a law and regulation filing office under the Law Committee, which is again under the Standing Committee of the National People's Congress. Although this organ is too low in administrative level to truly perform the function of judicial and constitutional review, it is still a small step in the right direction.

In a word, the dispute between socialism and capitalism has largely become a thing of the past, and this creates remarkable room for the development of China's system in the future.

Trend 3: Supranational Organizations' Restriction of Sovereignty

The third trend is the increasing presence of supranational organizations. The concept of the sovereign state formed in the eighteenth century is undergoing considerable changes, and it is increasingly acknowledged among countries that sovereignty should also be subject to certain restrictions. According to the traditional definition, the state is the paramount authority of its population. With democratic development since modern times, there is more emphasis on the restriction of the government's power, but as far as the state as a whole is concerned, the supremacy of its sovereignty remains undisputed. Therefore, the state has the capacity to make laws, serve as the only representative of all people in its territory, and enter into relations with other sovereign states and even start wars. If under the system of absolute monarchy, emperors and kings can claim that "I have supremacy in this state," now the opposite, that is, "the state has supremacy in its territory," holds true. However, in recent years, a significant change has been occurring in this regard. Take the European Union as an example: it is a supranational organization with the capacity of directly interfering with the affairs of its member states, and the laws adopted by the European Parliament are binding upon all its member states. Even a citizen of any member state of the European Union has the right to institute a legal proceeding against his government with the European Court of Justice, which may pass judgment on any individual and whose judgment shall be binding and enforced by the governments of all member states. One of the preconditions to becoming a member of the European

Union is the abolition of the death sentence. Such a supranational organization having its own legislature, executive, and judiciary was unheard of back in the middle of the twentieth century. Indeed, the European Union has increasingly greater power. Unlike the United Nations, which due to its great scale and coverage is unable to run like a government, the European Union succeeds in this regard. And this is not by mere chance, because historically European countries once submitted to the Vatican, which was exactly a supranational organization and had great authority over European countries in religious affairs as well as some secular affairs connected with religion. This serves as the historical context of the successful establishment of the European Union.

In China, however, sovereignty is still put above human rights. Although China has entered into many international conventions and declarations, their provisions are not directly turned into domestic laws. For example, China entered into the international conventions on human rights, which were signed by the Chinese government, but they remain unapproved by the National People's Congress because if they were ratified, China would have to honor the obligations in those conventions. If we examine what these conventions say about the various civil rights and restrictions on government's power, we will know their significance to China. Ratification of these conventions would mean that the country's sovereignty would be subject to the restrictions of the rules of conduct established by the international communities, depriving the country's ruling authorities of the license to do whatever they like domestically. In addition, a state's sovereignty is also subject to other less mandatory constraints, such as the international response to a state's domestic and foreign activities. In fact, the Chinese government itself has a precedent of criticizing and even condemning the domestic policies of other countries, such as the apartheid in South Africa. Today China seems to be more in favor of the doctrines of "noninterference in the internal affairs of states" and "sovereignty taking priority over human rights," and is in resolute opposition to any attempt of the Western countries to interfere in China's domestic affairs on the pretext of human rights. This is obviously self-contradictory. I believe, in the course of time, the subordination of sovereignty to some fundamental principles will be increasingly accepted. Isn't the reason for the establishment of and submission to the government that it promises a better life than in the absence of it? The government exists to safeguard liberty, not to exploit or deprive liberty. The government's abolition of the custody and repatriation system last year was a good action, and it answered the call of the people, but it is far from enough. We hope the government will make more effort and do a better job in this respect.

Trend 4: Global Expansion of Judicial Powers

The fourth trend of constitutional government is the expansion of judicial powers worldwide in the past half a century. The state's power is usually divided into executive, legislative, and judicial powers exercised by the executive, the legislature, and the judiciary, respectively. In many countries with separation and balance of powers, like the United States, there is a dynamic change in the position of each of the three powers as time passes. In the early period after the founding of the United States, the legislature had the greatest power and the executive and judiciary were in weaker positions. Early in its operation, the Supreme Court performed its duties in the basement of the Capitol Building because it did not have its own office; this reflected the insignificance of the judiciary. In the first half of the twentieth century, the executive held a dominant position. And after the 1950s, the balance of power has tilted toward the judiciary, and with constant expansion of its authority, it has become the most prominent of the three powers.

In the basic model for the exercise of judicial power, the disputing parties submit and cross-examine their evidence and argue with each other in front of a neutral third party who will make a judgment. In the United States, as observed by Alexis de Tocqueville as early as 170 years ago, all political issues will sooner or later change into legal issues to be solved in courts. The courts not only adjudicate on ordinary civil and criminal cases but are also an immense political force that maintains the balance of power between the legislature and the executive. When it comes to disputes concerning the transfer of power, violence is sometimes the only solution in quite a few countries, but in the United States, they are always solved through the judiciary. This supreme position enjoyed by the judiciary is powerfully attractive to people of high caliber. William Howard Taft, when he served as the president of the United States, did not think this position represented the highest actualization of his self-worth and set it his ultimate goal to become the chief justice of the country—which he achieved in the end.

Indeed, the most excellent of Americans generally do not have much interest in becoming the country's president because the president is elected, and to be the host of the White House, presidential candidates have to win the support of voters by showing all kinds of intimacy with them, including many things that these most excellent persons feel it beneath their dignity to do. Besides, the term of office is another factor. The president has a term of four years and often has to run for the second term by beginning a new round of playing up to voters. It is a disgrace if the president fails to win the second term, and even if he wins, after the second term he is again a "commoner." For example, after leaving the White House, Jimmy Carter went back to running his farm while Bill Clinton went on the lecture circuit.

The best profession is one that enables an individual to engage in it for an entire lifetime—and the profession of judges is for a lifetime. Furthermore, the difference between the president and a Supreme Court justice is also reflected in the way their powers are exercised. The executive power follows an order–compliance pattern, and although it may be based on internal discussion and demonstration, its external manifestation is very simple. In comparison, the way the judge exercises his power involves very complicated reasoning and the mobilization of knowledge and wisdom, a process that is highly satisfying to an intelligent mind. A justice of the U.S. Supreme Court once said that the only gratifying thing about being an appellate judge—the name for a judge of any appellate court and the Supreme Court—is that you can air different views from your colleagues. The nine justices of the Supreme Court jointly adjudicate cases and may have different views among them. The final judgment is made following complicated argumentation and majority rule. Justices whose views differ from those aired in the majority opinion may draft, issue, and publish their own versions of judgment; however, these do not have legal effect. Oliver Wendell Holmes was an extraordinary justice in U.S. history. He was best at writing dissenting judgments all his life, presenting himself as an exemplary dissenter. Diversity is always advocated in U.S. society. Once the community in which he was living proposed the building of a path, and it was agreed by every resident except himself. When asked about the reason, he simply said, "I have no particular reason of opposition. I just don't like everyone agreeing on something." As shown by published collections of his opinions as justice, he held minority views in most cases, but these views were later found to have prophetic historical insight.

With social changes over time, Holmes's minority opinions became mainstream judicial views. Therefore, the judicial profession is a highly challenging profession, where one has to think every day. The prospect of being a justice is indeed exciting. Holmes served as a justice of the Supreme Court until he was ninety-one years old. By then, with his black robe and white beard, hair, and eyebrows, he was a nationally influential figure famous for his knowledge, thought, and wisdom. His example illustrates how and why the judicial profession is highly attractive to excellent people in the United States. Even today, it is still true that the brightest minds are more likely to be found among judges rather than presidents. It is exactly because the judicial circle is composed of a large number of eminent figures that the judiciary has obtained the right to exercise judicial review of executive actions and even legislation.

After World War II, many countries began to introduce the kind of judicial review system initiated in the United States. This system is now as widespread as McDonald's and Hollywood movies. No wonder that sometimes globalization is equated with Americanization. In the case of Germany, its Federal Constitutional Court and Federal Court of Justice (supreme court) are both located in Karlsruhe, a small city with a population of 100,000. The constitutional court was established in accordance with the Basic Law of the Federal Republic of Germany after World War II. According to the Basic Law and the subsequently adopted Law of the Federal Constitutional Court, in a case heard by a common court where it cannot be advanced unless the constitutionality of relevant laws in question is established, then the court— and the parties concerned (as amended later)—may submit the case to the Federal Constitutional Court to decide whether the relevant laws are constitutional or not. The judgment passed by the Federal Constitutional Court is final and unchallengeable. The Constitutional Court's precedents are binding on similar cases, as per British and U.S. models. In addition, the profound influence of U.S. Supreme Court decisions on Germany's constitution and judiciary is also reflected in the content of the Constitutional Court's judgments. Although traces of judicial review in Germany's constitution before World War II can be found, it is obviously due to U.S. influence that the judiciary has come to have such great authority, especially the authority of judicial review over the constitutionality of legislation. This important influence of American constitutionalism upon German constitutional development is thus described by a German scholar:

> Through these contacts [with the U.S. constitutional jurisprudence and judicial circle], extensive academic works were written in Germany on almost all aspects of constitutional theories and practices in the United States. With cooperation between German scholars and their U.S. counterparts in the study of comparative law; enthusiastic discussions among visiting scholars, professors, and practicing lawyers in universities and professional associations; and easily accessible U.S. legal literature, Germany's constitutional theories and practice were strongly influenced by those of the United States. The constitutional system of no other country was held in so high esteem by German jurists.[5]

In addition to Germany, the U.S. judicial review system has also had an extensive and profound influence on almost the whole of Western Europe. In those countries that have traditionally doubted the value of the judiciary, such judicial review exercised by the constitutional court reestablishes the authority of the judiciary and transforms their political landscape, especially the relationship among their judicial, legislative, and executive branches.

Another sign of the expansion of judicial powers is that in an increasing number of countries, executive and legislative powers are often exercised using the judicial approach. A public hearing is just such an example. In Guangdong, which is on the frontline of political reform in China, there is an encouraging development in this regard, that is, the provincial people's congress often holds public hearings on major matters. Once even an environmental protection head was fired through a public hearing. In a way, a public hearing is a quasi-judicial method. It is an application of judicial practices in the exercise of legislative or executive powers. Since public hearings follow a format similar to a judicial procedure, it is very necessary that legal personnel or personnel with a legal background participate in the process.

Significance in the Chinese Context

The four global trends we have surveyed up to now are all closely related to China's reality. Since time does not allow me to discuss the connections one by one in detail, I will return to the subject of legislation and the judiciary that I am more concerned with and will provide a brief analysis of the implication of their relationship for building a constitutional government in China.

The first aspect is that we have arrived at a better understanding of the flaws of China's current constitutional system, particularly the People's Congress system. Some flaws, such as the absence of deliberation in the People's Congress system, are obvious. Deliberative politics requires careful consideration and debate by the legislature, but the People's Congress does not have debate, nor is it suitable for debate because its deputies are too numerous for effective debates. (In contrast, the parliaments of other countries usually have 500 or 600 members, making it possible to discuss and deliberate on some matters effectively.) Besides, the duration of the People's Congress is very short, usually twelve or thirteen days every year, and it was even shortened to less than ten days this year, despite a major legislative event—the adoption of an amendment to the constitution. The two or three days thus eliminated are said to have saved several million yuan. As far as I am concerned, it would save even more money if the Congress were not held in the first place!

The parliaments in Western countries have sessions for six or even nine months every year, and parliament members are professional meeting attendees who come together to review the government's budget, taxation, and other matters; this is how they effectively supervise the government. The Chinese government's spending of taxpayers' money, as revealed by Mr. Li Jinhua, auditor general of the National Audit Office, is indeed shockingly arbitrary! The loopholes in government spending make us taxpayers unsure where our money goes. A top official who returned to his hometown and found the local road not good enough ordered a fiscal allotment of several hundreds of millions to overhaul the road; a finance minister attending his alma mater's centennial celebration gave the school a gift of eighty million from the national treasury. Dear friends, you know these expenditures were not from their own pockets but from state revenue, ultimately from the taxpayers' own pockets! Has the People's Congress done anything to investigate such arbitrariness in fiscal spending? It cannot do so without holding sessions and having those officials appear for questioning. And how can such work be done without allowing a considerable amount of time?

Of course, the People's Congress system has other obvious flaws, the most prominent among them being the relationship between People's Congress deputies and the people. Be it the National People's Congress or provincial or municipal people's congresses, their deputies are appointed by relevant organs, and they are not representatives of the people, elected by the people. The essence of putting the people first is enabling everyone to participate in the political life of the country, and the foundation for that is the right of citizens to elect their own representatives to speak for them in the legislature. If the deputies to the People's Congress are not elected by the people and there is no relationship of agency between them and the people, they have no reason to be accountable to the people.

There is a nongovernmental organization called Sunny Constitutional Government. It recently arranged a small symposium on the role of the People's Congress and the building of constitutional government in China. It invited several deputies to the People's Congress of Haidian District of Beijing to share their experiences in their positions, and I also had the pleasure of being invited there as a commentator. I said at the symposium that it was indeed something to be celebrated that I finally had the honor to meet deputies to the People's Congress because usually they are simply nowhere to be seen, and you do not know what they are up to and have no way to check whether they are doing things for the people. We all know that this state of things is not normal or acceptable, and it is imperative to reform the People's Congress system, rectify major deficiencies in law, and enable legal professionals to participate in legislation. The Civil Code of the People's Republic of China, for example, with its numerous laws on special subjects, could not be successfully deliberated upon without the participation of personnel with relevant expertise.

Of course, we should also note that the system is changing gradually for the better, and many lawyers have shown intentions to become deputies to the People's Congress. Not long ago, I came to Guangzhou for the Third National Lawyers' Forum, and at the forum I talked with lawyers from across the country. Many of them have very big political aspirations, which I think is a good thing. I also think that with the rise of the lawyer group, there will be an increasing proportion of them in the People's Congress, and this will play a very positive role in changing that body's member composition, expertise level, and meeting procedures, and improving the quality of its legislation.

The second aspect of the judiciary and legislation is that judicial reform should be deepened to establish a truly impartial judicial system that can effectively restrict the government's exercise of power. This perhaps easily calls to mind administrative litigation. Indeed, administrative litigation is an effective mechanism to check the government's executive power within China's existing legal framework. However, the bad news is that in recent years the acceptance rate of administrative litigation cases nationwide has shown a downward trend, and ordinary citizens are also increasingly reluctant to take legal action against the government. So what's the reason then? We once flaunted to the world that the plaintiff success rate of administrative litigation cases reached up to 30 percent, something that was considered by people outside China to be an extraordinary achievement. They did not know, however, that if there were not great injustices involved, the plaintiffs would not have filed the cases in the first place! And even this plaintiff success rate of 30 percent should not make us optimistic as we all know that in many matters the judiciary fails to administer justice as it is supposed to. Why in disputes related to housing demolition and relocation do citizens often choose to take to the street or stage a sit-in before the government seat and in some cases even resort to self-immolation in Tiananmen Square rather than simply file an administrative litigation? The reason is that housing demolition and relocation projects are often jointly planned by enterprises and the government, motivated by mutual self-interest. In such matters, the role played by the court is only that of a servant of the government whose job is simply to translate the government's will into a legal judgment and order the relevant housing to be razed to the ground. Such a judicial system cannot reassure the people.

However, currently we have an opportunity: China may reform its administrative division. According to information disclosed on the Internet, China plans to increase the number of its provinces from thirty-two to fifty. This will bring a radical change to China's map of administrative divisions, where Guangdong will not be the same Guangdong because Shantou will be merged with southern Fujian to form Chaoshan Province, and Yuebei and the southern parts of Hunan and Jiangxi will be merged to form Nanling Province. This scheme, however, was later refuted by an official of the Ministry of Civil Affairs who said that it was only a proposal put forward by scholars, and it was far from implementation. At any rate, it is a very good proposal and a great opportunity, especially for China's judicial reform because if the scheme is implemented, the original thirty-three provincial entities will remain in the form of thirty-three higher courts, thus forming a separation between executive power and judicial power in terms of jurisdiction and giving judicial independence a firm guarantee. By then, when we open China's atlas, the first page will be the map of its administrative divisions, and the second page will be the map of its judicial divisions. Of course, judicial reform involves many more aspects than this. As for how my own efforts in this regard are concerned, they can summed up in two words—"judicial independence," which is what I pursue. Only judicial power can place powerful, effective restrictions on the government's power and give hope to the people, because this will address a serious problem in China's political arrangement: the absence of a neutral arbitrator between the people and the government.

Finally, I want to briefly discuss freedom of the press and how to safeguard it. It seems a little premature to talk about freedom of speech, just like the case during the three-year great famine in the early 1960s when the people were so starved that they had no thoughts at all about a sumptuous banquet but rather wished simply for a well-stuffed stomach. However, if we take a look at our constitution, we will see a different picture, where we are explicitly granted the freedom of the press, which is not yet reflected in our actual reality. This state of affairs demonstrates an "absence of constitutional government in the presence of a constitution." Of course, the system cannot be put right at one go but has to be advanced gradually, and although today's situation cannot be described as good, we do have some encouraging trends in sight. As I mentioned earlier, there are elements in the press that have never slackened their efforts to strive for the freedom of the press, and in them we see hope for the future. In addition, there are also other factors that are affecting the press environment, such as the commercial aspect of running newspapers. Be it *Guangzhou Daily, Yangcheng Evening News*, or *Southern Metropolitan Daily*, taking the local newspapers as examples, they all rely heavily on advertising. Advertising revenue is what sustains the existence of newspapers and decides whether they do well. Why do businesses choose to advertise in some newspapers while avoiding others? The reason is that they know what newspapers are mostly bought by private customers, and know that some newspapers are bought and read while others are not read, even when available free of charge. The fact that businesses choose to advertise in popular newspapers is an opportunity for the press circle. This is the commercial factor. However, there is also a political component. And the contradiction between the two is giving the press circle a hard time today. This "hard time," though, is a good sign of coming changes; a stagnant, lifeless press environment as it was in the past is what's truly horrible. The developments in Guangzhou point to a new future for the press in China.

In addition to the commercial factor, an improved judicial system will also play a positive role in creating a freer press environment. Yu Qiuyu, best known for his "cultural journey," recently embarked on a tough "legal journey" by accusing a critic of his of defamation and claiming RMB 100,000 in compensation for psychological damage.[6] An exclusive interview with Yu was carried by *Southern Weekend*.[7] Yu is a public figure, and frankly, as such, his reaction to media criticism is disappointing. The central issue of the lawsuit he filed recently was exactly the media's criticism. In the case, Yu accused Xiao Xialin of defamation because the latter wrote an article accusing him of turning culture into something of a commodity for fame and profit because he praised the culture of Shenzhen in exchange for a gift of luxury real estate from the city. Yu, in response, asserted that he had never received any luxury real estate. The court, however, rejected Yu's claim. The court is a place where reason rules. What do you guess is the reason given by the judge for the rejection? The judge reasoned, following something of the principle of proportionality, that Xiao, the author accused, had no means to confirm what he wrote about, that it was not feasible for him to travel a long distance to Shenzhen to check it for the purpose of writing an article, and that, in any case, it involves personal privacy. The defendant's lawyer was very smart and sought the testimony of Mr. Li Ming from the Chinese Academy of Social Sciences, who testified that "at the time, it was circulated among the cultural circle that Yu received luxury real estate." With this testimony, the judge thinks that the defendant's assertion is pardonable because, after all, the luxury real estate story was not fabricated by him. He simply mistook a rumor for the real thing and wrote it in his article. And Yu, as a public figure, should also have some tolerance for damage occasionally arising from unintentional misrepresentation. Of course, Xiao Xialin should be criticized for spreading unconfirmed, negative information about others, but this is not cause enough for a claim of RMB 100,000 in compensation.

Anyway, this case's judgment has given freedom of the press in China new hope. At the same time, it should be noted that China's judicial system is far from being in good order or consistent in its criteria, and cases with similar circumstances may face different judgments in different courts. In cases related to entertainment celebrities or figures like Yu Qiuyu, the court may be comparatively more detached, but when it comes to cases where the plaintiff has a certain political background, the possibility for the defendant—including the press—to win is very low.

Conclusion

In this discussion I have explored four major global trends related to constitutional government and their significance for China's legislative and judicial development. The example presented at the beginning of my speech about the disillusionment accompanying efforts to establish constitutional government in China illustrates that in this time-honored vast country, the introduction of a major system cannot be completed in one move but must be a gradual process. Some small countries have made great achievements in constitutional government over a relatively short period of effort, but in China, with its huge population and long historical tradition, it is much more difficult to carry out the same kind of reform. However, this difficulty is exactly the reason why we should apply our best efforts rather than use it as a pretext for inaction. Before this speech, I spoke with friends seated in the first row, and they expressed their support for what I have done in the past and gave praise especially for the letter jointly signed by five scholars, including me, and submitted to the Standing Committee of the National People's Congress. I don't think I really deserve their praise because the revocation of the more than twenty-year-old Measures for Custody and Repatriation of Urban Vagrants and Beggars by the State Council should be attributed not so much to the scholars' advocacy as to strong public opinion and demand expressed by millions of people in various media and particularly on the Internet, which formed a force and voice that the government could not ignore. Therefore, I would like to cite a line from our national anthem as our slogan: "Everyone must cry out until the very end." [*Loud applause*]

Of course, to make constitutional government a reality in China, just crying out is not enough, and we must make more intelligent and constructive efforts. There is a tendency in China to reject compromise, not only in the government but on the part of citizens as well. Yet sometimes it is very important for us to arrive at a compromise when necessary, with a rational attitude, especially when we face social ills in reality. I believe, with Guangdong pioneering in the frontline and people in various roles and professions having their voices heard and putting forth their own share of efforts, the prospects for constitutional government are still optimistic. Let us join together to make this exciting goal a reality! Thank you all! [*Loud applause*]

CHAPTER FIVE

REMARKS GIVEN AT THE
NEW WESTERN HILLS SYMPOSIUM

I am from the Law School of Peking University and a colleague of that professor [Gong Xiantian], just mentioned by President Gao [Gao Shangquan], who wrote an open letter against the adoption of the Real Right Law.[1] We

Author's note: After the Xinglin Villa meeting, the original transcripts of the meeting were widely circulated online, sparking a wide-ranging debate, especially regarding my remarks in the meeting. As a result of those fierce criticisms—more precisely, [the Cultural Revolution–style] criticisms—I feel that it is still difficult to have a rational discussion on the issues raised in my speech in present-day China. The fact that there is no way to have such a discussion reflects one of the biggest obstacles to China's progress. I have made some changes to the original transcripts in order to more accurately express my views and also to correct some errors. The basic ideas expressed in my speech were not changed. See my blog (http://blog.sina.com.cn/s/blog_48866320010006kn.html November 8, 2006).

Editor's note: The Chinese version of this chapter is based on the author's remarks at the symposium "China's Macroeconomics and Reform Trends," held at the Xinglin Villa in the Western Hills outside of Beijing on March 4, 2006. This symposium was later called the "New Western Hills meeting" (新西山会议). The main participants of the meeting included liberal scholars such as Zhang Weiying (张维迎), professor of economics at Peking University; Sun Liping (孙立平), professor of sociology at Tsinghua University; Yang Dongping (杨东平), professor of education at Beijing Institute of Technology; Shi Xiaomin (石小敏), economist at China Society of Economic Reform; and Li Shuguang (李曙光), professor of law at China University of Political Science and Law. Shortly after the meeting, the meeting minutes were leaked and published online, sparking a heated debate on the Internet. Leftist websites such as the "Banner of Mao Zedong" and "Utopia" launched critiques of the New Western Hills meeting. The prominent economist Ma Bin (马宾) wrote an open letter to Hu Jintao and the Politburo Standing Committee, accusing He Weifang and other like-minded liberal intellectuals of making "pro-American and anti-China traitorous remarks" in the meeting.

are quite a unique pair in the school, especially during the dissertation defense of law students, when he would choose the seat at the left end while I would sit at the right end. This often causes big trouble for the students who keep looking to the left and then to the right, at a loss on how to answer our questions, because our viewpoints tend to be diametrically opposite.

Up to now we have talked about quite a few issues in broad terms, including the issue pointed out by Professor Li Shuguang. As for the various challenges faced by China's reform agenda, I think there are two background issues that may be added here. The first is that, as Professor Li Shuguang has noted, these challenges come as the natural result of radical economic reforms not accompanied by political reforms. In his analysis of the French Revolution, Alexis de Tocqueville observes that great revolutions and social chaos in many countries were often triggered by nothing other than reforms themselves, and that the otherwise undisturbed social order may be thrown into confusion and violence by reform measures. If a major reform is not well thought out and planned, it will inevitably be unable to strike a balance among different concerns and even intensify existing conflicts, thus leading to social unrest. Therefore, China's reform must be pushed ahead comprehensively; otherwise it will give rise to problems of serious consequence. This issue merits some second thoughts, as do some slogans that were feasible in the past, such as "crossing the river while feeling for stones" and "do not argue."[2]

The second background issue is that, as we can see in the discussion about the general direction of China's reform—and to use readily understood terms of reference—people on the left often take a clear-cut stand under the banner of socialism, calling for, among other things, a return to the legislative tradition pioneered by the Soviet Union. They may say so without any risk, and not only that, they may sharply criticize what they perceive as a deviation from the path of socialism and inspire some misgivings on the part of the country's leadership. The solicitation of public opinions about the Real Right Law after the publication of the open letter against its adoption attested to this. In contrast, people who stand on the right often beat about the bush and speak vaguely about their advocacies, and are sometimes even very timid, for the simple reason that in the current political environment, they simply cannot come straight to their point. As the old saying goes, "When the map is unrolled, the dagger is revealed." Our dagger is so thickly wrapped in maps that we cannot draw it out to arm us, and indeed, it is forbidden to draw it out in the first place. So where are we going? We have a common goal, a path for which advocacy is forbidden and yet one that the country will inevitably follow—a path toward, for example, a multiparty system, freedom of the press, and true democracy safeguarding civil liberty, like what is practiced in Taiwan. We are all of the belief that this is the direction China should go, but for now we cannot express this belief openly. As a result, whenever we on the right get into a fight with those on the left, the losing party is also us, and that is why leftist preaching runs so rampant on the Internet. We do not have the platform on which to make our case, and so our cause has remained a losing battle up to now. During all these years, many people committed to this cause, including my seniors and peers here, have made great efforts especially regarding China's economic and political reform, but it has to be admitted that this process has indeed been very difficult and arduous.

Therefore, I side with Professor [Zhang] Weiying and other friends here in their call for full expression of intelligent thoughts. In this regard, I think a small community could be formed with some sort of division of labor. The scholars can present what is on their minds in a clearer and more definite way. If I have a certain social ideal, I make it a point to advocate fully for it, regardless of how this pursuit will be received and perceived. In my several speeches, which are widely circulated on the Internet, I explicitly advocate that the CCP split into two factions and that the military be under the command of the state, both of which I think are matters of fundamental principle. I make these proposals in a positive, constructive way. I also call for the freedom of the press, and an open letter addressed to the CCP Politburo Standing Committee and jointly signed by thirteen scholars, including me, was published in which we clearly expressed our views on the matter.[3] In the letter, we hold that the relevant government departments infringed upon freedom of expression and trampled on law. Furthermore, we state that it is organs without any legal status that have an absolute control of the media, and we doubt the validity of such a power system. This kind of act [banning] is in gross violation of the principle of constitutionalism and the provision of the country's constitution that any organization, political party, and individual shall carry out activities within the constraints of the constitution. The CCP Central Propaganda Department, the Communist Youth League Central Committee Propaganda Department, and even the CCP itself are all unregistered. In a country ruled by law, any organization must be a registered legal person to exercise any power and to have the legal capacity to sue or defend in court. However, in China, the CCP, a political party, does not meet this requirement at all. We have been members for many years, more than twenty years in my case, but it is not a properly registered legal entity. What is the power exercised by such a political party? It is power beyond law and a serious violation of the constitution and law. With this state of things, the leadership's advocacy of the rule of law is nothing but an insincere slogan. President Hu Jintao once emphasized that the National People's Congress and all levels of local people's congresses should rectify all unconstitutional and illegal acts, but given the existence of unregulated power beyond law, the so-called rectification of unconstitutional and illegal acts is only empty talk.

Will explicit and definite expression of views facilitate the formation of a rational discourse on reform? Some people holding the view that the reform has deviated from its proper path certainly have their own case, just as [Sun] Liping observed right now. It is not right to simplistically label these critics of the reform as antireformists; instead, sincere efforts should be made to investigate and analyze the reasons behind these criticisms. Meanwhile, the reform agenda should also be carefully examined to rectify inappropriate measures introduced in the name of reform. Those shouldering the mission of reform should continue to advance it amidst difficulties and misunderstandings and be more careful in their speech and deed. In addition, there is also the need for another group of people who do not stand at the opposite side of the establishment but have their own different views, and they may play a positive role in the formation of a better balance among different stances. In the past, this kind of third party was often deemed an antagonistic force. Even today there are still people emphasizing the existence of "contradictions between ourselves and the enemy," who like to sing out the alarm that foreign hostile forces are uniting and conspiring with some domestic groups. What is most alarming, indeed, is exactly this class struggle–charged ideology. Those who belong to what's called the "third" force are not really enemies but friends of the ruling authority. We all love this country and are worried about some of the ills we see in it, and we speak our minds because we love it. Therefore, I truly wish that a mechanism for constructive dialogue among different voices would be established.

In what follows, I would like to briefly survey several major problems related to the rule of law, because there is no time for elaboration. First, the power structure is highly disordered and a far cry from a true rule-of-law or constitutional model. For example, the tangle concerning the relationships between the CCP and the National People's Congress, between the CCP and the judiciary, and between the CCP and the government has reached a point where it must be unraveled. Professor Yang Dongping just mentioned the question of what is the biggest problem of education. I think the answer can also be found here: the primary question as relates to the relationship between the CCP and education is whether there is the need for universities to have their own CCP committees. That the overall power structure is unconstitutional is the first and the most consequential problem.

Second, the People's Congress is antiparliamentary. The National People's Congress is not so much a congress as a party—the greatest in the world at that—which is joined by deputies every year in the name of participating in the administration and discussion of state affairs. But as a matter of fact, they are there simply to "vote on" issues that have already been decided beforehand. Right now I received an SMS text message telling me that the duration of this year's National People's Congress sessions has been shortened to nine and a half days. I think it would be even better if it were not held at all. A mere look at how the National People's Congress performs its duty to financially supervise the government will show that in its present operation, it cannot be said to be a parliament at all.

Third, the political rights enshrined in article 35 of the constitution are generally not guaranteed, such as the freedom of association, of procession and demonstration, and of religious belief. These basic human rights exist only on paper and are not guaranteed in reality due to the absence of specific mechanisms to fulfill them or to the presence of a number of more specific laws and even administrative policies that are designed to gut them.

Fourth, there is no judicial independence. In recent years, the position of China's judicial system has been falling steadily. Not long ago, it was even reported that Xiao Yang, the president of the Supreme Court, was reporting to Zhou Yongkang, Politburo member and minister of public security, on the work of the Supreme Court, something that cannot be found in any country in the world that is ruled by law—having the chief justice report his work to the head of the ministry of public security! How then did this occur here? The arrangement was made during the Sixteenth National Congress of the CCP, which made a number of consequential adjustments to the country's political structure. A prominent aspect is the decreased independence of the judiciary. In recent years, the CCP has intensified rather than reduced its interference in the judiciary.

Fifth, the state's administration is divided and increasingly confusing. The Supreme People's Court announced that any case involving government-initiated demolition and relocation will not be accepted. However, whether the court is to accept a case or not is provided for in the law, and the court's announcement rejects cases that should be accepted according to the law. This is an instance of red tape prevailing over law.

Sixth, the collective ownership system, especially as relates to the land in rural areas and which most jeopardizes the interests of farmers, must be changed toward privatization in the next step, because private ownership is the foundation of civil law.

Seventh, there is no adequate guarantee of transaction security, which is the precondition for a sound and mature market economy. This also involves judicial independence, without which the courts will be under the sway of the local governments and rendered unable to adjudicate on cases in accordance with a unified set of standards. In an environment where the interpretation of a contract clause in a dispute must take into consideration the attitude of the local authorities, it is simply impossible to feel assured about transaction security.

In a word, China's economic reform has become increasingly intertwined with legal issues. We have all seen this trend, and this meeting is held precisely to highlight the need for us to join together to seriously address this problem.

PART III

The Expansion of Legal Education and the Legal Profession

China's Legal Profession

The Emergence and Growing Pains of a Professionalized Legal Class

The process of constructing the rule of law in China has been ongoing since the late 1970s. During this transitional "post–Mao Zedong" era, many factors have influenced China's quest for the rule of law, such as still-viable socialist theories; the historical inertia of various institutions built on these theories; the emerging market economy's need for a unified, stable, and predictable legal system; the directional uncertainties posed by the diversity of imported knowledge; and the difficulties posed by a virtually static political system.

In this chapter, I wish to emphasize how the current difficulties we face in building institutions relate to China's long and unique history. I focus especially on how it has affected dispute resolution, the lack of a professional judicature and legal experts, and the lack of precedential force in adjudication. This is the backdrop against which the rule of law must develop in China today. It is also the backdrop for discussions centered on the construction of a modern legal system and the difficulties this endeavor has faced in the past century. In analyzing these difficulties, I focus on issues in legal education, as it is one of the most important factors in molding the legal profession.

Part of the reason I wish to explore this topic is that, once more, a nationalist tide has recently risen, and certain scholars have specifically advocated that China reconstruct its modern political-legal system along Confucian political principles. Although it is not abnormal in many countries to have

Editor's note: An earlier English version of this chapter first appeared in the *Columbia Journal of Asian Law* 19, no. 1 (Spring-Fall, 2005): 138–51. The version here includes some stylistic editorial changes.

occasional tides of anti-Western sentiment, the mainstream of Chinese legal studies today, especially in areas such as civil law, criminal law, and criminal procedure law, is still based on Western knowledge and theories. It is, however, necessary to reflect upon the history of governance in China, not merely because of its historical significance but also because doing so will enhance our capacity for critical thinking in this age of intellectual "free trade." If this inquiry serves no other purpose, at least we will not become "lost lawyers."[1]

Traditional Background: The Contrast between China and the West

China's premodern society, in spite of its long history, failed to produce a legitimate and professionalized class of lawyers. Here, what set China apart from the West was its peculiar system of selecting officials, the impact this system had on the society's social structure, and the unique legal processes that resulted. For a millennium, until the abolition of the civil service examination in 1905, officials had been selected through examinations. Although the imperial examination system represented the traditional model of the knowledgeable ruling the ignorant, it failed to promote the diffusion of legal knowledge, and actually impeded it by hewing closely to the standards of Confucianism and poetic techniques. In the words of Max Weber:

> The Chinese examinations did not test any special skills, as do our modern national and bureaucratic examination regulations for jurists, medical doctors, or technicians. Nor did the Chinese examinations test the possession of charisma, as do the typical "trials" of magicians and bachelor leagues. . . . The examinations of China tested whether or not the candidate's mind was thoroughly steeped in literature and whether or not he possessed the ways of thought suitable to a cultured man and resulting from cultivation in literature. These qualifications held far more specifically with China than with the German humanist gymnasium.[2]

Though the individuals who succeeded in these examinations were subsequently tasked with the judgment and resolution of disputes, these officials' judicial activities did not contribute to the growth and development of independent and specialized Chinese legal knowledge because of the narrow focus of the officials' knowledge and background.[3]

As such, traditional Chinese legal concepts arose directly from a judicial process dominated by laymen. County officials usually had private secretaries help them decide cases.[4] The latter's training, however, was largely technical in nature. Secretaries thus did not pay attention to the inherent logic of law, such as the rules by which cases should be decided and the difference between legal and moral argumentation. At the same time, though secretaries played an important role in deciding cases and making policy, they focused more on helping their masters than strictly and precisely applying legal principles. They generally balanced all of the factors in a case, applying the law when favorable to their masters and ignoring the law when it was unfavorable.

As Qu Tongzu has noted, "Those secretaries studied law only to help their masters to decide cases, and they never intended to study law systematically."[5] In the middle of the Qing Dynasty, legal secretaries were sarcastically said to be "saving the living not the dead, saving the officials not the people, saving the important not the obscure, saving the old not the new."[6] Furthermore, as these secretaries were only assistants and were not responsible for any judicial decisionmaking, they were reluctant to fight for justice in any particular case.

In Western history, the emergence of legal professionals as an independent group originated from restricted access to the legal profession. The profession was based on the pursuit of profit, and according to American jurist Richard Posner, legal development was merely a side product of this profit-seeking cartel. As Posner remarks, "Professional ideology is a result of the way in which the members of the profession work, the form and content of their careers, the activities that constitute their daily rounds, in short, the economic and social structure of the profession."[7] While a body of specialized knowledge is indispensable for a profession to attain wider social resources, the way legal professionals work and the formality and nature of their work are also important sources of legitimacy.[8] Judges apply strict legal procedures to cases and make decisions without interference. Those decisions become authoritative if they are based on procedural validity. Such principles are often taken for granted in the West.

In contrast, judges in China were not lawyers and rarely received specialized training in law.[9] When they dealt with disputes or cases, there was no certainty of law. Rather, they applied a combination of law, moral guidelines, and community customs, none of which were that different from one another. When local officials handled cases, it was unlikely that Chinese judges would determine that a norm applied because of a normative structure defined by a hierarchy of related norms. At the same time, because of the judges' background and knowledge, they tended to rely on resources like Confucianism or historical works, which had no legal ramifications, in order to support their decisions. Examined from today's point of view, the records of some of the "famous trials" are more valuable for their literary or rhetorical merit than as legal documents.[10] County magistrates made decisions based on case-specific facts. They did not decide cases based on precedent or the continuity and coherence of rules established in previous cases. A French scholar, Jean Escarra, attributed this phenomenon to the inferior status of law in China's value system, in comparison to the West:

> The peoples of Western civilization have lived throughout under the Graeco-Roman conception of law. The Mediterranean spirit, while central to the patrimony of the Latin peoples, has also inspired large parts of the law of Islam, as also of the Anglo-Saxon, Germanic, and even Slavonic nations. In the West the law has always been revered as something more or less sacrosanct, the queen of gods and men, imposing itself on everyone like a categorical imperative, defining and regulating, in an abstract way, the effects and conditions of all forms of social activity. In the West there have been tribunals, the role of which has been not only to apply the law, but often to interpret it in the light of debates where all the contradictory interests are presented and defended. In the West the jurisconsults have built, over centuries, a structure of analysis and synthesis, a corpus of "doctrine" ceaselessly tending to perfect and purify the technical elements of the systems of positive law. But as one passes to the East, this picture fades away. At the other end of Asia, China has felt able to give to law and jurisprudence but an inferior place in that powerful body of spiritual and moral values which she created and for so long diffused over so many neighboring cultures. . . . Though not without juridical institutions, she has been willing to recognize only the natural order, and to exalt only the rules of morality
>   . . . Few indeed have been the commentators and theoreticians of law produced by the Chinese nation, though a nation of scholars.[11]

As was the case with Japan, China's traditional political and legal systems were transformed under pressure from Western powers. With increasing Sino-Western communications and corresponding legal disputes, Western dissatisfaction with the Chinese legal system began to mount. Thus the Treaty of Nanking and the Treaty of Humen signed after the Opium War not only demanded the cession of Hong Kong, the opening of port cities, and payment of tariffs but also explicitly provided that British citizens in China were subject only to the laws and courts of Britain, according to so-called "consular jurisdiction." For the Chinese living in the regent years of the Daoguang era (1820–50), this extraterritorial jurisdiction was not a matter of concern.[12] Rather, in their view, "It was no more than a matter of letting the barbarian rule the barbarian, which is supposed to be the most expedient solution without a fuss."[13] However, as conflicts occurred between Western countries and China, the political concept of the nation-state and the principle of sovereignty spread to China. As a result, extraterritorial jurisdiction acquired a stigma in the eyes of the country and the Chinese people as a whole.

After the Boxer Rebellion, a movement of growing strength emerged calling for Chinese legal reform according to Western standards. At the same time, extraterritorial jurisdiction became a factor that exacerbated Sino-Western conflict while protecting Western interests. Thus the Treaty of Commerce and Navigation of 1901 between China and the United Kingdom declared:

> China deems it as greatly desirable to reform its body of enacted laws and un-enacted case-laws so as to conform with the various states (of the West). The United Kingdom is ready to offer all possible assistance to facilitate China in achieving this end, and agrees to renounce the right to extra-territorial consular jurisdiction once it is satisfied that China has reformed with adequacy its body of enacted laws and un-enacted case-laws, its trial procedures, and all other relevant aspects.[14]

It was only at this point that China officially initiated legal reform. However, this early attempt had three key shortcomings. First, because the Chinese government was forced to reform, it was hard to know how sincere government efforts would be.[15] Second, as the Qing dynasty was established by the Manchu people—an ethnic minority within the greater Chinese population—long-standing conflicts between them and the Han crippled the progress of legal reform. Last and most important, officials emphasized short-term benefits over long-term efficaciousness. Basic prerequisites for successful judicial reform were brushed aside, and consequently the newly established legal system was inconsistent with China's social reality.

Nevertheless, influenced by the West's economic, political, and cultural experiences, a new political and legal system was established. The role of the missionary schools and universities established by Westerners cannot be overstated.[16] Likewise, domestic initiatives must not be ignored. Even though the Chinese government was not as zealous as certain nongovernmental advocates, more and more schools of law and politics were established, including many within national universities. When the Imperial Civil Service Examination was abolished, Western legal education was considered a close substitute, and younger generations found it especially appealing. In addition, as foreigners swarmed into China, there were more and more disputes between Chinese and foreigners. To resolve these disputes, the demand for legal professionals increased, and judicial reform and the arrival of a modern legal profession became inevitable.

The legal system continued to develop until Japan invaded China in the mid-1930s. During China's war with Japan, there was virtually no law in Chinese society. In 1945, when World War II ended, civil war broke out in China. While the war ended in 1949 with the victory of Mao Zedong and the Chinese Communist Party (CCP), social turmoil continued apace throughout the first three decades of the People's Republic of China. According to Marxism, law represents bourgeois interests and should be discarded. With the rise of Marxism in China, political discourse replaced legal discourse. In practice, law lost its autonomy and became the handmaiden of politics. As legal instrumentalism grew, Chinese law degenerated into legal anarchy. During the Cultural Revolution, law was replaced with a precarious balance between policy considerations and the capricious will of rulers. This state of anarchy lasted ten years, bringing not only unprecedented economic and humanitarian disaster but also a severe challenge to the legitimacy of CCP rule.

The Development of Legal Education in the Post-Mao Era

As a reflection of the historical lesson of the Cultural Revolution and in an effort to restructure the legitimacy of CCP rule, socialist democracy and the rule of law were proposed in the late 1970s. The past twenty years have witnessed rapid changes in the quality of legal education in China. The number of law schools has increased from 5 in 1978 to more than 300 in 2005. In 1978 there were only 600 law students in China. In 2005 Peking University Law School alone had more than 2,000 students. In 1998 the total number of university students studying law (excluding law postgraduates) reached 85,000, with an additional 29,000 students admitted that same year.[17] The progress made in legal education is evident not only in the surge of law students but also in the diversity of law degrees awarded. The majority of law students are undergraduates, but in some research-oriented universities, master's and Ph.D. candidates studying law now outnumber the undergraduates. Law is finding greater appeal among more qualified students and has now become one of the most popular majors in China.

The development of legal education has also improved the quality of the legal profession. Twenty years ago, judges had little legal education and could not be trusted with complex legal matters.[18] However, given the growing market economy and rising societal demand for an independent judiciary, legal professionals are now far better educated than their predecessors.[19] The Standing Committee of China's National People's Congress revised the Law on Judges and the Law on Procurators to introduce a unified national bar exam, further illustrating the growing importance of law. The first unified judicial exam, held in 2002, had 300,000 examinees and a 7 percent passage rate.

Given the growth in legal education, the establishment of the unified judicial exam, and the rising demand for democracy, Chinese legal professionals confront a historic opportunity, that is, the complete professionalization of lawyers in China. As a developing country in the age of globalization, China faces a number of challenges in the development of its legal profession. For one, the lack of a professional legal tradition in China weakens the development of ethical legal standards essential to a vibrant legal profession. As such, the belated professionalization of China's bar has been a process fraught with crises.

Challenges Facing Chinese Legal Education

China borrowed its method of professional legal education from Western countries. Influenced by the desire to abolish extraterritorial jurisdiction, mitigate the influence of Japan, and avoid the difficulty of transplanting common law, China adopted the Continental (European) legal model. As the Chinese legal system followed the Continental pattern, so did its style of legal education.[20] At the turn of the twenty-first century, China's legal education is up against a number of important challenges.

SYSTEM CHOICE

Like other countries that follow the Continental legal model, China focuses its legal education on statutes as opposed to case law precedent. In the early Republican Era, the goals of Chinese legal education, course design, and pedagogical method had been similar to those of Continental law. After an almost thirty-year interruption (1949–78), China's legal system again began to follow the Continental model. Even though some articles of China's constitution are colored by socialist ideology, China's civil law, criminal law, and procedural codes reflect a Continental influence. For example, the ongoing codification of China's civil code demonstrates China's acceptance of Continental methods. Contemporary Chinese legal education has also returned to the Continental pattern. Whereas American law schools admit only college graduates, Chinese law students attend law school directly after high school graduation. In terms of the goal of legal education, the primary objective is not necessarily to train professionals for legal practice but to foster cadres who work in both legal and nonlegal capacities in government service and corporate work. In addition, lecture, rather than the Socratic method, is the preferred teaching method in Chinese law schools.

Nevertheless, China's Continental methods have been influenced by some Anglo-American elements. The newly amended civil and criminal procedure laws, for example, both adopt the adversary system. China's adherence to the Continental system has waned not only in procedural law but also in substantive law. It seems that Anglo-American law is continually making inroads into Chinese legal institutions. The pursuit of comprehensive codification, an important tradition of Continental law, has recently been cast into doubt in China. Professor Jiang Ping, the former president of the China University of Political Science and Law, has suggested that "China should enact a civil code with an open spirit. The effective and efficient American legal system should be introduced into the design of property rule and contract rule of the to-be-enacted civil code."[21] As the Chinese legal system balances between the Continental pattern and the Anglo-American pattern, legal education inevitably oscillates between them as well. With ever more American legal rules and doctrines penetrating the Chinese legal system, Chinese legal education has moved closer to the Anglo-American style. Another reason for the great influence of American law on Chinese legal education is language. As the most widely used language in the world, English is the first foreign language for the majority of Chinese law students. Language is not only a tool but also a way of thinking. It is an issue of path dependency, as students are more likely to read an original legal treatise in English than in any other foreign language. As a result, there is a tendency for Chinese law students to think like common law lawyers.

Considering these influences, it is not altogether surprising that the American model has been proposed as the basis for Chinese legal education.[22] In fact, this suggestion was actualized in 1995 when the Department of Legal Education under the Ministry of Justice designed a J.M. (Master of Jurisprudence) program independent of undergraduate and graduate law degrees. In the same year, this proposal was adopted, and eight universities were granted the right to recruit J.M. students. This program has remained controversial in the past eight years.[23] The J.M. program has been criticized for its lack of clear differences from other programs offering formal legal education. The compromise of the two legal education methods resulted in chaos for China's legal education system. The debate will not end until one method is chosen over the other.

PROBLEMS OF QUANTITY

The expansion of law schools and the dramatic increase in law students mark an unusual development for legal education in China. This phenomenon reflects an increasing social demand for law students. However, it also reflects the questionable quality of Chinese legal education in three aspects. First, thanks to the weak and confusing administration by the Ministry of Education, it is very easy to establish a new law department in Chinese educational institutions without standards or requirements for faculty and facilities. As China's legal profession was separated from legal education, the profession exerts no substantial pressure on legal academia to address the low quality of Chinese law schools. Second, the explosion in the number of law students has diluted the quality of legal education on a per-student basis, undermining the reputation of judicial institutions. Third, the number of Chinese law students has grown to such an extent that the government has had to implement regulations to restrain the growth.[24]

There is no precise standard for how many lawyers a society needs. Among the G-8 nations, America has the highest percentage of lawyers while Japan claims the least. Different statistical methods, divergent attitudes toward alternative dispute resolution, and diversity of legal cultures may explain the differences across countries.[25] Nevertheless, China has far too many law students, and Chinese law schools are expanding too rapidly. This contrasts sharply with Western legal history. By setting the number of lawyers, regulating their services, and capping their fees, medieval lawyers' guilds in Europe played an important role in regulating the quality of legal services.[26] In comparison, China's current dilemma stems from two root causes: the uncontrolled explosion of Chinese legal academia and the Chinese legal profession's negligible influence on legal education.

BETWEEN AUTONOMY AND OPENNESS

China's legal community must attempt to acquire two important traits. On the one hand, law must attain autonomy; on the other hand, it must keep the door open to other academic disciplines and social sciences. Autonomy means the construction of an independent system of legal knowledge. According to Tocqueville, law is a professional discipline, and therefore not easily instilled in the greater, nonlawyer population.[27] Law has its own historical tradition, knowledge, genealogy, and methodology. The unique interpretative power of law lies in its autonomy, and law's specialized nature distinguishes it from politics and morality. In the past twenty years, Chinese legal scholars have touched on this specialized knowledge, and Chinese translations of foreign legal treatises have been ever more numerous. However, few conscious efforts toward systematic construction are made in China. Thus the Chinese legal community must work toward legal autonomy.

Similarly, legal history shows that law has never been a self-sufficient discipline and has always benefited greatly from the influence of other disciplines. Openness is essential to Chinese legal development, as the social sciences and various other disciplines play a significant role in legal academic work. Recently, the fields of anthropology, economics, and literary criticism have greatly enriched various areas of legal study. Furthermore, law is intertwined not only with academic theory but also with the world at large. Legal practice is ultimately meant to resolve disputes. This means that the law must be open to the real world. At present, Chinese society is undergoing a historic transformation. The pursuit of a market economy, the increasing demand for democratic politics, and the incremental separation of state and society have reshaped China's social structure and methods of political control. As a modern mode of governance, law continues to gain heightened legitimacy. Given such social conditions, it is important for legal academics to respond effectively and efficiently to the challenge of a transforming society. The long-standing separation between legal academia and practice has prevented China's legal practice from facilitating growth in legal theory, while the Chinese legal academic community is unable to grapple with practical legal causes and issues. The Chinese legal community as a whole must work toward bridging the gap between these currently separated disciplines.

The Western experience has seen law evolve through a dependent and derivative period to an era of independence and autonomy. According to Nonet and colleagues, as repressive law transformed into autonomous law, law has become an increasingly self-centered discipline because it has become too autonomous and is not able to respond to evolving social challenges.[28] They advocate a new legal order: responsive law. Postmodern legal theory is held in high regard by certain Chinese legal scholars. Because of postmodern legal theory's deconstructive nature, its openness to other disciplines, and its challenge to the existing social structure, the theory is widely popular among law students. Postmodern legal theory offers a distinctive perspective. However, as China is still in the process of establishing a fair and effective judicial system, postmodern legal theory is too radical a prescription for the country's current legal maladies.

Prospects and Conclusion

In the preceding discussion of issues affecting Chinese legal education and the Chinese legal profession as a whole, I have deliberately ignored the obstacles posed by China's current political system. It is, of course, a big problem. But under present circumstances, and from the standpoint of a legal scholar, the importance of the obstacles is diminishing. In fact, rule of law has become a major source of legitimacy for China's current government. The popularity of power discourse in China attests to this fact. A major part of this chapter has been devoted to a discussion of Chinese history because if one wants to build the rule of law and establish a democratic system in China—the country with the longest history of governance without the rule of law—time as well as human effort will be important elements.

In his book *Bird in a Cage*, Stanley Lubman took up the task of attempting to understand China through Chinese law.[29] By the same token, we must also observe and assess trends in Chinese legal institutions through understanding and studying Chinese society. We must not overlook the fact that Chinese legal professionals have received an education in imported knowledge and consequently apply this knowledge to create a new type of social relationship. From a long-term perspective, rule of law is the only way for China's ancient civilization to escape the historical cycle of order and chaos. As more and more Chinese citizens recognize this necessity, Chinese legal professionals should not be pessimistic, even given rule of law's uncertain future in China. Let me conclude with a saying praised by Confucius, even though it has a strong "rule-of-man" flavor: "Only if the right sort of people had charge of a country for a hundred years would it become really possible to stop cruelty and do away with slaughter."[30]

CHAPTER SEVEN

Foreign Models and Chinese Practice in Legal Education during the Reform Era

Lü: A university's academic atmosphere often has a huge influence on its students. You served as a visiting scholar at Harvard University for some time and experienced typical American or Anglo-American legal education, so I think you are well positioned to give us an informative introduction to Anglo-American legal education, like that offered by the Law School of Harvard University, as related to curriculum, sources of students, campus study, teaching methods, career directions of graduates, and so forth.

He: I did not stay there for long—only seven months—though, of course, I did get an impression of the legal education there. By the way, the term Anglo-American legal education is not quite appropriate because there are major differences between the United States and Great Britain in their legal education systems. An important characteristic of Western legal education is that it exists in rule-of-law societies, an environment that inevitably drives the development of legal education. After my return from Harvard, I was asked to give a presentation on my Harvard tour to my colleagues at the Law School of Peking University. The university is striving to develop into a world-class university, and a world-class university must have a world-class legal school. So what does it take to become a world-class law school? I was asked to share my Harvard experience with an eye to these issues. An important

Editor's note: The original Chinese version of this chapter was based on the author's interview with Lü Yaping, an editor of the Beijing University Press, in 2006 and first appeared in *Zhongguo faxue jiaoyu yanjiu* [Studies of China's legal education], no. 1 (2006). This chapter omits portions of the interview.

point is that a top legal school can only be established in a country with a strong legal and regulatory system. Few of us know what the legal education of Nepal or Tanzania is like, but most of us know one thing or two about the legal education of the United States, specifically, that it is offered by such universities as Harvard, Yale, Columbia, and Stanford.

This is so because America is the number one power in the world. So utilitarianism is also at work in the borrowing of culture—it is taken for granted that a strong country must have a strong culture. Of course, American legal education does have much to recommend itself, and the legal education offered by Harvard or Yale is indeed first rate. I think American legal education is a continuation of the traditional practice of the University of Bologna in Italy, where law is studied as a profession at the postgraduate level. This kind of framework is uncommon worldwide and has multiple benefits. First, legal education is exclusively dedicated to legal subjects—humanities education already has been completed in the undergraduate stage—with the definite objective of training legal professionals and experts, and in the three-year study, the students are only concerned with acquiring a comprehensive and systematic knowledge of the law.

The second benefit is the convergence of students with different academic backgrounds in the law school and the opportunity to see legal issues from different perspectives because graduates in whatever disciplines, however bizarre they are, can apply to law school. As we know, law is not a self-sufficient discipline, and its development has always been subject to input from other fields of knowledge. If there were not the legal thoughts contributed by Plato, Aristotle, and other Greek philosophers, Roman law would not have been so comprehensive and advanced. Romans benefited greatly from Greek philosophy, especially some abstract and natural law concepts. Enlightenment thinkers such as Locke and Montesquieu also played an important role in shaping the modern legal system, and their contributions to law are arguably even greater than those made by major jurists. In a word, American legal education is a melting pot of different kinds of expertise that serves to boost the development of legal education and legal research. I believe that it is no coincidence that for the major part of the last century, America held a leading position in the world in legal research, and this, I think, is closely related to its unique legal education system.

The legal education undertaken at the postgraduate level has still another benefit: the students are generally older. This situation suits the study of law very well because law is not pure knowledge and is closely associated with humankind's historical, social, and cultural development and the realities of daily life. And while younger people may be blessed with a better memory, they cannot rival older students in understanding the quintessence of the law.

What is law then? Law is a mechanism that develops for the purpose of solving disputes and conflicts among people, and to answer such questions as how these conflicts come into being, how to solve them effectively, and how to come up with a reasonable solution. Intelligence alone is far from enough in this endeavor; it requires life experience on the part of problem solvers. In Continental law countries, including China, a legal student usually begins the study of law at around age eighteen. Unlike in the Middle Ages, when an eighteen-year-old person was indeed an adult in every sense and might have been a parent with extensive life experience, in today's world, with the constantly increasing life expectancy, an eighteen-year-old still looks like a child; he is surely a child in his parents' eyes, and he largely deems himself a child. It is quite impossible for him to have the social experience reasonably expected of a mature adult.

This immaturity is less of an issue in America because eighteen is not the age at which students study law. A bachelor's degree is the most basic requirement of any applicant to a law school. Many students have already earned a doctor's degree in, say, economics before they apply to a law school. There is a big difference between an economist and a lawyer. We never call a businessman an economist. Most economics graduates embrace the practical business world, with only a few of them dedicating themselves to academic research in economics. Economics, in fact, is a highly theoretical subject. One does not need a degree in economics or to be certified in order to engage in the trade or any other business, but a certification is required for one to do a lawyer's work. The difference between professions that require certification and those that do not is both interesting and thought provoking. Many with doctorates in economics do not think that they are in any profession, and if they do not get a teaching position in a university, they are at a loss as to what to do next, feeling that they do not really belong to any profession. Some choose to apply to a law school, and it is only when they get a diploma in legal studies that they are assured that they are in a profession in the real sense of the word. Another example would be the study of history: the world simply does not need so many historians. So many history students turn to law after graduation.

As a result, applicants of law schools are often in their late twenties and thirties, and even in their forties, with quite a few degrees attached to their names, ready to earn a J.D. and become a lawyer and make a living by it. The classroom in a law school presents not only the convergence of different academic backgrounds but also the blending of different perspectives. In addition, there is a wide range of student ages, from fresh graduates to well-weathered people with extensive social experience. They can learn from each other both in knowledge and experience, enriching and deepening their understanding of the law as a social science. Not just the students but also the teachers can benefit greatly from their students' different backgrounds. The concept that teaching benefits teachers as well as students cannot be truer than in this case. This practice of teaching law at the postgraduate stage merits our special attention, and I will touch on this question later when talking about China's legal education.

In American legal schools, stress is placed on training in legal thinking as well as fostering the capability to handle practical legal affairs. Before entering law school, students have developed a fixed thinking pattern. Those previously studying economics are imparted with an economics mindset; those previously studying literature acquire a literary manner of thought, and so on. So after they enter law school, these students undergo a process of unlearning what is not in accord with the legal way of thinking, which they are to absorb and polish in law school.

In classroom instruction, what is called the Socratic method is used in some courses: students having already read extensively about the subject matter and arrived at an understanding of the related concepts and principles are asked by the teacher pertinent questions, and the questioning process goes on and on based on the students' answers, following the same fashion in which Socrates asked questions of Athenians on the street. For example, the students are asked how they will respond in different scenarios of dispute if they are lawyers. In these classes, students are forced to think deeply about the major issues involved, drawing on their extensive reading of monographs, precedents, and opinions of judges and lawyers. This is in keeping with the traditions of the profession and the discipline, and at the same time, it encourages innovative thinking and ingenious interpretations of and solutions to some problems.

The Socratic method is arguably the most typical teaching method used in American legal schools. Of course, there is also a place for taught courses, which account for a significant proportion of classes. The Socratic method is a very luxurious teaching method because it requires a lot of material, extensive reading, and a considerable amount of energy on the part of the teacher. And the process is time consuming, so that it often happens that the time is used up before the major issues are covered. This method therefore is criticized by some to be inefficient. However, I think the greatest value of this method lies in its enabling the student to realize that there is more than one way to look at and solve the same problem, that different things require different approaches, and that law is an art of balancing between justice and goodness. After students receive this education, they will adopt a more sophisticated way of thinking when they become lawyers or judges in the future, rather than approaching things with a fixed, oversimplifying pattern of thought. I think this is the aspect of American legal education that deserves our greatest attention.

Lü: As an example of legal education in the common law world, how does the American legal education pave the way for and interact with the country's legal profession?

He: Most noteworthy, I think, is that the legal profession in the United States is highly academic. In the confrontation model, the lawyers of both sides present their own facts, reasons, and references to specific legal provisions and precedents. In a word, the profession proceeds in an academic rather than anti-academic or anti-intellectual way. The American Bar Association's members include not only lawyers but also judges and prosecutors. They are what are called "academic lawyers." They run a periodical, which publishes legal articles and papers. In fact, many excellent legal papers in America are written by lawyers. Therefore, the American law profession is not one of "conspiring" with judges; instead, it primarily involves practitioners displaying their industry, knowledge, skills, and scholarship in the court. Those who cannot display these accomplishments are not competent lawyers. Judges often give a comprehensive elaboration on legal theories before passing judgment. It is often said that the best jurists in America are not in law schools but in courts. Passing judgment is also a form of academic pursuit and involves academic elements. This system interacts well with legal education and both challenges and boosts legal education. Court precedents themselves provide good learning material in legal schools and may have far-reaching influence on the development of legal thought and on the value orientation of the whole of legal education. In fact, many legal theories, such as sociological jurisprudence and legal realism, are closely related to the judiciary. So, first of all, we have to observe this kind of interaction between the academic and practicing worlds.

Also, we should note that classroom instruction in law schools is not isolated from but rather closely associated with the legal profession. In addition, the students have occasions to hear the voices of heavyweight figures in the legal profession because many influential judges, such as Justice Holmes, Judge Learned Hand, Justice Cardozo, and Judge Posner also taught in law schools on a part-time basis. Therefore, a new legal theory can originate in either law schools or courts, and the interaction between the two is an interesting subject. Although in China we often speak of the combination of theory and practice, those who are in the legal profession and those who are engaged in legal academic research are actually two highly incompatible groups of people, with the former accusing the latter of being too bookish and impractical and the latter accusing the former of falling behind the times. So I think we can draw on the American model to gradually form our own benign interaction mechanism.

Legal Education and Legal Unity under the Continental Model

Lü: Based on your study of comparative law, how do you think the legal profession and legal education operate in Continental law countries such as France, Germany, and Japan? And how does a legal student move into the legal profession in these countries?

He: I have not done any in-depth study on this subject, so I can only share what I currently know about it. There are many similarities between the European continent, Japan, Taiwan, and the Chinese mainland in their legal education systems, though there are some major differences between France and Germany in this regard. In Germany a person who sets his heart on the legal profession will first receive a legal education and get a certain amount of credits in university, then pass a national judicial examination, then do an internship at a judicial organ while taking some required courses, and at last pass another national judicial examination before entering the profession. The three professions of judges, prosecutors, and lawyers are separated at the beginning. In France, where legal education also starts at the undergraduate level, people with a bachelor of laws degree receive a lawyer's education to become lawyers or receive a judge and prosecutor's education (two years at the French National School for the Judiciary in Bordeaux) to become judges or prosecutors.

The situations in other countries are more or less the same. In the case of Japan, the most prominent characteristic is that the three professions are combined and subject to the same national judicial examination, and those who pass the examination will have one and a half years of training (two years in the past) at the Judicial Research and Training Institute under the Supreme Court before starting their career as a judge, prosecutor, or lawyer.

One noteworthy characteristic of legal education in the Continental law tradition is that it is more like a generalist education rather than what is called a professional education, where the legal education one receives is a necessary preparation for becoming a citizen with basic legal knowledge and consciousness. This characteristic determines its emphasis on the systematic instruction of theoretical knowledge over the training of practical skills in the legal profession, with the result that graduates are usually armed with a very systematic grasp of legal theories and laws and thus are capable of not only legal work but also government and business work. However, in comparison with their peers in the Anglo-American law tradition, the education they receive is less than professional, making them more knowledgeable in theory but less competent and skillful in specific affairs. However, we should not focus on the first half of legal education in the Continental law tradition to the neglect of its second half, such as the education that occurs after the first national judicial examination in the case of Germany, the postuniversity training at the French National School for the Judiciary in the case of France, or the training at the Judicial Research and Training Institute in the case of Japan. This second half of legal education provides training in practical affairs, and this stage may be extended in the future.

As far as the defects of legal education in the Continental law tradition, the primary one is its loose connection to the legal profession, a fact that is closely associated with the age at which the students receive legal education and with the targeted students and objectives of the education. This education places more emphasis on theoretical training and results in some problems in transitioning from legal education to the legal profession. This often leads to the accusation from the legal profession that the content of legal education is too general and impractical. Indeed, the image of legal education also largely shapes the image of the legal system. If a country's legal education is not professional enough, the country's legal system is also less than professional. An interesting development is that some Continental law countries such as Japan and Korea are turning toward the American model, a process of transition that is expected to be completed within ten years. This trend deserves our special attention.

Lü: In countries like France and Germany where the professions of judges, prosecutors, and lawyers are mutually separated from each other and lack communication, how do they form their own professional concepts, and how are these different professional concepts united?

He: This does have a remarkable influence on the unity of understanding and thinking of the practitioners in the different segments of the legal profession. If a person confines himself to the same segment of the legal profession, serving as a lawyer or prosecutor for his whole life, he indeed tends to have certain professional biases and difficulties in arriving at a good understanding of the other segments of the profession. With this situation, legal unity becomes a question of particular importance. In contrast, legal unity is vigorously promoted in the Anglo-American legal tradition, where precedents are conscientiously studied and compared both in courts and in classrooms at law schools, contributing to the formation of an increasing number of rules to be applied in adjudication and to the predictability and stability of the judicial process. In addition, the federal system also has a special need for legal unity, requiring that unity be maintained in the handling of federal affairs, basic rights, interstate cases, and trades while respecting local autonomy.

How is legal unity achieved in the Continental law tradition? This is not an easy question to answer, and it is a question that I have also been thinking about. Although there is inadequate communication among the three professions, those engaged in these professions have a common background, that is, they must be trained in law. The basic concepts and principles fostered in them during the process of legal training are helpful in maintaining a certain degree of unity in their decisionmaking processes. For example, they have the same understanding of the basic legal concepts such as *usucapion*, *negotiorum gestio*, and bona fide acquisition, to name but a few. This facilitates a unified understanding when they face similar issues. And then the instance of appeal and the supreme court play an important role in maintaining legal unity. I think there is a mechanism of coordination as to how to establish legal principles and how to construe legal provisions. If no party in a case heard by a lower court or first-instance court lodges an appeal, it means the dispute in question has been solved. If one party believes that the interpretation and application of the law in the first instance is wrong, then an appeal can be lodged in an appellate court. Different appellate courts need to be well coordinated in the interpretation of the law, and with this coordination, legal unity can be maintained. You know, Germany's appellate courts are highly specialized, with labor relations cases, administrative cases, civil cases, and criminal cases all having their own specialized appellate courts. In a word, the country's appellate court system has a multipyramid structure. This specialized division of labor among the appellate courts is effective in ensuring consistency in the handling of cases in each field.

In addition, I think legal scholars and professors are another important element in the judicial activities under the Continental European model. In Germany, for example, a mechanism of interaction between legal professors and legal practitioners had emerged in the era of Savigny. The German Civil Code is called a code of the professors because it is unintelligible to ordinary persons, and indeed, it is not intelligible even to professors not specializing in law, not even to professors specializing in criminal penalty. The code is so comprehensive and profound that the practicing legal community becomes reliant on legal academia; it may be exaggerating to use the word reliant, but it is beyond a doubt that there are important interactions and connections between the two. Legal professors' academic explanations of the development and meaning of Germany's Civil Code, of what interpretations should be avoided, and of what interpretations should be pursued have gradually become the mainstream theory of legal academia that is universally acknowledged. These mainstream explanations of the law in legal academia are a very important factor in shaping a unified judicial decisionmaking process.

Lü: As you noted earlier, some countries and regions such as Japan, Taiwan, and Korea are showing signs of turning from the Continental model to the Anglo-American model. What do you think of the operability of this transition, with all the issues involved taken into consideration? Given the differences between the Anglo-American and Continental legal systems in educational structure, which do you think is more operable? And which is easier to be introduced into a country with weaker rule of law?

He: I think this transition emerges under the influence of many different pressures. The value and advantages of the American model, as we discussed earlier, and the increasingly exposed defects in the Continental European model of legal education combine to drive the transition toward the Anglo-American style of legal education. However, it is inevitable that this transition will come at the expense of the balance within the existing model as the new model is introduced to establish a strong connection between the legal profession and legal academia. Up to now, I have not seen any analysis in this respect; indeed, I think maybe such analysis is impossible until the completion of this transition and the establishment of a new connection and balance.

It should be admitted that for a society with weaker legal infrastructure, the Continental European model is more suitable to be introduced and used to change the society's existing legal system and administrative model. It is more easily accepted. As a matter of fact, it is not by coincidence that different Western countries embraced the Continental European model in the process of modernization. The Anglo-American model is simply impossible to introduce exclusively by borrowing its written laws; if it is to be introduced, then legal practitioners in that system should also be introduced, because the introduced written laws and legal theories cannot replace the role played by legal practitioners working in that system. And it is impractical and impossible to replace a country's judges with Anglo-American judges. Therefore, the Continental European model is the only feasible option in the effort to quickly achieve legal modernization or Westernization. After the Continental European model is introduced and established, people realizing this model's defects begin to seek a model that is more professional and grapple with such questions as how to turn the law into a society-changing force, how to change the existing separation between legal circles and society and establish an effective interaction between them, and how to strengthen the rule of law. I think this effort should not focus exclusively on the existing model but should also consider the value of the Anglo-American model.

In France it is widely held that the American legal system best reflects the opinions of the legal circles, such as its approach to human rights protection and to such questions as how judicial judgments promote the development of legal studies and how the judiciary restricts the power of the government. In a word, the American system is thought to be highly successful. The power of judicial review, for example, plays an important role in checking the government's abuse of power and preventing the adoption of unconstitutional legislation. Of course, the Constitutional Council of France also plays a similar role by performing a constitutional review of proposed bills before they are adopted. However, whether a law or any provision of it is constitutional or not should be judged not only from the written text but also from the possibility of its application leading to unconstitutional results. These unconstitutional results can only be exposed by individual cases and in turn lead to the improvement of the relevant laws through amendments. As you see, the American model has a strong judiciary, which has supremacy over the legislature and the executive. Since World War II, there has been an increasing consensus in Continental European countries that a strong judiciary is an effective way to safeguard human freedom, restrict the government's power, and maintain a good social order. So I think the American model will have an even greater influence in the future.

Scale and Hierarchy of Legal Education

Lü: As you noted, the Continental model is easier to introduce to a country with weaker rule of law. China's legal system belongs to the Continental law system, and its legal education is provided at an undergraduate level. In contrast, legal education in common law countries, especially America, occurs at the postgraduate level. There are various legal programs in China, such as bachelor of laws, LL.M., and J.M., and this situation has caused some problems. In your article "China's Legal Education Should Embrace J.M. Education," you give an analysis of the goal of China's legal education and issues surrounding the legal education system.[1] What are your opinions on these issues?

He: The article you mentioned is part of an investigative report I participated in. I think China's current legal education is still in a very confusing state, with no definite answers to some of the most fundamental questions surrounding legal education, such as what kind of persons the legal education system is to train to meet what needs of society, what the proper scale of the legal profession is, and what the status of legal education should be. And this confusion is made even worse by poor management of legal education. In the past, there was a popular view, which has been proven to be mistaken, that China should educate a multilayer group of legal professionals through various channels and by various means. Under the influence of this thinking, China now has so many legal programs that range from vocational schools to the highest level of tertiary education and that cover so many different kinds of students that it is difficult to differentiate their graduates, even for insiders of the legal circles. A person may get a diploma in law without spending a single day at any university. Due to the popularity of legal education in recent years, there has been a sudden surge in the number of legal programs in various colleges and universities across the country so that there are up to 600 institutions of higher learning that offer legal programs under all kinds of names and titles, while back when I was a law student, there were only three to five legal programs in the whole country. When legal students are everywhere to be seen and legal degrees are looked down upon like dirt, it is by no means a good thing for the development of rule of law.

So, first of all, the proper scale of legal education, that is, the appropriate number of legal practitioners that are required by the society, should be determined. In actual fact, different countries have different requirements regarding the number of legal practitioners. As we know, America has a high percentage of legal practitioners, but the percentage in Japan, another affluent capitalist country, is very low, and it is even lower in some northern European countries. The percentage of legal practitioners among the population is no indicator of the status of rule of law in a country.

Another issue that was largely neglected in the past is how to strike a balance between legal knowledge and legal skills. It can be said that rule of law is a system under which legal principles are applied to the adjustment of all kinds of social relations, where actions that are against the law are punished and resulting damages are remedied. This system is set in motion by a group of professionals armed with legal knowledge, legal skills, and legal ethics. They are the mainstay in rule of law, and it is through them that social relations are adjusted, relevant legal provisions are construed, and the balancing art of law is applied to social adjustment. If different departments act on their own, and legal students are taught very differently, it is impossible to achieve consistent decisionmaking in legal affairs. As I just pointed out, legal unity in Continental law countries is highly dependent on different legal practitioners having the same educational background. In the absence of legal unity, there will be no good rule of law.

So I think it is a mistake to believe that the more legal practitioners and the more segmented they are, the better. I think everyone who has experienced a college life feels the indispensability of the campus to a genuine college education. The campus offers many opportunities that are not available elsewhere and that form an essential part of the college experience, such as communicating face to face with erudite teachers, having spirited discussions with dorm mates on topics of common interest, attending lectures on a variety of subjects, and having exchanges with students of different grades and from different departments, and much more. It is this kind of communication and the convergence of different knowledge fields that make university life what it is and that exert an imperceptible yet lasting influence on the students. Legal education, be it bachelor's or master's or doctorate programs, cannot dispense with concentrated study over a period of time or the exchange of ideas happening in a shared space. One cannot complete one's tertiary education on the street. That's why I do not support correspondence course programs or distance education programs, which are called "education on the air" in Taiwan and Japan but which I think should be better called "castle in the air." So I think it is advisable that the policy of recruiting an excessive number of legal students be changed to decrease the quantity and improve the quality of legal practitioners, otherwise it will do more harm than good to rule of law.

In a sense, legal practitioners are service providers, with the public being consumers. An economic analysis can be made of this process. In a well-regulated market, good legal services fetch high prices due to their high intrinsic value; but if the market is not well regulated, substandard services will appear and crowd the market with cheap price tags, with the result that undiscriminating customers choose them due to their lower prices. As providers of top-quality services are gradually squeezed out, the rule of law, as well as the whole legal profession, is sacrificed. This sounds like a naked interest analysis, but if we survey the history of the legal profession in Britain, we will find that this profession, when strictly regulated in all aspects—such as entrance requirements, training process, and certification—

is in the best interest of the public. So the two [strict regulation and the public interest] are consistent.

Lü: What do you think are the major problems created by China's current overcrowded, multilayered legal education system, covering as it does both tertiary legal education and short-term legal training programs? As you said, it is quite confusing. What do you think can be done to change this state of affairs?

He: My vision of how things should be is very clear. As I wrote in the article mentioned above, we can put a stop to undergraduate legal education within five to ten years and implement the law school model. And then the number of LL.M. degrees granted should be radically decreased. Universities like Peking University can recruit about ten candidates for the degree every year, imposing a strict standard to let in only those who are truly devoted to academic pursuit, making the LL.M. education no longer a path toward the practicing profession. Then most students in legal schools will be studying in the J.M. program, and all these students will be graduates from specialties other than law. Those who complete their three-year study at law school and then pass through the judicial examination will be qualified to enter the legal profession. As for whether to borrow the American-style appointment system where a judge can only be appointed from among lawyers or prosecutors with around ten years of experience, this issue can be addressed later.

In recent years, there have been a lot of comments and even charged debates on legal education, especially between LL.M. students and J.M. students, because in universities that enroll both LL.M. and J.M. students, the latter feel discriminated against in that they pay more tuition fees but get a lesser education than that received by LL.M. students. In many universities, J.M. students don't have advisers; no one is designated to guide and supervise their studies. My suggestion is that J.M. students be assigned advisers. They may be allocated at the beginning of the educational process in a random way, for instance, based on student numbers, and any teacher from junior lecturer to full professor can serve as an adviser. You know that many lecturers are also highly competent and may be given the opportunity to advise J.M. students. In this way, a teacher can serve as the adviser of one LL.M. student and several J.M. students so that every legal student has an adviser during his or her course of study. After one and a half years of legal study, students can choose their own professional mentors, going in for civil law or legal history, for example, as their interest dictates. Although different students may share the same adviser or mentor, to have an adviser at the beginning of their legal education will have a strong positive influence on them, and this will also help lessen the sense of discrimination felt by some students.

Regarding the instruction process, except for a very small number of teachers who hold a J.M. degree and a few J.D.'s trained overseas, most teachers in legal education hold an LL.M. degree. During my investigative study, a teacher at a university of politics and law displayed a strong prejudice against J.M. students, constantly comparing J.M. and LL.M. students, saying that he is least willing to lecture to the former because they are uninitiated. The fact is that the two groups of students are not comparable in the first place because the latter have received four years' study in law and gained a good understanding of basic legal concepts and principles, and it is therefore far easier for them to take some specialized courses than it is for J.M. students, and to expect J.M. students and LL.M. students to be equally knowledgeable in law is not fair. In fact, if they are compared in other fields of knowledge, J.M. students may prove far superior. I think we must be aware of the fact that teachers capable of teaching J.M. students effectively are still very few because this requires a diversified knowledge structure on the part of the teacher so as to mobilize the different knowledge bases of the students and establish their connection and relevance to the legal knowledge system. This poses a big challenge to teachers. To rise to this challenge, a virtuous circle featuring excellent interaction of different fields of knowledge both within and outside classes should be gradually established. It is also my hope that there will be an increasing number of J.M. graduates engaging in legal education so they can apply their undergraduate knowledge in different fields, like economics and anthropology, to enliven the imparting of legal knowledge. This is also the direction that China's legal education should follow in the future.

As for the courses offered, I think they must be designed to allow for the fact that although J.M. candidates have not received any formal training in law, they have completed a four-year study in their specialties other than law, with an eye to enabling them to gradually enrich their legal knowledge step by step.

Another important component of legal education is the entrance examination. The entrance examination for J.M. programs is controlled by law schools where only legal knowledge is tested, but the paradox is that those who apply for J.M. programs are not yet grounded in law. In this regard, I think the American LSAT examination model may be drawn upon. The primary task is to determine whether a person is suitable for receiving a legal education and to do so via a well-designed exam. But I have not seen any serious work done in this respect. In conclusion, with superfluous programs cancelled, the other programs streamlined, and the administrative matters straightened out, all problems will be smoothed and there will be no debates between LL.M. and J.M. students. Most conflicts are generated by the current system itself.

Establishment of a Unified Judicial Research and Training System

Lü: China currently has many judges' colleges, prosecutors' colleges, and administrative institutes of politics and law that offer accelerated legal education programs. What problems is this kind of education meant to solve?

He: This question relates to China's judicial research and training system. These accelerated programs come as something of a remedy for the defects of China's judge and prosecutor appointment system, which installs a large number of laypersons in the courts, and these programs are meant to make up their deficit in legal education. And what they get is usually no more than a rudimentary training in law, leaving many important subjects untouched. In fact, the judges' colleges and prosecutors' colleges are not many in number nor advanced in teaching facilities and faculties. I visited some of these colleges and found that they mostly are on a small scale, not really living up to the name of college. Some people who have not received a formal legal education but are appointed court presidents or chief procurators are required to get three months' legal training before assuming their positions. So these accelerated legal education programs are the result of the existing system. Now the country's judges' law and prosecutors' law have been amended, stipulating that no person without a college education shall be appointed a judge or prosecutor. In the meantime, a judicial examination system has been established. With these developments, what is now required is the establishment of a unified judicial research and training system.

I think the judicial research and training system serves as a crucial bridge between legal education and the legal profession. A person who has received a formal legal education in college does not have the necessary skills required to solve practical problems in the legal profession because experience is something that cannot be gained in classrooms. Law professors may have a rich stock of grand theories, but they are not really good at dealing with practical legal issues. This problem is increasingly recognized in the legal education circle, and efforts have been made to engage legal practitioners to train students. There is also an internship course meant to develop the student's practical abilities. These measures, however, are far from enough. But on the other hand, if these measures are too numerous, it will affect the mission of formal legal education to impart legal knowledge and theories in a comprehensive and systematic way. Therefore, it is necessary to create a bridge between legal education and the legal profession. The judicial research and training system is also the product of compromise in the power struggle between the practicing world and the education world. The question is how to establish a series of standards by which law graduates can become judges, prosecutors, or lawyers in the legal profession. In the British tradition, the practicing world holds a greater power and shapes its own image. But the Continental European law system is always influenced by rationalism, where legal education places more emphasis on theoretical acquisition. A person who has completed a formal legal education has to receive judicial training before becoming a legal practitioner capable of practical work. This role transition is primarily accomplished through the judicial research and training system.

I paid a visit to Japan in 1995 to study its judicial research and review system. Japan has always maintained a very small group of legal professionals, and this number is particularly small in comparison to Western countries. The profession is small in scale but has great strength, primarily because of its sound appointment model. Japan's Judicial Research and Training Institute is operated by the country's supreme court. Everyone who has passed the national judicial examination is required to receive training at the Judicial Research and Training Institute. People who work in one of the three branches of the legal profession come together to study the professional skills of the other two branches; this is unlike the French model, where lawyers-to-be are trained by the lawyers' association and judges- or prosecutors-to-be are trained by the National School for the Judiciary. The Japanese model facilitates mutual understanding of the three branches of the legal profession and the formation of shared perceptions among judges, prosecutors, and lawyers. Another characteristic is that judicial research and training is largely completed in the practicing professionals' work settings, with apprenticeships accounting for three-fourths of the time and classroom instruction for one-fourth. The apprentices stay with judges, prosecutors, and lawyers to familiarize themselves with practical matters and develop practical skills in the legal profession. The final aspect of the Japanese system is that the instructors at the Judicial Research and Training Institute are not academics but appointed from among senior judges, prosecutors, and lawyers.

In contrast, at China's colleges for judges and prosecutors, the instructors are often academics rather than practicing legal professionals. As far as I know, many instructors there have no experience working in courts and went to teach there directly after getting their doctoral degree in law. So there is a big problem in orientation. I think the training is best provided by practicing professionals, following the apprenticeship model, where the concept of the master-apprentice relationship is very important.

After I came back, I wrote an article summarizing my Japan tour in which I also proposed establishing a judicial research and training system in China. At that time, I thought a unified judicial examination was still unattainable, but I did wish for the establishment of a unified judicial examination and a judicial research and training system. Given the tens of thousands of people who pass the national judicial examination every year in China, how is the country's judicial research and training system to be established? It is not unfeasible to establish a national judicial research and training institute like Japan has. I think a solution is to establish a regionally based judicial research and training system in line with China's geographic divisions, with the regional institutes located in the central cities of those regions and the central institute located in Beijing or somewhere responsible for providing training for existing judges, prosecutors, and lawyers. The central institute of judicial research and training could provide various training programs on special issues, such as intellectual property rights protection for those judges having questions about or problems dealing with such cases. This approach, featuring regionally based judicial research and training facilities and division of labor would be easy to implement.

In 2001 China's national judicial examination was put in place, making a huge historic stride forward. However, the move was so sudden and hasty that a series of related issues have been left unresolved, such as how the examination relates to the existing legal education system and the personnel systems of courts and procuratorates. The establishment of a judicial research and training system was even more out of the question. So the endeavor left much to be desired and was far from being brought to fruition. In recent years, those who passed the national judicial examination are also beset by the question of how to enter the court system. As long as the transition from the judicial examination to the legal profession is not well regulated, the examination system remains incomplete. Efforts are far from enough to make the national judicial examination an effective mechanism in changing the actual operation of the legal profession and addressing its defects. Of course, this also has to do with the coordination of different departments. The national judicial examination is currently in the charge of the Administrative Department of Justice, but there is no coordination mechanism between the Administrative Department of Justice, which is a department under the State

Council, and the Supreme People's Court and the Supreme Procuratorate. I think this issue should be solved once and for all by the National People's Congress, either through making new laws or revising existing ones.

Lü: Like the legal education of the Continental law system, China's legal education is more academic than professional. Due to a lack of practical skills, many law school graduates find it difficult to go to work in courts, and when they are established as lawyers, it is even more difficult for them to join the ranks of judges. What's the proportion of law school graduates who manage to enter the court system? How are the employment problems faced by those failing to enter the court system solved?

He: There are indeed many law school graduates who are eager to but cannot enter the court system. The bridge for those who have passed the national judicial examination to work in courts has not been constructed yet. And how the national judicial examination is to position itself in and relate to other components of the legal system and profession has not been well planned out. This is the source of many problems. Questions asked by our foreign colleagues concerning the employment structure of our law school graduates and the numbers of those going to work in courts and those engaging in work irrelevant to legal affairs are often left unanswered because we simply don't have strict statistics for these questions. We haven't reached the point of what Mr. Ray Huang called the "numerical management."[2] Our management always proceeds in a general rather than exact fashion. Even China's state governance has a poetic style, being implicit, vague, and foggy. I think the main problem is one of coordination; it involves many aspects, such as how to make adjustments to the programs of law schools so as to meet the requirements of the judicial examination, and therefore requires overall thinking. There is a view that the threshold of the national judicial examination should be raised so that it is open only to those having received a bachelor's degree in law from a university, underscoring the indispensability of a campus-based formal legal education. And it is not enough to determine one's suitability for legal work simply by one examination. There is an even more dubious suggestion of allowing farmers to sit for the examination and giving them the chance of becoming judges. But I think what China's legal profession needs is professionalization, not professionalization with simultaneous democratization. As for the question of how to enter the court system after one passes the national judicial examination, this requires the establishment of a good mechanism of coordination among the lawyers' community, the Administrative Department of Justice, and the courts. Typical of many reforms in China, the judicial examination was introduced without adequate coordination with related parties, resulting in many otherwise avoidable problems. As long as the matters in question are smoothed out, those problems will disappear by themselves.

Using Theory to Shape Rule of Law

Lü: To follow up on the subject, what influence do you think the national judicial examination will have on China's legal education?

He: A unified national judicial examination certainly will have a strong influence on legal education. In a seminar held not long ago, my counterparts from Taiwan also shared the view that the judicial examination can be a tricky thing because it tends to shape legal education as to what to teach, or indeed what to learn and what not to learn on the part of students. The students often only concern themselves with subjects that are covered in the judicial examination and show particular interest in teachers who participate in the formulation of judicial examination papers, but they have little interest in subjects not covered in the judicial examination and are reluctant to attend those classes. In addition, with the introduction of a unified national judicial examination, a large number of private training organizations devoted to efficiently preparing students for the examination will mushroom outside the regular education. Many students spend a lot of energy on these exam-oriented private training programs. This results in a certain tension between legal education and the unified judicial examination.

Here I think it is in order to give a definition of the rule of law: it is a process of solving social disputes and conflicts using a set of comparatively abstract knowledge, methodology, and language that is considerably remote from the daily life experience. Based on this definition, it can be said that legal education is a process of differentiating legal professionals from ordinary people. As we know, Continental European law and Anglo-American law represent the two major legal traditions in the world. The Continental European legal tradition embarked on the path of professionalization as early as the ancient Greek and Roman periods. Professionalization means the recognition of division of labor and of legal professionals as a unique group of people. Their uniqueness is shown in various aspects and shaped through a formal legal education.

From this perspective, I think theorization in legal education is not a bad thing by itself because theories, by their very nature, distance themselves from everyday reality and derive their value from this distance. A "theory" that does not differentiate itself from reality does not fit the definition.

I think China's legal education is inadequate in theorization. It is full of various fancy theories that are not well digested and at the same time deemphasizes practical skills, so that the students are good at neither. So more effort should be made to strengthen theoretical training in our legal education. Legal theories play the important role of interpreting our society and the legal profession and ensuring legal unity and predictability in the judicial decisionmaking process. A deep understanding of legal theories cannot be achieved without a formal legal education. In recent years, there has been a gradual awakening to the real-world requirements of a legal education. Jurisprudence, which used to be filled with many ambiguous dogmas, for example, is becoming more practical. An increasing number of people realize that an autonomous legal profession can effectively transform society, and legal papers and monographs with a real-world orientation keep coming out, reflecting a movement in this direction.

The application of legal rules in actual life is not mechanical, where a problem is readily solved by applying a specific rule, but rather is subject to many factors including culture, social structure, customary preferences, and habitual behaviors. Thus the same case may lead to different scenarios depending on the individuals involved, their professions and countries, and applicable laws. For instance, in China we emphasize procedural justice and try to rectify the tendency to stress substantive matters to the neglect of procedural correctness. In this case, one has to study procedure consciousness and determine which judicial model is better able to solve disputes. In the past, the role of judge was filled by clan patriarchs in the rural area. The way they solved disputes was not mechanical but highly flexible and weighed many factors such as the social status of the parties concerned. It would make an interesting research project to study the acceptability of the concept of procedural justice in such a culture. When explaining the rural governance model, Fei Xiaotong gave a vivid example.[3] He said that a village head could conveniently solve the dispute of two quarrelling brothers by giving each of them a slap in the face and that this is what the rural governance model is about. Jurisprudence is always concerned with what can be called "universal theories" and does not have much interest in more situational theories. When we study English, we often encounter the expression "situational English," where people in a given situation speak in a way that departs from the standard taught in textbooks and is grammatically wrong, but that does not affect mutual understanding among the parties concerned. In the same vein, can we make a similar differentiation between universal legal principles and situational legal principles? I think with the understanding of social and cultural differences, one feels that rule of law can proceed differently in different societies. However, we must constantly work to advance the rule of law and the universal applicability of legal provisions while reducing situation-based uncertainty in legal application because the situational principle, if pushed to extremes, will destroy rule of law in the end. If every case is treated differently on the grounds that just as there are no two exactly identical leaves in the world, there are no cases that are exactly the same, then there will be no place for legal provisions and, ultimately, for rule of law. So I think this presents a big challenge to our legal theories, but to use a cliché, it is also a big opportunity for the creation of China's own jurisprudence. How our legal education system is to face this challenge and opportunity and make its fair contribution to the country's legal development is a thought-provoking question for those of us involved.

Lü: You wrote an article entitled "Ex-Servicemen of the PLA Now Serving at Court," in which you criticized the lack of legal education received by Chinese judges, and it was widely echoed in the practicing world but also gave rise to many different views.[4] Justice Holmes once said that "the life of the law has not been logic; it has been experience." Between theoretical knowledge and practical experience, which do you think is the most important for the legal profession? Is it necessary for judges to have received a tertiary legal education to bring about a good judicial environment?

He: The remark of Holmes is often cited as a dictum and used as a shield against logic and rationalism. But that's a misunderstanding of Holmes. Judging from the context in which the remark appears, it is obvious that Holmes was not negating the value of logic. What he meant to say is simply that the life of law lies in the incessant connections it has to social life. The article you mentioned, in fact, gave me some sort of fame among some people and notoriety among others, especially among soldiers-turned-judges who never seem to mention the article without feeling great hatred. Since 1979 when China began its reform and opening up, there has been an increasingly freer press environment, and now it is commonplace to see criticism of courts and judges on TV, radio, and newspapers. But such criticism was rarely seen before the 1980s because the courts were thought to be part of the state apparatus of proletarian dictatorship that was politically incorrect to criticize. Today, as I said, the criticism of courts, procuratorates, and the police is common to see, and many of those working in these branches are also accustomed to such criticism, but there remains a group of people, that is, those with a People's Liberation Army (PLA) background, who are generally thought to be above criticism due to their esteemed ideological position.

My article was the first to have ever expressed explicit doubt over this—of course, not this group of people but the phenomenon of deactivated soldiers going to work in courts—and it was indeed a little bold. In fact, the editor in charge had misgivings and did not decide to publish my article before being assured that I had published articles expressing similar views without triggering any problems. I did not tell him that I expressed the view only as a side comment in a long article in the past, with a nature quite different from the essay in question that was to be published in the widely circulated influential weekly *Southern Weekend*. The article did cause a stir nationwide and attracted subsequent articles published in newspapers with PLA backgrounds that criticized me for "going farther and farther in the wrong direction," in a manner that looked as if they were saving me from disaster. But as a matter of fact, up to now, I still hold firmly to my original view.

Of course, this issue also involves the cognition of the legal profession. If the role of rule of law in transforming the society is to be fulfilled, it has to be done through the community of legal professionals armed with a unique knowledge system and formatted mind that are the product of four or seven years of formal training. This training gives them a legal perspective in everything they approach. They rely on what they acquired from legal education to perform their professional duties of adjusting social relationships and applying the same criteria from various legal concepts such as default, *negotiorum gestio*, and bona fide acquisition. This consistency in understanding various concepts and, consequently, in applying legal provisions is the precondition for fulfilling another legal principle, that is, the same thing shall be treated the same way, and all people are equal before the law. In my classes, I often ask my students this question: in non–common law countries, what is the foundation of legal unity? Legal unity cannot be achieved simply through citing from the same laws. According to the Law of the People's Republic of China on the Protection of the Rights and Interests of Consumers, a consumer who bought a fake product from a business is entitled to a compensation amount equal to twice the value of the original product. But the provision can make things complicated if the concept of consumer is understood differently among judges, just as the consumer rights fighter Wang Hai experienced.[5] He got compensation in some jurisdictions but none in others because he was deemed a consumer in the former but not in the latter. Then how do we achieve this legal unity? I think this must be achieved through a unified legal education so that all those who have received this education will have the same mindset and will understand and apply the laws consistently.

If this thesis holds true, then what follows is self-evident. Those who have not received a formal legal education will have no way to experience the mind-formatting process and, as a result, will be unable to maintain uniformity in judicial decisionmaking. And besides, there are legal ethics to consider. A legal education imparts not only methods and skills but also the ethics to be observed by everyone in the legal profession. On this basis, judges are appointed following unified criteria, forming a professional community with shared values and consensus on good practices in the profession so that those who observe these values are praised and those who act contrary to these values are disdained. A person is very concerned with how he stands in the estimation of others, especially of what is called the "reference group" in anthropology. The selection of this reference group is extremely important in forming a person's evaluation of himself. A study finds that Japanese judges do not quite care about the opinions of people outside their profession but attach great weight to the opinions of their colleagues. This is also why in recent years I have always emphasized the importance of establishing a truly professional legal profession. People worried about various judicial problems have proposed a range of solutions such as administrative supervision, media supervision, and public trial, but I think these measures are all superficial rather than fundamental. The fundamental solution lies in establishing a professional community that observes the same professional ethics through the application of unified judicial appointment criteria.

Judges have a characteristic—the most important of all their characteristics—that distinguishes them from other officials such as executive officers and military officers: independence. Only lunatics will call for the independence of military officers, whose bound duty is to comply with the orders of their superiors. But independence is the pursuit of every judge who does not allow any form of interference in the exercise of his judicial power. This trait of independence, however, forms a sharp contrast to the deeply ingrained compliance consciousness of soldiers. This compliance was trained into them from their first day of military service, when they were forced to do various things for veterans such as washing socks and dishes. They are trained to do whatever they are commanded by their superiors. In this respect, there is no difference between China and any other country in the world. In the military, compliance is always the overriding virtue, above respect of persons. I had personal experience with this when I gave a lecture at a military college not long ago. As I was a guest, I was very cordially received. I did not even need to open the car door. In a word, for people who have spent many years in the military, compliance has become their second nature, and it is very difficult for them to transform into an independent judge.

Of course, the administrative model of China's court system also has defects. There is a high percentage of court heads who are laypersons without a formal legal education. Those who are obedient and flatter them often get quicker promotions. The percentage of ex-servicemen of the PLA who now serve as court officials at mid-level and above is also high. I once read a news report saying that soldiers-turned-officials accounted for more than 80 percent of one intermediate court. I think the application of different criteria to personnel appointments in the court system strongly influences the judiciary's power structure. Of course, my article about deactivated soldiers working in the courts also elicited different views from academia. Professor Long Zongzhi, then deputy chief procurator of the Military Procuratorate of Chengdu Military Region, wrote an article to express a divergent view on the subject.[6] In a chapter of his book *Sending Law to the Countryside*, Professor Zhu Suli also gave a comprehensive survey of the subject and expressed his different views.[7] I think this question has been largely settled, because with the establishment of a unified national judicial examination and amendments to the Judges Law and the Prosecutors Law, it is still possible for deactivated soldiers to work in courts, but it has become basically impossible for them to serve as industrial court judges.

Finally, it should be noted that this issue, in essence, is about legal professionalism because it is the result of different personnel appointment models in the court system. This question deserves more reflection. However, it is not something that can be solved overnight.

Lü: I read a striking sentence in Professor Zhao Xiaoli's preface to Professor Su Li's book *Rule of Law and Local Resources*, which reads: "The rise of professional training at law schools will spell the decline of their academic performance," underscoring the perceived contradiction between professional legal education and academic legal education.[8] On the one hand, law's foundation is practical reason, and therefore it behooves the legal education system to prepare students for legal practice. But on the other hand, emphasis on legal practice in legal education is detrimental to the development of legal studies. How do you think the two can be reconciled? Which model is more suitable to China's current conditions?

He: Jurisprudence is really a very time-honored discipline, and legal practice is one of the three oldest professions along with medicine and theology. In spite of the antiquity of jurisprudence, many people doubt whether it has its own theoretical foundation because it is so closely associated with actual social life, and its primary function is to solve the myriad practical problems in social life. It has always been a challenge to derive metaphysical theories from the practical problem-solving process. In a small article, I quoted the observation by fourteenth-century English bishop Richard de Bury that books on jurisprudence do not afford people the kind of ethical pleasure afforded by other books because jurisprudence is too much subject to the sway of the ruling establishment. Sometimes jurists themselves wish to see conflicts among people so as to enrich their theories.

Another criticism of jurisprudence is that it lacks a stable intellectual pursuit. As we know, the development of jurisprudence has been advanced by many other disciplines such as philosophy, ethics, economics, and sociology. The history of Western legal thought is dominated by many figures who themselves were not jurists but philosophers, such as Plato, Aristotle, Aquinas, Montesquieu, and Locke. So it is important to put the theoretical pursuit in legal education in the right perspective and combine theory and practice. I do not agree with the view that professional training in legal education weakens the academic advancement of jurisprudence. Above all, it has to be made clear what the purpose of theory is.

I think Max Weber was a paragon in combining theory and reality. His theories are profound and constitute a major contribution to the intellectual history of the twentieth century. Reading his works, you find that he was indeed a great jurist, highly accomplished in Roman law and the comparison of the legal profession in different places. His theoretical work is not removed from reality and can be used directly to inform and guide our practice.

American sinologist Philip A. Kuhn's book *Soulstealers: The Chinese Sorcery Scare of 1768* illustrates how the ruling class's response to rumors led to social disturbances and arrives at a deep understanding of the need to regulate the power of the monarch and subject the exercise of power to a well-defined system.[9] This is what the English did when they established the first constitutional monarchy in the world to check the formerly unlimited power of their monarch. In fact, rule of law is also such a process. Rule of law, in contrast to rule of man, is where everything proceeds according to established rules and where no power is beyond law. What Weber studied was the process by which the monarch's power is regulated and codified, where the monarch is required to exercise his power as provided for in the code. Philip A. Kuhn also studied the possibility of regulating and codifying imperial power in China. However, the emperor did everything to thwart any attempt to check his power and succeeded in doing so because China's social infrastructure was quite different from that of England. I think this had much to do with China's official appointment system and the absence of a professional bureaucracy. As a result, not only was the imperial power not checked, but the attempt driven by that unattainable wish eventually led to nationwide suppression. I think this touches upon a few major subjects that legal professionals may wish to study. We cannot say that it has nothing to do with us, or it is no help in solving social problems. In fact, theorizing in this realm could make a major contribution to our society. So it is wrong to equate theory with research and papers that have nothing do with our society and that are incomprehensible. On the contrary, theory entails a set of analytic methods, and their application can explain human behaviors and social phenomena. I think the advancement from the professionalism of the legal profession to the professionalization of legal education is very obvious in China. The unique identity of jurisprudence has to be established before it can generate its own theories. If jurisprudence is reduced to an annotation to other disciplines and plays the role of their helper—like Eve in *Paradise Lost*, who said to Adam, "As a woman, my most important virtue is ignorance, and I exist as a foil to set off your greatness"—then there will be no need for jurisprudence and legal education, and there will be no such thing as legal ethics. All legal scholars explore the value of jurisprudence by studying jurisprudential theories, and although we need to be acquainted with other disciplines, the primary and ultimate purpose of legal studies is to advance the research and theoretical development of jurisprudence.

Interaction between Academia and Professional Practitioners

Lü: At the present, there are many legal professors and researchers who plunge themselves into the business world and spend so much of their energies on their concurrent positions such as lawyers, advisors, managers, or booksellers that their teaching or research duties are largely neglected. There are also many scholars taking a temporary or permanent post in the judicial system and many academically oriented judges and prosecutors leaving the judicial system to teach or perform research at universities. Still, there are practicing lawyers who also participate in legal academia by teaching or giving lectures. Can this be seen as a fusion between legal professional education and legal scholarship? What do you think of this phenomenon?

He: First of all, it should be noted that the phenomenon of legal scholars serving as part-time lawyers had emerged as early as the 1980s. It is difficult for me to comment on this phenomenon since I don't have such experience, having never served as a lawyer. In that period, many otherwise brilliant legal scholars committed so much of their energies to external assignments that they sacrificed their academic careers. This, however, was not entirely their own fault and had much to do with the social environment at the time, when higher education was generally not highly regarded and an associate professor's monthly salary was only a little more than RMB 100 while even a cab driver could earn RMB 2,000 every month. Pressured by the demands of life, many teachers left schools and embraced the business world. In fact, I also was one of them, and I was more resolute because I did not do external assignments on a part-time basis but took up a full-time corporate job. However, I soon realized I was not meant for the business world and came back one year later.

The current social environment is similar to the one back then. Many people defending legal scholars who take part-time external assignments say that their research benefits when they acquire some familiarity with the practicing world by undertaking these assignments; however, I do not agree with this view because legal practice in China involves too many factors that are irrelevant to law, and although it does provide some understanding of actual proceedings, the academic price legal scholars have to pay for this acquaintance with practical affairs outweighs the benefits. And indeed, the incentive for taking on these assignments is not to advance their academic goals but rather to derive economic benefits. After all, the prospect of gaining tens of thousands or even hundreds of thousands of yuan simply by handling a single case is indeed too tempting to resist for some people. Some lawyers are so wealthy that they buy expensive luxurious villas in cash without any hesitation. For them, money is not an issue at all. This is how the actual world is, and everyone is subject to its influence. However, as far as academic research is concerned, one does not have to engage in the practicing world to arrive at a good understanding of it. If it was bragging in ancient times to say that one can know the world without even stepping out of the door, it is perfectly true in this Internet age with its ready access to a wealth of information. In addition, there are many other options for gaining such knowledge, such as investigative surveys, field research, and interviews with judges and practicing lawyers. In other words, we don't have to be part of the practicing world to understand the reality in which law operates.

In fact, the changes made to judicial practice and the overall judicial system in China in recent years have been mostly driven by those who are not practicing professionals. That's why we say that a distance should be maintained between the theory and the practice, and this distance not only gives a unique identity to each pursuit but also can transform into a society-changing force.

On the other hand, as you said, many practicing professionals are coming back to universities to teach, do research, or enroll in a J.M. or LL.M. program. Of course, there are also practicing professionals who give lectures at universities on a part-time, regular basis. However, a well-developed system to manage these two trends—legal professionals pursuing academic advancement and those teaching at universities—has yet to be established. If such a system is established, it will strengthen mutual understanding, exchange, and interaction among people from different branches of the legal system. As far as I know, there is already excellent interaction in such areas as the judicial system and legal reform. An example is the Criminal Law Forum sponsored by the Law School of Peking University, where people from both practicing and academic circles are invited to discuss various topics from their own perspectives. I remember a seminar on the death penalty led by Professor Chen Xingliang and attended by legal scholars, judges, lawyers, and journalists, and I found this model to be really very good.

To sum up, there are an increasing number of legal practitioners who are interested in theories or who are theoretically accomplished. A look at the youthful vice presidents of the Supreme People's Court illustrates this point. They are not only top performers in the practice of law but also accomplished scholars. Cao Jianming is highly knowledgeable in legal affairs related to international trade and international economic law; the same applies to Shen Deyong in criminal procedure, Zhang Jun in criminal law, Huang Songyou in civil law, and Jiang Bixin in administrative law.[10] In order for the judicial system to grow and improve, it must be led by such figures competent in both legal practice and legal theory. Furthermore, the appointment of judges who are both competent in legal practice and accomplished in legal theory is very important because it will help link the two. Besides their actual work, these judges are also well positioned to write books that will benefit legal education. Therefore I believe that the top priority is to staff the realm of legal practice with individuals who are both competent in practical affairs and firmly grounded in legal theory, and thus create a bridge of communication between legal practice and legal research.

PART IV

THE LEGAL PROTECTION
OF FREE SPEECH

Freedom of the Press: A Necessary Condition for Social Stability in China

Southern Weekend: The government is something of an agent who likes to be praised. If a country's media are full of the sound of praise, do you think it is a good thing for the government?

He Weifang: It is definitely not a good thing. It is true that the government is like an agent in some ways, and the government is a multilayer system comprising the central government, local governments, and grassroots governments. It is very important for governments at higher levels to have effective control of governments at lower levels. In the absence of such effective control, the governments at lower levels will have their own way and resort to various malpractices, and if the relationship between all levels of governments is confined to the transmission of formal documents, such malpractices of the lower governments will not be exposed.

The central government wishes to know the real conditions in the provinces. For example, it very much wants to know why there are so many people going to Beijing to petition, and it hopes that local governments will do a better job. However, if they make inspections in the provinces, they will only be shown good, but unreal, things. I remember when Hu Yaobang made inspections in the provinces; he used to leave aside his entourage and made it a point not to inspect where arrangements had already been made by the local governments, and he preferred to acquaint himself with the real local

Author's note: The original Chinese version of this chapter is based on my interview with Lin Chufang, a correspondent of *Southern Weekend,* which was published on February 28, 2003. Also see http://blog.sina.com.cn/s/blog_48866320010003cl.html.

conditions incognito.[1] This approach can solve some problems; but in modern society, many problems cannot be solved this way.

In this regard, the media can play an important role in addressing this information asymmetry. So the right approach is to reduce restrictions on the media. If the media are controlled by all levels of government, there will be no criticism heard.

Southern Weekend: What is the consequence of the truth being hidden?

He Weifang: If the national media only concern themselves with the activities of national leaders rather than focus on the news proper, the local media will follow suit. The result is that when you watch the local TV programs, there is nothing but whom the county party secretary or county head is meeting with and what conferences are held and the like, copying exactly the pattern of the national media.

If all media are filled with such reports, we cannot see through them to the real conditions of society. And if the real side of a society, especially negative situations, is hidden, it is a very dangerous thing, like putting the country on top of a volcano.

This is especially so in China, a country with a long tradition of centralized authority. Due to information asymmetry, many officials only answer to their superiors, with little pressure from ordinary citizens. Government supervision of the media and an absence of institutional restraints on power will only make things worse.

An Open Media Environment Is a Basic Condition for Social Stability

Southern Weekend: There is an oft-heard assertion that if the media are given too much freedom, they will cause social disturbances. Is it so?

He Weifang: More often than not, social disturbances are caused by suppression rather than openness of the media. On the other hand, there is the difference between a lesser evil and a greater evil: disclosure of disastrous events caused through the negligence of the government may lead to public dissatisfaction and even radical protests, but these minor disturbances may prevent greater disturbances that may result if channels for communicating dissatisfaction are suppressed, and good citizens are forced to turn to violence in despair. The latter scenario can be very horrible.

An important part of the social stability mechanism is to give the people the means to vent their dissatisfaction, just as the old saying goes, "To block peoples' mouths is worse than blocking a river." In this respect, the media play an important role. Therefore, greater media freedom is by no means a factor inducing social instability but rather an agent for effectively promoting social stability.

Southern Weekend: In the event of a major unexpected incident, the media naturally want to report it, but the government may consider this troublemaking. What do you think of it?

He Weifang: We have to admit that the media's reports are not always objective and true. This is a fact based on our daily experience. But the more the media report about an incident, the more likely that the truth behind it will eventually be exposed.

As far as I know, major unexpected incidents are customarily reported through the standard news releases issued by the Xinhua News Agency, and although Xinhua journalists are generally of high caliber, their horizons are very limited. When all media except Xinhua News Agency are denied the right to report on a major unexpected incident, the officials as well as the public will not be informed of the real conditions of the incident.

There are worries that giving the media too much freedom may have negative effects, but in this regard, we should remember the words of Alexis de Tocqueville, that "in order to enjoy the inestimable benefits that the liberty of the press ensures, it is necessary to submit to the inevitable evils that it creates. To expect to acquire the former and to escape the latter is to cherish one of those illusions which commonly mislead nations in their times of sickness." This is really very well put.

Southern Weekend: There are also concerns that if the media are given the right to criticize the government freely, the government's authority will decrease. Is it so?

He Weifang: I think the contrary is true; that is, if the media are given more freedom in reporting, the government will be held in higher esteem. In many countries, the government is attacked in the media every day, but their societies are very stable. A newcomer to the United Kingdom commented that reading its newspapers gives an ominous feeling that a revolution will soon break out in the country, because they are full of complaints and criticisms of the government, as if the people of the country were living in an abyss of suffering. But the fact is that since the Glorious Revolution in 1688, British society has always been very stable. The same is true with the United States. During press briefings, some White House correspondents seem determined to touch sensitive issues; that is, they make it a point to ask questions that the government wishes to avoid the most, and the president can do nothing about it. President Clinton's love affair with Monica Lewinsky was extensively covered by national media and drew sarcastic comments from all quarters. So before doing anything improper, government officials must consider what will happen if it is known by the media. Given that even such a private affair of the president was so keenly followed by the media, will not top political figures be more self-disciplined to avoid more serious misconduct?

Therefore, exemplary figures like Lei Feng and Kong Fansen in China are commonly seen in Western countries, and their conscientiousness in work is not the result of studying policy documents or practicing noble values; they are so because they cannot but be so because they work under a rigorous administration and supervision system.[2] In China, in contrast, the absence of media supervision and judicial independence has actually led an untold number of otherwise good officials astray.

Suppression of Media Freedom Is a Lose-Lose Situation for Both the Media and the Government

Southern Weekend: Is the suppression of media freedom also a bad thing for the government?

He Weifang: The suppression of media freedom will lead to a lose-lose situation. First off, it hurts the media, turning them into a mouthpiece of the government. For example, it is difficult for us to hear the voice of the people from TV channels, and on rare occasions when farmers are featured in the news, they speak in a formulaic way, and this is obviously the result of the journalist's manipulation and fabrication. The media, for their part, also take advantage of their unofficial status as the government's representative to pursue their own interests. In such an environment, the media cannot but degenerate and further depart from their proper role.

On the other hand, the government itself is also hurt by a restrictive media environment, which leads to deterioration in government operations. In the words of an official sentenced to death for corruption, "In China, government officials at the department or bureau level or above face no supervision at all." Is this a good thing for the officials? I don't think so.

Cheng Kejie, who was born into a poor family and rose to become a top national and party leader through his own industriousness and intelligence, was ultimately sentenced to death for corruption.[3] It was the country's tragedy as well as his own. I think it is nothing but common sense that the government should not put all reportage under its control because it hurts both the government itself and the media, causing the whole of society to deviate from its proper track.

Southern Weekend: Is there an inevitable trend toward more media freedom?

He Weifang: I do think the media will gain more freedom, and it is only a matter of time. This is not just because China made such a commitment when applying for World Trade Organization membership, but more important, because it will eventually dawn on the government that tight restriction of the media is detrimental to its own interests. On the other hand, an open media environment has two major benefits of further improving the international competitiveness of Chinese media and media professionals, and gradually accustoming the Chinese people to hearing different voices from the media.

In spite of Confucius's adage that "the gentleman seeks harmony without suppressing differences," China's tradition places emphasis on "agreement" and avoids differences and disagreements. We need to have these differences gradually recognized and accepted in some way and come to the realization that differences and disagreements have their own value.

I think it is impossible for a person or an organization to have a monopoly on what is right and correct. Only when the initiative and creativity of all people are mobilized can the country be governed well. And for this vision to come true, the media should be allowed to have their own and different voices, and different interest groups should be allowed to have their own media to represent them.

Preconditions for the Sound Development of the Media

Southern Weekend: The media circles are often criticized. What do you think are the reasons for the passive position of the media?

He Weifang: First of all, the intrinsic value of the press has never been duly recognized in China. For a long period of time, China did not have public organizations truly representing and serving the public. Chinese society has undergone profound changes, but many people still hold ambiguous and mistaken ideas about the press.

Second, there has always been a widespread view that more freedom of the press means more social chaos and disorder and more erosion of the government's authority.

Third, there is still another, and horrible, concept that views the press as a tool of social control. A government operating under this concept often imposes rigorous restrictions on the media so that they cannot have their own independent voices heard and are unable to play their watchdog role effectively. In a way, our media today are a far cry from those in the Republic of China era. In comparison with the *Ta Kung Pao*, a newspaper run by Zhang Jiluan (Chang Chi-luan) in that era, all our media today are far below par. However, when we blame the media circles, we should be aware of the fact that they are part of society and thus are subject to the influence of the overall social environment. Under such conditions, they simply cannot be independent, even if they wished to.

Of course, we have comparably good media outlets. Through my own experience, I find that newspapers that are more critical in their reporting usually have more upright journalists, and those that are affiliated with the government usually have some of the most corrupt journalists.

Southern Weekend: What conditions are needed for the media to develop along the right track?

He Weifang: To begin with, the media should have their own sphere of autonomy in which they can carry out their business undisturbed, following the universally recognized codes of conduct formed in the industry over the past several hundreds of years. If these codes of conduct are sacrificed due to unjustified interference from the authorities, it will result in the degradation of the industry. Second, the media should be governed by an intelligent system that rewards good journalists and punishes bad ones. Third, the media should not be put under the exclusive control of government officials because they will not allow the reporting of news unfavorable to them, with the result that news stories will not always truthfully reflect what has happened and that the cost of news reporting will increase. Finally, the freedom of the press should be safeguarded in law, especially in cases filed against the press. According to a recent study by Mr. Chen Zhiwu from Yale University, the plaintiff success rate in defamation cases against press organizations in China is much higher than in the United States in similar cases, almost to the point of incredibility.[4] If this worrisome situation remains unchanged, the freedom of the press can hardly survive over the course of time.

CHAPTER NINE

An Open Letter to the CCP Politburo Standing Committee Regarding Media Censorship

Dear Secretary General Hu Jintao, Dear Members of the Standing Committee of the CCP Central Committee,

We are writers for the *China Youth Daily*'s *Freezing Points* weekly.[1] On January 24, 2006, the Propaganda Department of the Communist Youth League Central Committee decided, on grounds that this weekly had published an article by Professor Yuan Weishi that considered modern Chinese history and history textbooks in a new light and that "created a negative influence on society and drew sharp criticism from relevant departments of the Central Committee," to issue critical reports to that newspaper's editor-in-chief and the chief editor of the weekly. The decision enjoined "the *China Youth Daily* to shut down and rectify the *Freezing Points* weekly, and impose economic sanctions on those persons responsible, with the *Freezing Points* weekly ceasing publication for rectification commencing January 25, 2006."[2]

Editor's note: The original Chinese version of this chapter is based on an open letter penned by thirteen Chinese public intellectuals and submitted to the Standing Committee of the Chinese Communist Party on February 14, 2006. He Weifang drafted the letter, and several others made changes. The letter's signatories were all contributors to the banned journal *Freezing Points*. They include: Cui Weiping (崔卫平), scholar; Ding Dong (丁东), scholar; Fu Guoyong (付国涌), scholar; He Weifang (贺卫方), scholar; Hao Jian (郝建), scholar; Jiang Xiaoyang (江晓阳), lawyer; Liu Xiaofeng (刘晓峰), scholar; Ma Shaohua (马少华), scholar; Qin Hui (秦晖), scholar; Tongda Huan (童大焕), editor; Zhang Yihe (章诒和), scholar; Zhao Mu (赵牧), editor; and Zhu Xueqin (朱学勤), scholar. For the Chinese version of the letter, see http://voyage.typepad.com/china/2006/02/_3.html.

After this incident occurred, it immediately elicited a strong reaction among domestic and foreign public opinion, and the sounds of protest lingered in the air, a fact that you would have known very well.

Please allow us to be outspoken to say that in fact it was the above decision itself that created "a negative influence on society" because not only was it illegal, it was also unwise, setting a bad precedent of denying citizens their most basic constitutional rights to speech and freedom of press. It should be pointed out that the shutdown of the *Freezing Points* weekly was by no means an isolated event. As a matter of fact, it has become a trend and a continuous movement that is hostile to the free dissemination of information, where any "unorthodox" comments from the media would be suppressed, with consequences ranging from disciplinary warnings to the closing of the responsible media organization and the termination of its employees. This indicates that the movement has its origin at the top levels of the country's leadership. It is you who are pushing or turning a blind eye to this suppression of freedom of speech, and the underlying reason, we conjecture, is the failure on your part to arrive at a sound understanding of the value of the freedom of speech, or rather how to realize this value in the proper ways. This is also the reason why we write this open letter.

We have no idea what you, as members of the CCP Politburo Standing Committee, think of the current state of freedom of speech and press in China, but we, as writers or members of the press, do think things have gotten worse in recent years, as more and more media organizations and journalists are being punished, and the room for speech and press is becoming increasingly limited. We never expected to bid "goodbye" to the "planned economy" only to be greeted by an even more absurd "planned press." It has become increasingly commonplace for all media organizations to copy the standard stance mandated by the propaganda department. The number of TV programs has increased, but the content they offer is monotonous and tedious. In spite of thirty years of reform and opening up, the field of journalism has become more close-ended with each passing day. Many websites of sundry kinds are blocked, including even the websites of some foreign universities. If basic information required for academic research is unavailable, it's simply building castles in the air to talk about "developing world-class universities." The Internet once ushered in an era of unprecedented access to information and free discussion, but in recent years private dissemination of information from foreign countries is discouraged, and any website or forum that is active in this regard risks being suppressed or shut down, with surviving websites all warning their users "Don't discuss state affairs" and their administrators busy deleting any sensitive posts. Is it possible that this is the "governing the country in accordance with law" that we are constantly hearing about, or the "harmonious society" that everyone is focused on realizing?

Rule of Law?

In recent years, members of the Standing Committee have repeatedly emphasized on different occasions governing the country in accordance with law. We think that, like us, you will not forget the inspiring words of General Secretary Hu during his first public activity after being elected general secretary, which happened to be at the meeting celebrating the twentieth anniversary of the promulgation and enforcement of the then-current constitution of the country:

> To comprehensively implement the constitution it is necessary to strengthen constitutional safeguards and ensure that the constitution is put into effect. Over the past twenty years, constant improvements have been made in the implementation of the constitution, and it has become a universal norm of conduct to do things in accordance with the constitution and laws. However, it should also be noted that, with the changes brought about after China's embrace of the socialist market economy and as a result of problems with flawed laws and systems and the ill-adapted quality of law enforcement personnel, there remain many problems in which laws are not being complied with, laws are not being strictly enforced, and violations of law are not being prosecuted, and there continue to be some unconstitutional situations at different levels. We must expeditiously study and implement constitutional supervision mechanisms and further clarify constitutional supervision procedures in order to redress all violations of the constitution. The National People's Congress and its Standing Committee must take as their starting point the fundamental interests of the nation and the people, and in the process of enacting legislation, they must ensure that the freedoms and rights of the citizens provided for in the constitution are fully protected. We must carry out the responsibility of supervising the implementation of the constitution and resolutely redress constitutional violations. And we must perform the duties to interpret the constitution and make necessary explanations and clarifications in light of any problems arising from the implementation of the constitution in order to facilitate its enforcement. On the part of the

people's congresses and standing committees at local levels, they must guarantee that the constitution is complied with and enforced in their own jurisdictions. And all government administrative organs, judicial organs, and procuratorial organs must resolutely enforce the constitution, carry out their duties in accordance with the law, and continuously improve the competence of law enforcement personnel. . . . No organization or individual may have any prerogative beyond that which is set forth in the constitution and law.

So General Secretary Hu: is it not obvious that the closure of the publication that has occurred before our eyes violates article 35 of our constitution? This constitutional article clearly stipulates that citizens "have freedom of speech, of the press, of assembly, of association, of procession, and of demonstration." We would like to ask: what part of the article by Professor Yuan Weishi is in violation of the constitution? The disciplinary action taken by the Propaganda Department of the Communist Youth League Central Committee, in plain fact, has no legal basis at all, nor do those various law-flouting antispeech actions taken by the propaganda authorities of the country in recent years. We ask again: over the last three years, what have you done to "redress all violations of the constitution"? Why is it that what we have seen is to the contrary; that not only have these violations not been redressed but rather been encouraged?

In a country ruled by law, a fundamental principle is that all exercise of public power must be pursuant to a grant by the constitution and law, and must give the relevant parties recourse to legal relief. This is to say that once people are subject to the effects of power and believe that relevant decisions violate the constitution or law, they may lodge a complaint and have the right to a fair hearing. But both the Propaganda Department of the Communist Youth League Central Committee that made this decision and the Central Propaganda Department that has consistently enforced policies silencing the mass media are, as far as the law is concerned, organizations completely lacking in legal character, and they exercise authority in a completely unscrupulous manner. As a result, the media and individuals are unable to offer any legal challenge. The reason is simply that they and other departments like them do not have any legal character, and that they are organizations that are beyond the law. Our nation's constitution's preamble states: "The people of all nationalities, all state organs, the armed forces, all political parties and public organizations and all enterprises and undertakings in the country must take the constitution as the basic norm of conduct, and they have the duty to uphold the dignity of the constitution and ensure its implementation." The statements of General Secretary Hu set forth above also emphasized that "no organization or individual may have any prerogative beyond that which is set forth in the constitution and law." Therefore, any organization that does not have a legal character lives outside the constitution and the law, and once this kind of organization issues its orders, they will be strictly enforced, and they have the authority to wield absolute control over media organizations. Is it possible that you cannot see that this is a "prerogative beyond that which is set forth in the constitution and law?"

Why the Freedom of Speech?

The freedom of speech is so suppressed in this country perhaps because many government officials, including you, the esteemed members of the Standing Committee of CCP Central Committee, are worried that as soon as we speak freely, certain negative effects will arise, with free speech triggering social unrest, hindering economic development, bringing about ideological chaos, and jeopardizing the power and prestige of the government. But if we open our eyes to the rest of the world, we will see that these kinds of fears are completely unfounded.

Any kind of social order that is able to be maintained over the long term cannot be founded on the basis of suppression. In a society going through a period of transition, traditional interest structures will be revised, and diverse interest groups need channels for public dissemination. The public dissemination of all kinds of speech will expose the true social situation for all to see, and encourage policies that have definite goals, while all that attempts to suppress dissent will accomplish will be to cause policymakers to be divorced from reality, to see the sky from the bottom of a well, and to be left unable to make rational policies. Quite often Standing Committee members will go see or investigate what things are like in the provinces, and quite often they are vexed by the deceptions of local officials, and in the process of carrying out their investigations, they will call upon the people to speak the truth; but in the end the truth is scant, even to the point where they have been completely duped. In fact, if there is freedom of the press and freedom of speech, then everything will be greatly simplified, and it will no longer be necessary to drag people out to carry out inspections, as a public media will be able to reveal the truth of all situations. You will have all of the kinds of information that you require, and then local officials will have no way of covering up anything. Not only that, the media have their antennae out to expose at the first opportunity all abuses of power or other corruption happening at all levels of society and in all places. The experience of countries where the freedom of speech is upheld shows that the pressure from the media is an important institutional factor that reduces corruption among government officials and promotes social stability. Besides, as you will no doubt agree from your own experience, psychologically it is important to provide channels by which the public can vent the pressure of social life and its frequent dissatisfaction with the government, and these channels, far from jeopardizing social stability, are indeed very effective measures to promote social stability.

Concerning the relationship between the freedom of the press and economic development, we think you will have good sources of information for reference. A survey of countries in the world points at a positive correlation between a country's economic achievement and its freedom of speech. A primary reason for the increasing number of enterprises knowingly or recklessly putting consumers in harm's way by making and selling dangerous, defective products—and reaping the bitter harvest they sowed when their malpractices were eventually exposed—is exactly the result of the absence of effective supervision and exposure of these acts from a well-functioning media circle. Frauds and irregularities in the stock market in recent years were also hidden for some time. (This point is well illustrated by the economist Professor Chen Zhiwu in his work "Market Economy Calls for an Open Press Environment.")[3] Admittedly, even with the lack of freedom of the press, China has still managed to achieve rapid economic growth in past years, but the members of the Standing Committee should be well aware that this growth has been underlined by a very low starting point and that much of the data is open to question. In addition, due to institutional defects, many economic decisions are less than well informed. With such a state of things, it is exactly the freedom of the press that can play a very effective role in ensuring the healthy development of China's market economy.

As for the impact of freedom of speech and the press on people's thoughts, it is obvious that, along with the ongoing social transformation in China, citizens' thoughts have also been undergoing transformation, transitioning from ideological rigidity to a higher degree of diversity and vigor; from uniform thinking to truly free thinking. In this process, a number of the most fundamental concepts and principles should be established, such as the recognition that truth is not measured in proportion to power or a person's status, and that no person or institution can monopolize the truth. A healthy state of mind of citizens is dependent on open and rational discussions, and the suppression of such discussions will only lead to a shallow alignment in appearance and the spread of various subversive doctrines. A forced suppression will also bring about the prevalence of falsehoods. In a country where those who speak the truth are suppressed, it is impossible to establish mutual trust, and in the course of time, people will hold each other in suspicion and disguise what they truly feel and believe, with the moral bottom line constantly sinking lower. It is inconceivable that a good mental state is possible in such an atmosphere. Just look at what we call "the mainstream media." Can a single thought of depth or a single comment of sincerity be found there? In this age of globalization, a country's competitiveness is reflected not only in its economic prowess but also, and more fundamentally, in the lively and critical vision of its citizens. What's the use of economic affluence if people do not have their own individuality and independent mind and know nothing but to obey! When the citizens become a mass of ignoramuses, the rulers will not become any wiser, because only citizens who have free, independent minds are capable of putting in place national leaders of true wisdom and authority.

Toward Democracy, Rule of Law and Constitutional Government

We believe that, like us, the esteemed members of the Standing Committee have a strong sense of responsibility to this nation, and we well understand that ruling a country as large as this is no easy matter. These days, on the one hand, you constantly emphasize building a harmonious society, while on the other hand a succession of social contradictions and conflicts emerges, growing more severe all the time. Your concern that relaxing controls on speech will trigger unrest is not completely irrational, but we must recognize that a society that is truly harmonious is also a society that appears as if it were filled with all kinds of conflict. Respecting different interests and diverging ideas, and simultaneously establishing a system that is just so as to allow different interests and ideas to openly and peacefully compete with one another—only in this way can a country truly move in the direction of great order. This was the rationale of our forefathers when they said, "Those that are the same cannot govern one another, and it is only when there are differences that a positive result can be achieved." In order to achieve this goal, we need to foster the concept of the people being the master of the country and provide channels enabling them to engage in the decisionmaking in national affairs, so that different groups of people have their representatives speaking for them within the law, and those oppressed by power have venues to openly express their dissatisfaction. This calls for an independent judicial system and a strict procedural model to govern the operation of politics. Above all, the public should be enabled to have its voice heard through all kinds of media. Of course, in this country that has had such a long tradition of autocratic rule, the process of establishing rule of law and constitutional government will be a gradual one. But even if the pace is slow, our direction must be correct. Regrettably, in recent years, high-handed policies toward the press are a movement in the wrong direction. The handling of the *Freezing Points* weekly was merely the most recent example.

Members of the Standing Committee, as we look back to three years ago when the ravages of "SARS" and the "Sun Zhigang incident" triggered the anger of the entire nation, we see that you were able to listen and respond to public opinion by relaxing controls over the press and abolishing the notorious Measures on the Detention and Repatriation of People Engaged in Begging in Cities, and for that you won the heartfelt support of the people and the praise of the international community. But what people cannot understand is how this situation could last for only a few months, after which there has been a continuous regression. This change for the worse has triggered a rising wave of dissatisfaction and aggravated social tension. Some officials, seeing in the escalation of dissatisfaction among the people an opportunity to serve their own purpose, conveniently attach the label of "neoliberalism" to all those who advocate continuing to push the country's reform ahead, and try every means to have various policies put in place over the past several decades of reform either reconsidered or adjusted. This has, in effect, posed a serious threat to the fundamental lines and policies initiated by Deng Xiaoping for reforming the Chinese society. As a matter of fact, as you have surely noticed, some comments reminiscent of the "Great Cultural Revolution" era have already begun to pop up. At this critical moment, it is hoped that you will stand on the right side of history and avail yourself of the present opportunity to reverse the ongoing worrisome trend and put the country back on the track toward a democratic country ruled by law and constitution. This meritorious endeavor of yours will surely make you shining heroes in the history of the Chinese nation!

"Make up your mind that happiness depends on being free, and freedom depends on being courageous." Let these inspiring words by the Greek statesman Pericles over 2,000 years ago, which remain so vibrant to this day, be a clarion call for us to move ahead!

PART V

THE LEGAL PROTECTION
OF HUMAN RIGHTS

CHALLENGING THE DEATH PENALTY
Why We Should Abolish This Barbaric Punishment

The topic I would like to discuss with you this evening is a heavy one; it's the death penalty. As we know, the death penalty is a focal issue in many countries around the world. As a matter of fact, the death penalty has been abolished or basically abolished in more than 120 countries worldwide. In other countries, such as the United States—a rare case among developed countries—the death penalty is still pronounced and executed. According to a recent news report, since 1976, when the death penalty was reinstated, a total of 1,000 executions have been performed in the United States. To perform 1,000 executions in thirty years means that there are only an average of 30 executions every year in the country. Given the large population of the United States, it is extraordinary. The lowest record of executions in a year in ancient China was 29 in the Tang dynasty, which had a population of around 50 million, far lower than the U.S. population today. However, the differences in historical context cannot be ignored. In ancient times, to perform only 29 executions in a year was already a miracle in human history.

Recently, the Supreme People's Court has been undertaking reform, that is, taking back the power of death penalty review, which has rekindled concerns over the death penalty and the hope that reform will help prevent the occurrence of misjudged cases. As we may still remember, there was a widely publicized news report last year about a case where the true culprit was captured ten

Editor's note: The original Chinese version of this chapter is based on the author's speech delivered at the East China University of Political Science and Law on December 15, 2005. It has been slightly edited for English usage.

years after the execution of the innocent suspect, raising concerns about the death penalty. Therefore, the most important motive behind the reform may be to prevent wrongful executions through stricter death penalty review.

We are also concerned about the question of how to reduce the number of executions. How many executions are performed in China every year? Professor You Wei, you are an expert on the death penalty issue; you may know the answer, but don't tell me, and I don't want to know about it because to know something one should not know is not a good thing and may have serious consequences, such as the leak of national secrets or the accusation of it.[1] How many executions are performed in China is a secret that the Chinese authorities make every effort to keep from the international community. Some international organizations are very eager to know how many executions are performed in China. In the past, a common way for them to get the answer was to make calculations based on our news reports on it. China used to take pride on death penalty enforcement, and executions were often covered by newspaper or TV news reports, such as the day the Shanghai No. 1 Intermediate People's Court announced the immediate execution of seventeen criminals, and then the Nanjing Intermediate People's Court and the Chengdu Intermediate People's Court made similar announcements, and so on and so forth. Those international organizations put those numbers together and were often appalled at the result.

Today, however, reporting about the exact number of executions is prohibited. As a result, courts' announcements on executions now follow another pattern, not on a number basis but on a group basis, such as the Shanghai No. 1 Intermediate People's Court announcing a group execution, and then the Chengdu Intermediate People's Court making a similar announcement, followed by the Nanjing Intermediate People's Court, and so on and so forth. This leaves foreign anti–death penalty organizations clueless as to how many executions are performed because it is impossible to translate the number of groups into exact numbers of individuals. In a word, the number of executions performed in China may be far greater than the executions in the rest of the world combined.

As you know, India and China are comparable in many ways, and the former is also a populous country. Then, one may ask, how many executions are enforced in India? The country has been troubled by the enforcement of the death penalty since the 1980s because of a lack of executioners. According to a recent report, the whole of India has only five hangmen left to carry out the special job of hanging, the way executions are performed in India, a craft that requires much training and is often handed down from generation to generation and is therefore far more complicated and cumbersome than straightforward shooting. As it stands, there are only a handful of hangmen left in India, and even they are not enthusiastic about the job, including one who is asking strongly for retirement. In India it is very difficult to enforce an execution because as long as the person to be executed cries, "I am innocent!" the court will order postponement of the execution to check whether the person is really innocent, and the investigation may take a long time—perhaps five or ten years. As a result, there are many prisoners waiting for execution in jails. Some have waited for it for more than ten years and are still waiting for their turn. Thus there are only a very few executions in India every year. In sharp contrast, China presents a radically different picture in this regard. As we know, resumption of authority by the Supreme People's Court to review the death penalty has been highlighted as a very important change in its second five-year reform outline. However, this reform is not a major structural change in the country's judicial system; to put it another way, it is simply a return to a basic stipulation in the Criminal Procedure Law that took effect in 1980, that is, all death sentences shall be subject to the review of the Supreme People's Court. According to the provision, if the court that initially gives the death sentence is an intermediate court, the second-instance court shall be a higher court, and if the higher court upholds the original death sentence, then the case shall be submitted to the Supreme People's Court for review.

The Supreme People's Court shall undertake the review, considering such aspects as whether the sentence is based on definite evidence and whether the judge's interpretation and application of law are appropriate. This provision was then considered to have drawn on China's ancient legal tradition, where the emperor had the ultimate power to decide cases. This stipulation of the 1980 Criminal Procedure Law was included to ensure the fair administration of the death penalty. Ironically, not long after this law was promulgated, the "Strike Hard Campaign" against crime was launched, and quickly the Standing Committee of the National People's Congress relegated the power of death penalty review concerning severe crimes, such as murder, arson, and robbery, to the higher courts of the provinces, with the result that provincial higher courts assumed the dual role of appellate court and death penalty review organ. In many higher courts, these two powers are exercised by the same group of judges, which in effect renders the death penalty review system null and as a result has led to the increasing number of executions in China.

Underlying this problem is a flaw in legislation. The Criminal Procedure Law of the People's Republic of China is a basic law of the country, a law that was deliberated upon and adopted at a plenary session of the National People's

Congress. However, the Standing Committee, the executive organ of the National People's Congress, has the power to tamper with the basic law by changing the death penalty review procedure provided for in the law. This indicates that in this country, law is not really taken seriously. Isn't it something decided by a few persons privately? Not only basic law, but even the constitution is not taken seriously.

Anyway, now this reform has been finally introduced. I believe this has much to do with external pressure because the great number of executions enforced every year in China has elicited great international concern. Recently, the Supreme People's Court has been occupied with designing a sounder death penalty review procedure. From several academic seminars on the issue that I have attended, I learned that the Supreme Court is going to recruit new people, at least in the Beijing region, providing a great opportunity for those with M.A. and Ph.D. degrees in criminal law and criminal litigation to work at the Supreme People's Court. Law professors teaching those subjects are particularly happy because not only are their students ensured employment, but they can make a beeline to the Supreme Court. The other day, when speaking of this matter, I said to a friend that this is simply not the proper practice because it is explicitly stipulated in the Judges Law that judges of a higher court shall be selected from excellent judges of a lower court. My friend replied that it is easy for me to stand by and criticize, but the Supreme People's Court must resort to this approach in order to solve staffing problems related to new recruits. If a senior judge from a lower court is introduced, the Supreme Court will have to attend to many related affairs, including the employment of the transferred judge's family members and the schooling of his children. To recruit graduates is the most convenient of all options. In refutation, I said death penalty review is a matter of life and death that cannot be compromised for the sake of convenience. How much understanding do M.A. graduates have of the seriousness of the death penalty? Young and lacking judicial experience, can they identify possible flaws in evidence on which the original death sentence is based and discern ambiguity in judicial interpretations? The response given is that for now, the Supreme People's Court cannot attend to these particulars, and the priority is to have those positions filled first. This is another deep-seated defect in China's system.

On the other hand, the Supreme People's Court itself lacks experience in death penalty review. Except for a few special crimes, such as economic crimes or spying, all death sentences are subject to the review of the Supreme Court, but many of its judges don't know much about how to undertake a death penalty review. Given this backdrop, there is close observation as to whether the resumption of death penalty review by the Supreme Court will effectively reduce the number of executions and misjudged cases in China, how to proceed with the review, and whether review judges will travel to other regions or stay in Beijing. If all death sentences are reviewed in Beijing, then all the condemned will be escorted to Beijing, and the CCP Central Committee and the State Council will not be happy to have so many condemned inmates in the capital. After all, the petitioners from the provinces are a nuisance enough, and think of adding to them all the condemned persons across the country! [*Laughter*] Therefore, it is not feasible to perform all death penalty reviews in Beijing. Therefore, Supreme Court judges will have to spend much time traveling by air in order to perform death penalty reviews. As you know, many condemned inmates are imprisoned in far-off counties or small cities. Therefore the traveling expenses will be a big financial burden on the Supreme People's Court. Furthermore, we are also concerned about whether each condemned prisoner will have the chance to receive face-to-face interrogation. If only document-based review is undertaken, how can it ensure that all misjudgments will be identified and put right? All these questions and concerns are under ongoing consideration, and relevant measures are yet to be promulgated.

What then is the next step? When asked about China's death penalty system in a press conference, Premier Wen Jiabao said that given China's unique national conditions, it is unrealistic to abolish the death penalty now, but China will make every effort to ensure that the death penalty is administered with caution and fairness. This is how Premier Wen stands on this matter. It seems, at least at the present, that the country's leadership is not considering the abolition of the death penalty. Even so, it is high time for us to have a thorough examination of this question: is the abolition of the death penalty in China likely?

In this audience there are judges, procurators, and quite a few law practitioners as well as students. What I present this evening here is only my own subjective or impressionistic views on the subject, something not backed by systematic research and therefore lacking in depth. And here I have to be frank that I am no expert in criminal law; the reason why I pick this subject for this lecture is that I think the issue of the death penalty is not the exclusive province of jurists specializing in criminal law or criminal procedure, and that it deserves attention from all people, particularly scholars of jurisprudence, legal history, and even sociology, ethics, history, and psychology. Therefore, I am very happy to see the series of articles on the death penalty published in *Beijing News* by Professor He Huaihong, my colleague at the

Department of Philosophy of Peking University. In fact, I also want to publish similar articles, but some newspapers seem to exercise too much self-censorship, and topics such as constitutional government and judicial independence are considered forbidden for discussion. The topic of the death penalty, however, is okay, but it should be discussed only from the perspective of how to improve the death penalty review system. I told their editors that to talk about how to improve the system is beyond me, but I do have some interesting views to share about the abolition of the death penalty, and this latter topic, this time, is beyond them. [*Laughter*] Therefore, since I cannot write about it, I am now here talking about it to show my concern about this subject.

Here let's have a brief analysis of the nature of capital punishment and the reason why it must be abolished. Before I proceed with this topic, I believe few among you agree with immediate and unconditional abolition of the death penalty. The proposal of such a move will even strike you as whimsical because, as you may reason, murders and economic crimes are becoming so rampant today in China, and it is neither practical nor responsible to abolish the death penalty at this point. In what follows, I will briefly discuss this issue, and I hope Professor You Wei will comment on my talk after I complete it.

So why should the death penalty be abolished? The first reason is that the death penalty, as has been pointed out by many people, has difficulty bringing about the intended effect of curbing crimes.

The death penalty is often seen as an instrument meant not only to punish the criminal but also to serve as a deterrent to those entertaining similar criminal motives. However, the effect of the death penalty in curbing serious crimes is doubtful because, according to experts on the death penalty and some international data, in countries where the death penalty has been abolished, there is usually not any significant change in the rate of serious crimes compared with the past, except for some minor fluctuations. In some federal countries where the death penalty is abolished in some states but not in other states, it is also found that there is not any remarkable change in the crime rate among these states. Indeed, in the case of Lithuania, after it abolished the death penalty, the rate of serious crimes has not only not increased but decreased. This is thought provoking. Why does the enforcement of the death penalty fail to achieve its intended effect of curbing crimes?

The famous French writer and philosopher Albert Camus, who is widely read in China, wrote quite a few articles related to the death penalty, including the novel *The Stranger* and a long coauthored essay titled *Reflections on the Guillotine*.[2] *The Stranger* is a portrayal of the mental state of a condemned criminal, with the story set in Algiers, then a French colony. A young man, hearing of his mother's death, hurried home to attend to the matter. In the room where his mother's coffin was placed, he smoked a cigarette, which was deemed morally offensive. He looked unfeeling during his mother's funeral and in the whole course did not shed a single tear. After the funeral, he returned to downtown Algiers and went for a swim the same day after work. When he was swimming, he encountered a former female acquaintance and suddenly the fire of passion was kindled between them. They went to the cinema and watched a comedy—on the very evening of the day of his mother's funeral. They then went to his apartment and performed their own special "play" together. [*Laughter*] Now on a weekend, he and several friends went to have fun in a place and for some reason got into a fight with others, and he shot a man to death using his friend's gun. He was then taken to the court, where he felt like an outsider to what was going on in the court, as if the case had nothing to do with him. He wanted to say something in his defense but was stopped by his lawyer. He said it was his own business, and he had the right to speak in his own defense, but the lawyer said no. Many questions were put forward during the court procedure. For instance, his smoking in front of his mother's coffin was cited as an example of his unfeeling indifference, which inevitably would lead him to murderous acts. In the end, he was sentenced to death. The novel touches on many challenging issues.

In his *Reflections on the Guillotine*, Camus cited statistics on executions in the early part of the twentieth century. As you know, in the past, criminals were often guillotined in a festive atmosphere, watched by crowds of people. According to a survey then, over 70 percent of condemned criminals had watched the executions of other criminals before, including many who had watched multiple times. They obviously were not deterred by the executions they had seen.

This gives rise to a question: among the factors that lead to murderous acts, which are avoidable and which are not? Let's take a recent case as an example. Early this year, a murder happened in Hangzhou, Zhejiang Province. The victim was a female student at a local university, allegedly a campus belle. She went out to take the college English test, level 6, but never came back, and now folks are saying that the test is really life-threatening. [*Laughter*] She took a taxi to the exam center, and after the exam, she took a taxi back home. On the way back, the driver took a sudden turn to dodge a truck ahead, and the girl hit her head against the car window as a result. The girl then accused the driver of bad driving, and the driver replied that he made the turn for safety purposes. Now the girl let out a stream of accusations in a superior air, saying that the driver was unqualified and uncouth.

The driver simply kept silent and drove on until they arrived at the destination. The girl took a look at the cab meter and found the fare was RMB 18. She said that was not the first time she took the route, and the fare was always RMB 16. The driver said that RMB 18 was what was displayed by the meter. The girl then said she would only pay RMB 16, and it was already very generous given the injury she had just suffered. The driver did not agree, and they got into a quarrel. At one point, the girl attempted to scratch the driver's face. This became the straw that broke the camel's back. The outraged driver suddenly seized the throat of the girl, and by the time he became aware of what had happened, it was already too late, and the girl was dead. The driver was sentenced to death and executed. Now we can only pray that their souls rest in peace.

Recently, a similar case happened in Beijing. A teenage girl living in my neighborhood was strangled to death on a bus. The girl was thirteen and the daughter of a seventy-three-year-old Tsinghua University professor. She and her elderly parents got on a crowded bus. The old professor's wife asked whether there was anyone who was so obliging as to offer his seat to her ailing husband, but no one responded. It happened that next to the conductress sat a forty-something woman in the bus company's uniform, and the professor's wife asked her whether she could offer her seat to her aged husband. However, the woman simply blurted out, "What right have you to ask me to do this?" And this caused a quarrel between them. The conductress, believing that her companion was wronged, came up with a method of revenge. She asked the girl and her parents to pay another RMB 1 each, insisting that they got on the bus at the stop previous to the one they actually boarded from. This again led to a hot dispute. The thirteen-year-old girl, in indignation, called the other party malicious and ill bred. Hearing this, the forty-something woman became very angry, approached the girl, and strangled her, using so much force that the girl soon weakened and fell to the floor. The old woman immediately called for help and asked to send her daughter to the hospital, but the driver was indifferent and said that they would first pay a fine at the bus station. Anyway, at the next stop, the girl was eventually sent to the hospital, but it was already too late. So the girl died, and the woman was arrested. The court judgment on the case is yet to come out.

In reality, which is more numerous: homicides committed by strangers or by acquaintances? According to statistics, more than 60 percent or even 70 percent of homicides are committed by acquaintances in China. There are children killed by mothers and husbands by wives and wives by husbands. And in many cases, homicides by acquaintances and even strangers are committed in the heat of passion, when the mind is not really fully conscious of what is going on. Homicidal acts in this category cannot be prevented by the death penalty. Then can the death penalty prevent premeditated murders? One fact suffices to prove that the answer is *no*; that is, impositions of the death penalty are followed by more impositions of the death penalty. The unceasing imposition of the death penalty for crimes shows that the death penalty is ineffective as a curb. If the death penalty were effective, crimes punishable by death would not be committed. For instance, after the sentencing to death of Cheng Kejie, a top corrupt official, corruption cases have not only not decreased but increased. Indeed, the worship of money has reached such a point in China that it is worth risking one's life. It gives the impression that the death penalty received by corrupt officials is but another form of martyrdom, that is, martyrdom for money, and for them decapitation is no more than having their hat blown away by the wind. [*Laughter*] What has one to fear when one has money? This is an issue that deserves more attention.

The second reason for the abolition of the death penalty is that it not only fails to deter crimes but actually incites them.

To cite a remark by Montesquieu, if to steal ten francs and to murder the king are both punishable by death, then people will choose to murder the king because then one not only steals the treasury and is immensely wealthy but also replaces the king and wields supreme power. As the saying goes, one life for one life breaks even; one life for two is a good bargain. Or as the Western saying goes, in for a penny, in for a pound.

If I committed a crime punishable by death and remained at large, I would have no scruples about committing more crimes. How else to explain the great number of cases in which robbers and thieves became murderers? Because even robbery and theft can be punishable by death, and if one's life is at stake either way, the criminals choose to commit even more serious crimes and, at the same time, try to destroy all evidence. This thinking pattern, obviously, encourages more crimes.

The celebrated Italian jurist Cesare Beccaria wrote a thin but highly influential treatise entitled "On Crimes and Punishments."[3] Nowadays, a scholar who in his whole life only wrote such a thin volume would even have no claim to professorship, but Cesare Beccaria has become a prominent name in the legal history of the world. His work has inspired generations of people to join the anti–death penalty cause. He said, "The minds of men, which like fluids always adjust to the level of the objects that surround them, become hardened. If punishments be very severe, men are naturally led to the perpetration of other crimes, to avoid the punishment due to the first. The countries and times most notorious for severity of punishment have always been those in which the bloodiest and most inhumane of deeds were committed." This is why the death penalty, rather than achieving its intended effect of curbing crimes, only incites more crimes. This quote shows great insight into human nature.

Nie Shubin was a wrongly executed young farmer, bright and very handsome, as shown by online photos of him. His case was reported by *Southern Weekend* and many other newspapers. The misjudged case emerged in February this year [2005] when a man detained by police in connection with a case in Zhengzhou, Henan Province, confessed to another case he committed in Hebei, in which he raped and killed a woman in the suburbs of Shijiazhuang. The police in Henan were overjoyed, because not only the present case but also an unsolved case from ten years before were now solved together, and they called the police authority of Hebei about the matter, only to be given the astonishing answer that the perpetrator of the rape-and-murder case was sentenced to death and executed ten years ago. The criminal was then escorted to Henan to check whether his confessed crime was the same crime, and the place he led police officers to turned out to be exactly the same site where the rape-and-murder case happened ten years ago. This shocking discovery was reported and caused a big stir among the public. People want to know how this outrageous thing could have happened.

This belated discovery also left Nie Shubin's mother bitter and grief stricken. She fell to the ground before her son's low grave, crying her heart out. Nie was barely twenty-one years old when he was executed. Over ten years, the family had been filled with humiliation because their son was executed for the crime. The victim's family, of course, also had no doubt that it was their son who committed the crime. Therefore, ever since then Nie's family had lived in shame. Now, even when the truth was exposed, their son's life could not be recovered. All that the poor mother could do was to simply cry and cry. However, in an article entitled *The Mystery Surrounding Nie's Case*, the author, a police officer who participated in the investigation of the case, insisted that Nie was the true perpetrator, saying that he confessed to his crime only after three days' continuous interrogation. The case, you know, is likely to end up with no definite outcome because rather than being reviewed by an independent party, as it should be, it is now under the investigation of a group organized by the Political and Judiciary Commission of Hebei Province and comprising officers from the police, the judiciary, and the procuratorate of the province. In other words, this misjudged case is now being investigated by exactly those responsible for the misjudgment. That's why they still hold that the original judgment is not wrong.

The issue is still in dispute. And the poor mother has yet to get a definitive ruling about her son's case.

Nie Shubin's case points to a third reason to abolish the death penalty, one arrived at by asking the following question: why do forced confessions and misjudgments keep emerging in China? For many reasons, torture is a common means of extracting suspects' confessions in this country. In spite of the fact that this practice has led to many wrongful convictions, there are still many people that defend it, saying that this practice is understandable and citing many supporting reasons, such as that the country does not have advanced interrogation equipment like other countries and therefore torture is a necessary method. What occurs during interrogation by torture is often very cruel, with the suspect's tightly handcuffed hands tainted with blood. The use of torture to coerce a statement has a long history and remains alive despite many attempts to eliminate it. Why is torture used in interrogations? It is seen by some as the simplest and most straightforward way to acquire the details of a crime, especially when it is very difficult or impossible to verify what really happened. However, as wittily put by the famous French writer and philosopher Montaigne, torture cannot bring out the truth of a case and seems to be a test of endurance rather than of truth. The man who can endure torture will not tell the truth, and the man who cannot endure it will tell untruths. [*Laughter*] In a word, the truth remains hidden. We should be grateful to Mr. Qian Zhongshu for this brilliant translation.

She Xianglin is another victim of a miscarriage of justice, which came to light and attracted nationwide concern this year. She, originally accused of murdering his wife, would likely have faced the death penalty if not for the decision of the Political and Judiciary Commission of Hubei Province to have the case heard by a lower court in the first instance on the grounds of some doubtful evidence. Upon hearing this decision, his lawyer told him that he had escaped the death sentence. She was curious and asked why, and was told that if the first-instance court is a lower court, it could not hand down a death sentence. Just as expected, She was only sentenced to fifteen years in prison. He would still be sitting in prison now had not a dramatic event happened: his wife, allegedly killed by him, returned home, after he had spent eleven years in prison for the alleged crime. And the corpse believed to be his wife was somebody else, whose identity remains unknown, meaning that another criminal case remains unsolved. Anyway, the return of his wife, who left home due to mental problems, cleared his name and exposed the former gravely wrongful conviction. On November 11, 2005, She Xianglin paid a visit to Beijing to show his thanks to the *Beijing News*, which played a major role in his release. He went to attend a celebration of the two-year anniversary of the newspaper. Thanks to the arrangement of friends at the *Beijing News*, I had a chat with him. He did not strike me as a normal person. I noticed that his index finger was only half its original length. He told me that the treatment he received during his interrogation was really too hard to bear. He was deprived of sleep for eleven days and nights in a brightly illuminated room and experienced all kinds of torture imaginable. At last, he gave up and said he would make whatever confession they wanted. When he was not threatened by beating, he could not help withdrawing his previous confessions, only to be subjected to a new round of tortures. Half of his index finger was beaten away during that period. In fact, there are tortures far crueler than this. I once received a petitioner from Jinan in Shandong Province, an old engineer. According to his documents, his son was arrested by the local police, and when he finally saw his son, he was appalled to find that his body was covered by poker-inflicted holes and four of his fingers were lost. It was truly heart wrenching.

How are we to prevent the use of torture during interrogation? The fact is that this practice not only is unchecked but is taking on new forms in addition to the traditional techniques that remain in use. Research on torture is a specialized discipline. The late professor Zhou Yeqian at the National Institute of Law of the Chinese Academy of Social Sciences, a scholar whom I highly respect, was truly an expert on the kinds of torture used during interrogation. He was so familiar with them that he could enumerate and describe them in meticulous detail, one by one, making your hair stand on end as you listened. [*Laughter*] Methods of torture, to use a catch phrase, are also "keeping pace with the times." Interrogators now know how to inflict serious internal injuries while maintaining a person's normal external appearance. The practice of sleep deprivation by continuous overillumination was unheard of in ancient times since there was no artificial, bright lighting back then. This was exactly what She Xianglin suffered, and he suffered so much that he said he avoids any place with strong illumination because his eyes cannot bear it. And he even avoids meeting strangers now. He said he has become an altogether different person after what he experienced in prison. During his imprisonment, his mother remained firmly convinced that her son was innocent, and she kept petitioning higher authorities. Because of her activism, she was imprisoned for three months and died soon after release. She Xianglin said it was for his sake that his mother died, and he does not know how to face his relatives. He told me that now he mostly spends his time indoors and avoids coming out, and when he does come out, he automatically moved sideways and then stays there motionless at the sight of strangers because it has become a conditioned response after the long years he had spent in prison after the sentencing. This is indeed spiritual torture. This way of handling things, indeed, has distorted the whole nation's mind.

During a visit to one county, I met a police officer who complained to me indignantly that the local authority of the Administration for Industry and Commerce arrested people and beat them. He said angrily, "They have no right to do that, to beat people. That's our exclusive business!" [*Laughter*] Indeed, arrests and corporal punishments are used not only by police but also by other government authorities, even including CCP discipline inspection commissions. Once a chief procurator in Shenyang was inspected, and his case was put in the charge of the procuratorate of Nanjing. A friend working in the procuratorate and close to the matter told me that it was only then that the chief procurator himself experienced what it was like to be deprived of sleep. It's really a very cruel thing. The widespread use of such practices, so to speak, has hardened the hearts of many people. When we see police officers beating their countrymen, we cannot help thinking of Mencius's teaching on human nature. The feeling of commiseration, he said, is essential to man, and one would be no different from a beast if he does not have this feeling.

Without doubt, the use of torture in interrogation has resulted in many wrongful convictions. The case of Du Peiwu is just such an example. He was accused of murdering his wife and a colleague of his wife's. Both Du and his wife were themselves police officers. His wife as well as the colleague were found beaten to death in a car, and he was suspected. Although there were major uncertainties involved in the case, Du was still sentenced to death with a two-year reprieve. Luckily, the true culprit was captured about one year later, and Du was released. After release, Du also narrated how he suffered torture during interrogation. He himself was a police officer, and now he was tortured by his peers. In a word, given the current framework of China's judicial system, it is simply inevitable that many wrongful death sentences will be given out.

Wrongful execution is fundamentally different from other wrongful convictions. When summarizing the work of East China University of Politics and Law in 2005, President He Qinhua can say that 95 percent of the work is well done, and the remaining 5 percent still leaves something to be desired, such as the Songjiang Campus being remotely located and the need for improving campus bus service. This, of course, is very normal. When it comes to criminal convictions, some flaws in the imposition of fixed-term imprisonment are tolerable, such as 5 percent of fixed-term imprisonments are too severe or lack a firm basis, because they are more or less compensable or remediable. Of course, in the case of She Xianglin, what he lost cannot be recovered, but at least he can receive around RMB 900,000 in compensation. The money cannot buy back what he lost, but it is at least a consolation to him. He gets sympathy wherever he goes and is more or less fortunate that things did not turn out even worse for him than they actually did. But what about those who are wrongly executed, like Nie Shubin? A life lost cannot be recovered in any way in the world! A court president cannot console himself by saying that of the more than 100 cases the court has heard, 95 percent are correctly adjudicated, and that, therefore, the achievements are in the majority. [*Laughter*] One's head is not like chives that keep shooting up after being cut. This is the primary reason why death sentences should be weighed with particular prudence.

There is a horrible photo of an execution scene during the Qing dynasty, taken by a Western photographer in the late nineteenth century. In the photo, a person to be executed looks around open-mouthed at the other person who has just been beheaded by the executioner. It was arranged this way on purpose, and the whole scene was watched by a big crowd of spectators. In the study of the history of the Roman Empire, there is a view that the combat of gladiators rendered the souls of Romans increasingly benumbed, inhumane, and cruel. The same thing, in fact, can also be said of executions in China.

There is another photo of a beautiful girl to be executed. This photo is less scary, but her expression is equally striking. She seems to be smiling, but it is a smile that saddens one. This was a case that happened in Guangdong, and the girl was from Henan. She and her ex-boyfriend murdered a woman. This was a very odd case. Having broken up with her ex-boyfriend, this girl carried on an affair with a married man, and when this affair was exposed, the man's wife came to her threatening such-and-such if she did not end the relationship. The girl, however, did not flinch. Instead, she called her ex-boyfriend and conspired to murder the woman. As a result, they tricked the woman into a hotel room where the woman was killed by the girl's ex-boyfriend. Eventually both the girl and her ex-boyfriend were sentenced to death, to be executed immediately. This was the scene before execution. As you can see, there was a rope around her neck. Today, executions are no longer performed openly. But in the past, especially during the Strike Hard Campaign, people sentenced to death were often shown to the public to serve as a deterrent. This practice, however, was actually encouraging cruelty. According to Cesare Beccaria, when the government treats the people ruthlessly, the people will also treat the government ruthlessly, resulting in ruthless confrontation between the two. I think this is reflected in what we might call the bloodthirsty attitude shown through the enforcement of execution. And this development would constitute the fourth reason for abolition of the death penalty.

There is a fifth reason for the abolition of the death penalty: is the state justified in enforcing executions? The government or the state is necessary for society. A detailed theoretical discussion of the origin of the state is out of place here. Suffice it to say that according to the social contract theory, the state is created for safeguarding our own interest, safety, and freedom. The government's authority is derived from the consent of the governed, but this consent absolutely does not include the authority of the government to take away our own lives. The conclusion drawn from the perspective of social contract theory, therefore, is that the government is not justified in enforcing executions.

Some opponents of the death penalty point to execution as fighting against evil with evil. Isn't it paradoxical that the government kills people for the purpose of stopping the killing of people by others? For detailed elaboration on this point, you may refer to relevant treatises. Though this argument is very convincing, it is also rather bookish and, perhaps for the common people, the least persuasive.

The sixth reason to abolish the death penalty is that it destroys a person's dignity. The process of execution is very cruel. As we know, the death penalty is meant to be a threat and deterrent to criminals. I observe a marked difference between China and the West in the time when the condemned are notified of their forthcoming execution. In Western countries, they are normally told in the morning when they just wake up that they are to be executed a moment later. But it is different in China. We notify them the last night before their execution. [*Laughter*] According to existentialism, the fear of death is the fount of all creative activities. Out of fear of death, we make every effort to leave as many traces of us in this world. All normal people fear death, which is something too mysterious to stare at closely. Why is it that man suddenly appears in this world and then, after some time, disappears from this world? Where will we go after death?

According to a BBC special program on near-death experiences, those who have undergone the experience, that is, those who were seized back from the hands of the Grim Reaper, all reported that it feels like falling down a dark hole at an increasing rate and then seeing an approaching spot of light before suddenly coming to life. Some also reported a flying experience. But the dark hole sensation was experienced by them all. However, there is no definite, positive research telling us what really happens after we die. [*Laughter*] Will we exist in this world in any other form after death? Will I change into a bird and hover over Shuzhou River to look at the campus of East China University of Politics and Law and at the students studying diligently here, and feel consoled at the thought that I once gave a lecture here? [*Laughter and applause*] Some say that the soul is imperishable while others contend that a dead man is a burnt-out candle never to be rekindled. However, personally, I have always believed that after death a person will continue to exist in this world in some form.

Whatever the case, death is a prospect that fills one with horror and fear. Even normal death is fearful. Many elderly often talk about their forthcoming death and do everything they can to delay the final day. Some engage in longevity practices. Behind these acts, the fear of death is the only motive. This death, at any rate, is normal. One person lives to his or her seventies, eighties, or nineties and dies, and that's the course of nature. Professor Fei Xiaotong recently passed away at a ripe age. He was considered an example of a virtuous man living a long life.

On the other hand, there is another kind of death. It often happens like this. A condemned prisoner is suddenly approached with extraordinary kindness and asked what he wants to eat for supper. [*Laughter*] Want to smoke? Well, okay, no problem, even the best cigarettes. Eat whatever you like, but no liquor is allowed. There are judges in this audience. I have a question to ask you: is it strictly banned for condemned prisoners to drink liquor before execution? If I met that fate, I would surely demand some liquor. [*Laughter*] The last supper, however sumptuous, is rarely enjoyed with relish. Indeed, many people find it hard to swallow, not because it is not delicious but for lack of the mood because they know this is the last supper in their life, and tomorrow they will die. This is a preplanned death, in contrast to the normal death that happens suddenly. The condemned prisoner is told that he is to die tomorrow and his head will receive a bullet. Many people suddenly collapse at the announcement. Some fall to dead silence and stare at a spot blankly, their eyes looking scared. You don't know what is on their mind. Some simply cry and cry, as if they were crying out all the suffering and grievances they have experienced in this life and will experience in the afterlife. Others laugh like fools. And still others choose to write, seizing the last opportunity to pour out their innermost thoughts and feelings. The night is really a sleepless one for many people. Anyway, how many people can sleep as usual when they are conscious that they will be executed the next day? Let's take a look at this picture. The person has his trousers fastened with red ropes on the knees. What's the reason? Because many people display fecal and urinary incontinence before the execution. Having their trousers fastened is meant to avoid leaving a dirty trail as they are escorted to the execution site. Some people are almost paralyzed by what they are to suffer and have to be dragged to the site. This is really a humiliation of human dignity. A person killed in the street has no time for fear, but a person sentenced to death faces great uncertainties surrounding the judicial procedure, and the result is a kind of mental torture. After being sentenced to death by the original court, the convicted will not be immediately executed, which would be straightforward; instead, he has the right to appeal to a higher court. Though with one leg already in the grave, he still entertains a flash of hope that the first judgment will be overturned. If after a long process of appeal the original death sentence is upheld, the mental tortures suffered will have been all in vain. I have no idea what it feels like when one is killed by a bullet. Without doubt it is very cruel. However, this is more than one life for a life; during the whole process, one feels as if one had been killed many times. I believe this is a violation of human dignity.

A man, whatever crime he has committed, nevertheless remains our peer and compatriot. He is entitled to human dignity like everyone else. Even in ancient times there were forced suicides where a person was ordered to kill himself by drinking a cup of poisoned liquor. The shooting used today is a lot more inhumane than that.

If a death for a death is justified, what's the justification for the death penalty used in economic crimes? Cheng Kejie, the former vice-chairman of the Standing Committee of the National People's Congress, was sentenced to death for accepting bribes amounting to more than RMB 30 million. Li Ping, his accomplice in the case, was a nice-looking lady and had a relationship with him like that between Monica Lewinsky and Clinton. [*Laughter*] Li Ping promised to marry Cheng Kejie, and Cheng put Li in charge of many things. During the period when Cheng served as the president the People's Government of Guangxi Zhuang Autonomous Region, they did quite a few things in violation of the law, either jointly or separately. After Cheng was originally sentenced to death, I wrote a letter to the judicial committee of the Supreme People's Court, calling attention to violations of proper judicial procedure in the case. For example, why were the two tried separately rather than together? After all, what they committed was a joint offense, and in a joint offense, as you know, there are often more conflicts among the defendants than between the defendants and the prosecution, and efforts must be made to ascertain who committed which crimes. In Cheng's case, if a crime had nothing to do with Cheng and was committed solely by Li, then Li had to account for it. However, as it was, Cheng and Li were tried separately, and it was impossible for Cheng's lawyer to meet Li. As a result, Li's testimony became almost the only basis on which Cheng was convicted. Most paragraphs within the body of the final judgment begin with witness Li Ping saying or admitting this or that. I think that was horrible because it was more than possible that Li would intuitively throw all crimes onto the back of Cheng in order to get a lighter punishment herself. All these points were covered in my letter to the Supreme People's Court. A chief justice of the court once informed me that my letter was received and circulated among the judges. He then smiled, and the matter was dropped. [*Laughter*] Eventually, Cheng was sentenced to death and executed, becoming the highest-level political figure to be executed since the founding of the People's Republic of China in 1949.

Economic crimes, you know, are motivated by greed for money, and as the severest punishment, the court may confiscate all properties of the criminal. But what's the need and value of putting the individual to death? I always hold that man's life is beyond price and therefore cannot be measured by money. You cannot sentence one to death simply for embezzlement. In an extreme case, a pretty accountant of a kindergarten was sentenced to death and immediately executed for embezzlement of only RMB 210,000. Oh, a human life! What is its value? However, if an online debate on this question is held, it is almost certain that this reason will cause the greatest indignation among the netizens, and anyone holding this view will be accused of defending corrupt officials. Some jurists promoting this pro-life view have the impression that their articles attract so many attacks online that if they met these numerous opponents in reality, their spit would be enough to drown them. [*Laughter*] Advocacy for abolishing the death penalty, at least for economic crimes, is seen by the public as the indulgence of corrupt officials. But as a matter of fact, the punishment of confiscating all their properties and putting them in prison where they spend their days weeping and repenting, I believe, is not a light punishment, not necessarily lighter than the death penalty. This is my seventh point against the death penalty, that economic crimes should not be punishable by death. The eighth reason to abolish the death penalty is that it is often used to serve purposes other than law enforcement.

There is a famous oil painting featuring Socrates, surrounded by a saddened crowded, speaking eloquently before drinking a cup of poisoned liquor and becoming the first martyr for free speech in human history. Socrates was an opponent of democracy as well as a great philosopher. He regarded the democratic government with hostility, believing that it was caus-ing the decline of Athens. He spent his whole life speaking out against democracy and his state. And his method of promoting his views was very effective. He often came up to a stranger in the street and asked, "Can you tell me what is good?" Then the man would proceed to give his own answer. When a defect in his reasoning was identified, Socrates would ask a new question about the defect, and asked why it was so, and then the man would again give his answer, and this pattern of Q&A went on and on until the man gave up and said, "Well, Socrates, I don't understand it." [*Laughter*] Though Socrates often said, "I know one thing, that I know nothing," he was, as a matter of fact, considered to be the most knowledgeable person.

During the period of the Great Cultural Revolution in China, it was a popular view that the more one knows, the more one tends to be reactionary. Such persons are thought to have complicated minds and believe in meritoc-racy, that is, the state should be governed by elites, by people of genuine knowledge and professional competence. According to Socrates, we seek the best shoemaker in the city to repair our shoes, the best barber to cut our hair, and the best tailor to make clothes for us, but when it comes to governing the state, it is ridiculous that people of all trades including shoemakers, barbers, and tailors flock together and claim that they are capable of the work! Socrates did not like such democracy and attacked it fiercely. Finally, he was charged with corrupting the youth and impiety. The court that heard Socrates' case was a genuine "people's court." China's courts, though bearing the same name, do not really live up to it because in the Western context, the people's court is a court where the people—men in the street and laypersons—serve as judges. [*Laughter*] The judges were chosen by lottery from a group of Athenian citizen volunteers. In Socrates' case, there were more than 500 judges involved. This group of people is sometimes wrongly translated as "jurors." In fact, the more than 500 Athenian citizens partici-pating in the trial of Socrates were all judges. Anyway, Socrates found himself in an awkward situation. He found that he got the sympathy of many of the judges, who did not think that he should be sentenced to death. His role, to use his own description of himself, as a "gadfly" of Athens was thought to be in the interests of the city-state. And he awakened in others awareness of their lack of knowledge. Such a person, in a word, should not be put to death. However, the problem, from the perspective of Socrates, was that if he was not to be sentenced to death and even declared innocent, it would show that the people's court was very tolerant and the democracy of Athens was a very great system, an image diametrically opposed to the negative assessment that he had espoused his whole life. He thought this would be too contradictory. If he were to remain alive, Athenian democracy would be proven to be good. However, this would go against his own conviction, and therefore, he resolved to use his own death to demonstrate his conviction that Athenian democracy was bad. And he succeeded in this. During the proceedings before the two rounds of votes, he kept making hostile and provocative remarks. In the first vote, a majority of the judges voted that Socrates should not be sentenced to death. Seeing this, Socrates became even more combative and assertive in his speech during the court proceedings before the second and last vote, claiming that he should be enshrined and that he was the greatest hero in Athens. As a result, a greater number of judges were provoked and angered. Finally, he was sentenced to death by a slight majority. Several days later, before his execution, Crito, a friend of Socrates, visited him in his cell and told him that they had arranged for him to flee and take refuge in the United States. [*Laughter*] The conversation between them, as you know, has become one of the most famous conversations in human history. Socrates argued eloquently why a convicted person should not break prison and why he needed to comply with the law to his own harm. I think this is an early expression of the social contract theory.

Socrates' death was the result of political persecution of dissent. How can a person be punished with death for his thoughts? In fact, one of those cases where people holding different political or ideological views are sentenced to death was heard by Confucius himself when he acted as prime minister of Lu, and the victim was Shaozheng Mao, another influential thinker at the time. Confucius was the first private teacher in Chinese history, and Shaozheng Mao was another private teacher. Both of them took it upon themselves to recruit students and impart to them their own teachings. For a time, Confucius was appointed as the prime minister of Lu. In the judgment handed down by Confucius to Shaozheng Mao, none of the charges had anything to do with murder or robbery. What then were the charges against Shaozheng Mao? Well, the first was that he had a mind of penetrating cleverness devoted to treachery. But can a treacherous mind by itself qualify as a crime? The second charge was that he was engaged in peculiar conduct with obstinate persistence. The third charge was that he defended false teachings and made others believe they were true. The fourth was that he had a memory that was comprehensive but recalled only wickedness. What does this mean? For example, our mobile phones often receive not only dirty messages but also, occasionally, political messages that poke fun at political leaders.

Shaozheng Mao had a particularly rich stock of such politically charged messages to share with and amuse his students. [*Laughter*]

One noteworthy anecdote is that during the period when Confucius served as a private teacher, Shaozheng Mao was running another private school near Confucius' school. Everyone who reads Confucius' *Analects* knows that he had no liking of people with glib tongues and praised those with strong wills but few words. In his words, "The firm, the enduring, the simple, and the modest are near to virtue," and "Fine words and an insinuating appearance are seldom associated with true virtue." He held that few virtuous people are eloquent in speaking. The group of people attacked by Confucius was represented by sophists like Deng Xi and Gongsun Long. They argued that a white horse is not a horse. The thesis is interesting because it goes against the common conceptualization. Why is a white horse not a horse? For instance, when we see a horse in the street, no one doubts it is a horse. However, according to Gongsun Long, it is not horse but a white horse. [*Laughter*] So a white horse is not a horse. You have seen people from different countries, such as Chinese, Germans, French, and Americans, but have you seen a human being? [*Laughter*] Just as one has never seen an abstract human being, a white horse is not a horse, and the Chinese is not a human being. [*Laughter*] Deng Xi, another figure in this group, was running a law school [*laughter*] where the students were asked to represent the plaintiff today and then represent the defendant tomorrow. They were trained to sharpen their tongues. These people, however, filled others with worry, particularly Confucians who considered their practices mind-corrupting. As a result, both Deng Xi and Shaozheng Mao were sentenced to death.

These major executions to a certain degree decided the direction of Chinese civilization's development. To this day, public debate is discouraged. In ancient China, there were no lawyers in the court because there was no place for them, since there was no place for debate. The ancient Greeks often made speeches in public squares, for which there was no equivalent in ancient China. People gathered together either to drink or revolt, not to debate. This is a characteristic or style of China's politics and a very serious problem. Even today, no debate is heard during the sessions of the National People's Congress, only speech, and that speech is often all about what achievements have been accomplished. But there is never public debate among national leaders. Chinese politics is completely averse to debate or rigorous speechmaking. In Chinese political culture, not only is debating not valued, but those who distinguish themselves in debate are often persecuted. The execution of Socrates, to this day, fills us with regret and makes us wonder why Athenian democracy made such a mistake.

Historically, religious persecution is another major reason people have been condemned to death. The crucifixion of Jesus is the best-known example.

The famous French statesman and jurist Maximilien Robespierre was trained as a lawyer. He put to death a great number of French aristocrats, and ultimately he himself was also put to death. The bold Chinese reformist Tan Sitong was another figure who took death as nothing, and when he was to be beheaded, he said heroically, "Do it quick, and be quick!"[4] This behavior is really typical of people from Hunan. Those in this audience who are also from Hunan have every reason to take pride in Tan Sitong, who was a truly a person of lofty ideals. The other day I published a short article in *Legal Daily*, and as an indirect expression of my advocacy for the abolition of the death penalty, I ended the article with the sentence, "If the death penalty were abolished in the Qing dynasty, Tan Sitong would not have been executed at the age of thirty-three." However, the editor was so sharp-witted that the last sentence was censored. [*Laughter*] This Saturday I will publish another article, with the determination that no single word of what I write should be deleted. I often write until two o'clock in the morning. I said to the editor that I take great pains to complete my articles, and I would not tolerate any censorship, not even censorship of a single word, and if my article is changed in any way, I will never publish a single word for the newspaper. The editor then assured me that this time no censorship would be exercised. [*Laughter*]

Nikolai Bukharin was one of the greatest communist theoreticians in Soviet history. He was put to death by Stalin in 1938. In his will, which he dictated to his wife before his death, he said: "Comrades, farewell to you. There is my blood in the banner under which you march unto Communism." Bukharin was highly appreciated by Lenin, and this caused Stalin to resent him because he posed a direct threat to him. In the end, Bukharin was executed as a common enemy of the people in 1938. People killed during the reign of Stalin far outnumbered those killed in the czarist era, reaching an almost unparalleled level in human history and making Hitler pale in comparison.

The martyr Zhang Zhixin was executed in 1975.[5] She was a very graceful and elegant woman and an amateur violinist. After graduation from college, she was assigned to work at the Organization Department of Liaoning Province. During the Cultural Revolution, she held views different from those of the majority, believing that Liu Shaoqi [then president of the People's Republic of China] should not be persecuted, and that indeed it was wrong to persecute Liu and to launch the Cultural Revolution movement.

She was reported to the authorities and as a result sentenced to life imprisonment. She continued to uphold and express her own views until she was executed in 1975. In the morning of the day when Zhang was executed, the medical department was ordered to cut off her tongue, preventing her from uttering any counterrevolutionary slogans or words that might make some people embarrassed, like "Down with such-and-such." Zhang was neither the first nor the last person whose tongue was cut off before execution. How could medical workers do such outrageous things?! According to the Hippocratic Oath, an oath that was taken by all Greek physicians, a physician should never give a lethal drug to anyone, even if asked, or advise such a plan. But the opposite did happen during the Cultural Revolution in a ruthless way.

Just as I said a moment ago, the enforcement of executions is an encouragement of killing that fosters cruelty and bloodthirstiness. This reached a peak during the Cultural Revolution, which saw countless people beaten to death. An old peasant was sentenced to death and immediately executed simply because he carried the portrait of Chairman Mao on his back with a rope in a way that looked as if Chairman Mao was being hanged. [*Laughter*] During that period, the Red Guards were the most horrible group of people, those teenage young people! They were capable of beating the wife of their schoolmaster to death and forcing the schoolmaster to dance before them while holding his dead wife in his arms. And people who were considered to be landlords, rich peasants, counterrevolutionaries, bad elements, and rightists were subjected to inhuman tortures until they breathed their last breath in a miserable state. This is our nation, with all the cruelties that happen in daily life. For example, a woman is beaten by several strong men, watched by a crowd with no one coming out to intervene. Is this what we call our brilliant Chinese civilization and harmonious society? To hell with such harmony! [*Laughter and applause*] In a word, the death penalty being used for political purposes is far from a thing of the past.

Now let's look at the ninth and last reason for the abolition of the death penalty. If the death penalty is to continue, a special profession, that is, the profession of executioners—the group of people who make a living by killing people—must be retained. Of course, there are also those who do the job on a part-time basis. [*Laughter*] In China, traditionally many executioners were part-timers, who butchered pigs in normal times and executed people when asked, for a higher payment than butchering pigs. However, in many countries, the enforcement of executions is a highly specialized profession. Now the job of executing is mostly carried out by the police. Camus found that executioners have a special subculture and terminology among them that is unintelligible to others. For example, when they said, "You unpacked the package real well yesterday," the package means head. You know it takes some courage even to kill animals. Many people make it a point never to kill anything, not even chickens. In rural areas, no one has the heart to slaughter an old ox, which has tilled the land for its whole life, and then they have to ask a communist to do the unwelcome job. [*Laughter and applause*] Therefore, if it is generally thought cruel to kill an ox, it would be even more cruel and horrible for one person to kill another human being. What kind of a profession is it, where a person is employed to perform executions? The process of performing this cruel job sometimes even fills the executioner with horror, especially so when a bullet fails to kill outright. Once an executioner failed to end the life of a condemned criminal, who then turned around and said encouragingly, "Buddy, shoot me right in the head please!" As a result, the executioner himself collapsed to the ground. [*Laughter*] In a word, if the death penalty is to be kept in place, the special profession of executioner must also be kept in place. This point needs no further elaboration.

In this evening's speech, I talked about the issue of the death penalty from the perspective of an ordinary person rather than a legal worker. It is meant to call attention to this issue. I believe that if you all make it a pursuit of yours to abolish the death penalty in your future legal work, then it will not be long before it is formally abolished in China. Of course, this is a tough cause. Given the difficulties involved, I don't think this goal will be attained within twenty years; but whether the death penalty will be eventually abolished sometime soon after that depends on whether we make sustained and concerted efforts in that direction. In China quite a few persons have engaged themselves in this cause. Professor Qiu Xinglong, dean of the Law School of Xiangtan University, for example, is an expert in research on the death penalty. He is highly accomplished in this field and has published many informative and enlightening articles and delivered many inspiring speeches. And there are many other persons, such as Professor Jia Yu of the Northwest University of Politics and Law and Dr. Hu Yunteng of the Supreme People's Court, who have made worthwhile efforts regarding the death penalty issue.

As a scholar studying legal history and the judicial system, I would also like to join in this cause because it pains me to think of the people who are wrongly convicted and executed or receive a death sentence that is incommensurate with the seriousness of their crimes. I believe the several cases of wrongful executions that were exposed this year are likely only the tip of the iceberg.

The human world cannot go on without compassion and sympathy for one another. Of course, we should sympathize with the victims of crimes, but our sympathy should also be extended to the criminals. In a word, our sympathy should be all-embracing rather than discriminating. Only with the increase of sympathy among people and the establishment of respect for everyone's dignity can we establish a truly harmonious society.

No one's heart will be truly at peace as long as there is a mother weeping before the grave of her wrongfully executed son in some corner of the world.

Thank you all!

CHAPTER ELEVEN

A Plea for Genuine Political Progress in China

Deutsche Welle: Professor He, you jokingly complained at the beginning of your speech earlier that the organizer inviting you to Germany did not tell you beforehand that the program's main subject is Tibet. So let's start our interview with this issue. Do you agree that the West's strong reaction to the issue of China's presence in Tibet is due to the media's biased reporting?

He Weifang: I think the West's recent strong reaction is the culmination of the interaction between China and the West in the past several years. Since the middle of the 1980s, China has been a popular topic in the West, which had expectations for a new political openness, economic growth, and democracy. In spite of the crackdown on the Tiananmen Square protests in 1989, the West still had hope for the future of China. But in recent years, with China's rapid economic development and the Chinese government flaunting its achievements, as well as the media hype about China's rise as a world power and its increasing presence in third-world countries, the West's attitude toward China gradually shifted from general praise and enthusiastic embrace to suspicion. Tibet only triggered the expression of this changed sentiment in the West.

Editor's note: The original Chinese version of this chapter is based on the author's interview with Deutsche Welle reporter Zhang Danhong (张丹红) in Bonn on April 8, 2008 (www.dw-world.de/dw/article/0,,3263153,00.html). The title was added by the editor. The interview was given after He's lecture on China's prospect for democracy and constitutionalism as part of the "Meeting China Week" in Bonn, April 2008, which was organized by the Federal Political Education Center and the Bonn Association of Chinese Studies.

Deutsche Welle: China has become increasingly unpopular among Western countries, as shown by the disruptions of the Olympic torch relay in London and Paris. As a Chinese, do you feel hurt when you see the video images of those scenes?

He Weifang: I think it is normal for a major event to provoke some protest, especially in Western countries. The Iraq War, launched in 2003, still inspires protest in the United States today. Other antigovernment protests are also commonly seen. So I think the disruption of the Olympic torch relay has two aspects: one is the overinterpretation by the media, and the other is the Tibet issue. I think China has the responsibility to handle the Tibet issue properly. In this regard, several questions must be answered: first, how to have friendlier and more active communication with the Dalai Lama; second, how to approach the prospect of a truly autonomous Tibet; third, how to effectively protect Tibet's cultural and religious tradition; and fourth, how to harmonize the relationship between Tibetans and Han Chinese. Westerners are very concerned about the assimilation of Tibetan culture into mainstream Chinese culture. However, just as no state or province in any Western country would be allowed to ban inhabitation by people of other ethnic groups on the pretext of preserving their local culture, it is impossible to exclude Han Chinese in Tibet. So the advocacy of a higher degree of harmonious coexistence is more practical. The Tibetan culture should be preserved, for sure, but it has to be achieved in the spirit of a republic, where different ethnic groups coexist harmoniously rather than being separated from each other. At this point in time, I think China should be more open and give more freedom of the press to Western journalists. Restriction of freedom of the press after the Tibet incident only fuels suspicion from foreign countries.

Deutsche Welle: China promised to give full freedom to journalists during the Olympic Games when it applied to host them in 2001. After the Tibet incident, do you think the promise will be honored?

He Weifang: It is not much of a problem in other regions outside Tibet. I have frequent contacts with foreign journalists in Beijing. They say the press environment is much freer now, and they don't need to obtain the approval of the Foreign Affairs Office for traveling to other regions, as in the past. Now the only exception is Tibet. I am a little worried whether the Tibet issue will become a hindrance to China's reform agenda. I expressed this misgiving to some German lawmakers in recent days. I think Western governments and politicians should deal with China in a more responsible way rather than expressing radical views simply to cater to their domestic political constituencies because the latter will elicit strong reactions from the Chinese government and fuel nationalism in China, thus causing China's reform process to stagnate or even regress.

Deutsche Welle: You mentioned in your speech that one of the characteristics of the socialism practiced by China in the past was the absence of press freedom. In China's current political framework, do you think it is possible to realize press freedom?

He Weifang: Socialism has always been evolving in China. It is a bag that can carry everything as long as it is given the modifier "Chinese-style." Indeed, China's socialism is not fundamentalist socialism but has been changing all along. For example, in China, press freedom is not labeled as such but rather is called "media supervision." In the past, the press scene was dominated by party newspapers, but now there have emerged quite a few influential metropolitan newspapers such as *Southern Weekend* and *Southern Metropolitan Daily*. As market actors, newspapers face the pressure of survival, and to attract more advertisements, they have to do their job well. All of these are important factors for the development of the media. I don't think there is press freedom in the real sense of the term in China, but the trend toward it is very obvious. Sooner or later, as progress follows this trend, the country may announce the lifting of restrictions on newspaper licensing and allow citizens to run newspapers as long as they have the means. I think this day will come eventually.

Deutsche Welle: You once said that the National People's Congress lacks legitimacy and suggested that the CCP should allow other parties to compete with it on an equal footing. Having aired such radical views, you are still allowed to visit Germany. Can this fact serve as a proof of freedom of speech in China?

He Weifang: Yes, I think this deserves special mention. My own example shows that China has taken a huge stride forward in its political and governmental systems. Back in the 1950s, many people expressing far less radical views than mine were labeled as rightists and put into prison. In contrast, I have systematically put forward my stance, but I have never experienced any persecution up to now. I can still give lectures freely at Peking University, and no one has ever told me what to talk about and what not to talk about. Although there are still some newspapers not daring to publish my articles, many others are very willing to do that. The blog I maintain used to have its entries on sensitive topics deleted, but now they are no longer censored. I can feel that society is changing for the better.

Deutsche Welle: The speech you gave today was on the democratization of China. Premier Wen Jiabao said that Western-style democracy does not tally with China's current national conditions. Do you agree that China has not reached the point of practicing Western-style democracy?

He Weifang: In fact, there is conflicting information in this regard. I have heard of the remark by Premier Wen that you mentioned, but recently when I read an article in *Foreign Affairs* by John Thornton, chairman of the Brookings Institution, on China's democracy, I noticed a seemingly significant shift in Wen's stance.[1] The author cited conversations with Wen Jiabao during his visit to China. He found that during their meeting, Wen devoted almost all of the time to discussing with him what democracy is and how to develop it. Wen holds that democracy is reflected in three aspects. The first is elections, enabling the people to elect their own national leaders. The second is supervision. And the third is judicial independence. His understanding of the subject is very good. So personally, I don't think it is easy to determine what the national leaders are really thinking about. First, if democracy is really so dependent on citizens' education levels, it would be inconceivable that England would have embraced the democratic system in the sixteenth and seventeenth centuries when the country's overall educational level was very low. Second, even if the judgment about the prerequisite of citizens' education levels stands, China's democracy should not start from the countryside. The democracy that we have now in China is reflected in the direct election of village heads in the rural areas, where the population has the lowest education level. Given the premise that democracy is feasible only in a well-educated society, then it should really start from the National People's Congress, China's top legislature. I think democracy is a way of living. At the village level, the local government that has been elected by the villagers should keep them informed of how the community's money is used, and at the national level, the taxpayers have the right to know exactly where their money goes. The people have the right to choose the country's top leaders through elections. Their choices are not necessarily always right, but even if the results of a democratic process are sometimes inferior to an authoritarian one, the people are willing to bear the consequences of their own decisions, feeling that they are the master of the country.

Deutsche Welle: Yes, not only can they vote on but also vote out national leaders. In your speech today you also mentioned Taiwan's democracy. You said that you are happy to see that Taiwan's major political leaders have legal backgrounds. In the case of the Chinese mainland, the fifth-generation leaders Xi Jinping and Li Keqiang allegedly also have legal backgrounds. Will China have a greater chance of achieving democracy when they lead the country?

He Weifang: Strictly speaking, only Li Keqiang has a legal background. He was enrolled in the legal department of Peking University in 1977. Xi Jinping did not study law but Marxism and Leninism. Both of them graduated with a legal degree. Xi's graduation thesis seemed to be about Marxist and Leninist education. There is an increasing presence of politicians with backgrounds in the humanities, while in the past, China's political scene was always dominated by engineers graduated from Tsinghua University. It is indeed rare for the Peking University–trained Li Keqiang to enter into the top leadership of the country. However, leaders' academic backgrounds are not the most important factor; what really matters is the country's decision-making mechanism. If the most basic human rights are not respected, then leaders' academic backgrounds are meaningless.

Deutsche Welle: My last question is that given the poor international image of China, as shown by the Tibet issue, the Chinese government is reported to be considering engaging a foreign firm to do some public relations work for it. What do you think is the best way for China to change and improve its international image?

He Weifang: I think the best way to achieve that is simply to substantially promote such universal values as democracy, rule of law, and constitutional government, and to make sincere decisions and implement them in earnest. If there is still difficulty in opening the traditional media, Internet censorship should be lifted first to make the Internet a free space where different voices and views are allowed. Efforts should be made to move to judicial independence. The people should be assured that the country is moving firmly toward the right direction, rather than vacillating to and fro. This is far more valuable than the service of the best public relations company in the world because if China steps firmly toward a reasonable goal, its footsteps will be heard throughout the world.

Notes

Introduction

1. The panel was entitled "The Top-Level Design of China's Judicial Reforms." This term (改革的顶层设计) was first used in the party documents of the fifth plenum of the Seventeenth Central Committee of the Chinese Communist Party in October 2010. The notion emphasizes the overall vision and structural coherence of political reform on the part of the party leadership. It highlights the importance of the direction, path, and possible breakthrough of reforms. He Weifang and Xu Xin apparently borrowed this concept to argue for the necessity of fundamental reform in China's judicial system.

2. Xu Xin (徐昕, 1970–), a native of Fengcheng, Jiangxi Province, is a professor of law and director of the Research Center of the Judicial System at the Beijing Institute of Technology. He received a Ph.D. in law at Tsinghua University and taught at the Southwest University of Political Science and Law before joining the Beijing Institute of Technology in 2010. More details on this panel can be found on He Weifang's blog; see Xu Xin and He Weifang, "Guanyu sifa gaige dingceng sheji de duihua" [The dialogue about the top-level design of China's judicial reform], December 12, 2011 (http://blog.qq.com/qzone/ 622009820/1323671026.htm).

3. The Central Commission of Politics and Law of the CCP, known as *zhengfawei* (政法委), oversees all legal enforcement authorities, including the Supreme People's Court, Supreme People's Procuratorate, Ministry of Justice, Ministry of Public Security, and Ministry of State Security, making it a very powerful organ. All the provincial, municipal, and county party committees have their own politics and law commissions.

4. Wu Bangguo is the second highest ranking leader in the Politburo Standing Committee of the CCP and is chairman of the National People's Congress (NPC). His famous "five no's" refer to no multiple party system, no pluralism in ideology, no checks and balances nor a bicameral parliament, no federal system, and no privatization. He made this

statement at the fourth plenary session of the Eleventh National People's Congress, held in Beijing on March 11, 2011. See *Zhongguo xinwenwang* [China newsnet], March 11, 2011 (www.china.com.cn/ 2011/2011-03/11/content_22114099.htm).

5. For examples of He Weifang's public speeches, see online videos at http://v.youku.com/v_show/id_XNDU2ODU3OTI=.html (October 5, 2008) and www.youtube.com/watch?v=8VJE2CFkTqE (December 3, 2011).

6. Cai Dingjian (蔡定剑, 1955–2010), a native of Xinjian County, Jiangxi Province, was a leading scholar of constitutional studies in China. He served as a staff member and deputy bureau chief of the Bureau of Staff of the Standing Committee of the NPC from 1986 to 2003. Prior to his premature death from cancer in 2010, he served as a professor of law and the director of the Institute of Constitutional Research at China University of Political Science and Law. His main publications include *Xianzheng jiangtan* [Constitutional forum] (Beijing: Law Press, 2010).

7. For example, see Guo Guangdong, "Weishenme zheme duoren jinian Cai Dingjian?" [Why do so many people commemorate Cai Dingjian?], *Nanfang zhoumo* [Southern weekend], November 26, 2010. Also see www.infzm.com/content/52858.

8. "The FP Top 100 Global Thinkers" (www.foreignpolicy.com/articles/2011/11/28/the_fp_top_100_global_thinkers?page=0,18 [June 27, 2012]).

9. Hu Shih, *The Chinese Renaissance* (University of Chicago Press, 1933). For an excellent study of the intellectual discourse about the May Fourth Movement, see Chow Tse-Tsung, *The May Fourth Movement: Intellectual Revolution in Modern China* (Harvard University Press, 1960).

10. Han Yongmei, "Jin Guantao jiaoshou: Wusi shi weiwancheng de qimeng yundong" [Interview with Professor Jin Guantao: The May Fourth Movement was an unfulfilled enlightenment movement], *Lianhe zaobao* [United morning news], April 19, 2009 (www.zaobao.com/special/face2face/pages1/face2face090419.shtml).

11. Zi Zhongyun, ed., *Qimeng yu Zhongguo shehui zhuanxing* [The enlightenment and transformation of Chinese society] (Beijing: Shehui kexue wenxian chubanshe, 2011), p. 164.

12. Xu Youyu, for example, asserted that when China is in the midst of a rapid economic rise but has lost in its political direction, public enlightenment is particularly essential. Xu Youyu, "Qimeng zai Zhongguo" [Public enlightenment in China], in *Qimeng yu Zhongguo*, edited by Zi, p. 101.

13. Zi, *Qimeng yu Zhongguo*, p. 171.

14. Ibid., p. 173.

15. Ibid., pp. 158–59.

16. Ibid. In the months preceding the Bo Xilai crisis, Su Wei, a scholar close to Bo at the Chongqing Party School, compared Bo and Chongqing mayor Huang Qifan to former leaders Mao Zedong and Zhou Enlai in comments circulated in both the Chongqing and national media. See Sina Global Newsnet, September 20, 2011(http://dailynews.sina.com/bg/chn/chnnews/ausdaily/20110920/18402783790.html).

17. Xu, "Qimeng zai Zhongguo," p. 102.

18. Ibid.

19. Wei Sen, "Xin qimeng yu Zhongguo shehui zhuanxing de yixie genbenxing wenti" [New public enlightenment and some fundamental issues in the transition of Chinese society]), in *Qimeng yu Zhongguo*, edited by Zi, p. 124.

20. He Weifang, *Jiaohuifa de lishi fazhan, hunyin zhidu ji dui shisufa de yingxiang* [A study of canon law: Its development, matrimonial institutions, and influence on secular law). LL.M. thesis, China University of Political Science and Law, Beijing, 1985.

21. He Weifang also made this point in many of his public talks in China in recent years. For example, see He Weifang, He Qinhua, and Tian Tao, eds., *Falü wenhua sanrentan* [A tripartite discussion of legal culture] (Peking University Press, 2010), p. 102.

22. He Weifang, "The Methodology of Comparative Study of Legal Cultures," *Asia Pacific Law Review* 37 (July 1994): 39.

23. Ibid., p. 40.

24. This discussion is based on He Weifang, "Cong xixue fanhui bentu" [Return to academic indigenization from the Western learning], March 1, 2010 (www.aisixiang.com/data/detail.php?id=31928).

25. Ibid. The Southwest College of Political Science and Law was later renamed the Southwest University of Political Science and Law.

26. Ibid.

27. Before 1983, China University of Political Science and Law was named Beijing College of Political Science and Law.

28. For the full citations of these translated books, see "Further Reading: The Writings of He Weifang" at the end of this volume.

29. See He Weifang's interview on Renmin website, October 8, 2007 (http://edu.people.com.cn/GB/8216/85218/104692/6349432.html).

30. He Weifang, "Wo weishenme likai Beida?" [Why did I leave Peking University?], July 18, 2008 (http://news.ifeng.com/opinion/200807/0718_23_660688.shtml).

31. For the views of both sides, see "Fang Zhouzi paohong He Weifang" [Fang Zhouzi bombards He Weifang], Duowei Newsnet (http://china.dwnews.com/news/2011-08-13/58008432.html [August 13, 2012]).

32. Wu Zuolai," Wo weishenme zhichi He Weifang?"[Why do I support He Weifang?], *Dongfang zaobao* [Oriental morning news], August 16, 2011. Yuan was quoted by Wu Zuolai.

33. Wang Zhaoxiang, "Xingyin falü de langman qishi" [The romantic knight who chants rule of law], *Dongfang fayan* [Oriental legal guardian], May 9, 2004.

34. Pan Congxia, "He Weifang: 'Shoumen laohe' de budao famen" [He Weifang: A Famennian gatekeeper], *Nandu zhoukan* [Southern metropolis weekly], December 5, 2008.

35. Jiang Hao, "Afterword," in He, He, and Tian, *Falü wenhua sanrentan*, p. 254.

36. Pan, "He Weifang: 'Shoumen laohe' de budao famen."

37. See http://blog.sina.com.cn/heweifang (accessed July 22, 2012). He Weifang has several other blogs; see www.bullogger.com/blogs/heweifang; http://blog.caijing.com.cn/heweifang; and http://heweifang2009.blog.163.com.

38. Peng Bo and Wang Lin, eds. *Keneng yingxiang ershiyi shiji Zhongguo de yibai ge qingnian renwu* [The 100 young people who may shape China in the 21st century] (Beijing: Zhongguo renmin chubanshe, 2001).

39. For a more detailed discussion of the Sun Zhigang case, see Yu Xiang, "Sun Zhigang's Death and Reform of Detention System," *China Human Rights Magazine* (China Society for Human Rights Studies) (www.humanrights.cn/zt/magazine/20040200482694708.htm [June 27, 2012]).

40. Chen Youxi, "Falüren shalong" [Legal professionals' salon], April 28, 2012 (http://wq.zfwlxt.com/newLawyerSite/BlogShow.aspx?itemTypeID=b3572aed-0599-4632-8969-9c2200730162&itemID=430fd40c-b0f8-40d8-9242-a04f0088aa35&user=10420).

41. For more on the Wu Ying case in 2012, see Chuin-Wei Yap, "China Court Spares Life of Millionaire," *Wall Street Journal*, April 21–22, 2012, p. A7; and "Wu Ying an nizhuan" [The reversal of the Wu Ying case], *Shijie ribao* [World journal], April 21, 2012, p. A12. For He Weifang's views and input in this case, see Kuang Ping, "He Weifang tan Wu Ying an" [He Weifang comments on the Wu Ying case], *Sanxiang dushibao* [Hunan metropolis daily], April 29, 2012.

42. Andrew Jacobs, "China Limits the Crimes Punishable by Death," *New York Times*, July 30, 2009, p. 12. In 2011 the Chinese government reduced the number of crimes punishable by death from sixty-eight to fifty-five. See "Zhongguo feichu shisanxiang sixing" [China abolishes 13 items of crimes punishable by death], Duowei Newsnet, May 2, 2011 (http://china.dwnews.com/news/2011-05-02/57676561.html).

43. Quoted from Jacobs, "China Limits the Crimes Punishable by Death."

44. He Weifang, "Yizhi baoyuan: He Weifang zaitan feichu sixing" [Using justice rather than revenge: The death penalty revisited], *Jingji guancha bao* [Economic observer], May 28, 2011.

45. Ibid.

46. See "Ying zhengshi Zhonghua Minguo" [To be realistic about "the Republic of China"], *Liaohe zao bao* (United morning news), October 13, 2011.

47. Zhou Xi, "Zhendui Chen Guangcheng shijian meiguo mingque jujue xiang zhongfang daoqian" [The United States firmly rejects China's request for an apology regarding the case of Chen Guangcheng], May 2, 2012 (http://boxun.com/news/gb/china/2012/05/201205062112.shtml).

48. Du Junli, "Kong Qingdong shidai de Beida" [Peking University in the era of Kong Qingdong], November 16, 2011 (http://cul.cn.yahoo.com/ypen/20111116/702822.html).

49. He Weifang, "Bo Xilai liyong shehui bingtai peizhi geren chongbai" [Bo Xilai uses social ills to cultivate his cult of personality], *Xianggang Jingji ribao* [Hong Kong economic daily], April 17, 2012.

50. Peter Foster, "Leading Chinese dissident claims freedom of speech worse than before Olympics" *The Telegraph*, April 27, 2009 (www.telegraph.co.uk/news/worldnews/asia/china/5230707/Leading-Chinese-dissident-claims-freedom-of-speech-worse-than-before-Olympics.html).

51. Chen Fang, "He Weifang: Bianjiang guilai" [He Weifang: Return from the borderland], October 21, 2011 (http://cul.cn.yahoo.com/ypen/20111021/652595.html).

52. Zi Zhongyun observed that courage is always part of enlightenment movements. Zi, *Qimeng yu Zhongguo*, p. 8.

53. Immanuel Kant, "*Beantwortung der Frage: Was ist Aufklärung?*" [Answering the question: What is enlightenment?], *Berlinische Monatsschrift* [*Berlin Monthly*] (1784).

54. For more discussion of Bo's campaigns in Chongqing, see Yawei Liu, "Bo Xilai's Campaign for the Standing Committee and the Future of Chinese Politicking," *China Brief* 11, no. 21 (November 11, 2011) (www.jamestown.org/single/?no_cache=1&tx_ ttnews%5Btt_news%5D=38660).

55. "Chongqing dahei yingxiong Wang Lijun 'qiwucongwen' yinfa weibo reyi" [Chongqing hero Wang Lijun's change of leadership posts triggers heated discussion in microblogs], *Xinwen wanbao* [Evening news], February 3, 2012.

56. *Chongqing wanbao* [Chongqing evening news], January 16, 2010.

57. For an excellent review of the left-wing intellectuals' support for Bo Xilai and his Chongqing model, see Rong Jian: "Benxiang Chongqing de xuezhemen" [The scholars who adored the Chongqing model], April 28, 2012 (www.21ccom.net/articles/zgyj/ gqmq/article_2012042858663.html).

58. "Beida jiaoshou Kong Qingdong liting Bo Xilai" [Peking University professor Kong Qingdong supports Bo Xilai], *Chongqing ribao* [Chongqing daily], August 23, 2011; also see "Beida jiaoshou Kong Qingdong liting Bo Xilai" [Peking University Professor Kong Qingdong supports Bo Xilai] (www.wenxuecity.com/news/2011/08/23/1451756.html). Some critics of Bo Xilai's campaign methods rejected Kong's assertions. Qian Liqun, also a professor of literature at Peking University, argued that Bo adopted two radical and potentially destructive economic policy initiatives. The first was radical land reform to seize farmers' lands in the name of urbanization, and the second was to promote socialist public ownership to consolidate state control over economic affairs, undermining the private sector. See Qian Liqun, "Lao hongweibing dangzheng de danyou" [Worries about the rule by the old Red Guards], *Wenzhai* [Readers' digest], February 19, 2012.

59. Wang Shaoguang, "Chongqing jingyan shi Zhongguo shi shehuizhuyi 3.0" [The Chongqing experiment is Chinese-style socialism 3.0], June 9, 2010 (www. sociologyol.org/shehuibankuai/shehuipinglunliebiao/2010-06-09/10387.html).

60. *Shijie ribao*, January 3, 2010, p. A2.

61. It was widely known among legal professionals and lawyers in the country that Wang Lijun, with the support of Bo Xilai, adopted an "innovative unlawful procedure" along with the generous use of torture in his campaign in Chongqing. "Chongqing dahei juzhang beiba" [Chongqing police chief purged], *Shijie ribao*, February 3, 2012, p. A11.

62. He Bing, "Cong 'xuemaoxuan' dao 'changhongge'" [From "study Mao's work" to "sing red songs"], April 24, 2011 [http://hebing1.blog.sohu.com/171382733.html].

63. He Weifang, "Gaige benshen jiushi gaibian guoqing" [China's reform is to change national conditions], *Huashang bao* [Chinese merchants daily], May 19, 2012.

64. He, "Yizhi baoyuan."

65. For example, Sida Liu, an assistant professor of sociology and law at the University of Wisconsin at Madison, called this case "the most important trial since the Gang of Four trial in 1980." See Sida Liu, "The Most Important China Legal Case since the Gang of Four Trial?" July 22, 2012 (http://practicesource.com/australian-asian-legal-eye/the-most-important-china-legal-case-since-the-gang-of-four-trial).

66. Ian Johnson, "Trial in China Tests Limits of Legal System Reform," *New York Times*, April 19, 2011 (www.nytimes.com/2011/04/20/world/asia/20china.html?_r=2&ref=world).

67. Xu and He, "Guanyu sifa gaige dingceng sheji de duihua."

68. See "Chongqing dahei diyian" [The first case of Chongqing's "striking the black mafia" campaign], Xinhua Newsnet, January 5, 2010 (http://news.xinhuanet.com/legal/2010-01/05/content_12759416.htm).

69. For more discussion of the details, see Xu Xunlei, "Lüshi Li Zhuang an shoupian baodao pouxi" [An analysis of the first media coverage of the lawyer Li Zhuang case], Renmin Net, February 23, 2010 (http://media.people.com.cn/GB/40628/11011197.html).

70. See Zhu Mingyong's court statement, March 11, 2010 (http://blog.sina.com.cn/s/blog_4b5857fb0100hauo.html).

71. Ibid.

72. Su Renyan, "Zhongguo shiliuwan lüshi duijue Bo Xilai" [China's 160,000 lawyers versus Bo Xilai], *Kaifang* [Open], May 2011, p. 16.

73. "Judicial Process and One Lawyer's Bold Stand," *Caixin Online*, April 22, 2011 (http://english.caixin.com/2011-04-22/100251590.html)

74. Quoted in Johnson, "Trial in China Tests Limits of Legal System Reform."

75. Many international journalists praised He Weifang's crucial role in defending Li Zhuang. See, for example, Jeremy Page, "China Leaders Laud 'Red' Campaign," *Wall Street Journal*, June 20, 2011.

76. Quoted from Chen Su, *Dangdai Zhongguo faxue yanjiu (1949–2009)* [Research on law in contemporary China, 1949–2009] (Beijing: Zhongguo shehui kexue wenxian chubanshe, 2009), p. 27.

77. Ibid., p. 26.

78. These two terms have exactly the same pronunciation in Chinese but quite different Chinese characters and thus meanings: "to use law to rule the country" (以法制国) and "to govern the country according to the law" (依法治国). Zhou Tianwei [Cedric T. Chou], *Fazhi lixiang guo: Sugeladi yu Mengzi de xuni duihua* [An ideal state of law: A virtual dialogue between Socrates and Mencius] (Taipei: Commonwealth Press, 1998).

79. Yu Keping, *Yifa zhiguo yu yifa zhidang* [Governing the country and the party by law] (Beijing: Zhongyang bianyi chubanshe, 2007), p. 2.

80. Chen, *Dangdai Zhongguo faxue yanjiu*, p. 239.

81. He, "Gaige benshen jiushi gaibian guoqing."

82. Cai Dingjian, "The Development of Constitutionalism in the Transition of Chinese Society," *Columbia Journal of Asian Law* 19, no. 1 (Spring–Fall 2005): 27.

83. Cai Dingjian, "Yifa zhili" [Rule of Law], in *Zhongguo zhili bianqian sanshi nian: 1978–2008* [China's political reform toward good governance: 1978–2008], edited by Yu Keping (Beijing: Shehui kexue wenxian chubanshe, 2008), p. 142.

84. Ren Miao, "Falü wenben chengxing, fazhi rentong shangyuan" [The texts of laws are all available, but the rule of law is still far off], *Duowei Times,* March 18, 2011, p. 17.

85. For discussion of a more optimistic view of China's legal development in terms of professional expansion, see Cheng Li and Jordan Lee, "China's Legal System," *China Review*, no. 48 (Autumn 2009): 1–3.

86. Chen, *Dangdai Zhongguo faxue yanjiu*, p. 13.

87. He, He, and Tian, *Falü wenhua sanrentan*, p. 87.

88. Chen, *Dangdai Zhongguo faxue yanjiu*, p. 114.

89. Gu Xin, "Revitalizing Chinese Society: Institutional Transformation and Social Change," in *China: Two Decades of Reform and Change,* edited by Wang Gungwu and John Wong (Singapore: Singapore University Press and World Scientific Press, 1999), p. 80.

90. See "Woguo lüshi renshu yi chao ershiwan" [The number of China's lawyers surpasses 200,000], China Lawyers' Network, January 10, 2011 (www.zgdls.com/2011/lvjieneican_0110/114973.html).

91. Ren, "Falü wenben chengxing, fazhi rentong shangyuan," p. 17.

92. He, He, and Tian, *Falü wenhua sanrentan*, p. 87.

93. Chen, *Dangdai Zhongguo faxue yanjiu*, p. 238.

94. Liu Donghua and Yang Xiaolei, *Gongyi falü yanjiu, diyijuan* [Public interest research], vol. 1 (Beijing: Falü chubanshe, 2010), p. 22.

95. Ibid., p. 19.

96. Ibid., pp. 119, 128.

97. He Weifang, "Fuzhuan junren jin fayuan" [Ex-servicemen of the PLA now serving at court], *Nanfang zhoumo* [Southern weekend], January 2, 1998.

98. He, "Gaige benshen jiushi gaibian guoqing."

99. He Weifang, "The Police and the Rule of Law: Commentary on 'Principals and Secret Agents,'" *China Quarterly*, no. 191 (September 2007): 671.

100. Ibid., p. 672.

101. "Kanshou Chen Guangcheng" [Watching Chen Guangcheng], *Shijie ribao*, May 3, 2012, p. A4.

102. He Weifang recently made a similar point on the convergence of money and power and the vested interest group claim to maintain social stability at all cost. See *Mingbao* [Hong Kong], March 23, 2012.

103. Sun Liping and others, *Yi liyi biaoda zhiduhua shixian shehui de changzhijiu'an* [Institutionalization of interest expression mechanisms and the realization of long-term stability], report delivered at the Tsinghua University Social Development Forum, April 19, 2010.

104. "越维越不稳怪圈" in Chinese. Ibid. Ma Jian, a Chinese writer who resides in the United Kingdom, made a similar point referring to China's problems in maintaining social stability: "The more policemen in a country, the less security in that country." Ma

Jian, "Zhongguo weiyi de anquan zhidi—Meiguo dashiguan" [China's only secure place: The U.S. Embassy], BBC, May 9, 2012 (www.bbc.co.uk/zhongwen/simp/chinese_analysis/2012/04/120430_us_embassy_chengguangcheng.shtml).

105. "大闹大解决，小闹小解决，不闹不解决" in Chinese.

106. He, "Yizhi baoyuan."

107. Xu and He, "Guanyu sifa gaige dingceng sheji de duihua."

108. He Weifang, "Wenzong zhencheng tui zhenggai" [Premier Wen sincerely promotes political reforms], *Mingbao* [Hong Kong], March 23, 2012.

109. In the recent leadership reshufflings in Guangdong, the heads of the politics and law committees at the municipal and prefecture levels no longer consecutively serve as heads of the Public Security Bureau, undermining the power of the police. *Shijie ribao*, June 6, 2012, p. A12.

110. For more discussion of the evolutionary changes of the PRC constitution, see Thomas E. Kellogg, "Constitutionalism with Chinese Characteristics? Constitutional Development and Civil Litigation in China," Indiana University Research Center for Chinese Politics and Business Working Paper 1, February 2008, pp. 1–41; and M. Ulric Killion, "Building Up China's Constitution: Culture, Marxism, and the WTO Rules," *Loyola of Los Angeles Law Review* 41, no. 2–4 (2008): 563–602.

111. Xia Yong, "Zhongguo xianfa gaige de jige jiben lilun wenti" [Several basic theoretical issues in China's constitutional reform], in *Zhongguo xuezhe lun minzhu yu fazhi* [Chinese scholars on democracy and rule of law], edited by Yu Keping (Chongqing: Chongqing chubanshe, 2008), p. 185.

112. Ibid., p. 186.

113. Quoted in Larry Cata Backer, "A Constitutional Court for China within the Chinese Communist Party: Scientific Development and a Reconsideration of the Institutional Role of the CCP," *Suffolk University Law Review* 43, no. 3 (June 22, 2010), p. 593. Backer, an optimist about Chinese constitutional development, rejected this notion.

114. Guobin Zhu, "Constitutional review in China: An unaccomplished project or a mirage?" *Suffolk University Law Review* 43, no. 3 (June 2010): p. 625.

115. Eva Pils, "Asking the Tiger for His Skin: Rights Activism in China," *Fordham International Law Journal* 30, no. 4 (2006): p. 1286.

116. M. Ulric Killion, "China's Amended Constitution: Quest for Liberty and Independent Judicial Review," *Washington University Global Studies Law Review* 4 (February 2005): p. 78.

117. Zhou, *Fazhi lixiang guo: Sugeladi yu Mengzi de xuni duihua*, pp. 174, 200.

118. Larry Cata Backer, "The Party as Polity, the Communist Party, and the Chinese Constitutional State: A Theory of State-Party Constitutionalism," *Journal of Chinese and Comparative Law* 16, no. 1 (October 2009): p. 155.

119. Ibid., p. 157.

120. Ibid., p. 101.

121. Backer, "A Constitutional Court for China within the Chinese Communist Party," p. 597.

122. Kellogg, "Constitutionalism with Chinese Characteristics?" p. 4.

123. Xia, "Zhongguo xianfa gaige de jige jiben lilun wenti," p. 201.

124. Zhu, "Constitutional review in China: An unaccomplished project or a mirage?" p. 625.

125. Michael William Dowdle, "Of Parliaments, Pragmatism, and the Dynamics of Constitutional Development: The Curious Case of China," *Journal of International Law and Politics* 35, no. 1 (2002–03): pp. 24–25.

126. Ibid., p. 30.

127. Yu, *Yifa zhiguo yu yifa zhidang*, p. 6.

128. Ibid., p. 3.

129. Ibid., pp. 13–14.

130. Wang Huning, "Wenge fansi yu zhengzhi gaige" [Reflections on the Cultural Revolution and the reform of China's political system], *Wenzhai* [Readers' digest], February 23, 2012; originally appeared in *Shijie jingji daobao* [World economic herald], May 1986.

131. He Pin, *Keyi queding de Zhongguo weilai* [China's future can be determined] (New York: Mirror Books, 2012), pp. 178, 419.

132. Zhang Lifan's blog, February 1, 2012 (http://blog.sina.com.cn/s/blog_4b86a 2630100zhuv.html).

133. "Xiang haiwai banqian" [Money flows overseas], *Shijie ribao*, April 20, 2012, p. A4.

134. Randall Peerenboom, "Law and Development of Constitutional Democracy: Is China a Problem Case?" *Annals of the American Academy of Political and Social Science, Law, Society, and Democracy: Comparative Perspectives* 603 (January 2006): p. 196.

135. Wei, "Xin qimeng yu Zhongguo shehui zhuanxing de yixie genbenxing wenti," p. 111.

136. Peerenboom, "Law and Development of Constitutional Democracy," p. 196.

137. Ibid., p. 194.

138. Dowdle, "Of Parliaments, Pragmatism, and the Dynamics of Constitutional Development," p. 195.

139. Ibid.

140. Ji Weidong, "The Mission and Authority of the Supreme Court," July 10, 2012 (http://english.caixin.com).

141. The epigraph is from Paula Bartley, *Emmeline Pankhurst* (London: Routledge, 2002), p. 100.

142. The epigraph is from Hu Shuli, Duan Hongqing, and Fang Xuyan, "Kanbujian de quanli" [Invisible power], *Caixin New Era*, June 5, 2012 (http://china.caixin.com/ 2012-06-05/100397117.html).

Prologue

All notes for the prologue are the editor's notes, unless otherwise indicated.

1. *Author's note:* The original letter contained the following footnote: "The author invites the media to republish this letter online or in print, and extends the invitation particularly to Chongqing media. There is no need to ask permission."

2. "The campaign against the underworld" (打黑), sometime translated as the "campaign to crack down on criminal forces" or "the campaign to strike black," was a punitive police operation led by former Chongqing party chief Bo Xilai and his hand-picked former Chongqing police chief Wang Lijijun in Chongqing City between July 2009 and February 2012. This ruthless social engineering-style campaign led to thousands of arrests and some executions of alleged corrupt officials, entrepreneurs, and gangsters in the city.

3. The Wen Qiang case (文强案) was part of a huge operation between July 2009 and February 2012, led by former Chongqing party secretary Bo Xilai, to crack down on illegal activities and arrest a large number of suspects (including several district police chiefs) in Chongqing, a city of more than 33 million people. Wen Qiang (文强 1956–2010) was the former head of the Justice Bureau of Chongqing and had also served as the city's deputy police chief. Wen was arrested in September 2009, charged with corruption on a massive scale, and sentenced to death in April 2010, found guilty of sponsoring and protecting gangs as well as committing rape and taking bribes. He was executed in July 2010. The Wen Qiang case has been seen as a significant personal victory for Bo Xilai. Many critics have argued that this use of the "campaign method" of combating crime (instead of an emphasis on legal procedure) could not bring about public safety or social justice, as new crime bosses with strong ties to government officials would likely emerge.

4. Li Zhuang (李庄 1961–), a graduate from the master's program in Civil and Commercial Law at the Chinese Academy of Social Sciences, is a defense lawyer in Beijing who represented an alleged Chongqing gang leader. Li was arrested in Chongqing in December 2009 on charges of falsifying evidence and jeopardizing testimony after a gang leader who was caught in a massive crackdown in Chongqing told the authorities that Li encouraged him to lie and say that he had been tortured by the police. Li at first denied the charges, but later, in a move that surprised many, revised his plea to guilty. Ultimately, Li denied the charges, claiming that his admission of guilt was the result of threats and pressure from the authorities. As this case received national attention, many Chinese defense lawyers have indicated that they have been experiencing increasing pressure because of overzealous authorities eager to win convictions. Several well-known lawyers signed a letter after Li's arrest claiming that the charge against Li had many flaws and, more important, that Chongqing authorities had violated the rights of Li's attorney. Li was sentenced to eighteen months in prison and was released in June 2011, despite efforts of the Chongqing police to extend Li Zhuang's sentence by leveling new charges.

5. *Economic Observer Online*, February 9, 2010 (http://wap.eeo.com.cn/).

6. Wang Lijun (王立军 1959–) has served as the police chief of Chongqing since 2009. In 2008 Chongqing party secretary Bo Xilai brought Wang, then policy chief of Jinzhou City, Liaoning, to Chongqing. Wang was known for his iron-fisted approach to securing sociopolitical stability, first in Liaoning and then in Chongqing, as manifest in Bo's "campaign against the underground." In May 2011, Wang was promoted to vice-mayor of Chongqing. It was also Wang Lijun who torpedoed his patron Bo's political career. In February 2012, Wang mysteriously fled into the U.S. consulate in Chengdu. It was widely believed that Wang's fears of retribution by Bo led him to take this incredible

action, which caused domino effects throughout China's political landscape on the eve of the Eighteenth Party Congress.

Chapter One

All notes for chapter 1 are author's notes unless otherwise indicated.

1. Hosea Ballou Morse, *The Chronicles of the East India Company Trading to China*, translated by Qu Zonghua, vols. 4 and 5 (Sun Yat-sen University Press, 1991), pp. 13–15, 25–29, and 36. This incident covered by Morse's work is also the opening story in Michael H. Hunt, *The Making of a Special Relationship: The United States and China to 1914*, translated by Xiang Liling and Lin Yongjun (Fudan University Press, 1993). See also Tyler Dennett, *Americans in Eastern Asia: A Critical Study of the Policy of the United States with Reference to China, Japan and Korea in the 19th Century.* (New York: Macmillan, 1922), pp. 87–88. Quoted from Li Dingyi, *A Diplomatic History between the United States and China: 1884–1894* (Peking University Press, 1997), p. 57. There is detailed but diametrically different narration of this incident in Chinese literature. See the memorial presented by the general governor of Guangdong and Guangxi to the throne on November 8, 1821, recorded in *Historical Sourcebook on the Qing's Diplomatic Relations (Reign of Daoguang)*, vol. 1, pp. 7–9.

2. Morse, *Chronicles of the East India Company.*

3. Ibid., p. 36.

4. For more legal conflicts happening around the time of the *Emily* incident, please see Morse, *Chronicles of the East India Company*, pp. 35–36; R. Randle Edwards, "Ching Legal Jurisdiction over Foreigners," in *Essays on China's Legal Tradition*, compiled by Karen Turner, Gao Hongjun, and He Weifang (China University of Political Science and Law Press, 1994), pp. 416–71.

5. See Tao Guangfeng, "Opium Wars and Conflicts of Chinese and Western Laws," *Journal of Comparative Law*, no. 2-3 (1992): 74–78. See also Edwards, "Ching Legal Jurisdiction."

6. Shiga Shuzo, "An Examination of Chinese Legal Culture: Forms of Litigation as Source Material," in *Civil Trials and Private Contracts in Ming and Qing Periods*, translated by Wang Yaxin and others (Beijing: Law Press, 1998), pp. 1–18.

7. See Ch'u Tongtsu (Qu Tongzu), *Local Government in China under the Ching* (Harvard University Press, 1962); Shuzo, "Examination of Chinese Legal Culture"; Yang Xuefeng, *Judicial System of the Ming Dynasty* (Taipei: Liming Cultural Enterprises Company, 1978); Na Silu, *The County Justice of the Qing Dynasty* (Beijing: Literature, History and Philosophy Press, 1982); Zheng Qin, *Essays on Judicial System of the Qing Dynasty* (Changsha: Hunan Educational Press, 1988); and Wu Jiyuan, *The Judicial Functions of Local Government in the Qing Dynasty* (Beijing: China Social Sciences Press, 1998).

8. *Editor's note:* Wang Huizu (汪辉祖 1730–1807), a native of Xiaoshan, Zhejiang Province, was an official during the Jiaqing Period in the Qing dynasty. For the quote, see Wang Huizu, "Diligent Governance," *School Governance Assumption.*

9. *Editor's note:* Ch'u Tongtsu (Qu Tongzu, 瞿同祖 1910–2008), a native of Changsha, Hunan Province, was a distinguished historian of modern China, famous for his studies of legal history and Chinese society. For the quote, see Ch'u Tongtsu, *Local Government in China under the Ching* (Harvard University Press, 1962), p. 443.

10. When he examined Chinese history, Max Weber was impressed with the much lower number of officials the Chinese government had in comparison with its European counterparts. See Max Weber, *Konfuziamismus und Taoismus*, Chinese translation by Wang Rongfen (Shanghai: Commercial Press, 1995), p. 99. He also sharply pointed out the correlation between the rough style of governance and the small number of officials. Compared with the traditional society, China today has a significantly larger number of officials, but the quality of performance required by rational governance has not seen a proportional growth. According to the data cited by one historian, "China's government employee to population ratio has increased 17 times from 1:600 in the early period of the People's Republic to today's 1:34, while in the same period the country's population increased by less than three times." See Ge Jianxiong, "Burden of the Whole Society," *Southern Weekly*, July 10, 1998.

11. See Shang Yanliu, *About the Imperial Civil Service Examination System* (Shanghai: Sanlian Books, 1958); Lu Simian, *A History of the Chinese Institutions* (Shanghai Classical Publishers, 1985), chap. 15; and He Huaihong, *The Selective System and Its End* (Shanghai: Sanlian Books, 1998).

12. See He Huaihong, *The Selective System*, pp. 107–13.

13. Weber, *Konfuziamismus und Taoismus*, p. 173. Weber's italics.

14. Historian Ray Huang holds that the organizational system of the traditional Chinese society was characterized by its enduring stability and "cost efficiency": "In the late period of the Qing Dynasty, the government's fiscal revenue never exceeded 100 million taels of silver, a very insignificant number given China's population and the world standards then. Because of the society's simple organization and shallow technological foundation, it was possible for so huge a country to be based on smallholder agriculture without need for lawyers and full-time judges until the Opium War." See Ray Huang, *Jindai zhongguo de daolu* [The road of modern China] (Taipei: Lianjing Publishing Company, 1995), pp. 72–73.

15. See He Weifang, "The Style and Spirit of Traditional Chinese Judicial Decisions: Based Mainly on the Song Dynasty and Comparing with that of England," *CASS Journal of Social Sciences*, no. 6 (1990): 188–217.

16. Ibid., pp. 210–17.

17. Tang Degang (T. K. Tong), ed. *An Oral Autobiography of Hu Shih* (East China Normal University Press, 1993), chap. 5, editor's note 23.

18. Fuma Susumu, *Mingqing shidai de songshi yu susong zhidu* [Litigation masters and the litigation system in the Ming and Qing Periods], recorded by Shiga Shuzo, "Examination of Chinese Legal Culture," pp. 389–430. It is interesting that Fu holds that "the litigation masters are monsters born by the state's civil examination system," and the important institutional factor that sustained the existence of litigation masters was "the litigation

system itself that follows the principles of documentary proceeding and the beneficiary bearing the cost" (pp. 418–19).

19. Robert Hart, "Bystander's View," in *Robert Hart and China's Early Modernization, His Journals, 1863–1866*, edited by Richard J. Smith, John K. Fairbank, and Katherine F. Bruner (Harvard University Press, 1991), pp. 282–93. Concerning western criticism of the Chinese system and its impact on the Hundred Days' Reform, see Wang Shuhuai, *Foreigners and the Hundred Days' Reform* (Shanghai Bookstore Press, 1988).

20. Ma Jianzhong, *Shang liboxiang yan chuyang gongke shu* [Letter to the prime minister on my European tour], appearing in *Shikezhai yanxing ji* [Account of speeches and activities at Moderation Studio], cited from Ma Zuowu, *Thoughts of Judicial Reform in the Late Qing* (Lanzhou University Press, 1997), p. 27.

Editor's note: Ma Jianzhong (马建忠 1844–1900), a native of Zhenjiang, Jiangsu Province, was a protégé of Li Hongzhang. Li sent Ma to France in 1876 to study international law. While in Paris, Ma served as an interpreter for Guo Songtao, then China's minister (ambassador) to the United Kingdom and France. Li Hongzhang (李鸿章 1823–1901), a native of Hefei, Anhui Province, was a prominent general and statesman of the late Qing dynasty.

21. Ibid.

22. *Editor's note:* The Hundred Days' Reform (戊戌变法 1898), led by the young Guangxu emperor and his reform-minded supporters, was a failed attempt at reforming the Chinese cultural, political, and educational system in the late Qing dynasty. The reform took place after the Chinese defeat in the Sino-Japanese War (1894–95).

23. *Editor's note:* Kang Youwei (康有为 1858–1927), a native of Nanhai, Guangdong Province, was a renowned Chinese scholar, prominent political thinker, and reformer during the late Qing dynasty. He led the Hundred Days' Reform, which aimed to establish a constitutional monarchy.

24. Kang Youwei, "Shang qingdi diyi shu" [The first memorial presented to the emperor), in *Wuxu bianfa ziliao congkan* [Sourcebook on the One Hundred Days' Reform), vol. 2, edited by Jian Bozan, (Beijing: Shenzhou guoguangshe, 1953), p. 128. Cited from Xiao Gongquan, "Modernization of the Administrative System: The Advocacy of Kang Youwei and Its Significance," in *Hong Kong, Taiwan and Overseas Chinese Scholars on Modern Chinese Culture*, edited by Jiang Yihua (Chongqing: Chongqing Chubanshe, 1987), p. 349.

25. Concerning Kang Youwei's elaboration on the government's organizational reform, see Xiao, "Modernization of the Administrative System." Concerning the measures introduced during the One Hundred Days' Reform, see Zhang Hao, "Ideological Changes and the One Hundred Days' Reform," in *The Cambridge History of China,* vol. 11*, Part. 2: Late Ch'ing, 1800–1911*, edited by John King Fairbank and Kwang-Ching Liu (Cambridge University Press, 1980), pp. 321–82.

26. For a discussion of the ideological and social changes elicited by the One Hundred Days' Reform, see Zhang, "Ideological Changes and the One Hundred Days' Reform."

27. Concerning the link between the reform initiated in 1901 and Kang Youwei's advocacies three years earlier ago, see Xiao, "Modernization of the Administrative System," pp. 258–361. Jiang Tingfu is also of the opinion that the reform directed by the Empress Dowager Cixi in the four years from 1901 to 1904 carried on and surpassed the reform measures promoted by Kang Youwei, who had the support of the Guangxu emperor. See Jiang Tingfu, *Modern History of China* (Changsha: Yuelu Publishing House, 1987), p. 90.

28. *Editor's note:* Yan Fu (严复 1854–1921), a native of Houguan, Fujian Province, was a renowned Chinese scholar and translator, famous for his translations of works by Baron de Montesquieu, Thomas Henry Huxley, John Stuart Mill, Herbert Spencer, Adam Smith, Charles Darwin, and others. Through his translation work, he tried to show that Western wealth and power did not lie in technological advances but rather in ideas and institutions.

29. Quoted in Wang Shi, ed., *Collected Works of Yan Fu*, vol. 4 (Beijing: Zhonghua Book Company, 1986), p. 969.

30. In a commentary in his translation of Montesquieu's *The Spirit of Laws* on the author's view that "it is natural for a republic to have only a small territory . . . a monarchical state ought to be of moderate extent . . . a large empire supposes a despotic authority in the person who governs," Yan Fu expressed his disagreement and said that "this view holds true only for the ancient times rather than the present time." Ibid., p. 960.

31. Yan Fu, "*Lun shibian zhi ji*" [On the speed of world change], in Wang, *Collected Works of Yan Fu*, vol. 1 (Beijing: Zhonghua Book Company, 1986), pp. 2–3.

32. Wang, *Collected Works of Yan Fu*, vol. 4, pp. 884, 930–32, and 981–82.

33. Ibid., p. 961.

34. Ibid., p. 970.

35. Ibid., p. 1000. In an 1895 article entitled "*Jiuwang juelun*" [On saving the nation from destruction], Yan Fu said that to save China from destruction, the first thing to do is to make reforms, and the first thing to do in the reforms is to abolish the eight-legged essay in the imperial civil examinations. In the article, he enumerated three principal harms: "shackling wisdom," "corrupting the mind," and "fueling negligence." Those who succeeded in the imperial examinations all had the firm conviction that "even by reading half the content of Confucius's Analects, one can govern the state well" and that "since there is nothing they can't elaborate as a student, there will be nothing they can't handle as an official. Such muddle-minded thoughts are simply beyond count." See Wang, *Collected Works of Yan Fu*, vol. 1, pp. 40–41.

36. Shen Yunlong, ed., *Qingmo choubei lixian dang'an shiliao* [Sources on the preparation for constitutional government in late Qing], vol. 1, Division of Ming and Qing Archives (Beijing: Palace Museum, n.d.), pp. 463–65.

37. Jiang, *Modern History of China*, p. 27. With a tradition lacking a strong consciousness of nationality and religious membership, which in Europe was emphasized as early as ancient and medieval times, and at a time before the concepts of a national country and sovereignty took root, it was only natural for people "completely ignorant of international laws and situations" during the reign of the Daoguang emperor to "fight for things that are not worth fighting for and give up things that should not be given up." For legal pro-

visions and practices concerning foreign-related cases throughout the dynasties in China, see Edwards, "Ching Legal Jurisdiction over Foreigners," p. 419; and Zhan Hengju, *Legal History of Modern China* (Taipei: Commercial Press, 1973), pp. 93–95.

38. *Editor's note:* The Boxer Rebellion (义和团事件 1898–1901) was an ultranationalist movement that opposed foreign imperialism and Christianity and attempted to drive all foreigners out of China.

39. Cited from Yang Honglie, *The Evolutionary History of Chinese Law* (Taipei: Commercial Press, 1930), p. 872.

40. Zasshi Sōgō raises doubts about whether the Qing court earnestly believed in the need for reform. He holds that the government was generally negative in its attitude toward reform before 1904. "The government did not have its reform agenda in the first place, and it only pretended to be committed to reform but actually did not care about the content of the reform at all." Although the government subsequently became more serious about reform, the motive or purpose of this seriousness was to maintain the Qing's rule amid rising pressures from the Han and foreigners. Besides, all figures and groups participating in the reform had their own private agendas, and their support was conditioned on the premise that the reform would maintain and expand their own interests. As a result, "the reforms only ended up accelerating the downfall of the dynasty." See Zasshi Sōgō, "Political and Institutional Reform: 1901–1911," in *The Cambridge History of China,* vol. 11, *Part. 2: Late Ch'ing, 1800–1911,* edited by Fairbank and Liu, pp. 459–63.

41. Shen Yunlong, ed., *Qingmo choubei lixian dang'an shiliao* [Sources on the preparation for constitutional government in late Qing], vol. 1 (Taipei: Wenhai Publishing, 1981), p. 471.

42. Shen Yunlong, ed., *Qingmo choubei lixian dang'an shiliao* [Sources on the preparation for constitutional government in late Qing], vol. 2 (Taipei: Wenhai Publishing, 1981), pp. 821–24. Another palace memorial recorded in the same book (pp. 591–96), presented by Zhang Renjun, viceroy of Liangjiang, also presented a rigorous argument for the gradual transition of the judicial system from the traditional model to the modern model.

43. *Editor's note:* Wu Fang (吴钫) was an official in the Ministry of Civic Affairs in the late Qing dynasty period. He served as governor of Zhejiang in the early years of the Republic of China.

44. Shen, *Qingmo choubei lixian dang'an shiliao,* vol. 1, pp. 463–65.

45. Ibid.

46. Wang, *Collected Works of Yan Fu,* vol. 4, pp. 900–01.

47. Ibid., p. 952.

48. Articles 48 through 51. Chai Degeng and others, eds., *The Revolution of 1911,* vol. 8 (Shanghai People's Publishing House, 1957), pp. 35–36.

49. Andrew J. Nathan, "A Constitutional Republic: The Peking Government, 1916–28," in *The Cambridge History of China,* vol. 12, *Part 1: Republican China, 1912–1949,* edited by John King Fairbank, Chinese translation by Yang Pinquan (Beijing: China Social Sciences Press, 1998), p. 310.

50. Ibid., p. 315.

51. *Editor's note:* The 1911 Revolution (辛亥革命) was a nationalist democratic revolution that overthrew the Qing dynasty and marked the beginning of the republic.

52. Yang, *Evolutionary History of Chinese Law*, p. 872.

53. Concerning Shen Jiaben's contributions to China's judicial reform, see Li Guilian, *A Chronicle of Shen Jiaben's Life* (Taipei: Cheng-Wen Publishing, 1992); Li, *Shen Jiaben and China's Legal Modernization* (Guangming Daily Press, 1989).

54. Wu Tingfang, *Zhonghua minguo tuzhi chuyi* [Preliminary suggestions on the governance of the Republic of China] (Shanghai: Commercial Press, 1915). The article is included in Ding Xianjun and Yu Zuofeng, eds., *Collected Works of Wu Tingfang* (Beijing: Zhonghua Book Company, 1993).

55. See Ding and Yu, *Collected Works of Wu Tingfang*, p. 594.

56. *Official Gazette by Categories*, vol. 36 (n.d.): 9–10. Cited from Xu Xiaoqun, "The Fate of Judicial Independence in Republican China," *China Quarterly* (1997): 5.

57. Ibid.

58. *Official Gazette*, vol. 301 (March 9, 1913): 136–41.

59. *Official Gazette*, vol. 961 (January 11, 1915).

60. Xu, "The Fate of Judicial Independence in Republican China," p. 6.

61. *Editor's note:* Yuan Shikai (袁世凯 1859–1916), a native of Dingcheng, Henan Province, was a powerful Chinese general and politician famous for his role in events leading up to the abdication of the last Qing emperor, his autocratic rule as the second president of the Republic of China following Sun Yat-sen, and his short-lived attempt to revive the Chinese monarchy.

62. The chiefs of the Department of Justice were frequently changed during this period. Among the more than ten chiefs, the first chief, Wang Chonghui, was a Yale-trained doctor of law; Zhang Zongxiang graduated from Meiji University; Lin Changmin and Jiang Yong were graduates of Waseda University; Dong Kang studied law for two years in Japan; Zhang Shizhao studied law for four years at the University of Edinburgh; Ma Junwu had a doctorate in engineering from Berlin Institute of Technology; and Luo Wengan had a master's degree in law from Oxford University. Only one chief, Liang Qichao, did not have the experience of studying overseas.

63. See Xu, "The Fate of Judicial Independence in Republican China," pp. 7–9.

64. *Editor's note:* Liang Qichao (梁启超 1873–1929), a native of Xinhui, Guangdong Province, was a foremost intellectual leader of China in the first two decades of the twentieth century and was especially known for his leadership in reform movements.

65. See *Falü pinglun* [Law review], no. 1 (July 1, 1923): 1. However, in a question-and-answer article concerning the drafting of the constitution published in the fourth year of the Republic of China, Liang Qichao gave a low evaluation of the judicial situation then, and even held that, since the promulgation of the Provisional Constitution, its provisions concerning civil rights and the judicial system "have not been duly implemented at all, nor are there any signs that they will make efforts to ensure their implementation. They are nothing but lip service." *Collected Works of Liang Qichao*, vol. 33 (Tianjin: Tianjin

guji chubanshe, 2006). He was also highly critical of the judicial system in the Beiyang government era. See Zhang Guofu, *A Brief Legal History of the Republic of China* (Peking University Press, 1986), pp. 174–82.

66. *Editor's note:* The Northern Expedition (北伐战争 1926–28) was a military campaign led by the Kuomintang while it was allied with the communists; it aimed to unify China by ending the rule of northern warlords.

67. Zhang, *Brief Legal History*, pp. 220–21. *Editor's note:* Li Dazhao (李大钊 1888–1927), a native of Leting, Hebei Province, was the cofounder, along with Chen Duxiu, of the Chinese Communist Party in 1921. The May Thirtieth Patriotic Movement (五卅反帝爱国运动 1925) was a series of strikes and demonstrations precipitated by the killing of thirteen labor demonstrators by British police in Shanghai. This anti-imperialist labor movement later encompassed people of various classes from many parts of the country.

Editor's note: Feng Yuxiang (冯玉祥 1882–1948), a native of Caoxian, Anhui Province, was a powerful Chinese warlord in the early years of Republican China and controlled a large part of northern China from 1918 to 1930.

68. Published in the Chinese newspaper *Ta kung pao* (Changsha), December 24, 1926. Cited from Zhang, *Brief Legal History*, p. 220.

69. *Republican Daily News* (Shanghai), September 20, 1926. Cited from Zhang, *Brief Legal History*, p. 221.

70. Ju Zheng, "Sifa danghua wenti" [Issues on partisan control of the judiciary], *Eastern Miscellany* (Shanghai) 10 (1934): 6–19. The cited passage is from page 7.

Editor's note: The Three Principles of the People (三民主义) is the ideological framework developed by the Chinese Nationalist leader Sun Yat-sen (1866–1925). The three principles are nationalism, democracy, and people's livelihood.

71. Ibid. According to Ju Zheng, from Cicero and Aquinas to Hobbes and Kohler, "The theory of natural law has often been used by reactionary scholars as a smoke bomb to attack revolutionary forces. Those not armed with the sharp perspective of social philosophy are often deceived by them."

72. Ibid. See also Karl Marx, "The German Ideology," in *The Complete Works of Marx and Engels*, vol. 3 (Beijing: People's Publishing House, 1956).

73. Ju, "Sifa danghua wenti," p. 11.

74. *Law Review*, no. 185 (January 1927): 17.

75. See Xu, "The Fate of Judicial Independence in Republican China," pp. 10–13.

76. *Shibao* [Times], February 22, 1929.

77. *Official Gazette of the Judicial Yuan*, no. 29 (March 25, 1935): 1–3.

78. See Xu, "The Fate of Judicial Independence in Republican China," p. 14.

79. See Sun Yat-sen, "Reply to Kuomintang Sichuan Branch," in *Complete Works of Sun Yat-sen*, vol. 6 (Beijing: Zhonghua Book Company, 1981), p. 573; "Speech at the Party Meeting in Guangzhou," *Complete Works of Sun Yat-sen*, vol. 8, p. 258. It is a general view that Sun Yat-sen had a considerable amount of Western knowledge and his political thoughts were influenced by the Western system, but as a revolutionary, his political and social thoughts differed greatly from prevailing Western concepts. His Three Principles of

the People were strongly influenced by socialism, and his conceptualization of China's political system had an obvious resemblance to that of the Soviet Union. For instance, he held that "Russia's practice of one political party running the state is superior to the multiple-party system of Britain, the United States and France. . . . The Russian revolution, in essence, was an application of the Three Principles of the People, in that it put the party above the state" (*Complete Works of Sun Yat-sen*, vol. 9, p. 104). He also showed a great interest in the "people's dictatorship" in Russia. See *Complete Works of Sun Yat-sen*, vol. 9, p. 314.

80. In Taiwan judicial independence had not been achieved until recently.

81. Benedetto Croce, "History and Annals," in *Selected Works of Modern Historical Schools in the West*, translated and edited by Chen Quan, Tian Rukang, and Jin Chongyuan (Shanghai: People's Publishing House, 1982), pp. 333–46.

82. *Black's Law Dictionary*, 5th ed. (West Publishing, 1979), p. 728.

83. See Shu Li, "Rule of Law in China's Modernization," in *Ideas and Problems of China* (Nanchang: Jiangxi Education Press, 1998), pp. 170–214.

84. See Ji Weidong, "Positioning of the Legal Profession: Japan's Practice of Restructuring the Power Structure," *Social Sciences in China*, no. 2 (1994).

85. A good example of this power relationship can be found in He Weifang, "Social Justice through the Judiciary: An In-depth Look at the Current Status of Judges in China," in *Sifa de linian yu zhidu* [The Idea and System of Justice] (China University of Political Science and Law Press, 1998), p. 53. See also p. 55 for the analysis of the example.

86. This insight had been long expressed by the ancient Chinese, as shown in the Justice Administration part of *The Rites of Zhou*: "The judge adjudicates on cases by five hearings, namely, of speech, of complexion, of breath, of reaction, and of eyes."

87. During July and August in 1996, I had the pleasure of paying a visit to the United States (along with a Chinese judicial delegation) to study its judicial system. Through communications with their U.S. counterparts, what the Chinese judges (including chief justices and deputy chief justices, of course) found most inconceivable was not the great power enjoyed by the courts there but the little sway the chief justices had over their "subordinates." What puzzled the Chinese judges was that, without the leadership of the chief justice or other leaders, it would seem that the judges being given the right to handle cases at their own discretion would throw the court and even the whole judicial system into a chaotic state and lead to widespread corruption. Concerning the administrative powers of federal chief justices of the United States, see Lawrence Baum, *American Courts: Process and Policy* (Boston: Houghton Mifflin, 1986), p. 37 onward.

88. When explaining the Judges Law of the People's Republic of China to the Standing Committee of the National People's Congress, Ren Jianxin, president of the Supreme People's Court, said that "the characteristics of judges require them to have high caliber," and he also added that "there are even higher requirements on judges of courts of higher levels." See Zhou Daoluan, *A Sourcebook for Studying the Judges Law of the People's Republic of China* (Beijing: People's Court Press, 1995), pp.16–17. In fact, judges of courts of different levels should have equally high requirements imposed on them. Everyone familiar with how judicial work proceeds knows the great importance of preliminary judges'

competent performance of their duties for maintaining the overall judicial system and safeguarding citizens' rights. In some Western countries, a special effort is made to keep the qualification criteria largely consistent for court judges at all levels and their emoluments within a relatively narrow range. This arrangement reduces the incentive for lower court judges to pursue promotion to higher-level courts, thus preventing such motivations from affecting judicial independence and attracting more high-caliber judges to work at lower-level courts. It also has the effect of decreasing the appeals rate: when higher-court judges are presumed to be of higher caliber than those of lower courts, concerned parties then have an incentive to have their case adjudicated by the ostensibly more competent judges in the higher courts in order to get more favorable results, which thus increases the costs of the judicial system.

89. Similar provisions are made in article 10 of the Organic Law of the People's Procuratorate of the People's Republic of China and in articles 17 and 30 of the Organic Law of the People's Courts of the People's Republic of China.

90. See Alexis de Tocqueville, *Democracy in America*, vol. 1, translated by Dong Guoliang (Shanghai: Commercial Press, 1997), p. 303.

Chapter Two

All notes for chapter 2 are editor's notes unless otherwise indicated.

1. The May Fourth Movement (五四运动) was an intellectual movement growing out of student demonstrations that occurred in China on May 4, 1919. This anti-imperialist, cultural, and political movement initially aimed to protest the Chinese government's weak response to the Treaty of Versailles, and it later spurred the reorganization of the Nationalist Party (Kuomintang) and stimulated the birth of the Chinese Communist Party. For more discussion of the subject, see Chow Tsetsung, *The May Fourth Movement: Intellectual Revolution in Modern China* (Harvard University Press, 1960).

2. *Fortress Besieged* (围城 1947), a novel by renowned writer Qian Zhongshu, is famous for its theme based on an original Western notion: "Marriage is like a fortress besieged: those who are outside want to get in, and those who are inside want to get out." This sentiment is not limited to marriage but can also refer to choices in many other situations. See Qian Zhongshu, *Fortress Besieged*, translated by Jeanne Kelly and Nathan K. Mao (New York: Penguin Books, 2006).

3. Jiang Qing (蒋庆 1953–), a native of Xuzhou, Jiangsu Province, graduated with a law degree from Southwest University of Politics and Law in China. He taught at his alma mater for six years after graduation; in 1988 he transferred to the Research Center for Western and Eastern cultures in the Shenzhen Institute of Administration. Jiang has dedicated himself to research on Chinese culture, especially Confucian cultural studies.

4. "Zhuangzi, Mengzi, and Shihezi" refer to, respectively, the names of two great Chinese philosophers (Zhuangzi and Mencius) and the name of the city in Xinjiang where he was transferred.

5. The Lin Biao incident (林彪事件) refers to the September 1971 plane crash that killed Minister of Defense Lin Biao (1907–71) in Mongolia after what appeared to be a failed coup attempt by Lin to oust Mao Zedong.

6. Mencius (also Meng Zi or Meng Tzu, 孟子 372–289 BCE), a native of the State of Zou, now Zoucheng County (originally Zouxian), Shandong Province, was a Chinese philosopher in the Confucian school of thought. His fame among Confucians is second only to Confucius himself. *Mencius*, the book with his name as the title, was based on his conversations with kings of the time and is one of the Four Books containing the core of orthodox Neo-Confucian thought.

7. Tang Degang, ed., *An Oral Autobiography of Hu Shih* (East China Normal University Press, 1993).

8. *Author's note:* Hsiao Kung-chuan (Xiao Gongquan, 肖公权 1897–1981), a native of Taihe, Jiangxi Province, was a distinguished scholar in political philosophy. He studied at Tsinghua University and received his Ph.D. from Cornell University; his dissertation was entitled *Political Pluralism.* Hsiao served as a professor at the Law School of Sichuan University during World War II and subsequently taught at Washington University in Seattle from 1949 to 1981.

9. Yi Zhongtian (易中天 1947–), a native of Changsha, Hunan Province, is a writer, historian, and professor of literature at Xiamen University. In recent years he has become a television celebrity in China, known for his popular talk shows on history, politics, and culture.

10. *Author's note:* See "Book 1, Part 2, King Hui of Liang," *The Works of Mencius.*

11. Song Zuying (宋祖英 1966–), an ethnic Miao and a native of Guzhang, Hunan Province, is a popular folk singer in present-day China.

12. *Author's note:* See "Book 1, Part 2. King Hui of Liang," *The Works of Mencius.*

13. Zhu Guangqian (朱光潜 1897–1986), a native of Tongcheng, Anhui Province, was a professor at Peking University. He is considered the founder of the study of aesthetics in twentieth-century China.

14. *Author's note:* See Sima Qian, "Rulin liezhuan" [Forest of scholars], in *Records of the Grand Historian.*

15. Chen Sheng (陈胜) and Wu Guang (吴广) were the leaders of the peasant uprising against the reign of Qin Er Shi, the first emperor of China.

16. Guo Moruo (郭沫若 1892–1978), a native of Leshan, Sichuan Province, was a historian, archaeologist, and poet who served as vice-premier in the State Council and president of the Chinese Academy of Sciences during the Mao era.

17. Jiang Qing (江青 1914–91), a native of Zhucheng, Shandong Province, was Mao Zedong's last wife and was most well known for her major role in promoting the Cultural Revolution (1966–76). After Mao's death in 1976, she was convicted in 1981 of "counter-revolutionary crimes" and was imprisoned for life. She committed suicide in 1991. See Roxanne Witke, *Comrade Chiang Ch'ing* (Boston: Little, Brown, 1977).

18. Liu Shaoqi (刘少奇 1898–1969), a native of Ningxiang, Hunan Province, was the president of the People's Republic of China from 1959 to 1968. Once considered the heir

apparent to Mao Zedong, Liu was purged by Mao in the late 1960s during the Cultural Revolution.

19. The Sun Zhigang (孙志刚 1976–2003) case refers to an incident that occurred on March 20, 2003. Sun, a 27-year-old native of Hubei, arrived in Guangzhou for employment but was arrested by police for not carrying proper identification. He was beaten to death by eight patients at a penitentiary clinic just hours after being arrested. In May several Chinese law professors requested that the Standing Committee of the National People's Congress review the "Regulation for Deportation of Urban Vagrants and Beggars." Their request was widely covered in the Chinese media. In June Premier Wen Jiabao announced that the State Council had decided to repeal these discriminatory regulations against migrant workers.

20. Joseph Levenson, *Confucian China and Its Modern Fate* (New York: American Council of Learned Societies, 2008).

21. Edward Coke, *Coke's Reports* (1600).

22. The Sun Weiming (孙伟铭) case refers to the situation in which Sun Weiming, a native of Guangan, Sichuan, was sentenced to life imprisonment and deprived of political rights for life for the crime of "endangering public safety with dangerous methods." In late 2008 Sun was drunk driving without a license and was involved in an accident that killed four and seriously injured one. This case led to a nationwide debate on the maximum penalty for drunk driving and other similar violations.

23. Henry Wheaton, *Elements of International Law: With a Sketch of the History of the Science* (London: B. Fellowes, 1836).

24. Lin Zexu (林则徐 1785–1850), an official during the Qing dynasty, is often seen as a national hero in contemporary China. Lin's forceful opposition to the opium trade on moral and social grounds is considered the primary catalyst for the First Opium War of 1839–42. Lin was also a proponent of the revitalization of traditional Chinese thought and institutions, which became known as the Self-Strengthening Movement.

25. W. A. P. Martin, trans., *Wanguo gongfa* [Elements of international law] (Beijing: Jingdu chongshiguan, 1864).

26. *Author's note:* See "Book 7, Part 1. Jin Xin," *The Works of Mencius.*

27. Cedric T. Chou, *Fazhi lixiangguo—Sugeladi yu mengzi de xu ni dui hua* [An ideal state of law: A virtual dialogue between Socrates and Mencius] (Beijing: Shangwu yinshuaguan, 1999).

28. *Author's note:* See "Book 6, Part 2. Gaozi," *The Works of Mencius.*

Chapter Three

All notes for chapter 3 are editor's notes unless otherwise indicated.

1. Xia Yong (夏勇 1961–), a native of Jingzhou, Hubei Province, is currently director of the State Secrets Bureau. An accomplished legal scholar, Xia previously served as director of the Institute of Law at the Chinese Academy of Social Sciences.

2. In Chinese, the pronunciation of *xinan*, meaning "southwest," sounds very close to *xilan*, meaning "rotten."

3. Qian Zhongshu (钱钟书 1910–98), a native of Wuxi, Jiangsu Province, was a well-accomplished literary scholar, writer, and translator in twentieth-century China.

4. He Weifang, *Juti fazhi* [The detailed rule of law] (Beijing: Law Press, 2002), chapter entitled "Toupiaoxiang de miaoyong" [The magic of the ballot box].

5. Hu Xiaoming, "Jinqian pujiu baigonglu" [The money-paved path to the White House], *Fujian Daily*, March 16, 2000, p. 4.

6. The term "southern tour" (南巡) refers to an imperial inspection trip to the south of China, including those of Qing dynasty emperors Kangxi and Qianlong. During the reigns of Kangxi and Qianlong, each had six southern tours. More recently, this term has been used to refer to Deng Xiaoping's inspection trip to Wuchang, Shenzhen, Zhuhai, and Shanghai in January-February 1992, during which he promoted further economic reforms in the wake of the 1989 Tiananmen incident.

7. Babaoshan (八宝山) refers to the Babaoshan Revolutionary Cemetery, which is located in western Beijing. It is China's most famous resting place for revolutionary heroes, high-ranking government officials, and in recent years, any individuals deemed important due to their contributions to the country.

8. Hua Guofeng (华国锋 1921–2008), a native of Jiaocheng, Shanxi Province, was Mao Zedong's designated successor in the mid-1970s. After Mao's death in 1976, Hua ousted Mao's widow Jiang Qing and the other three members of the Gang of Four from political power. However, Hua himself was outmaneuvered a few years later by Deng Xiaoping, who forced Hua into early retirement.

9. Attributable to William Pitt the Elder, in Parliament in 1763, referring to the sanctity of an individual's home. See http://thinkexist.com/quotation/the-poorest-man-may-in-his-cottage-bid-defiance/537178.html.

10. The May 31 speech (5.31 讲话) refers to Jiang Zemin's speech at the Central Party School in Beijing on May 31, 2002, in which he provided a new conceptualization of the Chinese Communist Party and its representation.

11. *Author's note:* In Jiang Zemin's May 31 speech (see preceding note), he argued that the Chinese Communist Party not only should represent the fundamental interests of the majority (that is, the working class) but also should represent two other forces: advanced social productive forces (meaning entrepreneurs and capitalists) and the progressive course of China's advanced culture (meaning cultural elites and intellectuals). This concept becomes known as the "three represents" (三个代表).

12. Gu Zhun (顾准 1915–74), a native of Shanghai, was a well-known economist and a pioneer of post-Marxist Chinese liberalism. He was a communist official and served as head of the Bureau of Finance in the Shanghai municipal government. He was a victim of "anti-Rightist" purges and the Cultural Revolution, and he spent the latter part of his life in prisons and reeducation centers. See "Gu Zhun" (http://en.wikipedia.org/wiki/Gu_Zhun).

13. Liu Xiaoqing (刘晓庆 1955–), a native of Peiling, Chongqing, and a Chinese movie star, was arrested in 2002 for evading nearly RMB 6.7 million in taxes from 1996 to 2001 in connection with her company, Beijing Xiaoping Culture and Arts Company, Ltd. She was fined RMB 7.1 million and imprisoned for one year.

14. Tang Degang, *Wanqing qishinian* [Seventy years in the late Qing dynasty] (Taipei: Yuanliu Publishing House, 1998).

15. Paul A. Cohen, *Discovering History in China,* 2d ed. (Columbia University Press, 1997).

16. Wang Baosen (王宝森 1939–95) was vice-mayor of Beijing in charge of financial affairs for the city. Due to a spate of corruption charges, Wang committed suicide in the Huairou countryside near Beijing. Kong Fansen (孔繁森 1944–94) was portrayed by the Chinese authorities as a role model for communist officials. Kong spent many years in Tibet, an arduous work environment. In November 1994, he was killed in a traffic accident.

Chapter Four

All notes for chapter 4 are the editor's notes, unless otherwise indicated.

1. The Sanyuanli Anti-British Incident (三元里抗英) was an armed conflict between British and nongovernmental Chinese forces in Sanyuanli on the outskirts of Guangzhou during the first Opium War. In May 1841, criminal behavior by British soldiers, including looting and rape, spurred 10,000 locals from Sanyuanli and other nearby villages to besiege the British. This incident marked the first large-scale spontaneous defense of the homeland against foreign aggression by local citizens in modern Chinese history.

2. Francis Fukuyama, *The End of History?* (Washington: National Affairs, 1989).

3. Jiang Qing, *Political Confucianism: Its Turn, Characters and Development* (Beijing: Sanlian Publishing House in Beijing, 2003).

4. Hu Feng (胡风 1902–85), a native of Qichun, Hubei Province, was a Chinese writer and literary theorist. He embraced Marxist theory in political and social matters but not in literature. He criticized the manner in which Mao Zedong's realism in art and literature had become overly politicized. Hu's views were condemned as counterrevolutionary, and from 1955 to 1979 he was imprisoned.

5. *Author's note:* Helmut Steinberg, "Historic Influence of American Constitutionalism upon German Constitutional Development," in *Constitutionalism and Rights: The Influence of the United States Constitution Abroad*, edited by Louis Henkin and Al Rosenthal [Chinese translation] (Beijing: Sanlian Books, 1996), p. 276.

6. Yu Qiuyu (余秋雨 1946–), a native of Yuyao, Zhejiang Province, is a well-known contemporary Chinese cultural and literary figure. He was president of the Shanghai Theater Academy. In addition to commercial success resulting from his popular writing and talk shows in China, his bold and direct criticisms of certain cultural phenomena have earned him respect and detestation in equal measure.

7. *Southern Weekend* (南方周末), based in Guangzhou and owned by the independent-minded news organization Southern Daily Group, is one of the most popular newspapers

in present-day China. The *New York Times* has described *Southern Weekend* as "China's most influential liberal newspaper."

Chapter Five

All notes for chapter 5 are the editor's notes.

1. Gao Shangquan (高尚全 1929–), a native of Shanghai, was the president of the China Society of Economic Reform, which has been under the leadership of the National Development and Reform Commission. As a prominent economist, Gao has participated in drafting many important documents on Chinese market reforms in the past three decades. The other professor referenced, Gong Xiantian (巩献田 1944–), is a native of Zibo, Shandong Province. Gong obtained a doctoral degree in law from the University of Sarajevo, Yugoslavia, in 1987. Gong has been known for his open letter in August 2005 in which he argued that the NPC Standing Committee's draft of the "Private Property Law of the People's Republic of China" was unconstitutional.

2. The notion of "crossing the river while feeling for stones" (摸着石头过河) was first put forth by Chen Yun, the CCP leader in charge of economic planning, at a Government Administration Council meeting on April 7, 1950. He stressed the need for price stability. This expression was used in the 1980s by Deng Xiaoping, who called for brave and pragmatic experiments in economic reforms. The expression "do not argue" (不争论) originated with Deng Xiaoping during his "southern tour" in 1992. Deng believed that ideological debates might make economic reforms more complicated and thus would be a waste of time. This notion reflects Deng's pragmatism toward China's market reforms.

3. This refers to the letter that protested the CCP authorities' ban of the journal *Freezing Points* in early 2006. For the whole letter, see chapter 9.

Chapter Six

All notes for chapter 6 are the author's original notes unless otherwise indicated.

1. The notion of "lost lawyers" comes from Anthony T. Kronman, *The Lost Lawyer: Failing Ideals of the Legal Profession* (Belknap Press of Harvard University Press, 1995).

2. Max Weber, *The Religion of China: Confucianism and Taoism*, edited and translated by Hans H. Gerth (London: MacMillan, 1964), p. 121. Examining the Chinese government, Weber found that the number of officials in China was much lower than that of European governments, and he connected this state of affairs with the country's rough style of governing.

3. Inadequate budgeting for legal services contributed to China's failure to develop a professionalized legal class. Ray Huang has noted long-term stability and "low price" as two important characteristics of the organization of traditional Chinese society, including its legal system. Huang explains: "The annual revenue of the government in the late Qing dynasty had never exceeded 100 million silver ounces, a figure that was very insignificant

when measured against either China's population or the general yardstick of the world at the time. The crudeness of organization together with the shallowness of technology made it possible for such a big country to be based on a petty-agrarian economy and to dispense with the need for lawyers and professional judges, even though the population was hundreds of millions. This situation remained until the Opium War." Ray Huang, *The Road of Modern China* (Taipei: Lianjing Publishing), pp. 72–73.

4. Qu Tongzu, *Selected Papers in Law of Qu Tongzu*, 1st ed. (China University of Political Science and Law Press, 1998), p. 460. Qu describes the division of labor between county officials and their private secretaries.

5. Ibid., p. 413.

6. Ji Yun, "Jottings of Close Observations at the Thatched Abode—Part IV: Just Listen to Them," in *General History of Chinese Culture: Law*, edited by Guo Jian and others (Shanghai People's Publishing House, 1998), p. 327.

7. Richard A. Posner, *Overcoming Law* (Harvard University Press, 1996), p. 35.

8. Ibid., p. 37.

9. Qu Tongzu noted that due to the complexity of the law and the pressure of daily work, it was difficult for county officials to conduct a specialized study of law, and so they had to rely on their private secretaries. Yet he also pointed out that "it is a basic requirement for county officials to be well-versed in law when they are involved in the administration of justice, for otherwise they will not be able to render a judgment based on law." See Qu, *Selected Papers*, p. 460.

10. He Weifang, "The Style and Spirit of Traditional Chinese Judicial Decisions," *Zhongguo shehui kexue* [Social sciences in China] (December 1990): 203–19, as translated in *Social Sciences in China* (September 1991): 74–95; see also He Weifang, *The Idea and System of Justice* (China University of Political Science and Law Press, 1998), p. 188.

11. Jean Escarra, *Le Droit Chinois: Conception et evolution, institutions legislatives et judiciare, science et enseignement* (Peking: Editions H. Vetch, Librairie du Recueil Sirey, 1936), p. 3. Quoted in Joseph Needham, *Science and Civilization in China*, vol. 2 (Cambridge University Press, 1956), p. 521.

12. *Editor's note:* Extraterritorial jurisdiction (域外管辖权) refers to the legal ability of a given government to exercise authority beyond its normal boundaries (for example, in a special external territory in a foreign country). More specifically, some countries have implemented laws that allow their nationals to be prosecuted by their own courts for crimes even when the crime is committed extraterritorially.

13. Jiang Tingfu, *A History of Modern China* (Changsha: Yuelu Press, 1987), p. 27. See also R. Randle Edwards, "Ch'ing Legal Jurisdiction over Foreigners," in *Essay on China's Legal Tradition*, edited by Jerome Cohen, R. Randle Edwards, and Fu-mei Chang Chen (Princeton University Press, 1981), p. 222; Zhan Hengju, *Modern Chinese Legal History* (Taipei: Commercial Press, 1973), pp. 93–95.

14. Quoted in Yang Honglie, *History of China's Legal Development* (Shanghai: Commercial Press, 1930), p. 872.

15. See Chuzo Ichiko, "Political and Institutional Reform, 1901–1911," in *The Cambridge History of China*, vol. 11, *Part 2: Late Ch'ing, 1800–1911*, edited by John King Fairbank and Kwang-Ching Liu (Cambridge University Press, 1980), pp. 375, 413.

16. A most successful example is Soochow University Law School, established by American missionaries in 1915. See Alison W. Conner, "Training China's Early Modern Lawyers: Soochow University Law School," *Columbia Journal of Asian Law* 8, no. 1 (1994): 8.

17. These numbers are drawn from data from the Center of Education Information, Ministry of Education, and Department for Legal Education, Ministry of Justice. See "The Establishment of Uniformed Legal Education in China: A Report on the Reform and Development of the Education toward a Master's Degree in Law," in *Documentary Book on the J.M. Program Education in China*, edited by He Weifang and Huo Xiandan (Beijing: Law Press, 2001), p. 375.

18. According to data compiled by China's court system in 1980, only 3.6 percent of the 58,000 personnel surveyed within China's court system graduated from university-affiliated law schools or law departments. See Tang Mengsong and others, *A Concise History of Chinese Legal Education* (Beijing: Law Press, 1995), p. 410.

19. He Weifang, "The Realization of Social Justice through Judicature: A Look at the Current Situation of Chinese Judges," in *Zouxiang quanli de shidai—Zhongguo guomin quanli fazhan yanjiu* [Toward an age of rights: A study of the development of civil rights in China], edited by Xia Yong (Beijing: Shehui kexue wenxian chubanshe, 2007), pp. 142–97; Stanley B. Lubman, *Bird in a Cage: Legal Reform in China after Mao* (Stanford University Press, 1999), p. 253.

20. Since the 1940s, the diverse educational backgrounds of China's leading lawyers have caused confusion about the choice of model for China's legal education and legal system. See Roscoe Pound, "First Report on Legal Education," in *Zhongguo falüjiaoyu zhilu* [The development of legal education in China], edited by He Weifang (China University of Political Science and Law Press, 1997), p. 298.

21. See generally Jiang Ping, "Several Thoughts on the Enactment of the Civil Code" (http://lawthinker.com/show.asp?id=1010 [April 6, 2006]).

22. The current legal education regime seems relatively undesirable not only in China but also in Japan and South Korea. In recent years, the introduction of the American model of legal education has been a popular topic among scholars from East Asian countries at some of the conferences in which I have participated.

23. Wang Jian, "A J.D. Program in China? A Critique of Education towards a Master's Degree in Law," in *Zhongguo falüjiaoyu zhilu*, edited by He, p. 83.

24. See Yang Yinhang, *Laopu yi wen ji* [Collected essays of Yang Yinhang] (Wuhan: Changjiang wenyi chubanshe, 1993), pp. 806–07.

25. Henry Walter Ehrmann, *Comparative Legal Culture* (New York: Prentice Hall College Division, 1976), pp. 55–79.

26. See Posner, *Overcoming Law*, p. 39.

27. Alexis de Tocqueville, *Democracy in America*, translated by George Lawrence (New York: Harper Perennial Modern Classics, 1988), p. 264.

28. See Philippe Nonet and others, *Law and Society in Transition: Toward Responsive Law* (New York: Transaction Publishers, 2001).

29. See Lubman, *Bird in a Cage*.

30. *The Analects of Confucius*, 1st ed., translated by Arthur Waley ((Hopkinton, Mass.: Vintage Books, 1989), p. 174.

Chapter Seven

All notes for chapter 7 are the editor's notes.

1. He Weifang, "Cong alüjiaoyu xiang JM jiaoyu de zhuanxiang" [China's legal education should embrace J.M. education], *Renmin fayuan bao* [People's court daily], May 10, 2002.

2. Ray Huang, *Zibenzhuyi yu ershiyi shiji* [Capitalism and the twenty-first century] (Shanghai: SDX Joint Publishing, 2006).

3. Fei Xiaotong (费孝通 1910–2005), a native of Wujiang, Jiangsu Province, was one of the foremost Chinese social anthropologists in the twentieth century, noted for his studies of village life in China and Chinese ethnic groups.

4. He Weifang, "Fuzhuan junren jin fayuan" [Ex-servicemen of the PLA now serving at the court], *Nanfang zhoumo* [Southern weekend], January 2, 1998.

5. Wang Hai (王海 1973–), a native of Qingdao, Shandong Province, is often dubbed the "Ralph Nader of China" for his crusades on behalf of consumers against certain business practices. He started his campaign making thousands of RMB by returning counterfeit goods in Beijing in the mid-1990s. He also opened a telephone hotline through which consumers could report infringements of their rights.

6. Long Zongzhi, *Lilun fandui shijian* [Theory versus practice] (Beijing: Falü chubanshe, 2003.)

7. Zhu Suli, *Songfa xiaxiang* [Sending law to the countryside] (China University of Political Science and Law Press, 2000).

8. See Zhao Xiaoli's preface in Su Li, *Fazhi jiqi bentu ziyuan* [Rule of law and local resources] (China University of Political Science and Law Press, 1996).

9. Philip A. Kuhn, *Soulstealers: The Chinese Sorcery Scare of 1768* (Harvard University Press, 2006).

10. Cao Jianming (曹建明 1955–), a native of Shanghai, is the procurator-general of the Supreme People's Procuratorate of the People's Republic of China. A legal scholar, Cao previously served as president of East China University of Political Science and Law. Shen Deyong (沈德咏 1954–), Zhang Jun (张军 1956–), Huang Songyou (黄松有 1957–), and Jiang Bixin (江必新 1956–) have all served as vice presidents of the Supreme People's Court of the People's Republic of China. They all received advanced degrees in law. In 2008 Huang Songyou was detained by Communist Party disciplinary officials in connection

with a corruption scandal. Subsequently, he was removed from his post as the vice president of the court and two years later was sentenced to life in prison for receiving about RMB 4 million in bribes while serving as a Supreme People's Court judge.

Chapter Eight

All notes for chapter 8 are the editor's notes.

1. Hu Yaobang (胡耀邦 1915–89), a native of Liuyang, Hunan Province, was general secretary of the Chinese Communist Party from 1980 to 1987 and chairman of the CCP from 1981 to 1982. In 1987 he was forced by conservative hardliners in the party to resign for his liberal views and his "laxness" on "bourgeois liberalization." Following Hu's funeral in April 1989, some 100,000 Chinese students marched on Tiananmen Square, leading to the Tiananmen Square protests of 1989.

2. Lei Feng (雷锋 1940–62), a native of Changsha, Hunan Province, was a soldier in the People's Liberation Army. He was characterized as a selfless and modest person who was devoted to the Communist Party and Chairman Mao Zedong. In the posthumous "Learn from Comrade Lei Feng" campaign, initiated by Mao in 1963, Lei became a symbol in nationwide propaganda for his blind obedience and absolute devotion to communism. See also chapter 3, note 16, for background on Kong Fansen.

3. Cheng Kejie (成克杰 1933–2000), a native of Shanglin, Guangxi Province, was chairman of the People's Government of Guangxi Zhuang Autonomous Region and vice chairman of the Ninth National People's Congress. Cheng was sentenced to death for accepting more than RMB 41 million in bribes in 2000. He was one of the highest-ranking officials to have been executed in PRC history.

4. Chen Zhiwu (陈志武 1963–), a native of Chaling, Hunan Province, is an economist and a professor at the Yale School of Management. He is a prolific author with many best-selling volumes on finance and economics.

Chapter Nine

All notes for chapter 9 are the editor's notes unless otherwise indicated.

1. *Freezing Points* (冰点周刊) was a news journal and weekly supplement to *China Youth Daily* (中国青年报). *Freezing Points* was often controversial due to its criticism of Communist Party officials. On January 24, 2006, officials temporarily shut down the journal over controversy surrounding the journal's criticism of the content of Chinese government–mandated history textbooks. The journal was allowed to reopen in March of the same year, albeit without former editor Li Datong (李大同) and well-known Taiwan-based columnist Lung Yingtai (龙应台).

2. Yuan Weishi (袁伟时 1931–), a native of Xingning, Guangdong Province, was a professor in the Department of Philosophy at Sun Yat-sen University. Yuan was known for his independent thinking and his critique of distortions in history textbooks in communist

China. Yuan's article in *Freezing Points* that diverged from the CCP's official view of the Boxer Rebellion was the primary reason for the journal's shuttering.

3. *Author's note:* See chapter entitled "Kaifang de xinwen meiti shi shichang jingji de biyao zhidu jizhi" [Market economy calls for an open press environment] in Chen Zhiwu, *Meiti, falü yu shichang* [Media, law, and the marketplace] (China University of Political Science and Law Press, 2005).

Chapter Ten

All notes for chapter 10 are the editor's notes.

1. You Wei (游伟), an expert on criminal law and professor at East China University of Political Science and Law, was the host of this seminar.

2. Albert Camus, *The Stranger*, 1st. American ed. (New York: Alfred A. Knopf, 1946); Arthur Koestler and Albert Camus, "Reflections on the Guillotine," in *Réflexions sur la peine capitale* (Paris: Calmann-Lévy, 1957).

3. Cesare Beccaria, *Dei delitti e delle pene* [On crimes and punishments], 1st ed. (Rome, 1764).

4. Tan Sitong (谭嗣同 1865–98), a native of Liuyang, Hunan Province, was a well-known Chinese politician, scholar, thinker, and revolutionary in the late Qing dynasty. As a main supporter and architect of the Hundred Days' Reform, he was executed when the reform failed.

5. Zhang Zhixin (张志新 1930–75), a native of Tianjin City, was a dissident during the Cultural Revolution who became famous for criticizing the political fanaticism and ideological indoctrination of Mao Zedong thought. Due to her views, she was imprisoned for six years (1969–75), tortured, and ultimately executed.

Chapter Eleven

1. *Editor's note:* John L. Thornton, "Long Time Coming: The Prospects for Democracy in China," *Foreign Affairs* 87, no. 1 (2008): 2–22.

Further Reading

The Writings of He Weifang, 1984–2010

Books

2010

《法律文化三人谈》 *Falu wenhua sanrentan* [A tripartite discussion of legal culture], co-authored with He Qinhua and Tian Tao. Peking University Press.

《四手联弹》 *Sishou liandan* [Collaboration], co-authored with Zhang Yihe. Guangxi Normal University Press.

2007

《走向权利的时代》 *Zouxiang quanli de shidai* [Toward a time of rights: A perspective on civil rights development in China], revised ed., co-edited with Xia Yong (chief editor) and others. Social Sciences Academic Press; see also 1st ed., China University of Political Science and Law Press, 1995.

2004

《美国学者论中国法律传统》 *Meiguo xuezhe lun zhongguo falu chuantong* [Recent American academic writings on traditional Chinese law], expanded ed., co-edited with Karen Turner and Gao Hongjun, Tsinghua University Press; see also 1st ed., China University of Political Science and Law Press, 1994.

2003

《超越比利牛斯山》 *Chaoyue biliniusishan* [Surmounting the Pyrenees: China's legal reform]. Beijing: Law Press.

《法边馀墨》 *Fabian yumo* [Marginal notes on law], 2d. ed. Beijing: Law Press; see also 1st ed., 1998.

2002

《具体法治》 *Juti fazhi* [The Detailed Rule of Law]. Beijing: Law Press.

《运送正义的方式》 *Yunsong zhengyi de fangshi* [Delivery of justice]. Shanghai: SDX Joint Publishing Company.

2001

《20世纪的中国：学术与社会（法学卷）》 *Ershi shiji de zhongguo— xueshu yu shehui (faxue juan)* [Twentieth-century China: Academia and society (volume on law)], co-edited with Su Li and others. Jinan: Shandong People's Publishing House.

Documentary Book on the J.M. Program Education in China, co-edited with Huo Xiandan. Beijing: Law Press.

1998

《司法的理念与制度》 *Sifa de linian yu zhidu* [The idea and system of justice]. China University of Political Science and Law Press.

1997

《中国法律教育之路》 *Zhongguo falujiaoyu zhilu* [The development of legal education in China], editor. China University of Political Science and Law Press.

1992

《外国法制史》 *Waiguo fazhi shi* [Foreign legal history], co-edited with You Rong (chief editor) and others. Peking University Press.

1988

《新波斯人信札: 变化中的法观念》 *Xin bosiren xinzha: Bianhua zhongde faguannian* [New Persian letters: The changing legal culture in a changing society], co-authored with Liang Zhiping and others. Guiyang: Guizhou People's Publishing House.

1985

《教会法的历史发展、婚姻制度及对世俗法的影响》 *Jiaohuifa de lishi fazhan, hunyin zhidu ji dui shisufa de yingxiang* [A study of canon law: Its development, matrimonial institutions and influence on secular law], LL.M. thesis. China University of Political Science and Law.

Book Translations

1998

《美国法律辞典》 *Meiguo falu cidian* [The American law dictionary, by Peter G. Renstrom], co-translated with others. China University of Political Science and Law Press.

1993

《法律与革命：西方法律传统的形成》 *Falu yu geming: Xifang falu chuantong de xingcheng* [Law and revolution: The formation of the Western legal tradition, by Harold J. Berman], co-translated with Gao Hongjun and others. Beijing: China Encyclopedia Publishers.

《比较法律传统》 *Bijiao falu chuantong* [Comparative legal traditions, by M. A. Glendon, M.W. Gorden, and C. Osakwe], co-translated with Mi Jian and others. China University of Political Science and Law Press.

1992

《比较法总论》 *Bijiaofa zonglun* [Introduction to comparative law, by K. Zweigert and H. Koetz], co-translated with Pan Handian and others. Guiyang: Guizhou People's Publishing House.

1990

《比较法律文化》 *Bijiao falu wenhua* [Comparative legal cultures, by Henry Ehrmann], co-translated with Gao Hongjun. Shanghai: SDX Joint Publishing Company.

Selected Articles and Book Chapters

2010

"司法如何获得国民的信赖：评孙伟铭案" "Sifa ruhe huode guomin de xinlai: Ping Sun Weiming an" [How China's judicial system earned the nation's trust: On the Sun Weiming case], *Xibu faxue pinglun* [Western law review], no. 3: 1–4.

2007

"通过司法实现社会正义：对中国法官现状的透视" "Tongguo sifa shixian shehuizhuyi: Dui zhongguo faguan xianzhuang de toushi" [The realization of social justice through judicature: A look at the current situation of Chinese judges], in Xia Yong and others, eds., *Zouxiang quanli de shidai—Zhongguo guomin quanli fazhan yanjiu* [Toward a time of rights: A perspective of civil rights development in China]. Beijing: Social Sciences Documentation Publishing House, pp. 142–97.

"The Police and the Rule of Law: Commentary on 'Principals and Secret Agents,'" *China Quarterly*, no. 191: 671–74.

2005

"China's Legal Profession: The Nascence and Growing Pains of a Professionalized Legal Class," *Columbia Journal of Asian Law* 19, no. 1: 138–51.

2003

"司法考试、司法研修及法律职业化" "Sifa kaoshi, sifa yanxiu ji falu zhiyehua" [Bar examination, legal research and training, and legal professionalism], *Yuedan Journal of Law* (Taipei), no. 4: 219–25.

"中国的法院改革与司法独立：一个参与者的观察与反思" "Zhongguo de fayuan gaige yu sifa duli" [Judicial reform and judicial independence in China: A participant's observation and reflections], *Zhejiang shehui kexue* [Zhejiang journal of social science], no. 2: 83–86.

"宪政三章" "Xianzheng sanzhang" [Three chapters of constitutionalism], *Faxue luntan* [Legal forum] 18, no. 2: 11–16.

"统一之道" "Tongyi zhidao" [Road to legal unification], *Henan shehui kexue* [Henan journal of social science], no. 1: 21–24.

1998

"司法与传媒三题" "Sifa yu chuanmei santi" [The judiciary and the media: Three problems], *Faxue yanjiu* [Journal of law], no. 6: 21–26.

"司法：走向清廉之路" "Sifa: zouxiang qinglian zhilu" [The judiciary: The road to honesty and integrity], *Faxuejia* [Jurists], no. 1: 112–15.

1997

"中国司法管理制度的两个问题" "Zhongguo sifa guanli zhidu de liangge wenti" [Two problems of judicial administration reform in China], *Zhongguo shehui kexue* [Social sciences in China], no. 6: 117–30.

1995

"对抗制与中国法官" "Duikangzhi yu zhongguo faguan" [The adversary system and Chinese judges], *Faxue Yanjiu* [Studies in law], no. 4: 85–92.

1992

"比较法律文化的方法论问题" "Bijiao falu wenhua de fangfalun wenti" [On the methodology of comparative legal cultures], *Zhongwai faxue* [Peking University journal of law], no. 1: 30–35; for the English version, see *Asia Pacific Law Review* (Special Issue), no.1 (1994): 37–44.

"契约与合同的辨析" "Qiyue yu hetong de bianxi" [The true meaning of contracts and its correct translation in Chinese], *Faxue yanjiu* [Studies in law], no. 2: 36–40.

1990

"中国古代司法判决的风格与精神" "Zhongguo gudai sifa panjue de fengge yu jingshen" [The style and spirit of traditional Chinese judicial decisions], *Zhongguo shehui kexue* [Social sciences in China], no. 6 (December): 203–19; English version appears in *Social Sciences in China* 12, no. 3 (1991): 74–95.

1986

"天主教婚姻制度及教会法对世俗法的影响" "Tianzhujiao hunyin zhidu ji jiaohuifa dui shisufa de yingxiang" [Catholic matrimonial institutions and the influence of canon law on secular law], *Shijie Zongjiao Yanjiu* [Studies on world religions], no. 1: 73–89.

1984

"英国陪审制史略" "Yingguo peishen zhidushi" [The origin and development of the English jury system], *Shehui kexue* [Journal of social sciences (Shanghai)], no. 4: 67–69.

INDEX

ABA. *See* American Bar Association

Abdul Jalil, Mustafa, xix

Administration for Industry and Commerce, 203

Administrative Department of Justice, 160, 161

Agriculture, 13

American Bar Association (ABA), 148

Americanization. *See* United States

Analects of Confucius, 45–46, 110

Antigone (Sophocles), 80

Apprenticeships and internships, 149, 158, 159–60

Aquinas, Thomas (priest), 80, 168

Arab Spring (*2010*–present), xlii

Aristotle (philosopher and teacher), 85, 98, 145, 168

Arts and literature, 52, 85

Article 71, 49, 50

Backer, Larry (professor), xlv

Ba Jin (writer), xxxiii

Basic Law of the Federal Republic of Germany, 117

BBC, 205

Beccaria, Cesare (jurist), 199, 204–05

Beijing Children's Legal Aid and Research Center, xxxix

Beijing Legal Aid Office for Migrant Workers, xxxix

Beijing News, 195–96, 201–02

Beiyang era (*1912–28*), 27–29

Bird in a Cage (Lubman), 143

Black society (criminal gangs), 4

Blair, Anthony Charles Lynton ("Tony"; prime minister; UK), 50

Boxer Rebellion (*1898–1901*), 16, 22, 137

Bo Xilai (Politburo member), xx, xxiii, xxix, xxxi–xxxiii, xxxvi, xlii, xlvi

Breyer, Stephen (Supreme Court justice; U.S.), xvii, xlix

Britain. *See* Great Britain

Bukharin, Nikolai (theoretician; Soviet Union), 212

Bury, Richard de (bishop; England), 168

Cai Dingjian (constitutional scholar), xix–xx, xxxviii

Caixin magazine, xxxv

Campaign against the underworld. *See* Chongqing

"Campaign-method governance" (*yundongshi zhili*), xlii

Camus, Albert (writer; France), 196–97, 213–14

Cao Jianming (vice president, Supreme People's Court), 171

Capitalism. *See* Economic issues

Capital punishment. *See* Death penalty

Carter, Jimmy (president; U.S.), 116

Catholic Church and Catholics, 76, 77

CBS, 69

CCP. *See* Chinese Communist Party

CCP Central Propaganda Department, 127

CCPL. *See* Central Commission of Politics and Law

CCP Politburo Standing Committee, 127, 181–88

CCTV, 73

Central Commission of Politics and Law (CCPL), xviii, xlii, xliii

Central Committee of the Communist Party, 43, 112. *See also* Chinese Communist Party; Communism and the Communist Party

Central Daily News (party newspaper; Taiwan), 86

Central Propaganda Department, 184

Challenger disaster (*1986*), 85

Chen Guangcheng (human rights activist), xx, xxx, xlii

Chen Sheng (leader of peasant uprising), 47

Chen Shimei (opera character), 81, 98

Chen Xiang (utopian Socialist), 42, 54–55

Chen Xingliang (professor), 171

Chen Zhiwu (professor and economist), 180, 186

Chiang Ch'ing (Mao's last wife). *See* Jiang Qing

Chiang Kai-shek (generalissimo), 102

China. *See* People's Republic of China; Republic of China; *individual subject headings*

"China's Legal Education Should Embrace J.M. Education" (He), 153–54

"China's Macroeconomics and Reform Trends" (symposium; *2006*), 125–30

China Youth magazine, xxviii, 63

China Youth Daily's Freezing Points (weekly), xxix, 181–88

Chinese Association of Constitutional Law, 68

Chinese Communist Party (CCP): cases involving CCP members, 32; Chinese civil war and, 138; criticism of, xviii–xx; constitution of, xlvi; constitutionalism and, xlv, xlviii, 70; education and, 128–29; fears of, xliii; finances of, 85–86; Kuomintang and, 102; loss of legitimacy of, xlvii; monopoly over the legal system, xli; newspapers and, 68–69; party affiliation with, 108; reforms and, xliii, xlvi; representation of, 94; resistance of, xix; Xu Qian and, 30

Chinese ethnic groups, 43, 96, 217

Chengdu Intermediate People's Court, 53

Cheng Kejie (corrupt national and party leader), 178, 199, 207–08

Chongqing, 1–6

Chongqing Evening News, xxxii

Chou, Cedric T. (lawyer), 58

Christianity, 76–78

Ch'u Tongtsu (historian), 12

Civil Code of the People's Republic of China, 119–20

Civil service examination system. *See* Imperial civil service examination system

Civil War (*1945–49*; China), 102, 138

Classes, social. *See* Society

Clinton, William J. ("Bill"; president; U.S.), 73–75, 116, 177–78, 207

Clinton, Hillary, 74

CNN, 69

Cohen, Paul A. (historian, professor), 95

Coke, Sir Edward (chief justice; Britain), 52

Committee for Judicial Reform (China), 32

Communism and the Communist Party, 111–12, 127. *See also* Chinese Communist Party

Communist Youth League Central Propaganda Department, 127, 181, 184

Comparative Law (Bijiaofa yanjiu; Chinese quarterly), xxv–xxvi

Comrade Chiang Ch'ing (Witke), 48

Confucian China and Its Modern Fate (Levenson), 52

Confucianism: competition for political positions and, 13; core concepts of, 109; Jiang Qing and, 109–10; legal predicament of, 58, 135; Mind Confucianism, 41, 108–09; Neo-Confucianism, 41, 108–09; reliance of judges on, 14–15; rule of law and, 40, 58, 108; technocracy and, 59; third wave of Confucianism, 41, 107; Western theories and values and, 109

Confucius (ancient philosopher): dialogues and discussions of, 85, 98; Jiang Qing and, 41–42, 109–10; as prime minister of Lu, 210; as a private teacher, 211; relationship between sovereigns and ministers, 44; sayings praised by, 143, 179; view of his words, 79

Congress (U.S.), 72

Constitutional Council of France, 153

Constitutional government: end of the socialism-capitalism dichotomy and, 110–13; global expansion of judicial powers and, 115–18; increasing justification for and,

103–10; significance in the Chinese context, 118–23; supranational organizations' restriction of sovereignty and, 113–14. *See also* Government

Constitutionalism, xliii–xlix, 50–51, 101

Constitutional issues: China's readiness for constitutional government, xliii–xlix, 93–95, 101–03, 104–10; conscience of constitutional jurisprudence, 67–68; constitutional government as a game of the rich, 98; constitutional review system, 112–13; dimensions of constitutional government, 76–87; freedom of speech and the press, 97, 121–22, 123, 126–27, 175–88; logic of constitutional argument, 69–70; pluralistic interests and class society, 81–82; political rights, 129; purpose and legitimacy of the constitution, 88; questions and answers, 87–100; religion and the church, 76–80; resistance to constitutional government, 104, 107; rule of law and legal professionals, 86–87, 96; taxation and representation, 82–86; text and reality of constitutional rights, 68–69; tradition of natural law, 80–81; types of constitutions, xliii–xliv

Constitution of the People's Republic of China: article 35 of, 129, 184; article 71 of, 50; article 127 of, 38; article 132 of, 38; CCP and, xlvi; constitutional rights of, 50; Continental influence on, 139; criticism of, xliii, xliv–xlv, xlvi, 82, 101–02; freedom of the press and, 68–69, 121–22, 123, 126–27; freedom of procession and demonstration and, 69; freedom of religion and, 69; history of, xliii–xliv; Hu's remarks on its implementation, 183–84, 185; optimistic views of, xlv, xlvi; political versus legal accountability in, xliv; preamble of, 184–85; provisional constitution, 27; relationships between higher and lower courts and, 38; role of the party leadership, xlv; separation of powers in, xlv; study of, 68

Court cases, 2–3, 4, 53. *See also individual cases by name*

Court system and courts: absence of review power in, xliv; administrative structure of courts, 37–38, 167; appeals and appellate courts, 37, 151; Confucianism and, 13, 14–15; deactivated soldiers working in,

xl, 164–65, 167; death-penalty executions, 192, 193; debate in, 211; drunk driving cases, 54; judicial proceedings without adversity, 15–16; respect for, 5. *See also* Judges; Judicial system

Crime, 196–204

Criminal law, 53

Criminal Law Forum (Peking University Law School), 171

Criminal penalties, 99–100

Criminal Procedure Law (*1980*), 193–94

"Criticize Lin, Criticize Confucius" (*pi lin pi kong*) campaign, 42

Croce, Benedetto (politician, philosopher), 33

C-Span, 73

Cuba, 110

Cultural Revolution. *See* Great Cultural Revolution

Custody and repatriation system, 112, 114

Dalai Lama, 217

Daoguang era (*1820–50*), 136–37

Death, 205–07

Death penalty, xxix–xxx, 114, 191–215

Decisionmaking, 71

Democracy: arguing for and experiencing democracy, 70–76, 97; beauty of debate, 71–72; election of the president, 73; governance cost, 72–76; magic of the ballot box, 71; in modern China, 96, 126–27, 218–19; national leaders in, 74–75; socialist democracy, 138; Socrates and, 208–09; supremacy of sovereignty and, 113

Deng Xi (dialectician), 15, 211

Deng Xiaoping (leader of the CCP), xxxviii, 93–94, 111, 188

Department of Justice, 27, 28, 29, 30, 160–61

Department of Legal Education, 140

Detailed Rule of Law, The (He), 70

Deutsche Welle, 216–20

Dialogues, 45–46

Ding Weiliang. *See* W. A. P. Martin

"Disastrous encounter with the West." *See* Opium Wars

Discovering History in China (Cohen), 95

Dissidents and dissension, 102

Division of Check and Filing, xlv

Dole, Robert (congressman, U.S.), 73–74

Domestic violence, 78

Dowdle, Michael (professor), xlv–xlvi

Du Peiwu (falsely accused of murder), 203

Dynasties, 43

Dynasties—Qing (*1644–1912, 1917*): constitutional monarchy and, 43; execution during, 204; formulation of constitution during, 101; Germany and, 106–07; governmental structure during, 104; legal and judicial systems of, 16; legal secretaries during, 135; overturning of, 96; pettifoggers during, 15; reforms during, 18, 21, 22–27, 30; social changes and, 95

Dynasties—specific: Han, 46, 93; Ming, 43; Qin, 43, 45, 46, 93; Shang, 19; Song, 15; Southern Song, 86; Tang, 191; Xia, 19; Zhou, 19

East China University of Politics and Law, 203

Economic issues: capitalism, 94; China's economic reforms, 126, 186; China's illegal capital outflows, xlvii; economic crimes, 207–08; end of the socialism-capitalism dichotomy, 110–13; freedom of the press and economic development, 186; interaction between academia and professional practitioners, 169–71; legal practitioners as service providers, 155; legislation, xxxviii; market economy, 93–94, 110–11, 130; peasant economy, 81; standards of living, xliv; transaction security, 130

Economics and economists, 146

Educational issues: American legal education, 145–49, 150; Anglo-American legal education, 144, 150, 152; CCP and education, 128–29; challenges facing Chinese legal education, 139–43, 156–58; China's legal education, 67–68, 138–42, 149, 153–56, 159–60, 162–63, 165; colleges and college campuses, 155; colleges specializing in politics and law, xxxviii–xxxix; confrontational method, 148; entering and working in the court system after graduation in China, 161–62; establishment of a unified judicial research and training system, 158–62; ethics and, 166; exam-oriented private training programs, 162; generalist vs. professional education, 149–50; interaction between academia and professional practitioners, 169–71;

judges' and prosecutors' colleges, 158; judicial examination system, 158, 161–64; judicial research and training system, 158–61; law school admission test (LSAT), 157; legal education and unity under the Continental model, 149–53, 159; legal unity and, 165–66; Master of Jurisprudence (J.M.) program, 140; recommendations to improve China's legal education system, 156–57, 160–61, 163; scale and hierarchy of legal education, 153–56; Socratic method, 147–48; theorization in legal education, 162–63; Western legal education, 137, 144–45

Edward VIII (king; England), 82

Eight-Nation Alliance, 16. *See also* Boxer Rebellion

Elements of International Law (trans. W. A. P. Martin), 56

Emperor. *See* Dynasties; Monarchy

Empress of the Red Capital (Witke), 48

England, 103–04, 168, 219. *See also* Great Britain; Magna Carta; United Kingdom; *individual kings*

English (language), 140

Enlightenment and Transformation of Chinese Society, The (Zi), xxii

Enlightenment movements, xxii–xxiii, xxxi

Escarra, Jean (scholar; France), 136

Eto Shinpei (statesman; Japan), 105

Europe, 79, 104, 110, 117–18. *See also individual countries*

European continent, 149, 154

European Parliament, 113

European Union (EU), 113. *See also individual member states*

Executioners, 213–14. *See also* Death penalty

"Ex-Servicemen of the PLA Now Serving at Court" (He), xl, 164–65, 167

Fairbank, John K. (historian), 95

Fang Zhouzi (critic), xxvii

Federal Constitutional Court (Germany), 117

Federal Court of Justice (supreme court; Germany), 117

Fei Xiaotong (professor and anthropologist), 163, 206

Feng Yuxiang (warlord), 30

Foreign Affairs, 239

Foreign Policy, xxi
Fortress Besieged (Qian), 41
France, xlv–xlvi, 105, 149, 150, 153, 159
Freedom of the press. *See* Constitutional
    issues; Constitution of the People's
    Republic of China; Media
*Freezing Points. See China Youth Daily's Freez-
    ing Points*
French National School for the Judiciary,
    149, 150
French Revolution (*1789–99*), 126
Fukuyama, Francis (political scientist), 107
Fuma Susumu (scholar), 15
Fu Zitang (professor), 88–89, 95, 96

Gaddafi, Muammar (ruler; Libya), xix
Gao Shangquan (economist and professor),
    125
Germany: appellate courts in, 151; China
    and, 106–07; constitution of, 80–81,
    117; German Civil Code, 151–52;
    humanist gymnasiums of, 134; judicial
    examination in, 150; legal profession in,
    149
Global Financial Integrity, xlvii
Globalization, 117
Glorious Revolution (*1688*; England), 177
Go (emperor), 46–47
Gong Gangmo ("mafia" businessman), xxxiv
Gongsun Long (dialectician), 15, 211
Gong Xiantian (professor), 125
Government: authorization of the people
    and, 104; enforcement of executions and,
    205; local autonomy, 106; rule of law
    and, 112; socialism and constitutional
    government, 112. *See also* Constitutional
    government
Government—China: accountability in, 96;
    administration of, 129; administrative lit-
    igation and, 120; anticonstitutional prac-
    tices in, 102; Beiyang government period,
    27–29; coalitions with business elites, xlii;
    compromise in, 27, 87–88, 124; concen-
    tration of or separation of powers, 12–13,
    96, 112, 115; constitutional review sys-
    tem, 112–13; corruption in, 97; costs of,
    72–76; difficulty of compromising in,
    102; five-power constitution model of,
    21; forced separation of powers, 22–27;
    freedom of the press and, 175, 177–78;
    government spending, 119; government

structure and functions of ancient China,
    11, 12–13; local autonomy and, 106;
    modern separation of powers, 16–21, 35;
    professionalism in, 54; rule of knowledge
    in, 13–14; rule of unspecialized knowl-
    edge in, 14–15; significance of constitu-
    tional government in the Chinese con-
    text, 118–23. *See also* Constitutional
    government; Court system and courts;
    Democracy; Judicial system
Grand Council (*junjichu*), 17
Great Britain, xlvi, 49, 50–51, 105–06, 108,
    155. *See also* England; Magna Carta;
    United Kingdom; *individual kings*
Great Cultural Revolution (*1966–76*): causes
    of human rights violations during,
    xlvi–xlvii; China's constitution and, 68;
    closing of colleges during, xxxviii–xxxix;
    degeneration of Chinese law during, 138;
    executions during, 213; meritocracy dur-
    ing, 209; myths about, xxiii; nostalgia for,
    xxxiii; post-Mao era and, xxii; return to,
    188; socialist system and, 111; suffering
    during, 2, 48, 57
Great thinkers, 58–59
Greece, 80, 145. *See also* Antigone; Plato;
    Sophocles
Guangdong, 10, 49, 65, 118, 124
Guanghua Law School of Zhejiang Univer-
    sity, xxxi
Guangxu (emperor), 20, 22–23
Guangzhou, 9, 30, 32, 56, 111, 122
Guangzhou Daily, 122
Guo Moruo (historian, archaeologist, and
    poet), 48
Guo Songtao (ambassador), 19
Gu Zhun (intellectual and economist), 79

Hart, Robert (consular official), 17
Harvard University (U.S.), xxvi, 144
He Bing (law school dean and professor),
    xxxiii, xxxv
He Huaihong (professor), 195–96
He Pin (political analyst), xlvii
He Qinhua (university president), 203
He Weifang (law professor): advocation of
    reforms by, xxiii–xxiv, 127, 218; back-
    ground and education of, xxiv, xxv–xxxi,
    42, 63–67; as a CCP member, 85, 94;
    challenging of Bo Xilai and Wang Lijun,
    xxxi–xxxiii; China's First Steps to Consti-

tutionalism lecture, 64–100; China's legal development and, xx–xxi; commitment to constitutionalism and rule of law, xlviii, 40; criticism and punishment of, xxvii, xxx, xxxi; death penalty and, xxix–xxx; Great Cultural Revolution and, xxxiii; reading Mencius, 42–43; letters, 1–6, 181–88; Li Zhuang case and, xxxiii–xxxvi; plea for political progress in China, 216–20; proposals of, xviii, xxviii–xxix; transfer to Shihezi University, 42; view of China's constitution, xliii; view of Taiwan, xxx; view of totalitarian countries, xxx; views of lawyers and judges, xxix, xxxviii–xliii, xli, xliii; writings, 68, 70, 82–83, 85, 90, 243–47

"He Weifang phenomenon," 65–66

History, 33, 48

History of the Peloponnesian War (Thucydides), 85

HMS *Hero of Malown*, 9

Holms, Oliver Wendell (judge), 116

Holy See, 77. *See also* Catholic Church and Catholics

Homicide. *See* Murders and homicides

Hong Kong, 22, 136

Housing demolition and relocation, 120

Hsiao Kung-chuan (scholar and philosopher), 44

Hua Guofeng (Mao's designated successor), 75, 85

Huang, Ray (historian and philosopher), 161

Huang Sheng (scholar), 46–47

Huang Songyou (vice president, Supreme People's Court), 171

Huang Yongyu (professor), 103

Hubei Institute of Finance and Economics, xxxix

Hu Feng (writer and theorist), 111

Hu Jintao (CCP general secretary), xxix, 43, 128, 183–84, 185

Hu Shih (intellectual), xxii, xxvii

Hu Yaobang (political leader), 175–76

Hu Yunteng (department head, Supreme People's Court), 214

Human rights. *See* Constitutional issues; Constitution of the People's Republic of China; Death Penalty; Media

Hundred Days' Reform (*wuxu bianfa*; 1898), 18

Hutton, James Brian Edward ("Lord Hutton"; lawyer), 50

Ideal State of Law, An: A Virtual Dialogue between Socrates and Mencius (Chou), 58

Imperial civil service examination system (*keju kaoshi*), 13–14, 19–20, 34, 35, 52, 59, 81, 134

Imperial University of Peking (Peking University), 42, 56

India, 192–93

Inner sageliness (*nei sheng*), 108

Innocent III (Pope), 83

Institutional development, 38–39

Internet, xlii, 5, 123, 170, 182, 220

Intermediate People's Courts, 192

Iraq War, 57–58, 217

Islam, 136

James I (king; England), 52

Japan: correspondence courses in, 155; examination system of, 35; judicial research and review system, 159; Judicial Research and Training Institute, 149–50, 159; lawyers in, 141; legal code in, 105; legal education system in, 149, 150, 152; legal practitioners in, 154; war with China, 138; Western pressures on, 136

Jesus, 212

Jiang Bixin (vice president, Supreme People's Court), 92, 171

Jiang Ping (professor), xxxv, 140

Jiang Qing (Mao's last wife), 48, 75–76. *See also* Mao Zedong

Jiang Qing (professor), 41, 43, 108, 109

Jiang Shan (professor), 66

Jia Yu (professor), 214

Jie of Xia (king), 45, 46

Jilin University, xxxix

Jing of Han (emperor), 46, 47

Ji Weidong (law school dean), xlviii

John (king; England), 50–51, 83

Judges: American judges, 148; banning from political affiliations, 29–32; Chinese judges, 135; Confucianism and, 135; death-penalty executions and, 194; decisionmaking by, 36–37, 163; education and practice of, xl, 14–15, 35, 52–53, 138–39, 164–67; judge and prosecutor appointment system, 158; judicial power,

116; judiciary specialization (*sifa zhuanye-hua*), xl; hierarchical system of, 36–37; independence of, xl, 166; lifetime appointment of, 116; replacement with Anglo-American judges, 152; in rural areas, 163; staffing problems of, 194; unified judicial research and training system, 158–61, 166; unified national judicial examination, 167; Western judges, 135

Judges—specific: Cardozo, Benjamin N., 148; Fu Mingjian, 3; Holmes, Oliver Wendell, 148, 164; Learned Hand, Billings, 148; Posner, Richard, 148; Wang Lixin, 2. *See also* Supreme Court (U.S.); Supreme People's Court (China and Japan)

"Judicialization of the constitution" (*xianfa sifahua*), xlv

Judicial systems: American model of, 153; appeals and appellate courts, 151; exercise of judicial power, 115, 116–18; global expansion of, 115–18; judicial review systems, 117, 153; need for strong judiciaries, 153. *See also* Legal issues

Judicial systems—China: administrative division and litigation, 120–21; case referral system in, 38; challenges facing Chinese legal education, 139–43; Chinese Communist Party and, xli; concepts and practice of, 9–10, 14, 15–16, 38–39, 149; county magistrates, 135–36; development of, 87; judicial examination system, xl, 139; judicial independence during the Beiyang government period, 27–29; judicial independence in modern China, xl, xli–xliii, 21–27, 35–39, 76, 121, 129–30; judicial review system, 67, 87, 121; old tradition of, 11–16; partisan control of the judiciary, 30–33; pettifoggers and, 15–16; press environment and, 122; principle of judicial independence, 26; private secretaries, 134–35; professionalization of, xxxviii–xli, 161; Provisional Constitution and, 27; reforms of, 41–42, 120–21. *See also* Constitutional issues; Legal issues; Supreme People's Court

Judiciary. *See* Courts; Judges; Judicial systems

Jurisprudence, 31, 67–68, 98, 136, 148, 163–64, 167–69

Ju Zheng (politician), 31–32

Kang Youwei (scholar and reformer), 18, 107

Kant, Immanuel (philosopher), xxxi, 59, 91

Kellogg, Thomas (legal scholar), xlv

Kelly, David (arms expert), 50

Kelsen, Hans (jurist and philosopher), 32

Killion, M. Ulric (writer), xliv

Kim Jong-il (supreme leader; North Korea), 47–48

Kong Fansen (Tibetan cadre), 178

Kong Qingdong (professor), xxx, xxxii

Kosovo, 75

Kuhn, Philip A. (professor), 168

Kuomintang (political party), 29, 30, 31, 32, 86, 102

Law of the Federal Constitutional Court, 117

Law of the People's Republic of China on the Protection of the Rights and Interests of Consumers, 165

Law on Judges, 139, 158, 167, 194

Law on Procurators, 139, 158, 167

Law School Admission Test (LSAT). *See* Educational issues

Law School of Peking University. *See* Peking University Law School

Laws of Nations, The (de Vattel), 56

Lawyers. *See* Courts; Judges; Judicial systems; Legal issues

Leaders and leadership, 43, 47–48, 79. *See also individuals by name*

Lee Kuan Yew (politician; Singapore), 108

Legal Daily, 212

Legal issues: Anglo-American legal tradition, 151, 152, 162; application of legal rules in actual life, 163; arbitrariness of Chinese legal system, 53–54; bar exams, 139; China's legal framework, xxxviii, xliv; China's legal profession, 133–43; civil and criminal procedure laws, 140; clash of East and West legal system, 9–10; compliance with the law, 71; Continental legal model, 139, 146, 151, 152–53, 162; contrast between China and the West, 134–38; development of Chinese legal system, 10–11, 14–33, 34–39, 105–06, 165; economic reforms and, 130; equality before the law, 165; features of Western legal system, 26; increase in number of licensed lawyers, xxxix; integration of moral and political authorities, 58–59;

interaction between academia and professional practitioners, 169–71; international public law, 56–58; introduction of Western legal thought into China, 59, 134–38, 153; legal aid programs and institutions, xxxix; legal history of China, 33; legal order and conflict, 33–34; legal professionalism, xxxvi–xlix; legal unity, 151, 155, 165–66; nature of law, 33; political and cultural issues, xxxvii–xxxviii, 115, 138; postmodern legal theory, 142; private secretaries, 134–35; professional concepts of, 150–51, 162, 165; public interest litigation, xxxix; reforms, 126, 127–28; rights protection lawyers (*weiquan lüshi*), xxxix; role of legal scholars, 4; tradition of natural law, 80–81; status of law in China's value system, 136; what is law, 146. *See also* Constitutional issues; Court cases; Educational issues; Judges; Judicial system—China; Legislation; Regulation

Legal issues—rule of law: China as a rule-of-law country, 112, 133, 143; legal capacity, power, and rule of law, 127–28; legal principles and, 154; legal professionals and, 86–87; using theory to shape rule of law, 162–69; World Bank rule of law index, xlvii—xlviii

Legislation: in China since the Cultural Revolution, xxxviii; Chinese conventions and declarations and, 114; in democratic vs. nondemocratic countries, 72; natural law tradition and, 80, 81. *See also* Legal issues; Regulation; *individual measures and laws*

Lei Feng (soldier), 99, 178

Lenin, Vladimir (communist revolutionary; Russia), 212

Levenson, Joseph (scholar), 52

Lewinsky, Monica (political intern; U.S.), 73, 74, 177–78, 207

Liang Qichao (intellectual and chief, Department of Justice), 29, 107

Li Changqing (professor), 87–88, 93

Li Cheng (director of research, Brookings Institution), xvii–xlix

Li Dazhao (founder CCP), 30

Li Hongzhang (statesman), 17–18

Li Jinhua (auditor general), 119

Li Keqiang (political leader), 219–20

Li Ming, 122

Lin Biao (minister of defense), 42, 79, 112

Lin Xiangrong (professor), 66

Lin Zexu (official), 56

Li Ping (accomplice of Cheng Kejie), 207–08

Li Shuguang (professor), 126

Lithuania, 196

Liu Junxiang (professor), 88, 94, 95

Liu Shaoqi (revolutionary and statesman), 48, 212

Liu Xiaoqing (film artist), 83

Li Zhuang case (*2010*), xxxiii–xxxvi, 2–3, 4

Locke, John (philosopher), 145, 168

Long Zongzhi (professor), 167

LSAT (Law School Admission Test). *See* Educational issues

Lubman, Stanley, 143

Luo Jun (professor), 91, 98

Lü Yaping (editor), 144, 148, 152, 153–54, 156, 158, 162, 167, 169

Lu Yunbao (professor), 66, 89–90, 96–97

Magistrates, 12, 15

Magna Carta (Great Charter of Liberties; England; *1215*), 50–51, 83–84, 104

Ma Jianzhong (protégé of Li Hongzhang), 17–18

"Market Economy Calls for an Open Press Environment" (Chen), 186

Marriage, 77–78

Mao worship, xxiii, xxxiii

Mao Zedong (chairman of the CCP): comments on law and meetings, xxxvii; designation of his successor, 75; killings during Mao's political campaigns, 48; readings in He's education, 42; view of himself, 112; view of the PRC, 67; view of the West, 93. *See also* Jiang Qing

Marxism, 31, 41, 98, 138

May Fourth Movement (*1919*), xxii, 40, 110

May Thirtieth Patriotic Movement (*1925*), 30

"May 31 speech" (*2002*), 78

Measures for Custody and Repatriation of Urban Vagrants and Beggars, xxviii, 123

Measures on Aid and Management of Urban Vagrants and Beggars, 50

Measures on the Detention and Repatriation of People Engaged in Begging in Cities, 188

Media: advertising in, 122; control of, in China, 127; coverage of death-penalty executions, 192; criticism of the courts and judges, 164; defamation cases against, 180; development of, 180; international media organizations, 69; newspapers, 68–69, 218; open letter to CCP Politburo Standing Committee regarding censorship, 181–88; preconditions for the sound development of, 179–80; press conferences, 45; privately owned press, 69; social stability and, 176–78; suppression of media freedom, 178–79; television and television channels, 73. *See also individual outlets*

Media—freedom of the press: China's current political framework and, 218; China's progress toward, 126–27; effect on government officials, 97; freedom to journalists during the *2001*, 217–18; judicial system and, 122; open letter to CCP Politburo Standing committee regarding, 181–88; reality of, 121; social stability and, 175–80

Mencius (philosopher): as a dialogist, 45, 85, 98; eloquence of, 42; filial piety and, 58; human rights vs. sovereign rights and, 56–57; international law and, 56–58; monarchical power and responsibilities and, 43–45, 46–50, 51–53, 54–55; punishment of tyrants, 57; teaching on human nature, 203

Middle Ages, 76, 77, 78

Midsummer Night's Dream, A (Shakespeare), 107

Military issues, 166–67. *See also* "Ex-Servicemen of the PLA Now Serving at Court"

Mind Confucianism. *See* Confucianism

Ministry of Civil of Affairs, 121

Ministry of Education, 141

Mitsukuri Rinsho (statesman and scholar), 105

Mo Jingping (associate professor), 92

Monarchy and monarchs: aligning power of monarch with needs of the people, 51–52; ancestors' mandates for, 104; in ancient China, 11, 16–17; constitutional monarchy, 43, 106; limiting the power of, 58–59, 168–69; monarch as despot, 47–48; monarch as Son of Heaven, 104; punishment of tyrants, 57; reforms and, 104; regression of monarch into "robber and ruffian," 47–48, 49–51; relationship

between monarchs and ministers, 46; role of the emperor, 43–45, 104; role of the ministers, 44, 45. *See also* Dynasties

"Money-Paved Path to the White House" (Hu), 73

Mongolia, 110

Montaigne, Michel de (writer), 201

Montesquieu, Charles-Louis de Secondat, baron de La Brède et de (political thinker), 19, 20, 26, 145, 168, 199

"Moral enlightenment and prudent punishment" (Chinese tradition), 98

Morse, Hosea Ballou (scholarly writer), 9–10

Murders and homicides, 197–99. *See also Stranger, The*

Mystery Surrounding Nie's Case, 200–01

Nanjing Nationalist government period, 29, 30

Nathan, Andrew (U.S. expert on Chinese affairs), 102

National Audit Office (China), 119

Nationalism, 107, 133–34, 217–18

Nationalist government (Guangzhou), 32

National People's Congress (NPC): appointment of deputies, 119; committees of inquiry and, 49; debate in, 85, 107–08, 118, 211; deputies to, 72, 84–85; duration of, 118, 129; flaws of, 118–19; investigations of government spending by, 119; lawyers in, 120; model of government under, 21; need for reform and, 85–86, 88, 119–20, 128; as a political party, 129; role in adjudication and judicial review, xlv; special committees under 50

National School for the Judiciary (France), 159

Nation states. *See* Sovereignty and sovereign states

Natural law. *See* Legal issues

Nazis and Nazism, xxxiii, 107

Near-death experiences, 205–06

Neo-Confucians. *See* Confucianism

Netherlands, xlvi

Newspapers. *See* Media

NGOs. *See* Nongovernmental organizations

Nie Shubin (executed farmer), 200–01, 204

"Nine squares" system, 93

Nonet, Philippe (professor), 142

Nongovernmental organizations (NGOs), 119

Northern Expedition (*1926*), 30
North Korea, xxx, 110
NPC. *See* National People's Congress

Obscurantism (*mengmei zhuyi*), xxiii
Olympic games, xxix, 217
"On Crimes and Punishments" (Beccaria), 199–200
Opium trade, 56
Opium Wars (*1839–42, 1856–60*), 22, 93, 105
Oral Autobiography of Hu Shih, An, (Hu), 42
Oration and oratory, 85
Orthodox Church, 79
Outer kingliness (*wai wang*), 108

Pankhurst, Emmeline (political activist), xvii, xlix
Paradise Lost (Milton), 169
Parker, Peter (missionary and doctor), 56
Parliaments, 71, 118–19
Peerenboom, Randall (scholar), xlvii
Peking University, xxvi, xxxi, xxxix, 42, 56, 64, 69, 218
Peking University Law Journal, xxvi
Peking University Law School, xxvi, 138, 144, 171
Peng Zhen (CCP leader), xxxviii
People's Congress. *See* National People's Congress
People's Daily (newspaper; China), xxxii–xxxiii, 86
People's Liberation Army (PLA), xxviii–xxix, 164
People's Republic of China (PRC; *1949*–present), 21, 38, 67, 103, 110, 138. *See also* Constitution of the People's Republic of China; National People's Congress
Pericles (statesman, orator), 85, 188
Petition letters, xlii
Pettifoggers (shyster lawyers), 15–16
PLA. *See* People's Liberation Army
Plato (philosopher, mathematician), 45, 145, 168
Police, xli–xliii, 5
Politburo, 112
Political Confucianism (Jiang), 41, 108
Political issues: Chinese politicians, 90; Chinese reforms, xlvi, 126; Chinese traditional political system, 95–95; debate and speechmaking, 211; enforcement of the political system, 50; integration of moral and political authorities, 58–59; legal issues and, 115, 138; parliamentary politics and debate, 107–08; political activities of judges, 29, 32; political leaders, 79; political reform in China, 118; political rights, 129; political tutelage, 89; rectifying mechanisms, 48–49; subjugation of the judiciary to politics, 30–32; suppression of protest, 49
Political parties: anticonstitutional practices and, 102; need for in China, 94; party affiliations, 108; in rule-of-law countries, 86; taxpayer money and, 86; using the political party to run the state (*yi dang zhi guo*), 33
Political parties—specific: Kuomintang, 29, 30, 31, 32, 86, 102; Republican Party, 29. *See also* Chinese Communist Party
Posner, Richard (jurist), 135
Power, xl, 12, 79, 127–28, 129, 184
PRC. *See* People's Republic of China
"Preliminary Suggestions on the Governance of the Republic of China" (*Zhonghua minguotuzhi chuyi*), 28
Presidents, 116. *See also individual presidents by name*
Press conferences. *See* Media
Property issues, 81, 111–12, 129–30
Property Rights Law, 41
Protests, xlii, 69
Provinces, 121
Provisional Constitution of the Republic of China (*1912*), 27
Public enlightenment (*qimeng*), xxii
Public hearings, 118

Qian Zhongshu (author), 41, 64, 99, 201
Qing dynasty. *See* Dynasties—Qing
Qiu Xinglong (professor and law school dean), 214
Quotations from Chairman Mao, 99
Qu Tongzu (writer), 135

Reagan, Ronald (president; U.S.), 79, 85
Real Right Law, 125, 126
Reflections on the Guillotine (Camus), 196, 197
Regulation, xxxviii, 155–56. *See also* Legal issues; Legislation; *individual measures and laws*

Regulation for Internment and Deportation of Urban Vagrants. *See* Measures for Custody and Repatriation of Urban Vagrants and Beggars

Rehnquist, William (chief justice; U.S.), 74

Religious issues: doctrine of original sin, 76–77; freedom of religion, 69; marriage, 77–78; religion as a transcendent force, 76–80; religious persecution, 212. *See also individual religions and denominations*

Renewed Treaty of Commerce and Navigation (*1901*), 22

Republic, The (Plato), 45, 112

Republic of China (*1912–49*), 21, 27, 28, 89–90, 139, 179. *See also* Taiwan

Research Center of Economic Laws, xxxviii

"Review of Classical Chinese Thoughts on International Law, A" (Martin), 56

Revolution of *1911*, xix, 28

Revolutions, 126

Rhetoric (Aristotle), 85

Rites of Zhou, The, 104

Robespierre, Maximilien de (lawyer and politician), 212

Roman Empire, 76, 145, 204

Roosevelt, Theodore ("Teddy"; president; U.S.), 79

Rule of law. *See* Legal issues—rule of law

Rule of Law and Local Resources (Su), 167

Rule of man, 98

Rule of virtue, 98, 99–100

Rural enlightenment movement, 97

Sanlian Publishing House (SDX Joint Publishing), 41

Sanyuanli Anti-British Incident (*1841*), 105

SARS. *See* Severe Acute Respiratory Syndrome

Sending Law to the Countryside (Zhu), 167

Severe Acute Respiratory Syndrome (SARS), 188

Shaozheng Mao (ancient official), 210–11

Shen Deyong (vice president, Supreme People's Court), 171

Shen Jiaben (official), 27–28, 30

She Xianglin (falsely accused of murder), 201–03, 204

Shiga Shuzo (Japanese scholar), 10

Shihezi University, 42

"Significance of NPC Review of Government Budget, The" (He), 82–83

Simpson, Wallis (wife of King Edward III), 82

Singing of red anthems, xxxii, 5–6

Smith, Adam (political economist), 26

Social contract theory, 205, 210

Socialism: China's reforms and, 126; end of the socialism-capitalism dichotomy, 110–13; freedom of the press and, 218; as a great experiment, 111; political philosophy of, 111–12; power of the paramount leader in, 112; remaining socialist countries, 110–11

Socialist democracy, 138

Socially Vulnerable Group Protection Center, xxxix

Social order, 71, 126, 175—80

Society: bureaucratic class, 52; Chinese class society, 81–82, 110; Chinese intellectual ferment (*1970s*), xxii; freedom of speech and the press and, 186–88; imperial civil service examination and, 81; literati-official class, 52; organization and unified action of, 51–52; pluralistic interests and class society, 81–82; relations between structure of government and, 11; role in decisionmaking, 71; social classes, 81, 100. *See also* Black society; White society

Socrates (philosopher), 208–10, 211–12. *See also Republic, The*

Socratic method. *See* Educational issues

Song Jiangping (constitutional scholar), 94

Song Yubo (professor), 68, 88, 95

Song Zuying (folk singer), 45

Sophocles (tragedian), 6

Soulstealers: The Chinese Sorcery Scare of 1768 (Kuhn), 168

Southern Metropolitan Daily, 122, 218

Southern Weekend (weekly publication), 68, 70, 82, 90, 122, 165, 175–80, 200, 218

South Korea, 150, 152

Southwest University of Political Science and Law (SWUPL), 1–2, 4, 64–65, 94

Sovereignty and sovereign states, 113–14, 115, 137

Soviet Union, 30, 31, 93, 104, 110, 126

Spirit of Laws, The (Montesquieu), 19, 20, 26

Stalin, Joseph (premier; Soviet Union), 212

Stalinism, 111

Standing Committee of the National People's Congress, 113, 193, 194

State Council (China), 160–61

States. *See* Sovereignty and sovereign states

Stranger, The (Camus), 196–97
"Strike Hard Campaign" (against crime), 193, 204
"Striking the black mafia" campaign, xxxii, xxxiv, xxxvi
Su Li (professor), 167
Sun Liping (professor), xlii, 128
Sunny Constitutional Government (non-governmental organization), 119
Sun Weiming case (*2008*), 54
Sun Yat-sen (revolutionary and president; China), 19, 33, 89, 93, 106
Sun Zhigang incident (*2003*), xxviii, 49, 50, 112, 188
Supranational organizations, 113–14
Supreme Court (Japan), 149
Supreme Court (U.S.), 115, 116, 117
Supreme People's Court (China), 38, 59, 129, 160–61, 171, 191, 193–95

Supreme People's Procuratorate (China), 160–61
Sweden, xlvi
"Sweep Colorful Expressions out of Legal Papers" (He), 83
Switzerland, 105
SWUPL. *See* Southwest University of Political Science and Law

Taft, William Howard (president, chief justice; U.S.), 115
Taiwan, xxx, 127, 149, 152, 155, 219
Ta Kung Pao (newspaper), 179
Tang (minister, king), 45, 46, 47
Tang Degang (T. K. Tang; historian), 15, 42, 93
Tan Sitong (reformist), 212
Taoism, 15
Tao Ying, 58
Taxation and representation, 82–86, 104
Terranova, Francis (seaman), 9–10
"Third" force, 128
Third National Lawyers' Forum, 120
Thornton, John (chairman, Brookings Institution), 219
Thrasymachus. *See Republic, The*
Three Principles of the People, 31
Tiananmen Square (China), xxii, 103, 216
Tibet, xix, 216–17
Tocqueville, Alexis de (political thinker), 76, 115, 126, 141, 177

Tong Zongjin (associate professor), xxvii
Torture, xxxiv, 200–01, 202, 213
"Treat Officials Well" (He), 97
Treaty of Bogue or Humen (*1843*), 22, 136
Treaty of Commerce and Navigation (*1901*), 137
Treaty of Nanjing or Nanking (*1842*), 22, 136
Tsinghua University, 220
Turkey, 105

UK. *See* United Kingdom
UN. *See* United Nations
United Kingdom (UK), 137, 177. *See also* England; Great Britain
United Nations (UN), 114
United States (U.S.): Americanization, 117; death penalty in, 191; difficulty in copying laws of, 105–06; freedom of the press in, 177; governance costs in, 73; handover of political power in, 74; influence of American constitutionalism, 117–18; judiciary in, 115, 153; lawyers and law profession in, 141, 148; legal education in, 144–48; legal system of, 140; as a model of Chinese constitutionalism, 105; presidents in, 74–75, 115–16; separation and balance of powers in, 115; taxation in, 104
University independence, 78
University of Bologna (Italy), 145
University of Michigan (U.S.), xxvi
U.S. *See* United States
USS *Emily*, 9–10

Vatican, 114
Vattel, Emmerich de (jurist), 56
Victoria (queen; England), 56
Vietnam, 110
Villager autonomy, 97

Wang Hai (consumer rights fighter), 165
Wang Huitsu (official), 13
Wang Huning (aide to Hu Jintao), xlvi
Wang Lijun (police chief), xx, xxxi, xxxii, xxxiii, xxxvi, xlii
Wang Lixin (judge), 2
Wang Shaoguang (professor), xxxii
Wang Xuehui (professor), 91–92, 98
W. A. P. Martin (Ding Weiliang; university president), 56

Wars, 10, 56, 57. *See also* Opium Wars
Washington Post, 69
Wealth of Nations, The (Smith), 26
Weber, Karl Emil ("Max"; sociologist, philosopher, political economist), 14, 134, 168
Wei Sen (professor), xxiii
Wen Jiabao (premier), xxviii, 195, 218–19
Wen Qiang (former police chief), xxxii, xxxvi, 2, 5
West and Westerners: Chinese legal education and, 139; Chinese Westernization, 21–22, 40–41, 66, 107, 152–53; Chinese contempt for and appreciation of, 17–18, 93, 101; Chinese interest in Western legal system, 16, 41; constitutional government in, 103, 107; contrast between China and the West, 134–38; emergence of legal professionals, 135; executions in, 205; independence of legal professionals, 14; monogamy and, 78; Neo-Confucians and, 41; parliamentary sessions in, 71–72; purity of blood lines and, 82; social and historical development in, 76–87; spread of the Western system, 107, 110; status of law in Western value systems, 136; taxation in, 83; thinkers and, 79; Western constitutional theory, 52, 81; Western judicial system, 26; Western legal education and thought, 59, 137; Western view of China, 216–18; Western view of Chinese legal system, 10, 136. *See also* Opium Wars
"What Is Enlightenment?" (Kant), xxxi
White society (clean society), 4
Wills and will-making, 77
Witke, Roxane (writer), 48
Works of Gu Zhun (Gu), 79
Works of Mencius (Mencius), 42, 45–46
World Bank, xlvii
World Trade Organization (WTO), 67, 179
World War II, 80, 138, 153
WTO. *See* World Trade Organization
Wu (minister, king), 45, 46, 47
Wu Bangguo (senior leader), xix
Wu Fang (official, governor), 23–25
Wu Guang (leader of peasant uprising), 47
Wuhan University, xxxix
Wu Tingfang (lawyer, official), xix, 27–28
Wu Ying (entrepreneur), xxix
Wu Yu (critic of Confucian ethics), 40

Xianzheng yecong (Constitutionalism studies; translation series), xxvi
Xiao Xialin (writer), 122–23
Xiao Yang (president, Supreme People's Court), 129
Xia Yong (scholar and director of State Secrecy Bureau), xliii, xlv, 64
Xi Jinping (political leader), 219, 220
Xinhai Revolution (*1911*), 28
Xinhua News Agency, 177
Xuan of Qi (king), 44–45, 46, 47, 54, 57, 58
Xu Qian (chief, Department of Justice), 30–31
Xu Xin (law professor), xviii–xix
Xu Xing (philosopher), 54
Xu Youyu (scholar), xxiii

Yan Fu (scholar, translator), 19–20, 26, 101, 107
Yangcheng Evening News, 122
Yang Dongping (professor), 128
Yi Tian (professor), 65
Yi Zhongtian (historian and professor), 44
You Wei (professor), 192, 196
Yuan Dehui (translator), 56
Yuan Gusheng (scholar), 46
Yuan Shikai (general and politician), 29
Yuan Weishi (professor), xxvii, 181, 184
Yu Keping (scholar), xlvi
Yu Qiuyu (writer), 122–23

Zhang Guofu (writer), 30
Zhang Jiluan (Chang Chi-luan), 179
Zhang Jun (vice president, Supreme People's Court), 171
Zhang Lifan (scholar), xlvii
Zhang Shaoyan (professor), 63, 64
Zhang Sizhi (lawyer), xxxv
Zhang Weiying (professor), 127
Zhang Zhiming (professor), 69–70, 86–87
Zhang Zhixin (dissident), 212–13
Zhao Xiaoli (professor), 167
Zhou of Yin (king), 45, 46
Zhou Yeqian (professor), 202
Zhou Yongkang (Politburo member), 129
Zhu Guangqian (professor), 45
Zhu Mingyong (lawyer), xxxv
Zhu Suli (professor), 167
Zi Zhongyun (scholar), xxii–xxiii